Traveling

C000132144

ALSO BY CATHY AND VERNON SUMMERLIN

Traveling Tennessee
Highroad Guide to the Tennessee Mountains
Traveling the Southern Highlands
Traveling the Trace

BY VERNON SUMMERLIN WITH JIMMY HOLT

Tennessee Outdoorsman Cookbook

BY VERNON SUMMERLIN WITH DOUG MARKHAM

The Compleat Tennessee Angler

Traveling Florida

CATHY AND VERNON SUMMERLIN

JOHN F. BLAIR, *Publisher* Winston-Salem, North Carolina

Published by John F. Blair, Publisher

Copyright © 2002 by Cathy and Vernon Summerlin
All rights reserved under International and
Pan American Copyright Conventions

The paper in this book meets the guidelines
for permanence and durability of the
Committee on Production Guidelines for
Book Longevity of the Council on Library Resources

All photographs courtesy of Cathy and Vernon Summerlin unless otherwise noted.
Cover photograph by Vernon Summerlin
Book design by Debra Long Hampton
Composition by The Roberts Group
Printed in Canada

FOR CALEB

Contents

Preface

After spending decades visiting Florida and two years researching this book, we're even more fascinated with the state than when we started.

Looking through the table of contents, you'll notice that we cover a lot of territory, from the oldest towns to those that popped up in the last century. In the course of our travels, we paddled canoes down the second-tallest waterfall in the state, jumped out of a perfectly good airplane, ate buckets of raw mollusks, fed thousands of mosquitoes, spent a couple of hours smoking an Ybor City special, got drunk on orchids, giggled with Mickey, laughed at children laughing at manatees, lost a staring contest with a pelican, applied balm to an elbow a tarpon tore up, tried to catch a mermaid, launched rockets over the Atlantic, squeezed oranges at breakfast, looked through the bottom of a boat at million-gallon springs, contemplated Dali's watches, tasted the sweet winds off the Gulf . . . The list goes on and on.

Florida is a large state in size and content. It stretches 700 miles from Pensacola to Key West, yet no part of the state is more than 60 miles from the Gulf of Mexico or the Atlantic Ocean. Of its 58,560 square miles, 4,300 are rivers and lakes, and that doesn't include the largest underground aquifer in the United States. Its fertile estuaries are among the largest in the nation; you can't count all the things that go on there.

We love the water and welcome the opportunity to share information about all sorts of water-related activities. Whenever possible, we direct you to areas that offer a taste of Florida as it was before men wrought their many changes—building roads, draining swamps, and erecting great, gleaming cities where panthers, camels, mammoths, giant sloths, and fierce saber-toothed cats once roamed.

We also try to give you a sense of the story of man in the areas we cover. Indian tribes were here at least 12,000 years before whites arrived. Among the distinct Native American cultures in Florida were the Apalachees in the north, the Timucuas in the central and eastern parts of the state, the fierce Calusas in the south, and, finally, the Seminoles. The recorded history of the United States began here. Florida was the claimed possession of five sovereign nations. Amelia Island flew eight different flags.

We likewise focus on the splendid beaches the state is known for, indulgent bed-and-breakfasts, snazzy seaside resorts, and delectable dining spots. We include a wide assortment of popular tourist destinations in the hope that you will find places that suit your tastes.

We begin our journey through Florida in the northwestern corner on the Panhandle and continue down the Gulf Coast before turning our attention to Central Florida and the Atlantic Coast from Amelia Island to Key West. In some chapters, we invite you on a loop tour that explores off-the-beaten-path attractions and returns you to your starting point. In others, attractions are centrally and easily located, so we leave you to choose your route based on your preferences.

Websites are a boon to both travelers and the travel industry. We recommend that you visit a website or two about your destination before you leave home. Two excellent sites are flausa.com and floridatravelusa.com. For details about Florida's state parks, visit www.dep.state.fl.us/parks. And don't forget to try search engines like Google.com and Askjeeves.com.

Be sure to contact the area visitor bureaus listed at the end of each chapter. The very helpful folks at these places can supply you with detailed information. In some cases, they'll even tailor a trip just for you.

Acknowledgments

Many thanks go to Carolyn Sakowski, the president of John F. Blair, Publisher, for giving us the opportunity to write *Traveling Florida*. We have looked forward to working with her for several years and are delighted with our collaboration. Also, sincere thanks to our editor, Steve Kirk, who has shared his expertise and helped make this project so enjoyable.

Our deep appreciation also goes to the countless people we met on the roads, on the water, and on the trails of Florida who shared their knowledge, their time, and their favorite places with us as we crisscrossed the state. Among these were Vern's new fishing buddies Ralph Allen, Reno Alley, Terry Segraves, Big Al Hubbard, Greg Burnett, Rick Rawlins, Ben Evans, Brian E. Smith, Chris Oaks, Charles Wilson, Gene Kingery, and Gary Thompson.

Also very helpful were Abby Montpelier, Amber Peterson, Anita Gregory, April Sollars, Bill Voliva, Bishop Clark, Bonnie Holub, Captain Marian Schneider, Cindy Malin, David Harraden, Dean Fowler, Debbie Geiger, Deborah Bell, Diane Delaney, Diane Kinchen, Don Lesh, Ed Stone, Frank Gamsky, George Billiris, Georgia Turner, Ginny Gutierrez, Jay Humphreys, Jayna Leach, Jim Lawson, John Pricher, JoNell Modys, Kelly Earnest, Kelly Yatcko, Ken Lutzenberger, Kriss Titus, Lee Rose, Leon Corbett III, Lindsay Gowing, Lori Smithberger, Lorraine Moore, Maggie Pearson, Megan MacPherson, Meredith McCormack, Mitzi Coleman, Nancy Hamilton, Nicole Spruill, Pat McSweeney, Paula Ramsey Pickett, Rachel Bray-Stiles, Rebecca Dawes, Renee Wente, Richard Dunham, Jr., Rob Ondo, Shelley Knox, Shelley Yancey, Sherri Martin, Sherry Rushing, Stacy Badics, Stacy Garrett, Susan McClain, Tom Bartosek, Trisha Chason, Wade Berry, Ed Engel, Captain Jack Taylor, and Wayne Vaughan.

Last but not least, our thanks go to Kathie German, Bobbie McAllister, and Darlene Gibson for keeping the home fires burning while we were exploring and to Holly Sherwin, Bill Vandeford, and Rita Venable for sharing stories of their Florida days with us.

Traveling Florida

Pensacola-Pensacola Beach-Perdido Key-Milton-Navarre

HIGHLIGHTS

HISTORIC PENSACOLA VILLAGE AND SEVILLE SQUARE HISTORIC DISTRICT

BEACHES AT GULF ISLANDS NATIONAL SEASHORE

FORT PICKENS

NATIONAL MUSEUM OF NAVAL AVIATION

MILTON, THE "CANOE CAPITAL OF FLORIDA"

Since the sun shines here an average of 343 days each year, it should come as no surprise that the 20 miles of sugary sand beaches between Pensacola and Perdido Key near the Alabama state line are popular with summer vacationers. In addition to national franchises from Hampton Inn and Holiday Inn to Ramada Inn and Comfort Inn, choices for lodging include beach cottages, high-rise condominiums, historic bed-and-breakfasts, and camping along the largely undeveloped coast of Gulf Islands National Seashore.

Begin your visit at the modern, spacious **Pensacola Convention and Visitor Information Center**, located on the mainland at Gregory Street just before you start over the Pensacola Bay Bridge toward Pensacola Beach. The old bridge at Wayside Park behind the visitor center parallels the new bridge and is now a 1.5-mile fishing pier with access by both foot and car.

Although St. Augustine, on Florida's Atlantic coast, is the nation's oldest continuously occupied city settled by Europeans, Pensacola was the first settlement, predating St. Augustine by five years. Pensacola has been under the rule of the Spanish, the British, the French, the Confederacy, and the United States since the conquistadors arrived in 1559, some 46 years after Juan Ponce de Leon discovered Florida. Don Tristan de Luna y Arrelano set sail from Mexico with 500 Spanish soldiers, 1,000 civilians, and big plans to settle Pensacola Bay. However, a hurricane scattered the ships, and soldiers, settlers, and cargo were lost. The locals—the Ochuse and Panzacola Indians—were not inclined to help, which forced the remaining soldiers and settlers to abandon their plans and return to Mexico two years later.

According to Charlton Tebeau in *A History of Florida*, after this first attempt to settle Florida failed, Pensacola remained "lost" until Juan Jordan de Reina described it as "the best bay I have ever seen in my life" following its rediscovery by Juan Enriquez Baroto and Antonio Romero in 1686. Pensacola was permanently established in 1698 by the Spanish but was later occupied by the British. In 1763, it served as the capital of British West Florida, the 14th American colony. Pensacola returned to Spanish rule in 1781 before General Andrew Jackson led occupying forces to Pensacola twice and became the first United States governor of Florida in 1821.

Pensacola is situated on the mainland overlooking the deepest natural harbor on the northern Gulf of Mexico. To the west are Pensacola Naval Air Station and Perdido Key, to the east are Eglin Air Force Base and Navarre, and to the south is a pair of bridges leading to Pensacola Beach, its 1950s-era 40-foot neon billfish sign pointing the way.

Historic Pensacola Village, a three-block-square area in the heart of one of the oldest historic districts in the Southeast, offers visitors glimpses of local history and culture daily Monday through Friday except for state holidays. The tree-lined streets of the **Seville Square Historic District** are home to historic buildings open for

Historic Pensacola Village is a complex of museums and historic buildings within Pensacola's Seville Square Historic District.

Pensacola's former city hall is home to thousands of items displayed in the T.T. Wentworth, Jr., Florida State Museum.

touring, as well as several small cafés, art galleries, and antique shops.

A couple of blocks away on Jefferson Street, the imposing brick Renaissance Revival building that houses the **T. T. Wentworth, Jr., Florida State Museum** was once Pensacola's city hall. Beginning with a coin found on the beach in 1906, Wentworth added automobile license plates, woodworking tools, and Indian artifacts before branching out to acquire the world's largest and smallest shoes, a petrified cat, and even a shrunken head. He eventually donated over 100,000 items to the state of Florida, and they're displayed here.

The neighboring **Pensacola Museum of Art** has gallery space on two floors and a small gift shop.

The **Pensacola Historical Museum**, located on Zaragosa Street, is operated by the Pensacola Historical Society. It is closed Sundays and holidays. The museum offers exhibits on Indian, maritime, and military history, along with special exhibits.

The **Colonial Archaeological Trail**, between

Zaragosa and Government Streets, preserves what remains of the evidence of structures that existed here between 1752 and 1821.

Veteran's Memorial Park, on Bayfront Parkway at Ninth Avenue, honors vets of all wars. It includes The Wall South, a replica of the Vietnam Veterans Memorial in Washington.

As you might expect, there's a lot of fresh seafood in town.

Many locals get seafood to prepare themselves at **Joe Patti Seafood Company**, located at the foot of A Street.

Better yet, you can ease back and let yourself enjoy the view from the deck while taking lunch or dinner at the popular **Fish House** on Barrack Street. The menu ranges from lightly blackened Strip Steaks gently flavored with Creole spices to Grits à Ya Ya, a concoction of jumbo shrimp with seasoned vegetables sautéed with bacon and served over a hot bed of Gouda Cheese Grits. The Fish House offers an adventurous sushi bar, light, interesting salads, and a menu that includes Pecan-Crusted Catch of the Day, Soft-Shell Crab, and Ginger-Crusted Grouper. What better way to end a day than sitting on a sprawling wooden deck overlooking the harbor, sipping Bushwhackers, and watching the sun set?

Another popular restaurant, **McGuire's Irish Pub** on Gregory Street, is relatively sedate at lunch, but don't be surprised if some boisterous blarney develops as the evening rolls on. Patrons are exhorted to kiss not the Blarney Stone, but rather a moose, an ass, or a leprechaun to get into a proper McGuire's attitude. The menu ranges from traditional pub fare like Fish and Chips and Irish ale brewed on site to 32 different combinations to dress up the ¾-pound burgers. The choices range from the sedate, award-winning

Old-Fashioned Burger to the likes of Onion, Garlic, Jalapeño, and Olive burgers, Peanut Butter Burgers, and Hot Fudge Burgers. There's even a patty with bit of everything in the kitchen. It's called the Garbage Burger.

If you're staying on the beach, be sure to try **Flounder's Chowder and Ale House**, which boasts live entertainment on weekends and an invitation to "eat, drink, and flounder."

Spring Street in the North Hill Preservation District is home to the historic **Pensacola Victorian Bed and Breakfast**, a lovingly restored Queen Anne Victorian that was once the home of ship captain William Hazard Northup.

Down the street, another Queen Anne Victorian, the **Springhill Guesthouse**, offers two suites with phones and internet hookups, laundry facilities, and breakfast at the landmark **Hopkins House** across the street daily.

The **New World Landing** on Palafox Street in the Palafox Historic Business District offers the **New World Inn**, which has 14 rooms and two suites with distinctive décor relating to Pensacola's past. Originally a 19th-century box factory, the New World Landing retains vestiges of those days, blended seamlessly with modern amenities. The **New World Restaurant** serves continental cuisine for lunch and dinner Tuesday through Saturday in three distinctly styled dining rooms.

The **Crowne Plaza Pensacola Grand Hotel** on Gregory Street is an elegant marriage of the historic Louisville and Nashville Railway Depot and a gleaming, modern glass-and-steel addition with luxurious guest rooms and suites.

The Pensacola Bay Bridge leads south toward Gulf Breeze, a small community sandwiched between Pensacola and Pensacola Beach. Gulf Breeze had the dubious distinction of being a hotbed of

UFO sightings during the early 1990s. Here, before reaching Pensacola Beach on Santa Rosa Island, you'll find a visitor center at the 1,400-acre **Naval Live Oaks Reservation**, the nation's first timber preserve, now part of Gulf Islands National Seashore. Originally valued for its strength in shipbuilding and its ability to repel cannonballs, the majestic, salt-spray-tolerant live oak is well suited for life along the coast from Virginia to Texas. Some of the live oaks in Florida are hundreds of years old and have expansive, gnarled branches covered in elliptical leaves. Those branches are dramatically draped with Spanish moss and sport resurrection ferns after rains. Though it sheds leaves like other oaks, the live oak is never totally bare.

Established by Congress in 1971, **Gulf Islands National Seashore** consists of 11 separate units stretching from Mississippi's West Shipp Island to Navarre on Santa Rosa Island.

Santa Rosa Island, one of Florida's many barrier islands, was most likely created by steady deposits of sand on bars and shoals. The island protects the mainland from the full force of tropical storms. Here, beach lovers savor the aquamarine water, the rolling dunes, the wildlife, the salt marshes, and the historic sites along the largest protected shoreline in Florida.

The two other Florida visitor centers for the national seashore are at Fort Barrancas, located on the mainland slightly west of downtown Pensacola at the Pensacola Naval Air Station, and at Fort Pickens, located on the western tip of Santa Rosa Island.

Built between 1829 and 1834, **Fort Pickens** was part of a triangular defense system that included Fort Barrancas across Pensacola Bay and Fort McRae near Perdido Key across the Gulf.

Fort Pickens is of interest to historians as well as nature enthusiasts.

After the Civil War, Fort Pickens and other forts like it became obsolete, as the new generation of rifled cannons was able to pound masonry to rubble. From 1886 to 1888, Fort Pickens achieved a measure of notoriety while holding Geronimo and other Apaches captive. During their incarceration at Fort Pickens, the Apaches were used by local promoters as a tourist attraction. Today, Fort Pickens is a great spot for biking and birding. It is open daily. In addition to soaking up the sun on the white-sand beaches, visitors enjoy boating, hiking, camping in the 200 available sites, and fishing from the pier or the jetties. The on-site bookstore has a good selection of books about Florida.

The navy has been in Pensacola, site of the first naval air station in the United States, since 1826. Naval aviators proudly tell their story at the **National Museum of Naval Aviation**, located at the Pensacola Naval Air Station west of downtown Pensacola. Use the main entrance to the air station about a mile south of Barrancas Avenue (FL 292) on Navy Boulevard (FL 295) to reach

Allow a half-day to view the hundreds of aircraft on display and take in an IMAX show at the National Museum of Naval Aviation.

the museum. Thanks to an IMAX theater that shows seven shows daily, more than 240 aircraft, and lots of hands-on interactive exhibits, this is one of the 10 most-visited attractions in Florida. One of the three largest aviation museums in the world, it has nearly a million visitors each year. It is open daily except for Thanksgiving, Christmas, and New Year's. Among the displays is the very first naval aircraft, a 1911 Curtiss Triad A. George Bush's trainer plane is also housed here. Bush Senior was one of the youngest naval aviators ever granted officer status. Staffed by about 300 dedicated volunteers, the museum conducts four guided tours daily; the tours last just under two hours. If you want to take in the IMAX show and have time to enjoy lunch in the faithfully reconstructed on-site café—an officer's club from Cubi Point Air Station at the mouth of Subic Bay in the Philippines—you'll need to spend at least a half-day here. A luncheon menu offering soups, salads, and sandwiches is served. A tour bus carries visitors to the restored hangar behind the

museum. The gift shop has everything from flight jackets to a well-stocked collection of books. Museum admission is free. Prices for IMAX tickets vary.

Just down the street from the bustle of the museum is the **Pensacola Lighthouse**. The peaceful beauty is enough to make this worth a visit whether you're a history buff or not. The original lighthouse was constructed in 1825, making it the first built by the United States government on Florida's Gulf coast. A replacement was constructed in 1858 and lighted on New Year's Day 1859. In 1965, the structure was automated, saving the lighthouse keeper the climb up the 177 steps leading to the tower. At 191 feet above sea level, the light can be seen 27 miles away. A white picket fence accented with splashes of brilliantly colored flowers surrounds the old keeper's cottage and lighthouse. The southern view looks to Pensacola Bay and the Gulf beyond. If you'd like a tour, it's best to call ahead to arrange it with members of the United States Coast Guard Auxiliary, unless you're here on a Sunday afternoon, when the lighthouse is open to the public. According to local legend, three ghosts haunt the lighthouse. They were nowhere to be found when we visited.

As you head west from Pensacola, the last community you'll come to before entering Alabama is Perdido Key, a barrier island that is part Alabama, part Florida, and more than half state and federal parks and preserves.

Along this section of the Gulf coast, you'll find beach cottages, high-rise condominiums, resorts, and national motel franchises, as well as camping in a portion of Gulf Islands National Seashore off Johnson Beach Road. You'll have to hike to the ruins of **Fort McRae** and the campground on the

Each Florida lighthouse has a distinctive appearance and identifying flash pattern. On the Pensacola Lighthouse the lower third is white and the upper two-thirds are black.

eastern end of Perdido Key unless you take a water taxi. The land Fort McRae sat on long ago gave way to the longshore currents and slipped into the Gulf, taking the fort with it. Hurricanes like Elena, Juan, and Kate have taken their toll on what remains. South of Fort McRae just off Pensacola Pass, the wreck of the USS *Massachusetts* is a big attraction for scuba divers.

Along the way, Gulf Beach Highway passes

Big Lagoon State Recreation Area, a 712-acre park with 75 campsites on a pine ridge nestled along the southern edge of the mainland. Forty-nine of the sites have electricity, some are RV-sized, and others are handicapped-accessible. A pair of handicapped-accessible nature trails and an observation tower at the East Beach area offer great views of Big Lagoon, the Intracoastal Waterway, and Perdido Key with the Gulf beyond. Big Lagoon also has a boat ramp with a dock that provides easy access for watersports such as canoeing, boating, swimming, snorkeling, crabbing, and fishing for redfish, bluefish, sea trout, and flounder. Sea-turtle beach walks are available by reservation on Saturdays during July and August. Big Lagoon is also popular among bird watchers hoping to spot migratory birds and shorebirds.

Perdido Key is also the home of a famous roadhouse, the **Flora-Bama Lounge and Package**. Sitting precisely on the Alabama-Florida line, it is a bastion of West Florida culture. It looks a little off-kilter and well used, like any really good roadhouse should. The last weekend in April, the Flora-Bama hosts an infamous benefit mullet toss. Tossers heave the hapless fish (usually served fried or smoked in these parts) 150 feet or more from Florida into Alabama. The Flora-Bama also hosts a song-writing festival in November and the **Polar Bear Plunge** in January to start the new year off right. Most folks content themselves to grab a cold brew and some raw oysters while waiting for the evening's entertainment to begin.

Pensacola Bay is connected to Escambia Bay, Blackwater Bay, and East Bay, an area covering more than 140 square miles. The resulting estuary—an area where river water mingles with seawater—is the fourth-largest in Florida. The combination of mud flats, sea grasses, wetlands, and sand bars creates an extremely rich habitat for invertebrates, fish, and birds.

Local companies offer canoes, kayaks, and guided fishing trips to help visitors spend some quality time on the water. Inshore fishing trips for speckled trout, redfish, bluefish, flounder, and Spanish mackerel are popular, as are offshore trips for red snapper, grouper, and amberjack. You may also make arrangements for custom trips for billfish or do some scuba diving at one of the wrecks or artificial reefs.

There are several public-access areas that will get you quickly to the edges of grass beds and quiet waters on the rivers, bays, and bayous if you're traveling with your own canoe, kayak, or shallow-draft boat. Eglin Air Force Base allows public access to thousands of acres for hunting, fishing, boating, canoeing, and camping.

North of town, the Blackwater River near Milton, the self-proclaimed "Canoe Capital of Florida," is a gentle, shallow river popular with canoeists and kayakers. **Blackwater River State Forest** offers several hiking trails, including the **Bear Lake Loop Trail**, and at least one famous inhabitant, the red-cockaded woodpecker, which nests in the hard wood of healthy, old seed pines in the long-leaf pine savannas surrounding the lake. **Adventures Unlimited** on Coldwater Creek offers canoeing, kayaking, rafting, and tubing for a couple of hours or a couple of days along spring-fed rivers through the state forest. The **Adventures Unlimited Schoolhouse Inn** has eight rooms with private baths, 12-foot ceilings, hardwood floors, and bead-board walls.

From Pensacola, you can make a short drive east on US 98A to visit Navarre, another of the Panhandle's sparkling residential beach communities. Named for a Spanish province, it was founded in 1925. Although only 10 miles from I-10, Navarre and its beach community across Santa Rosa Sound have managed to preserve much of their beauty. A one-mile waterfront boardwalk wanders along Santa Rosa Sound before reaching the **Panhandle Butterfly House**, noted for its butterflies and native plants. The eight miles of white-sand beaches here are part of Gulf Islands National Seashore. The **Navarre Pier** on FL 399 is a popular destination for anglers. Lodging choices range from beach houses and condominiums to national franchise properties including Best Western, Comfort Inn, and Holiday Inn.

Drive east on US 98 to visit Fort Walton Beach, Destin, and Sandestin.

All of the following are in Pensacola and use the 32501 zip code and 850 area code, except where noted.

ACCOMMODATIONS

Adventures Unlimited Schoolhouse Inn and Cottages—Rt. 6, Box 238, Milton, FL 32570; 800-239-6864 or 623-6197

Crowne Plaza Pensacola Grand Hotel—200 E. Gregory St.; 800-348-3336 or 433-3336

New World Inn—600 S. Palafox St.; 432-4111

Pensacola Victorian Bed and Breakfast—203 W. Gregory St.; 800-370-8354 or 434-2818

Springhill Guesthouse—903 N. Spring St.; 800-475-1956 or 438-6887

Tristan Towers—1200 Fort Pickens Rd., Pensacola Beach, FL 32561; 800-342-9980

ATTRACTIONS

Adventures Unlimited—Rt. 6, Box 283, Milton, FL 32570; 800-239-6864 or 623-6197

Fort Barrancas—Building 3822, Taylor Rd., Pensacola Naval Air Station; 455-5167

Historic Pensacola Village—205 E. Zaragosa St.; 595-5985

National Museum of Naval Aviation/IMAX Theater—1750 Radford Blvd., Pensacola Naval Air Station; 800-327-5002 or 452-3604

Pensacola Historical Museum—115 E. Zaragosa St.; 433-1559

Pensacola Lighthouse—Radford Boulevard, Pensacola Naval Air Station; 455-2354

Pensacola Museum of Art—407 S. Jefferson St.; 432-6247

T. T. Wentworth, Jr., Florida State Museum—330 S. Jefferson St.; 595-5990

CAMPING

All Star RV Resort—13621 Perdido Key Dr., Perdido Key, FL 32507; 800-245-3602 or 492-0041

Big Lagoon State Recreation Area—12301 Gulf Beach Hwy.; 492-1595

Blackwater River State Park—7720 Beaton Bridge Rd., Holt, FL 32564; 983-5363

Gulf Islands National Seashore/Fort Pickens National Park—Fort Pickens Rd., Pensacola Beach, FL 32561; 800-365-2267 or 934-2622

DINING

Bayside Grill—14 Via De Luna, Pensacola Beach, FL 32561; 932-9898

Billy-Bob's Beach Barbecue—911 Gulf Breeze Pkwy; 934-2999

Fish House—600 Barracks St.; 470-0003

Flora-Bama Lounge and Package—17401 Perdido Key Dr., Perdido Key, FL 32507; 492-3048

Flounder's Chowder House—800 Quiet Water Pkwy. (at the traffic light at Pensacola Beach), Pensacola Beach, FL 32561; 932-2003

McGuire's Irish Pub—600 E. Gregory St.; 433-6789

New World Landing Restaurant—600 S. Palafox St.; 434-7736

Screaming Coyote—796 N. Palafox St. (corner of Palafox and Gregory); 435-9002

Wisteria Café—221 E. Zaragosa St., Seville Square Historic District; 438-8188

E V E N T S

January—Polar Bear Plunge

February-March—Mardi Gras

April—Pensacola Jazz Fest

April—Crawfish and Creole Fiesta

April—Interstate Mullet Toss at the Flora-Bama Lounge and Package

May—Lobster Festival

June—Fiesta of Five Flags

August—Bushwhacker Festival

September—Seafood Festival

November—Blue Angels Homecoming Air Show

November—Great Gulf Coast Arts Festival

November—Frank Brown International Songwriters Festival

 F O R   M O R E   I N F O R M A T I O N

Blackwater River State Forest—11650 Munson Hwy., Milton, FL 32570; 957-4201

Eglin Air Force Base—Natural Resource Division, 501 DeLeon St., Suite 101, Eglin Air Force Base, FL 32542; 882-4164

Gulf Islands National Seashore—1801 Gulf Breeze Pkwy., Gulf Breeze, FL 32561; 800-365-2267 or 934-2600

Pensacola Convention and Visitor Information Center— 1410 E. Gregory St.; 800-874-1234 or 434- 434-1234; www.visitpensacola.com

Perdido Key Visitor Information Center—15500 Perdido Key Dr., Perdido Key, FL 32507; 800-328-0107 or 492-4660; www.perdidochamber.com

HIGHLIGHTS

INDIAN TEMPLE MOUND MUSEUM

FISHING IN DESTIN

BEACHES

GOLF AT SANDESTIN

OFFSHORE FISHING

Collectively known as the Emerald Coast, the 24 miles of beautiful beaches in Fort Walton Beach and Destin are sparkling white, and the Gulf is an emerald color with touches of aquamarine and shimmering turquoise. Located on the mainland overlooking Choctawhatchee Bay and its sister city, Destin, to the east, Fort Walton is joined to Okaloosa Island by a bridge heading southeast. A second bridge connects Okaloosa Island to Destin, which is known as "the world's luckiest fishing village," a title that reflects the outstanding sportfishing here.

About 60 percent of the oceanfront property along the Emerald Coast is publicly held. The rest is densely developed with accommodations that range from high-rise condominiums to national franchises and oceanfront resorts.

Archaeological evidence from the Fort Walton area indicates visitation by nomadic hunters who migrated from Asia across the Bering Strait as early as 12,000 years ago. It is believed they followed game to the Southeast and eventually to what is now Okaloosa County, an area containing Fort Walton Beach, Okaloosa Island, and Destin on the coast, as well as Mary Esther, Niceville, Crestview, and portions of both Blackwater River State Forest and Eglin Air Force Base inland. There's some discussion about the meaning of Okaloosa, but there's little doubt that it is of Indian origin. While it could mean "Black Water," it may also mean "Place of Rest" or "Pleasant Place." Native Americans permanently settled the area around 500 B.C.

A temple mound located along US 98 in Fort Walton was explored by the Smithsonian Institution in 1883 and has been excavated several times since. The **Indian Temple Mound Museum** adjoins the mound. It contains more than 6,000 artifacts of stone, shell, bone, and clay, including the largest collection of prehistoric Fort Walton Period pottery in the Southeast. You'll also find exhibits on European explorers and pirates like the infamous Brit William Augustus Bowles, a.k.a. Billy Bowlegs, whose exploits are celebrated each June during the **Billy Bowlegs Pirate Festival**. The museum is open daily during the summer. It is closed on Sundays from September through May.

The flat area at the base of the mound was used as a campsite by a small Confederate militia

Indian Temple Mound Museum introduces visitors to the Florida Panhandle's prehistoric people.

unit that was organized to guard East Pass during the Civil War. Those men became known as the Walton Guards and their camp as Camp Walton. It subsequently became Fort Walton. Then, in 1953, in a public-relations coup, the word *Beach* was finally added to the name.

In 1937, some 55,000 acres of Panhandle property became Eglin Air Force Base, the largest air-force base in the free world. It was named for Lieutenant Colonel Fredrick Eglin, who had been stationed at Maxwell Air Force Base and had recently died in a plane crash. The **Air Force Armament Museum**, just outside the base's main gate, exhibits artifacts of air combat from World War II through Operation Desert Storm. Reconnaissance planes, fighters, bombers, and spy planes are on exhibit. A 30-minute film tells Eglin's story.

Another good stop on a rainy day, the **Gulfarium** on US 98 offers a close look at dolphins and sea lions during its daily shows. Built in 1955, the Gulfarium is one of many Florida attractions offering interactive dolphin programs.

Perennially voted "Best Beach in the South"

and one of the top three "Favorite Family Vacation Destinations" by the readers of *Southern Living,* **Destin** is a small seaside resort town that offers a wide assortment of vacation options. Agreeably sleepy during the off-season, US 98 buzzes with traffic during the summer months.

Fishing, diving, snorkeling, and sailing are some of the most popular ways to enjoy being on the water here. Divers consider this one of the top five areas in the world for shelling. Offshore sand bars, crystal-clear water down to 100 feet, and a limestone reef about three miles out provide fertile ground for shell seekers. Landlubbers will enjoy the golf links, tennis facilities, and hiking opportunities available in the area.

Strategically located Destin has the fastest access to deep water on the Gulf. These waters yield more billfish each year than all the other Gulf ports combined. Fishing events and festivals are held year-round, from the spring and summer cobia and shark tournaments to the fall fishing season, which brings both the **Destin Fishing**

The Gulfarium's interactive dolphin programs are popular with the young and young at heart. Photo courtesy of the Emerald Coast Convention and Visitors Bureau.

The "world's luckiest fishing village," Destin has the largest charter fishing fleet in Florida.

Rodeo and the **Destin Seafood Festival**. In short, Destin offers big-time big-game fishing and the largest charter boat fleet in Florida.

I caught my biggest fish ever, a 26-pound jack cravalle, here. Although I was worried I'd lose the skipper's tackle before I landed it, the guys strapped the fighting belt on me, Vern cheered me on, and we all hoped for the best. My behemoth earned only a second-place standing in the tournament in which I was entered, and that for only a few days. It's true what they say about there always being bigger fish in the sea.

Vern has had lots of success fishing for blues from the jetties on the Destin side of the bridge in spring. The small boat ramp on the Okaloosa side of the bridge offers quick access to the Gulf or the bay, depending on the weather and the size of your boat.

If you don't feel you're quite ready for the big time, try the party boats. You'll fish alongside folks with varying degrees of experience. There's no need for finesse here. Just drop your line on cue, set the hook when you get a bite, and reel 'em in.

The action tends to be fast paced, and the deck hands really earn their tips, constantly changing bait and removing hooks. One of the newer party boats, the *Destin Princess*, can carry up to 45 anglers. The activity is much more relaxed on the three-hour cruises aboard the *Nathaniel Bowditch*, a 54-foot traditionally rigged schooner that can carry 22 people on sailing adventures. The 65-foot, wooden *Southern Star* is family owned and operated by an experienced husband-and-wife team. This classic boat, built in 1959, carries up to 75 people on two-hour cruises searching for bottlenose dolphins. There's also a 72-foot wooden replica schooner, the *Daniel Webster Clements*. You can join this boat for a morning dolphin cruise or an afternoon snorkel-and-sail cruise that comes complete with snorkeling gear and instruction. All you need is a towel, a bathing suit, and sunscreen. All these boats and many more depart from the Destin harbor.

Henderson Beach State Recreation Area is located east of Destin on US 98. Luckily for Okaloosa County beachcombers, the Henderson family donated this beautiful 208-acre site to the Florida state parks system in order to preserve it. Now surrounded by high-rise developments, the recreation area's 1.3 miles of protected shoreline are home to sea turtles, sanderlings, and black skimmers. Boardwalks allow access to the beach without damaging the sand dunes. The recreation area offers day-use activities like swimming, sunbathing, fishing, and picnicking. It also has a campground with 30 RV-sized sites, showers, and a dump station.

In addition to most national franchises, lodging choices in the area include the Henderson Park Inn and the Sandestin Golf and Beach Resort.

Built in 1992, the **Henderson Park Inn** is tucked

The award-winning Sandestin Golf and Beach Resort contains more than 700 accommodations on 2,400 acres of beach and bay-front property. Photo courtesy of Sandestin Golf and Beach Resort.

away on a quiet road on the eastern boundary of Henderson Beach State Recreation Area. It has a heated swimming pool and overlooks more than a mile of unspoiled beach. There are 35 guest rooms, most with a Jacuzzi, a refrigerator, a microwave, tasteful Victorian reproduction furnishings, fine linens, and a king- or queen-sized four-poster, canopied, or iron bed. The morning meal is complimentary. Lunch and candlelight dinner may be arranged in **The Veranda**, the inn's dining room. The Henderson Park Inn does not accommodate children.

On the other hand, lots of families get together for a week at the beach at the **Sandestin Golf and Beach Resort**, a 2,400-acre property split by US 98 (also called Emerald Coast Parkway) about 10 miles east of Destin. The property—divided into beach-side, bay-side, and link-side communities—has more than 700 vacation rentals. The resort is a complete destination offering 73 holes of golf, including a course designed by Robert Trent Jones, Jr., and a high-tech golf training

center with golf schools, computer analysis of golfers' swings, and auditory biofeedback that allows individuals to train at their own pace. Visitors also enjoy the world-class tennis courts with a variety of surfaces, the health club and day spa, the 7.5 miles of sandy beach and sparkling bay-front property, and the 98-slip marina overlooking Horseshoe Bayou on Choctawatchee Bay. Pontoon boat rentals, fishing charters, and kayaks are available out of **Baytowne Marina**. Both the *Jennifer Marie*, a 70-foot schooner that can carry up to 49 passengers, and the *Spanish Moon*, a 34-foot sailing sloop, depart from Baytowne Marina on half-day, sunset, and lobster cruises. **Premier Sailing** offers sailing lessons.

Sort of a resort within a resort, the **Hilton Sandestin** is northwest Florida's largest Gulf-front hotel. Its 600 suites include executive suites with a parlor area, a refrigerator, and a wet bar, junior suites with bunk beds for the kids, and parlor suites with a couch seating area, a wet bar, a refrigerator, and a bunk-bed alcove. Casual dining choices at the Hilton include the **Beachside Grill, Picnix Deli**, and **Sandcastles**, which serves three meals daily. **Seagar's** offers fine dining. The Hilton also has a heated indoor pool, two outdoor pools, and a full-service spa.

For a culinary night on the town, visit the **Elephant Walk**, Sandestin's signature restaurant. The coastal cuisine here has won more than its share of awards, and the view from the patio is worthy of mention. You will appreciate the lunch menu as well.

More than two dozen trendy shops, an island playground, and a series of children's programs at both the Sandestin Golf and Beach Resort and the Hilton guarantee that everyone has something fun to see or do.

If you happen to be here the third weekend in October, you really ought to check out the **Boggy Bayou Mullet Festival**. Once known as Boggy Bayou, the town of Niceville decided it needed a festival to liven things up a bit in the mid-1970s, and the mullet festival was born. About 12,000 folks live here, but 50,000 people showed up the first year of the festival. Recent festivals have attracted three times that number and national attention on *Good Morning America* and in publications like *National Geographic Traveler* and *Country Living*.

Ease back on the throttle and continue east on US 98 to visit the beaches of South Walton along CR 30-A, one of our favorite spots on this gorgeous stretch of the Gulf coast.

All of the following are in Fort Walton Beach and use the 32547 zip code and 850 area code, except where noted.

ACCOMMODATIONS

Henderson Park Inn—2700 US 98, Destin, FL 32541; 800-336-4853, 837-4853, or 654-0400

Sandestin Golf and Beach Resort—9300 US 98, Sandestin, FL 32550; 800-277-0800 or 267-8150

ATTRACTIONS

Air Force Armament Museum—FL 85, 100 Museum Dr., Eglin Air Force Base, FL 32542; 882-4062

Baytowne Marina—9300 US 98, Sandestin, FL 32550; 267-7777

Gulfarium—1010 Miracle Strip Pkwy., US 98; 244-5169 or 243-9046

Indian Temple Mound Museum—139 Miracle Strip Pkwy., US 98; 833-9595

Nathaniel Bowditch *Sailing*—Harborwalk Marina, East US 98, Destin, FL 32541; 650-8787

Southern Star—Harborwalk Marina, East US 98 (P.O. Box 1713), Destin, FL 32541; 888-424-7217 or 837-7741

CAMPING

Henderson Beach State Recreation Area—17000 Emerald Coast Pkwy., Destin, FL 32541; 837-7550

DINING

Elephant Walk—9300 US 98, Sandestin, FL 32550; 267-4800

Flamingo Café—414 US 98, Destin, FL 32540; 837-8890

Marina Café—404 US 98, Destin, FL 32540; 837-7960

Pandora's Restaurant—1120-B Santa Rosa Blvd.; 244-8669

EVENTS

March—Cobia Tournament

April—Fort Walton Beach Seafood Festival

May—Blessing of the Fleet

May—Mayfest

June—Billy Bowlegs Pirate Festival

August—Dog Days Open Billfish Tournament

August—Greek Festival

October—Destin Fishing Rodeo

October—Destin Seafood Festival

October—Boggy Bayou Mullet Festival, Niceville

FOR MORE INFORMATION

Emerald Coast Convention and Visitors Bureau—P.O. Box 609, 32549; 800-322-3319 or 651-7131; www.destin-fwb.com

3   Beaches of South Walton–
DeFuniak Springs

HIGHLIGHTS
_____

EDEN STATE GARDENS

GRAYTON BEACH STATE RECREATION AREA

CHAUTAUQUA AT DEFUNIAK SPRINGS

Scenic CR 30-A is a two-lane, 19-mile drive that meanders through 13 delightful beach communities ranging from grand old Grayton Beach to Seaside, an architect's pastel dream come true. CR 30-A leaves US 98 east of the 2,400-acre Sandestin Golf and Beach Resort and rejoins it west of Panama City Beach's Miracle Strip. If you need information, stop by the attractive information center at the intersection of US 331 and US 98.

Unlike many of Florida's beaches, summer is peak season here. Temperatures are generally mild year-round. Highs from October to March tend to be in the mid- to upper 60s and 70s. The crowds are gone and lodging rates are discounted.

You won't find honky-tonk bars, high-rise hotels, McDonald's golden arches, or go-cart tracks, but you will find historic communities and nearly 25,000 acres of public land within south Walton County's 52,000 acres. The people here have made an effort to preserve a connection with Florida in its wild, natural state. Both the Atlantic loggerhead sea turtle and the green sea turtle nest along the beaches of CR 30-A from May through

The Gulf waters are incredibly clear along the beaches of south Walton County.

October. Strict zoning ordinances limiting the height of buildings to four stories guarantee that visitors will continue to enjoy views of the ever-changing Gulf.

Composed of quartz—or silicon dioxide—that originated in granite formations such as Georgia's Stone Mountain and North Carolina's Grandfather Mountain, the grains of sand along this 19-mile stretch have been buffed to their present sugary texture by the rigors of a long journey. The Gulf is incredibly clear here because its river sources are filtered by Apalachicola Bay to the east and a series of barrier islands that trap most of the sediment. The emerald color is the result of light reflecting off the white sand of the Gulf floor, while the blue results from color absorption at greater depths. The effect is nothing short of magical.

You can enjoy the usual beach pursuits at communities like Dune Allen, Santa Rosa, Blue Mountain, Grayton, and Seagrove. And the area's dozen-plus fresh and brackish lakes and Choctawhatchee Bay are perfect for boating and fishing. There's a snazzy RV resort, a lovely oceanfront state park, lots of condominiums, and best of all, beach houses old and new. Some have fireplaces, hot tubs, and decks; others even provide canoes and rowboats.

A wide, paved biking and hiking trail runs along much of CR 30-A. And there are sandy biking and hiking trails at **Point Washington State Forest** between Seagrove and US 98. Loops of 3.5, five, and ten miles wind through coastal sand-pine scrub, longleaf pine woods, and wet prairies. For a longer ride, continue on CR 395 across US 98 to historic Point Washington, about five miles due north of Seagrove on Choctawhatchee Bay.

Once the center of a bustling lumbermill operation, **Eden State Gardens** thrives beneath an incredible canopy of 500-year-old live oak trees that dominates the lush, green lawn as it gently slopes toward the small fishing pier on the bay. A guided tour of the 6,900-square-foot Wesley Mansion, built in 1895 by lumberman William Henry Wesley, is offered Thursday through Monday. The grounds, gardens, fishing dock, and picnic area are open daily.

The lovely grounds at Eden State Gardens offer a pleasant spot for a picnic.

When wealthy author and publisher Lois Maxon purchased Wesley Mansion for $12,500 in 1963, it looked like anything but a mansion. She spent $1 million renovating the 1890s house into the gracefully columned antebellum home seen by visitors today. She came home from a European shopping spree with the second-largest collection of Louis XVI furniture in the United States. When she donated the house and its furnishings to the state on Christmas Eve 1968, the antique collection alone was valued at $2.25 million.

CR 395 ends near the entrance to Eden State Gardens at a small boat ramp that's a good put-in for exploring the eastern end of Choctawhatchee Bay. The Nature Conservancy has obtained much of the land surrounding the mouths of the rivers at the eastern end of the bay. This land is not only a fishing hot spot but is scenic as well. One sunny New Year's Day, we lost count of the brown pelicans and cormorants flying overhead.

During our many trips to explore this area, we've found a variety of great places to lodge, even one that allowed our beloved golden retriever to stay with us for an extra fee. We started out more than a decade ago in a one-bedroom oceanfront condo at **Journey's End**, then rented a house on Stallworth Lake at the western end of CR 30-A. We loved them both. We've also enjoyed the **Sugar Beach Inn Bed and Breakfast** in Seagrove and several other bed-and-breakfasts, including **Josephine's French Country Inn** in Seaside, **A Highlands House**, and **Hibiscus Guest House** in Grayton Beach. At Seagrove Beach, we stayed in a two-bedroom oceanfront condo at **Walton Dunes**. It offered great views from the master bedroom and the living room. We could step out the front door to the Gulf or walk 100 yards and launch a canoe on Eastern Lake. A nearby firm not only rents canoes but will bring them to patrons' doors. **Commodore's Retreat** is perfect for families. It has bunk beds in the hall area, a small swimming pool, and easy access to the beach. Since this area offers more than 9,000 rooms, deciding where to stay is definitely part of the adventure.

Although Seagrove Beach is currently our favorite place to stay, there's no denying that **Seaside** is also fun to visit. Seaside's developer, Robert Davis, visited the land owned by his grandfather as a child. In 1981, after he inherited 80 acres, he began to create a modern version of his childhood days at the beach. Architects Andres Duany and Elizabeth Plater-Zyberk built a planned community in which no two houses are alike but all are bound by common threads, including attractive landscaping, porches, picket fences, and designs that celebrate sun and sand. The results are internationally recognized by urban planners and architects and thoroughly enjoyed by anyone with an interest in home or garden design. Seaside is intended to be a way of life that emphasizes the

Seaside is an upscale resort designed to recapture an old-fashioned sense of community and the architecture of days gone by.

pleasures of strolling along quiet streets, to the beach or the semicircular town center, where you'll find shops selling everything from beachwear to soaps and fragrances. Pedestrians enjoy the user-friendly surroundings, but parking may be a bit of a challenge to those coming for the afternoon on a busy summer weekend. The public parking closest to the Seaside shops and restaurants is located along CR 30-A and around the town center. One of the most popular restaurants in the area, **Bud and Alley's**, overlooks the Gulf. Across CR 30-A is a Seaside landmark, **Modica Market**, which offers an excellent selection of gourmet grocery items, wines, and sandwiches.

We've launched canoes in most of the lakes that line CR 30-A, including Western Lake at Grayton Beach, where there's a public ramp with very limited parking off Hotz Avenue. Grayton Beach is feeling the pressure of rising tourism. Many of the streets here are still sandy lanes, and houses date back to the 1920s and 1930s, although the first settlers arrived more than 100 years ago.

Grayton Beach was platted in 1890 and named for Major Charles T. Gray. According to Carol McCrite of Memory Lane Historic Tours, Grayton Beach, the oldest coastal community between Pensacola and Apalachicola, was a popular turn-of-the-century beach resort. By 1911, visitors from neighboring communities like DeFuniak Springs found that traveling the 30-mile distance could take nearly all day across rough roads and a river crossing at a cattle ford. In 1919, a group of Iowa bankers purchased property at Grayton Beach and started building a road from Point Washington.

During the Roaring Twenties, W. H. Butler built the Grand Hotel, which served cold, home-brewed beer for 10 cents a bottle, a real bargain considering that 200-pound blocks of ice had to be hauled from Pensacola twice weekly on a small freight boat to Point Washington, then hauled overland packed in sawdust. A grand piano floated down from Pensacola provided live music for Saturday-night dances, a hand-cranked Victrola filling in as needed during the week. A hurricane in 1936 blew the porches off both stories of the hotel, bringing the dancing and good times to an abrupt end. Constructed in 1937, Butler's Store picked up where the old hotel left off. The big dance floor lined by booths along the walls is now home to a one-of-a-kind restaurant and bar, the **Piccolo Restaurant and Red Bar**. While waiting for your food to arrive, be sure to check out the funky décor.

Across the street and scattered around the village are colorful galleries, specialty shops, restaurants, and even a bed-and-breakfast. Despite the arrival of greater numbers of tourists each year, Grayton Beach manages to retain a sense of itself.

Located east of Grayton Beach, 1,133-acre

Grayton Beach State Recreation Area has a mile of unspoiled shoreline. Its shimmering white dunes, capped with trembling sea oats, overlook the Gulf as it shifts from emerald to turquoise and aqua. This has been rightfully called the number-one beach in America. The recreation area offers canoe access to Western Lake. The park is open for day use for those interested in canoeing, swimming, saltwater fishing in the surf, or fishing for fresh and saltwater species in the brackish lake. The 37 wooded campsites are equipped with picnic tables, grills, water, electrical hookups, and the occasional marauding raccoon. Cabins, opened in 2001, are nestled in the pines a short walk from the beach. Each cabin has a screened-in back porch, two bedrooms, one bath, a fireplace, a microwave, a dishwasher, and a kitchen equipped with utensils and cookware, but no telephone or television to disturb your peace and quiet. A paved bike trail connects the gated cabin area to Grayton Beach and Seaside. Linens are furnished, and a two-night minimum is required. Handicapped-accessible cabins are available upon request.

Grayton Beach State Recreation Area's newest additions are two-bedroom cabins, only a short walk from the beach.

The 1,600 acres of **Topsail Hill Reserve State Park** are among the most pristine in coastal Florida. The dunes here—including one 25 feet high—were formed when huge quantities of sand were moved to the west by longshore currents about 10,000 years ago. Nodding sea oats stabilize the dunes with an extensive root system that grows both vertically and horizontally. The dunes in turn offer protection against storm surges of 15 to 20 feet. When the dunes are overwhelmed, as they were after Hurricane Opal in 1995, sea-oat plantings are the foundation of beach restoration programs. Signs warn you to stay off the dunes. Because they are such an important part of this ecosystem, they are protected by state law. Topsail is an important nesting site for loggerhead and green sea turtles, least terns, and piping plovers. It is also home to 14 different plant communities and the rare Gulf coast lupine.

Accessed via the western end of CR 30-A, **Gregory E. Moore RV Resort**, part of Topsail Hill Reserve State Park, is one of the highest-rated resorts in North America. It offers daily, weekly,

Bayou Art and Antiques is an off-the-beaten-path shopping adventure offering a wide range of items with Florida and nautical themes in a lovely woodland setting.

and monthly rentals of its 168 spaces. A pool, restrooms, showers, a laundry, and storage facilities are available. There's even a heated pool for the winter months.

If you're searching for garden gift ideas, the **Gourd Garden and Curiosity Shop** has lots of herbs, perennials, and annuals outside. The treasures inside this old Florida cottage turned shop range from folk art and colorful watering cans to birdhouses, beautiful earrings made of gourds, and clay feet in the form of turtles and frogs for your flowerpots. If you like plants, you'll love the Gourd Garden.

Speaking of colorful gifts, **Bayou Arts and Antiques**, off FL 393 at Cessna Park, is filled with colorful paintings, old and new garden statuary, furniture, and interesting nautical gifts. The setting overlooking Hogtown Bayou is as inspiring as the items you'll find inside. Perhaps the most unusual is the wildlife chapel a short stroll down the lush pathway.

Fresh Gulf seafood is readily available.

The Gourd Garden and Curiosity Shop is a great source of gardening information, inspiration, and gifts.

Whether you choose fine dining at **Café Thirty-A**, **Criollas**, or **Bud and Alley's**, area restaurants stack up against the best Florida has to offer. On a recent visit, we found the Crab Cakes, Tuna Sushi, and wine selections at **Vintij** to be excellent. Far more casual but equally to our liking are **Goatfeathers Restaurant** and **Nick's On The Beach**. We are addicted to carry-out from **Cocoon's**, where we get delicious Shrimp Salad Sandwiches, Cajun Chips, and Texas Caviar (known as black-eyed pea salad in some circles) for our daily picnic lunches. If you're in the mood for a really good burger and freshly cut fries or a delicious omelet with crabmeat and shrimp, look no farther than **Las Palmas Café and Bakery**. No matter how full you are, you'll have a tough time leaving without a bag of pastries once you catch a glimpse of what's in the display cases.

In 1881, Colonel W. D. Chipley came upon a nearly perfectly round lake 30 miles north of the beaches and the Gulf while surveying for the railroad. He was so taken with it that he returned to found **DeFuniak Springs** along its shores in the 1880s. Named for Fred R. DeFuniak, who held a high office in the L & N Railroad, the lake is fed by a spring. Today, visitors may drive north from the beach across the US 331 bridge to DeFuniak Springs, then cruise along Circle Drive or stroll the lake's one-mile circumference to enjoy the grassy slopes and historic homes that line it.

In 1884, DeFuniak Springs was chosen as a winter home for the famed New York Chautauqua, founded in 1874 to teach Sunday-school instructors contemporary education techniques. That system evolved into an effort to inspire self-discovery, self-discipline, and self-enrichment. The movement grew to include some 100 chautauquas across America.

The historic Hall of Brotherhood in DeFuniak Springs, which was the site of lectures during Florida's early Chautauqua, continues to welcome visitors today.

When the first Florida Chautauqua was held in 1885, DeFuniak Springs found itself cast as a cultural center. It hosted lectures by prominent speakers, classes, and workshops during educational retreats that attracted thousands of visitors. The Florida Chautauqua was an annual event for 36 years until World War I and the Great Depression interfered. It was revived during the 1990s and is going strong again today. Tickets are available for workshops and lectures during the three-day event, as well as for special events like Victorian teas, concerts, and heritage-arts demonstrations and workshops.

Although the back portion of the historic Hall of Brotherhood was destroyed by Hurricane Eloise in 1975, a portion of the ornate building remains. It serves as an information headquarters for DeFuniak Springs and the chautauqua. Thirty-three historic homes, which ring the nearly perfectly round lake, show off their turrets, verandas, and gingerbread trim in styles ranging from Folk Victorian and Prairie

Gothic to Queen Anne. An additional 150 historic homes are in the immediate vicinity.

While you're in town, check out the cast-iron frying pans, handmade soaps, and crocks at **The Little Big Store**, a re-creation of an early-1900s general store. The neighboring **Big Store** sells fine antiques, as do several other shops in town.

Just down Eighth Street, **Hotel DeFuniak**, built in 1920 and recently restored, offers four suites, eight rooms, and a very popular dining room. Another choice for dining is **Mom and Dad's**, which serves tasty Italian dishes, steaks, and sandwiches.

Return to US 98 and continue south to the beaches, or head east to visit Panama City Beach.

All of the following are in Santa Rosa Beach and use the 32459 zip code and 850 area code, except where noted.

 A C C O M M O D A T I O N S

A Highlands House—P.O. Box 1189; 267-0110

Dune Allen Realty—5200 CR 30-A; 888-267-2121 or 267-2121

Garrett Realty—3723 CR 30-A, Seagrove Plaza, Seagrove Beach, FL 32459; 800-537-5387 or 654-3866

Grayton Beach State Recreation Area—357 Main Park Rd.; 231-4210

Hibiscus Guest House—85 DeFuniak St., Grayton Beach, FL 32459; 231-2733

Hotel DeFuniak—400 E. Nelson Ave. at Eighth St., DeFuniak Springs, FL 32433; 892-4383

Josephine's French Country Inn—P.O. Box 4767, Seaside, FL 32459; 800-848-1840 or 231-1940

Sandi Nichols Associates—4987 CR 30-A; 800-648-5833 or 231-5785

Seagrove on the Beach Realty—3010 South County Hwy. 395, Seagrove, FL 32459; 800-443-3146 or 231-4205

Seaside—P.O. Box 4730, CR 30-A; 888-732-7433 or 800-277-8696

Sugar Beach Inn—3501 CR 30-A, Seagrove Beach, FL 32459; 231-1577

 A T T R A C T I O N S

Bayou Arts and Antiques—Cessna Park and FL 393; 267-1404

Eden State Gardens—P.O. Box 26, Point Washington, FL 32454; 231-4214

Gourd Garden and Curiosity Shop—4808 CR 30-A, Seagrove Beach, FL 32459; 231-2007

Memory Lane Historic Guided Tours—654 Eden Dr.; 231-1581

Topsail Hill Reserve State Park—CR 30-A; 267-1868

CAMPING

Grayton Beach State Recreation Area—357 Main Park Rd.; 231-4210

Gregory E. Moore RV Resort—7525 W. CR 30-A; 877-232-2478 or 267-0299

DINING

Bud and Alley's—2236 CR 30-A, Seaside, FL 32459; 231-5900

Café Thirty-A—3899 CR 30-A, Seagrove Beach, FL 32459; 231-2166

Cocoon's—4101 CR 30-A, Seagrove Beach, FL 32459; 231-4544

Criollas—170 CR 30-A, Grayton Beach, FL 32459; 267-1267

Goatfeathers Restaurant—3865 CR 30-A; 267-2627

Hotel DeFuniak—400 E. Nelson Ave. at Eighth St., DeFuniak Springs, FL 32433; 892-4383

Las Palmas Café and Bakery—4935 CR 30-A, Seagrove Beach, FL 32459; 231-3456 or 231-0842

Mom and Dad's—2184 US 90 West, DeFuniak Springs, FL 32459; 892-5812

Piccolo Restaurant and Red Bar—70 Hotz Ave., Grayton Beach, FL 32459; 231-1008

Vintij—10859 W. Emerald Coast Pkwy., Suite 103, Destin, FL 32550; 650-9820

EVENTS

February—Florida Chautauqua at DeFuniak Springs

May—ArtsQuest

September—Seaside Institute Environmental Program

October—Paxton Heritage Festival

December—Christmas Reflections at DeFuniak Springs

December—Eden Candlelight Tour

FOR MORE INFORMATION

Beaches of South Walton—P.O. Box 1248; 800-822-6877; www.beachesofsouthwalton.com

Point Washington State Forest Field Office—5865 E. US 98; 231-5800

HIGHLIGHTS

St. Andrews State Park

Gulf World Marine Park

Falling Waters State Recreation Area

Florida Caverns State Park

Situated on a peninsula between the Gulf of Mexico and St. Andrews Bay, Panama City Beach, on Florida's Panhandle, is a favorite destination for families seeking sun, surf, and sand, and it welcomes them with open arms. Surrounded by the Gulf, East Bay, West Bay, North Bay, and St. Andrews Bay, the area offers endless opportunities for watersports. The beaches here ranked among the top 10 "Most Healthy Urban Beaches" in America in 2000, according to a report produced by the Surfrider Foundation, an international nonprofit organization dedicated to protecting the beaches and oceans of the world.

Panama City Beach has several piers and marinas. Both fishing and diving charters are available. Charter boats run out of **Captain Anderson's, Treasure Island, Lighthouse, Bay Point**, and **Hathaway Marinas**. Known as the "Wreck Capital of the South," the area boasts more than 46 artificial reefs that attract sea life ranging from tropical fish to giant manta rays. Historic wrecks include the 130-foot coastal steamship SS *Tarpon*. Resting in 95 feet of water 7.8 nautical miles from

shore, the freighter went down in high seas in 1937. In April 1997, the *Tarpon* was designated Florida's sixth State Underwater Archaeological Preserve. Submerged mooring buoys have been placed around the wreck.

The traffic creeps along Front Beach Road on holiday weekends, but it's easy to find your way around. There are only three main east-west thoroughfares, although they go by several different names. Front Beach Road (or Miracle Strip, as US 98 Alternate is known) caters to vacationers with its high-rise hotels and condominiums overlooking the Gulf and its attractions ranging from amusement parks and miniature golf to bungee jumping and go-cart tracks. Middle Beach Road (or Hutchinson Boulevard) has a combination of tourist attractions, restaurants, a post office, and a supermarket. Back Beach Road, Panama City Beach Parkway, and US 98 are all names for the same road. Exit signs labeled *A* to *N* direct you to cross streets near your desired location on the Miracle Strip to help you avoid some of the congestion during the peak spring-break and summer seasons. The visitor information center at the

The beautiful beach welcomes sunbathers to St. Andrews State Park.

corner of Panama City Beach Parkway and FL 79 at Exit I has maps and additional information.

Shell middens along St. Andrews Bay reveal the early presence of Native Americans. The land that now forms **St. Andrews State Park** was poorly valued by colonial settlers, who were far more interested in farmland than scenic beauty. It was for that reason that the area remained sparsely settled.

The first known resident was a Norwegian sailor named Theodore Tollefsen. "Teddy the Hermit," as he came to be known, found his way here when he was shipwrecked in his 26-foot boat during a hurricane in 1929. He remained for 25 years. Even more remarkably, he never paid taxes! He died in 1954 at the age of 74, leaving behind little but his legend. Tollefsen's shack stood near where sites 101 and 102 are located at the recreation area's campground today.

St. Andrews Park encompasses more than 1,200 acres. It is well known to locals, who enjoy the day-use facilities and partake of the excursions across "the Pass" to Shell Island, which is accessible only by boat. A shuttle departs from the rec-

reation area every 30 minutes, so you can shell and snorkel all day or just for an hour or two. The snorkel package includes all equipment and round-trip fare. The undeveloped island is seven miles long and up to a mile wide in places. Legend has it that pirates stashed their plunder on Spanish Shanty Point, but you're much more likely to find sand dollars than gold coins while you're here.

The park has 176 campsites with electrical hookups, five bathhouses, and two playgrounds, as well as a reconstructed "Cracker" turpentine still, the only surviving example of the many such distilleries once found in North Florida and central Florida. This particular still operated near Bristol, Florida. Circular cannon platforms that served during World War II as part of the St. Andrews Sound Military Reservation remain near the jetties.

In 1995, St. Andrews was designated the number-one beach in America by Dr. Stephen Leatherman, a University of Maryland coastal

Pine gum, or resin, was collected from trees using slashes that directed drippings into clay cups whose contents were eventually distilled into turpentine at stills like this one at St. Andrews State Park.

geologist. He based his evaluation on environmental, biological, and human factors.

Each fall, St. Andrews hosts **Nature's Gallery**, an award-winning historical and environmental festival of fine arts and crafts. Other activities at St. Andrews include fishing from the jetties and fishing piers, snorkeling, birding, boating, camping, hiking, picnicking, swimming, kayaking, and some surfing, although this is not an area known for great waves. Kayaks and fishing boats are available for rent through the **Shell Island Shuttle**. The overlook at Buttonwood Marsh is a perfect spot to watch rookeries of egrets and herons, to listen for pig frogs sitting on the lily pads, and to follow the slow progress of a gator as it makes its way across the marsh to bask on the shore.

Ever been kissed by a dolphin? Those who don't know the story behind the big sign at **Gulf World Marine Park** should stop by for a visit. Licensed under the provisions of the Marine Mammal Protection Act, Gulf World has been a presence on the beach for 32 years and is still growing.

The lively stars of the shows here are dolphins and sea lions. With no other audience present, we watched one day as the dolphins played ball among themselves like frisky pups. Clearly used to humans, one would occasionally lay the ball on the side of the pool and look at us in what seemed an obvious entreaty to play, only to have another dolphin sneak up and race off with the ball, starting the game all over again.

Co-owner Ron Hardy designed the impressive pump and filtration system that provides millions of gallons of sparkling water for the delightful creatures. He is also deeply involved with their protection and rehabilitation as the area coordinator for the Marine Mammal Stranding Network. Ron explained that dolphin strandings

Gulf World Marine Park offers vacationers the opportunity to enjoy tropical birds, alligators, and otters as well as dolphins and sea lions.

are usually due to an animal's being injured or sick, so it's best to call for help right away. He told us about the stranding of a dolphin named Granny. When she beached herself, helpful folks kept trying to push her back out in the water. Unfortunately, no one knew the importance of calling for help and putting a wet towel over her surprisingly delicate skin. She sustained third-degree sunburn before trained help arrived, but she survived.

Most of the dolphins at sanctioned sites like this were bred in captivity or were unable to be returned to their native pods after strandings. Problems arise when dolphins are fed by humans, which adversely affects the cooperative feeding behavior so important to survival in the wild. The last time any of Gulf World's animals were captured from the wild was 1989. The captive breeding population is sustainable unless a need arises for genetic diversification.

The entertainment here includes a laser light show and a performing parrot show. Education is also an important part of Gulf World's mission.

Lucky visitors can sign up for the "Trainer for the Day" program to get a behind-the-scenes view of the goings-on. Others participate in the "Swim with the Dolphins" program, which puts them in the tank for a close encounter of the best kind, ending with a quick peck on the cheek. Day camps are offered for children ages eight to 13. But people of any age with an interest in dolphins will enjoy a visit to Gulf World.

We stayed down the street at the **Flamingo Motel and Tower.** It has two pools and an outdoor spa surrounded by a tropical garden overlooking the Gulf. Some rooms have small refrigerators or microwaves, while others have a complete kitchenette. If you come during the off-season, you can even stay in a seventh-floor tower penthouse without breaking the bank. Monthly rentals are offered for snowbirds—a term meant to include all of us who take a break from the cold, gray winter to head for some Florida sunshine. Who could want more?

Golfers might want to consider the **Marriott Bay Point Resort Village.** The resort's **Lagoon Legends** course is consistently rated highly by *Golf Illustrated* and *Golf Digest*. The 1,100-acre resort offers two PGA championship golf courses. Condominiums, villas, and town homes are available for rent. At the 356-room Marriott, lodging choices range from guest rooms to one- and two-bedroom golf villas overlooking the Lagoon Legends fairways. Among the resort's five restaurants and lounges is **Bayview**, a favorite for breakfast, lunch, or dinner. Those in a more casual mood will enjoy **Teddy's Back Bay Beach Club**, which may be accessed by boat or by the pier behind the Marriott. The resort's 200-slip deepwater marina is one of the largest on the Gulf. Bay Point also offers three outdoor pools, one indoor pool, four tennis courts,

The award-winning Captain Anderson's features delicious seafood, steaks, and Greek specialties in a dockside dining room.

10 miles of paved surface suitable for biking, a workout room, and jogging trails. There's even an excursion boat to take you to Shell Island.

There are more than 20,000 hotel, motel, and condominium units in Panama City Beach. You'll find everything from national franchises like Ramada Inn, Best Western, Holiday Inn, Days Inn, and Quality Inn to mom-and-pop establishments.

Speaking of mom-and-pop operations, how about an award-winning restaurant run by brothers? **Captain Anderson's** was originally owned by the Anderson brothers, Walt and Captain Max. The Patronis brothers, Johnny and Jimmy, bought it in 1967. With the help of Jimmy's four sons, the brothers carry on the fine family tradition today. Captain Anderson's has retained most of its valued staff for decades and has grown in both size and excellence. It has been named one of the state's top 10 restaurants by *Florida Trend* magazine and one of America's top 50 by *Restaurants and Institutions.*

The rambling waterfront restaurant seats more

than 600 diners. Its season runs from February to November. The food is so good that we had to leave the gift shop with a copy of *The Captain's Classics Cookbook* and several bottles of Greek Salad Dressing. Never before or since have we had Grouper Cheeks! If they're on the menu, you owe it to yourself to try them. The somewhat bizarre-looking morsels are flaky, lightly fried, incredibly tender, and absolutely delicious. In addition to mouth-watering charcoal-broiled fish and seafood, the menu includes pasta, delicately fried seafood, and charcoal-broiled Angus beef. The special Greek Salad—which includes fresh crabmeat, shrimp, ripe olives, and feta cheese on a bed of lettuce, served with Greek Salad Dressing—is so big you'll be forced to share. The breads and desserts are all freshly made. The restaurant is open daily except Sunday. Early diners can watch the fishing fleet unload the fresh catch at the marina.

The Patronis family also owns a first-magnitude natural spring in northwestern Florida. It began to market the water, called Ecofina, in the spring of 1995.

We sampled the tasty Grouper Sandwich at **Schooners**, tucked among the sand dunes on Gulf Drive. Considered by many to be the last local beach club, this is a popular spot for boaters and divers. When the surf is calm, boats anchor and patrons wade in for the fresh local seafood, wine by the glass, and cold beer. This is one of the spots where locals take their friends for a casual night on the Gulf.

Each September, Schooners hosts the **Lobster Festival and Tournament**. After the weigh-in on Saturday afternoon (some of the past winners have been more than 12 pounds!), the feast begins with lobster grilled, fried, broiled, steamed, and blackened. The proceeds are donated to the Panama

City Marine Institute. Festival visitors can also enjoy a sand-sculpting contest, live music, and plenty of cold beer.

If you're in the mood for fresh scallops, you can gather your own. Scallop season runs from July 1 through August 15 and on weekends from August 16 to Labor Day weekend. Found in the bay hiding among the sea grasses, scallops have 30 to 40 brilliant blue eyes around the edge of their two-part, or bivalve, shells. When startled, the creature snaps its shell shut, which forces the water out and propels the scallop up to three feet away.

Vern had the pleasure of fishing Panama City Beach's beautiful bay waters and coastal beaches with Captain Greg Burnett, a local native with 20 years' experience on these waters. His guide service is located at **Bay Point Marina**. Greg's 18-foot *Osprey* is designed for working the shallow flats but is still capable of fishing open bay waters and coastal beaches. The bays have both deep and shallow areas where the fish concentrate, depending on the tide. Greg's experience puts you in the right place at the right time. Whether you're searching for an adventure that lasts a half day, a full day, or several days, you'll enjoy a first-class, stress-free experience aboard the *Osprey*. Your tackle, bait, fishing license, and ice are provided. Guests need to bring food, drinks, and sunscreen.

In general, if you're booking a charter and the captain is unknown to you, it's a good idea to check out a few basics beyond the boat itself. The equipment should be clean and in good repair, and the electronics should also be in good shape. Safety equipment should be available for all on board. Some fishing charters provide live bait, while others expect customers to pay an additional fee.

If you're fishing on your own, check with the

Florida Fish and Wildlife Conservation Commission or the Florida Marine Patrol for current regulations. Out-of-staters can buy Florida fishing licenses by calling 888-FISH-FLO. You'll need separate licenses for saltwater and freshwater species, if you're not covered by a charter-boat captain's license while angling.

If you're a diving enthusiast, you may want to visit the **Museum of Man in the Sea**, where you'll find 19th-century diving artifacts and pieces of equipment stored in every nook and cranny from floor to ceiling. A video and five aquariums tell the story of man's diving efforts from the 1500s to modern recreational and commercial diving. The museum is open daily. Plans are in the works to relocate to a new 50,000-square-foot facility next to the naval base.

While you're staying in Panama City Beach, consider a couple of interesting day trips across the Hathaway Bridge, then north along US 231.

Located an hour's drive from the beach, **Falling Waters State Recreation Area** is home to a Florida rarity—a waterfall. Falling Waters cascades 67 feet before disappearing into a sinkhole 100 feet deep and 20 feet wide.

This is also a good spot to get the skinny on one of the Florida stories that periodically grabs the attention of the national media—the state's infamous sinkholes. They're created when rainwater acidified by carbon dioxide in the air and decaying vegetation on the ground seeps into the underlying limestone bedrock. Over time, enough limestone is dissolved below the ground to cause a collapse, and—voila!—a sinkhole is formed, taking whatever was sitting on top of it as it falls.

Nearly 1,000 feet of boardwalks meander around the various sinkholes in the 155-acre recreation area. Visitors can swim and fish at a small

lake accessed by the **Wiregrass Trail** and the **Terrace Trail**. There are also facilities for picnicking. The camping area has 24 sites with electrical hookups, a restroom with showers, and a dump station.

An additional 30 minutes of driving time will bring you to another rarity—**Florida Caverns State Park**, the state's only limestone caverns open to the public. The largest of the caves is the only one available for viewing without a researcher's permit.

Begin your tour at the historic visitor center, constructed by the Civilian Conservation Corps following the Great Depression. The visitor center offers exhibits and a short video about the park. Visitors may also purchase tickets for a guided cave tour offered daily except for Thanksgiving and Christmas. The park has a 32-site campground with electrical hookups, restrooms with showers, and a dump station. It also offers canoe rentals for those interested in exploring a portion of the Chipola River, which bisects the park. Within the park's 1,300 acres are six miles of hiking, biking, and horse trails, an equestrian campground, and plant habitats commonly found in the Appalachian Mountains, but left here when the glaciers of the Pleistocene retreated. Animals ranging from the river otter to the endangered gray bat roam freely.

Return to US 98 and head east to begin your exploration of Florida's delightful "Forgotten Coast."

All of the following are in Panama City Beach and use the 32413 zip code and 850 area code, except where noted.

ACCOMMODATIONS

Flamingo Motel and Tower—15525 Front Beach Rd.; 234-2232; www.flamingomotel.com

Marriott Bay Point Resort Village—4200 Marriott Dr.; 800-874-7105 or 234-3307

 ATTRACTIONS

Falling Waters State Recreation Area—1130 State Park Rd., Chipley, FL 32428; 638-6130

Florida Caverns State Park—3345 Caverns Rd., Marianna, FL 32446; 482-9598

Gulf World Marine Park—15412 Front Beach Rd.; 234-5271

Museum of Man in the Sea—17314 Panama City Beach Pkwy.; 235-4101

Osprey Fishing Charters—Bay Point Marina, 3824 Hatteras Lane; 233-1959

Shell Island Shuttle—St. Andrews State Park, Thomas Dr.; 800-227-0132

 CAMPING

St. Andrews State Park—4607 State Park Ln.; 233-5140

 DINING

Captain Anderson's—5551 North Lagoon Dr.; 234-2225

Schooners—5721 Gulf Dr.; 235-3555

 EVENTS

September—Lobster Festival and Tournament

October-November—Nature's Gallery

 FOR MORE INFORMATION

Panama City Beach Convention and Visitors Bureau—P.O. Box 9473, Panama City Beach, FL 32417; 800-327-8352; www.800PCBEACH.com

5 Apalachicola-St. George Island-Carrabelle-St. Joseph Bay

HIGHLIGHTS

APALACHICOLA OYSTERS

HISTORIC DOWNTOWN APALACHICOLA

ST. GEORGE ISLAND

LITTLE ST. GEORGE

ST. VINCENT NATIONAL WILDLIFE REFUGE

ST. JOSEPH PENINSULA STATE PARK

Once upon a time, the Gulf coast community of Apalachicola and its neighbors were accidentally left off a map given to tourists visiting Florida. Capitalizing on the mistake, the "Forgotten Coast" was born. The funny thing is that the name actually fits Apalachicola, with its handsome Victorian homes, lovely bed-and-breakfasts, and oystermen harvesting the shellfish off the bay floor with long-handled tongs in the time-honored tradition.

Located about midway between Panama City and Tallahassee, Apalachicola is a must-see for those who enjoy Florida history, fishing, bird watching, shell collecting, wildlife, and estuarine reserves. There are miles of sandy beaches, uninhabited islands, and historic sites to explore.

The famous Apalachicola oysters were harvested commercially as early as 1836. Today, Apalachicola Bay provides 90 percent of the state's and 10 percent of the nation's oyster harvest from more than 10,000 acres of carefully tended beds. You'll never get them any fresher than what is served here.

This is one of Florida's last big, healthy coastal ecosystems. Apalachicola Bay and the rivers that feed it 16 billion gallons of water a day combine to create one of the best fishing environments in the United States. There are miles of shallow bays and meandering rivers.

The town is named for the Apalachees, a tribe of Native Americans who lived in the area prior to the arrival of Spanish missionaries. Apalachicola has been translated as "Place of the Ruling People" and as "Land of the Friendly People." According to Charlton W. Tebeau in *A History of Florida*, the Apalachees and related tribes in the western Florida Panhandle numbered about 25,000 at the time of the arrival of Europeans. Jesuit and Franciscan missionaries soon followed the Spanish explorers. The first priests reached the

Apalachicola Bay supplies 10 percent of the nation's oysters.

Apalachees in 1633. Over the next 20 years, they established a chain of missions built about 20 miles apart that crossed the Apalachicola River and went on to Port St. Joe. According to Michael Gannon in *Florida: A Short History*, the Franciscans had only humanitarian, rather than military, goals in mind. However, James Moore, the British governor of neighboring Georgia, had a different plan, leading raiding parties to destroy the missions of the Apalachees. According to Gannon, three Franciscans died defending their

charges, most of the mission compounds were destroyed, and many of the mission Indians were killed or captured and sold into slavery. Thus ended any humanitarian efforts in dealing with Florida's native people.

After 200 years of Spanish domination, Florida was sacrificed to the victorious British at the conclusion of the French and Indian War (1754-1763) as the price for the return of Cuba. The British proceeded to carve out two colonies from a Florida that at that time extended well beyond its present borders. The Apalachicola River formed the boundary between East Florida, which had its capital at St. Augustine, and West Florida, which had its capital at Pensacola.

Soon, the American Revolution fully occupied the British. At its conclusion, Spain briefly regained Florida. In 1821, Spain relinquished control of Florida in a deal made with the newly formed United States of America. This deal forgave Spanish debts and abandoned United States claims to Texas.

Apalachicola was ideally positioned to transfer bales of cotton brought from Alabama and Georgia on the Flint, Chattahoochee, and Apalachicola Rivers to the sailing ships anchored in the deeper waters of Apalachicola Bay. In 1822, President James Monroe officially appointed a port collector. A boom period began that peaked about 15 years later, when Apalachicola was the third-largest port on the Gulf. Thousands of bales of cotton were shipped from Apalachicola to New England and Europe.

During the long, hot summers, residents were susceptible to the ravages of the dreaded yellow fever, a subtropical disease carried by mosquitoes. Following an epidemic in 1841, Dr. John Gorrie of Apalachicola laid the groundwork for modern refrigeration and air conditioning when he began working on a way to cool the rooms of his yellow-fever patients. By 1844, he developed an ice-making machine that employed the same basic principle still in use today. Unfortunately, Dr. Gorrie died in 1855 broke, discouraged, and unaware of the far-reaching effects of his invention. The original machine is in the Smithsonian Institution in Washington D.C., but you can see a replica and learn more about his story at the **John Gorrie State Museum** on Sixth Street. It's open Thursday through Monday except for Thanksgiving, Christmas, and New Year's.

With the arrival of railroads in the 1850s, the cotton trade cooled, a decline that continued through the Civil War. For a time, sponging was an important local industry. By 1888, Apalachicola was harvesting a third of all the sponges brought to market in Florida. Next came the timber industry, which dominated the area's economy until the 1930s. During that time, lumber magnates built large Victorian homes overlooking Apalachicola Bay. Now part of a 200-home historic district, several of these have been converted to bed-and-breakfasts.

If you're interested in taking a scenic walking tour in Apalachicola, you can obtain a map at the chamber of commerce on Market Street. The walking tour begins at the John Gorrie State Museum and ends at Lafayette Park.

As you enter town from the east, you'll cross the John Gorrie Bridge. At its base, the **Gibson Inn** holds court over the entrance to the downtown area. This 1907 landmark has wraparound porches, gorgeous wooden accents, 31 guest rooms with private baths and televisions, and a full-service restaurant featuring an inspiring menu and a good wine list. After extensive renovations

The Gibson Inn offers beautifully restored classic accommodations in downtown Apalachicola.

that took two years, the Gibson Inn is shipshape these days. It sits at the forefront of the rebirth of Apalachicola's downtown. Some of the rooms on the second floor have French doors that open to a covered porch. Others are more like suites. Room 315, for example, has a large four-poster bed with lamps strategically placed on both sides, a sitting area, and a large bath. Some rooms have twin beds, but most have queens and kings. The bar is a vision of dark, lustrous wood and shuttered windows. Meals are served in the steamboat-style dining room. Executive chef Adam Mitts prepares tempting seafood dishes like Almond-Crusted Sea Scallops and Bronzed Tuna with Ginger Soy Honey Glaze. The restaurant is open nightly for dinner and serves breakfast and lunch on weekends.

The couple of blocks of Market Street beyond the Gibson House are lined with restaurants and shops like the whimsical **Chez Funk**. Its shelves are loaded with fun items—sweets labeled as "Training Treats for New Husbands," a lamp made from a minnow bucket, quirky garden sculptures, and other such things.

Located farther down Market Street, **Apalachicola Seafood Grill** claims to have the world's largest fried Fish Sandwich. It's a whopper, all right, about as big as a dinner plate, filled with flaky, white tilefish. Salads featuring char-grilled yellowfin tuna, grouper, and Atlantic salmon are correctly listed as "Meal Salads." The oysters are big and fresh, and the Key Lime Pie is really good, too. The grill offers a full bar. It's open for lunch and dinner every day except Sunday.

Across the intersection, **Tamara's Café Floridita** serves seafood, Caribbean cuisine, and South American dishes for lunch and dinner Tuesday through Saturday.

Around the corner on Water Street, you can get your oysters served 17 different ways for lunch or dinner at **Boss Oyster**. You can have the staff shuck you a couple of dozen fresh ones, then head out to the deck overlooking the river with a cold beer for some truly delectable dining. Boss Oyster is open daily.

Located on the other side of Market Street are the **Tin Shed** and the **Grady Market**, where you'll be hard pressed to prowl through all the nautical items without finding something you absolutely must have.

You can explore the area by sea aboard the *Governor Stone*, an authentic 1877 Gulf coast schooner. This National Historic Landmark is docked at Apalachicola's **City Marina**. Two-hour charters are offered.

A few blocks away at the corner of Sixth Street and US 98 is the **Coombs House Inn**, built in 1905 by a former Union officer from Maine who fell in love with a Southern lady and the balmy climate in Apalachicola. The home he built for his wife is now a beautifully restored, award-winning inn, classically furnished with elegant

One of Apalachicola's historic bed-and-breakfasts, the Coombs House Inn offers a variety of guest rooms with elegant antique furnishings.

antiques. The floors are of tiger oak and the wall panels of dark cypress. The hand-carved stairway is a marvel of craftsmanship in oak. The nine guest rooms and one Jacuzzi suite have private baths, cable television, and telephones. A full breakfast is served, but you'll find treats like cookies and tea to refresh you throughout the day.

Lodging is also available in **Coombs House East**, a smaller Victorian down the street that offers eight rooms, including a honeymoon suite with a massive, hand-carved Indonesian bed and a Jacuzzi with lovely stained glass overhead. The inn's Carriage House is a one-bedroom efficiency with a small kitchen and a trundle bed. Children are welcome as long as their parents are well behaved.

Just down the street, **Brigitte's Romantic Retreat** offers classic Old World hospitality, from wine in the evening to a bountiful breakfast featuring German Pancakes, Egg Cups, fruit, ham, and Tupelo honey. This lovingly restored bed-and-breakfast offers a suite with a private dining

For those who prefer staying on St. George Island, the St. George Inn has generous rooms and suites conveniently located for enjoying the Gulf or the bay.

area and a fireplace, as well as guest rooms in shades of rose, blue, and gold. The rooms have private baths and antique furnishings designed to put you in a romantic frame of mind.

On St. George Island, a barrier island linked to the mainland by a causeway, you can rent a beach house or stay at the gorgeous, three-story **St. George Inn**. Although it has many classical features, the inn is a modern facility designed to meet the needs of today's visitors. Each of its generous rooms and suites was designed with creature comforts in mind—big, comfortable queen or king beds, full baths, cable television, refrigerators, coffee makers, and telephones. We stayed on the first floor in the Sandpiper Suite, which had a full kitchen, a fireplace, and a sitting area. The second-story rooms offer Gulf views to the south and comfortable perches where you can curl up with a good book. The newest two-room suites are on the third floor. Each has a king bed, a large bath, a sitting room with a queen sleeper, and a large, private balcony that overlooks either the

Gulf or the bay. A continental breakfast is served downstairs each morning.

There are several restaurants to sample while you're on St. George Island. **Finni's Grill and Bar** offers fresh seafood, pasta, and steaks for lunch and dinner. The **Island Oasis Restaurant and Lounge** serves breakfast, lunch, and dinner, specializing in such items as Peel-and-Eat Shrimp and Soft-Shell Crabs. Across the causeway at Eastpoint, **That Place on 98** is a popular spot for fresh seafood, pasta, and homemade desserts served overlooking Apalachicola Bay.

Located at the eastern end of the island, **St. George Island State Park** offers camping and the longest beach of any state park in Florida. You'll also find canoe launches, nature trails, and picnic areas. This is a popular destination for birding on the Gulf during the spring and fall. Large, highly visible nesting colonies of least terns take advantage of the sands along the edge of the causeway leading back to the mainland. The traffic doesn't seem to disturb them in their preparation for parenthood.

Little St. George—or Cape St. George, as it's also known—was formed when the United States Army Corps of Engineers dug a permanent pass through St. George Island to the Gulf in 1957 for the fishing boats from Apalachicola. Little St. George was purchased by the state in 1977 under the Environmentally Endangered Land Program and is managed as part of the Apalachicola National Estuarine Research Reserve. Little St. George is accessible only by boat. Local outfitters including **Journeys of St. George Island** offer adventure tours to the island. From March through December, canoe, kayak, and fishing trips are available, as are rentals. A four-hour excursion to Little St. George includes a hike to the 148-year-old lighthouse, the third lighthouse built here, the others having been wiped out by storms. The walls of the 72-foot tower are four feet thick at the base, built to withstand tides and time. Little St. George also offers opportunities for wildlife viewing and primitive camping at designated sites at West Pass and Sikes Cut.

Northwest of Little St. George, **St. Vincent National Wildlife Refuge** is another barrier island accessible only by boat. It is believed that the island was named by Franciscan missionaries in the 1600s. Once a private hunting and fishing preserve, the 12,358-acre barrier island has 10 separate habitats ranging from tidal marsh to stands of cabbage palm and slash pine. Initially established for waterfowl, St. Vincent is a bird watcher's delight. It also provides protected habitat for endangered wildlife ranging from loggerhead turtles to red wolves. Wolf pups are bred here and taken to reintroduction sites after they are weaned. All recreational use is for daylight hours only, unless you're taking part in one of the hunts for deer and feral hogs. The refuge manager's office is located at the north end of Market Street in Apalachicola.

The educational center for **Apalachicola National Estuarine Research Reserve** is also located at the north end of Market. Here, you'll find exhibits on the area's flora and fauna, a nature trail, and publications about wildlife and the environment. Resource management, research, and education are the top priorities at the educational center.

If you're in a sporting mood, Captain Charles Wilson, a fourth-generation Apalachicola fisherman, uses his 22-foot, 200-horsepower boat to get clients to the fishing holes quickly and comfortably. He handles angling for speckled trout, redfish, Spanish mackerel, white trout, tripletail, black drum, flounder, tarpon, and more. And he char-

Oystermen on Apalachicola Bay use traditional long-handled tongs to pluck the delicacies from the floor of the bay.

ters offshore trips for the really big boys: cobia, amberjack, dolphin, snapper, and king mackerel.

Vern got to wet a hook with Captain Charles and his nephew, Chet, on the Apalachicola River, where the streams and cutoffs are so numerous that a first-timer would be lost in no time. The ride was filled with trees laden with Spanish moss, alligators sunning on the banks, an osprey nibbling on a recent catch high in a tree, and silence punctuated by bird chatter. They landed redfish and sheepshead and had a blast.

The peak fishing season begins in March and runs through Christmas. That's not to say fish can't be caught in the off months. They can, but they aren't in big schools.

There are several interesting day trips from Apalachicola.

You may want to visit **Apalachicola National Forest.** Established in 1936, it contains more than a half-million acres. Camping, boating, fishing for bass and bream, and hunting for deer, quail, and bear are popular pursuits here. **Fort Gadsden State**

Historic Site is part of Apalachicola National Forest. This was the site of a bloody battle between United States forces and a combination of Native Americans and runaway slaves on July 27, 1816. Located on the east bank of the Apalachicola River, it may be accessed via FL 65. The fort has long since been destroyed, but a miniature replica is used to interpret the site. According to *Boone's Florida Historical Markers and Sites*, the British built Fort Gadsden in 1814 as a rallying point for the Seminoles, who wanted to fight with the British against the United States. After the British abandoned the fort, it was occupied by a band of free Negroes until it was destroyed by order of Major General Andrew Jackson.

Located farther north, **Torreya State Park** is one of the best places in Florida to enjoy fall foliage. The park is named for the rare torreya tree, which lives only along a few miles of bluffs on the Apalachicola River. Unfortunately, the future looks bleak for the torreya, since young trees started being struck by disease during the 1960s. The park's 150-foot bluffs are forested with trees commonly found in the southern Appalachian Mountains. The historic **Gregory House**, originally built across the river in 1849, is open for tours daily. The park's campground offers showers, a dump station, and 30 sites, about half of which have electrical hookups. Visitors may also rent a domed tent called a Yurt that is 10 feet in diameter and has flooring, air conditioning, heat, a table and chairs, and a futon. Fifteen miles of hiking trails introduce visitors to the park's natural beauty.

To the east of Apalachicola is Carrabelle, a coastal fishing village with the distinction of being the home of the world's smallest police station, housed in a phone booth along US 98 in the middle of town. Carrabelle was named in 1897, two years after a lighthouse was completed

Towering sand dunes overlook the Gulf at St. Joseph Peninsula State Park.

west of town at Crooked River. The lighthouse's fourth-order lens started operating in the fall of 1895. It continues to warn mariners of the eastern end of the Panhandle portion of the Intracoastal Waterway. There are more than 150 miles of open Gulf between Carrabelle and the resumption of the Intracoastal Waterway near Tarpon Springs. The lighthouse's iron skeleton tower rises against the sky southwest of Carrabelle.

If secluded beaches and native beauty suit your taste, head east from Apalachicola on US 98 and CR 30 about 25 miles to Cape San Blas and the incredible 2,516-acre **St. Joseph Peninsula State Park**.

On your way, you'll pass a local landmark, the **Indian Pass Raw Bar**, a very laid-back, very local, no-frills operation with plenty of delicious oysters and a loyal following across the Southeast. As you continue toward the park, you'll pass a radar station, followed by a turnoff to the **Cape San Blas Lighthouse**, a skeleton tower whose light is visible 25 miles at sea. The lighthouse is presently closed to visitors, and the keeper's quarters are under renovation. If you're looking for a place to stay, the **Turtle Beach Inn** at Indian Pass offers guest rooms with private baths, a Jacuzzi suite, and one- and two-bedroom cottages. Breakfast and afternoon refreshments are served on covered porches and in the oceanfront dining room.

The main road at St. Joseph Peninsula State Park follows the narrow peninsula as it curves into the Gulf, partially encircling St. Joseph Bay. St. Joe is the only embayed body of water in the eastern Gulf without an inflow of fresh water. As a result, the bay's 73,000 acres of water have the same salinity as the Gulf. St. Joseph Bay supports a significant population of bay scallops. Manatees are commonly seen during the summer months,

perhaps drawn by the sea-grass beds. This area has the largest numbers of nesting sea turtles on the Panhandle. Spotted trout, redfish, flounder, and sheepshead prowl the sandy bottoms and grassy beds.

Portions of the park have a wildness and remoteness that feel like no other place. The dunes here are so high that they block the view of the Gulf until you climb the steps of the boardwalk and see the long, unbroken expanse of beach below. Look the opposite way and you'll see the shallow bay, which is breathtakingly beautiful.

The park's two campgrounds have 119 sites, including nearly 100 with electrical hookups. Restrooms, showers, and dump stations are available. A one-way road leads to the gray, weathered cabins overlooking the bay. You'd better make reservations well in advance if you're planning to stay here. Each cabin has two stories, a fully equipped kitchen, a screened porch, and a boardwalk leading to a private bench by the bay.

Across the bay is Port St. Joe, a community making the transition from an industrial city to an eco-tourism economy. Downtown is all dolled up with brick sidewalks. There's a new marina. Thursday through Monday, stop by the **Constitution Convention State Museum** to learn more about Port St. Joe's role in Florida's statehood.

Continue east along US 98 to visit Panacea, Sopchoppy, Wakulla Springs, and St. Marks.

All of the following are in Apalachicola and use the 32320 zip code and 850 area code, except where noted.

ACCOMMODATIONS

Anchor Vacation Properties—119 Franklin Blvd., St. George Island, FL 32328; 800-824-0416

Apalachicola River Inn—123 Water St.; 653-8139

Brigitte's Romantic Retreat—101 Sixth St.; 888-554-4376 or 653-3270

Coombs House Inn—80 Sixth St.; 653-9199

Gibson Inn—57 Avenue C, P.O. Box 221; 653-2191

Gulf Coast Realty—45 E. First St., St. George Island, FL 32328; 800-367-1680

St. George Inn—135 Franklin Blvd., St. George Island, FL 32328; 800-332-5196; www.stgeorgeinn.com

St. Joseph Peninsula State Park—8899 Cape San Blas Rd., Port St. Joe, FL 32456; 227-1327

Turtle Beach Inn—140 Painted Pony Rd., Port St. Joe, FL 32456; 229-9366

ATTRACTIONS

Apalachicola Maritime Museum—Apalachicola Chamber of Commerce, 99 Market St.; 653-9419

Apalachicola National Estuarine Research Reserve—261 Seventh St.; 653-8063

Captain Charles Wilson Charters—653-9008; www.captcharlescharters.com

Constitution Convention State Museum—200 Allen Memorial Way, Port St. Joe, FL 32456; 229-8029

Fort Gadsden State Historic Site—P.O. Box 579, FL 20, Bristol, FL 32321; 643-2282

Governor Stone Charters—Apalachicola Chamber of Commerce, 99 Market St.; 653-9419

John Gorrie State Museum—Sixth St. and Avenue D, P.O. Box 75; 653-9347

Journeys of St. George Island—240 E. Third St., St. George Island, FL 32328; 927-3259

St. George Island State Park—1900 E. Gulf Beach Dr., St. George Island, FL 32328; 927-2111

St. Joseph Peninsula State Park—8899 Cape San Blas Rd., Port St. Joe, FL 32456; 227-1327

St. Vincent Island Shuttle Service—690 Indian Pass Rd., Port St. Joe, FL 32546; 229-1065

St. Vincent National Wildlife Refuge—P.O. Box 447, Apalachicola, FL 32329; 653-8808

CAMPING

Cape San Blas Campground and Cabins—1342 Cape San Blas Rd., Cape San Blas, FL 32457; 229-6800; www.capesanblas.com/capecamp

Indian Pass Campground—2817 Indian Pass Rd., Port St. Joe, FL 32456; 227-7203

St. George Island State Park—1900 E. Gulf Beach Dr., St. George Island, FL 32328; 927-2111

St. Joseph Peninsula State Park—8899 Cape San Blas Rd., Port St. Joe, FL 32456; 227-1327

Torreya State Park—Rt. 2, Box 70, Bristol, FL 32321; 643-2674

 DINING

Apalachicola Seafood Grill—100 Market St.; 653-9510

Boss Oyster—123 Water St.; 653-9364

Gibson Inn—Avenue C and Market St.; 653-2191

Indian Pass Raw Bar—8391 CR 30-C (Indian Pass Rd.), Port St. Joe, FL 32456; 227-1670

Island Oasis Restaurant and Lounge—101 E. Gulf Beach Dr., St. George Island, FL 32328; 927-2639

Owl Café—Avenue D and Commerce St.; 653-9888

Tamara's Café Floridita—17 Avenue E; 653-4111

That Place on 98—500 US 98, Eastpoint, FL 32328; 670-9898

 EVENTS

March—St. George Island Chili Cookoff

April—Apalachicola Antique Boat Show

November—Florida Seafood Festival

 FOR MORE INFORMATION

Apalachicola Chamber of Commerce—99 Market St.; 653-9419; www.baynavigator.com

A charming Southern city of more than 220,000 residents, Tallahassee offers fine restaurants, parks, art galleries, museums, and other cultural amenities supported in large part by the two major universities in town, Florida A & M and Florida State. More than 5,000 rooms are available for visitors. The accommodations range from historic bed-and-breakfasts to national franchise hotels and motels.

Situated 25 miles north of the Gulf of Mexico and 14 miles south of the Georgia line, Florida's capital city is much more closely related to the plantations of Georgia than the beaches of South Florida. So how did a town closer to Atlanta than Miami become the center of government for the Sunshine State?

According to Mary Louise Ellis and William Warren Rogers in *Tallahassee and Leon County: A History and Bibliography*, Congress established the Territory of Florida and President James Monroe signed the bill into law on March 30, 1822. That first year, the legislative council met in Pensacola. The following year, it met in St. Augustine. It

On a clear day, visitors see Tallahassee spread out beneath the observation deck at the top of the state's New Capitol.

quickly became apparent to all the legislators that the long and dangerous journey between the two settlements necessitated finding a permanent, centrally located capital. In the interest of fairness, Territorial Governor William Pope DuVal decided to send lawyer John Lee Williams in a boat from Pensacola and Dr. William Simmons on horseback from St. Augustine. The two men explored the area between the Ochlockonee and Suwanee Rivers, met in the middle, so to speak, and agreed that Tallahassee would be the site.

In December 1824, the legislative council met for the first time in Tallahassee in a capitol built of logs. Despite complaints that travelers were unable to "walk the streets without being armed to the teeth," the town grew quickly. Not even a yellow-fever epidemic followed by a terrible fire could stop the wheels of progress.

A good place to begin your exploration is the **Tallahassee Convention and Visitor Bureau** at 106 East Jefferson Street, open Monday through Saturday. Or you might start at the excellent museums in the Capitol Hill area. In most cases, the museums are open daily, and admission is free.

The **Old Capitol** on Monroe Street is now a museum. Rather than tear down the 1845 Greek Revival structure, it was decided in the late 1970s to restore it to its 1902 American Renaissance appearance. Inside are restored legislative chambers and exhibits on Florida's political history. The Old Capitol Museum is open daily.

Current legislative functions take place next door in a gleaming white monolith rising 22 stories above the ground. The **New Capitol** tops out at 512 feet above sea level. The glass-walled observation areas on the top floor are a good place to get a bird's-eye view of the city spreading in a sea of green across seven rolling hills, a seldom-seen landscape in Florida. A gallery of attractive artwork on the interior walls showcases Florida artists and invites visitors to linger in the newest state capitol in the continental United States. The New Capitol is open daily.

If you're interested in the state's past, be sure to visit the **Museum of Florida History** on Bronough Street. Here, a nine-foot-tall mastodon

The gleaming, new Florida State Capitol Building is a landmark in downtown Tallahassee.

taken from nearby Wakulla Springs during the 1930s introduces visitors to Florida's prehistoric past, beginning with the emergence of the peninsula from the ocean 28 million years ago.

A simple but helpful display uses a lever to reveal the coastline as it was at the end of the last Ice Age around 12,000 years ago, when Paleo-Indians arrived to hunt and fish in Florida's coastal areas. Indians of that period used chipped pieces of a flint-like rock called chert to hunt grazing

The Museum of Florida History has exhibits from Florida's prehistory to present times.

Another exhibit describes how Florida's geographic position helped Spain protect the route of the Plate Fleet, which transported gold and silver from Mexico, Central America, and South America back to Spain. The Plate Fleet—derived from *plata*, the Spanish word for silver, began sailing in 1537, not long after Cortez first plundered Aztec gold. As more gold arrived from the New World, Spain's power increased proportionately. The Plate Fleet sailed for the last time in 1778.

You'll also learn that five Civil War battles took place in Florida. Displays explain that Gainesville, Olustee, and Natural Bridge were won by the Confederacy, while Marianna was won by the Union. The fighting at Santa Rosa Island was inconclusive. The Confederate victory at Natural Bridge saved Tallahassee from capture, making it the only Confederate capital east of the Mississippi River not to be taken by Union forces.

The photo exhibit of Florida cowboys is especially interesting if you've always believed cowboys lived only in the wild, wild West. It turns out they were an important part of wild, wild Florida as well.

Of course, oranges are a central part of Florida history. Originating in Southeast Asia and spreading westward, they reached the New World in 1498, carried aboard ships commanded by Christopher Columbus. In 1773, noted naturalist William Bartram reported an abundance of wild oranges in Florida. But it wasn't until the mid-1870s that the potential for commercial citrus production developed. One of Florida's many natural disasters struck the fledgling citrus industry a one-two punch during the great freezes of 1894 and 1895, when every tree in the Citrus Belt was damaged or killed. Fortunately, America's thirst for

mammoths, forest-browsing mastodons, and other large animals. The settlements the Paleo-Indians made along the coast have long since been covered by rising sea levels. Ancient people followed the retreating coastline inland between 7,500 and 1,000 years ago. Archaic sites remain in the Panhandle and around Tampa Bay. Stone, bone, and antler tools are displayed, as is early Indian weaving from the Windover site in Brevard County near Cape Canaveral.

citrus persisted, and the industry boomed again farther south by the 1920s.

About the same time, another Florida industry came into full swing with the advent of Tin Can Tourism. Motorized wanderers traveled Highway 1A, the Tamiami Trail, and the Dixie Highway to escape Northern winters.

The Museum of Florida History is open daily.

The **Mary Brogan Museum of Art and Science** on Kleman Plaza is also open daily. Its three floors of art and family-friendly science exhibitions have common content themes. For example, a lighthearted look at city life offered by artist Red Grooms is complemented by a scientific look at the way Florida cities work. The second floor has permanent, hands-on science exhibits suitable for a wide range of age groups. The third floor houses art galleries. An admission fee is charged.

One of the city's many historic homes, the **Knott House**, is open for public tours Wednesday through Saturday. Admission is free. Built in 1843, the Knott House has seen Tallahassee's story unfold. The Emancipation Proclamation was read in front of this house on May 20, 1865. The furnishings date to the 1930s, when William and Louella Knotts moved in. The lady of the house liked to write poems and put them on furnishings ranging from iron hall trees to silver teapots, earning the residence the title "the House That Rhymes." William and Louella's son, Charlie, never married. In his will, he gave the house and its contents to the state of Florida, to be used as a museum.

Once one of Tallahassee's largest plantations, **Goodwood Plantation** dates to 1837. Now run by a private foundation, it is open to the public Monday through Saturday. The lovely grounds feature sago palms more than 100 years old and huge live oaks. Mid-March is the best time to

Goodwood Plantation was the center of an 8,000-acre plantation that was one of Tallahassee's finest in 1837.

see the gardens, though the grounds are lovely year-round. Admission to the grounds is free Monday though Saturday. An admission fee is charged for tours of the main house, which are available on Thursdays and Fridays.

Alfred B. Maclay State Gardens on Thomasville Road offers picnic areas, a swimming area, seven miles of hiking trails, a 161-acre lake with bass and bream fishing, and 1,200 acres of beautiful gardens ranging from formal to woodland. More than 1,000 types of plants are found here, including the endangered torreya, a tree related to the yew that is native only to the banks of the Apalachicola River. Peak blooming season runs from January to the end of April, when outstanding displays of camellias, rhododendrons, and azaleas put on a show. But something is blooming here year-round. Guided garden tours are conducted on Saturday and Sunday during the peak season. The estate's historic home was originally a hunting lodge built in the early 1900s. A wealthy New Yorker, Alfred Maclay, purchased it in the 1920s. The property was donated to the state by

The Alfred B. Maclay State Gardens include beautiful camellias representing about 150 varieties.

Mrs. Louise Maclay in 1953. It is open daily. An admission fee is charged.

The **Tallahassee Museum of History and Natural Science** is on Museum Drive. The 52-acre property offers nature trails and animal exhibits that include bobcats, the endangered red wolf, and the rare Florida panther living in natural-habitat enclosures. This is also the location of the **Murat House**, or Bellevue, as Princess Catherine Willis Murat knew it after she pur-

chased it in 1854. Catherine was the widow of Achille Murat, the exiled prince of Naples and the son of Napoleon Bonaparte's sister, Caroline. According to Mary Louise Ellis and William Warren Rogers in *Tallahassee and Leon County: A History and Bibliography*, Achille Murat's "eccentricities reached epic proportions." He and Catherine were "popular and flamboyant residents of early Tallahassee." The house was moved here in 1967 and is furnished with period antiques. The museum is open daily. Living-history demonstrations are conducted at the 1880s farm, school, and church on weekends.

Although no mission structures remain standing in Florida, the site of the **Mission San Luis de Apalachee** is located on Mission Road off Tennessee Street. This was the location of an Apalachee Indian town and the capital of the western Spanish missions in Florida from 1656 to 1704. The Spaniards burned the mission in 1704, rather than risk having it taken in raids by the British and their Creek allies. According to Henry Cabbage in *Tales of Historic Tallahassee*, the Apalachee population had dropped to about 25,000 in the 1600s. The tribe was near extinction when the mission burned. The few Apalachees who remained were absorbed by the Creeks and Seminoles.

The visitor center at the mission site has an orientation film and displays of some of the artifacts uncovered during the annual excavations here. This is the most thoroughly studied Spanish mission in Florida. Outdoor exhibits interpret the areas that once housed more than 1,500 people and were the site of the Apalachee council house, the Spanish fort, and the Franciscan church. Admission is free. The site is open Tuesday through Sunday except for Thanksgiving and Christmas.

Another important archaeological site is located along the shores of the 4,000-acre Lake Jackson. **Lake Jackson Mounds State Archaeological Site** has six temple mounds dating to around 1200 A.D. It is open daily until sunset. Lake Jackson has a peculiar tendency to drain itself completely every 20 years or so. When water levels are normal, it's a popular venue for bass anglers. **Red and Sam's Fish Camp** offers bait, boat rentals, fishing guides, fishing licenses, cabins, and RV and tent camping sites.

Hernando De Soto State Archaeological Site nearly became an office complex. Although it was widely known that De Soto led an expedition into what is now Florida in 1539, there was no archaeological confirmation of his journey through the Southeast. In March 1987, an archaeologist visited a construction site that included the home of former governor John W. Martin and made the surprising discovery that the house had been built on top of De Soto's 1539 winter camp. This is currently the only confirmed De Soto site in North America. The more than 40,000 artifacts that have been removed from the property range from copper coins from the early 1500s to links of chain-mail armor. Each January, historical reenactors gather for an event called the **Hernando De Soto Winter Encampment**.

If all this sightseeing works up your appetite, you'll be glad to know there is no shortage of dining options in Tallahassee.

The fun, funky **Kool Beanz Café** has a loud, lively atmosphere, good food, and entertaining décor. Appetizers like Calamari with Lemon-Jalapeño Vinaigrette, Buttermilk-Battered Quail with Spicy Cornbread, and Blue Crab Cakes with Saffron Mayo are designed to please the palate. Entrées range from Seared Tuna to Seafood

Chez Pierre serves award-winning French cuisine to appreciative Tallahassee diners.

Jambalaya to Sirloin Steak.

The chef at **Chez Pierre**, Eric Favier, is from a small town between Cannes and St. Tropez. He has treated Tallahassee diners to 25 years of award-winning French cuisine. Guests step inside the sunlight-filled 1920s home that's been restored with a Country French flavor to enjoy lunch or dinner Monday through Saturday. Sunday brunch is also served. Outside dining is offered on the patio beneath a canopy of live oaks. The menu includes appetizers like Caviar, Escargots, Crab Cakes, and Gingered Scallops. Entrées range from Wild Mushroom Fricassee to grouper, venison, lamb, beef, and veal dishes. You should really try your best to save room for Chez Pierre's decadent pastries, made in the finest French tradition. Even if you've overindulged, have a taste of the Mango or Black Raspberry Sorbet.

For more than 60 years, the award-winning **Silver Slipper** has served Tallahassee politicians its famous steaks and fresh seafood. The original Silver Slipper was designed for dining and dancing, but the private dining rooms are the hallmark of this legendary establishment today. From movie stars to presidents, when they come to Tallahassee, they come to the Silver Slipper. The menu includes salads, soups, and vegetables, but the succulent steaks top the list. From Delmonico to Châteaubriand flamed table-side, they're prepared just the way you like. Veal, lamb, and seafood dishes round out the menu. An extensive selection of wines, beers, and mixed drinks is also available. The Silver Slipper is open for dinner daily.

Located within easy walking distance of the Capitol, the Adams Street Common at South Adams Street is the pedestrian-friendly home of the **Governor's Inn**. This creative reconstruction of a classic downtown business building has 40 luxurious rooms, each named for a Florida governor and equipped with antiques and a variety of amenities from fireplaces to whirlpool tubs. The space is creatively used. You'll note the odd ceiling angles, the skylights, the interior hallway windows, and the exposed beams hinting at the building's industrial past. The Governor's Inn has no elevators, but the ambiance, the proximity to downtown attractions, the continental breakfast, the exemplary service, and the complimentary

The Adams Street Common is home to the Governor's Inn and Andrew's Capital Grill and Bar.

evening cocktails more than make up for any slight inconvenience. You'd better plan ahead if you want to stay here while the Florida legislature is in session or during a Florida State home football game.

Other downtown accommodations are available down the street at the **Doubletree Hotel Tallahassee**, which offers 244 guest rooms, seven suites, a pool, a fitness center, a restaurant, and a lounge.

Several national chains—including Best Western, Comfort Suites, Days Inn, Holiday Inn, Quality Inn, Marriott, and Radisson—have franchises within a mile or two of the Capitol. Many others are located within a five-mile radius.

The only downtown bed-and-breakfast is the **Calhoun Street Inn**, located in the Calhoun Street Historic District. This two-story frame inn has four guest rooms with private baths, televisions, and telephones. The inn boasts a big front porch complete with a swing and a garden complete with a pond. Six fireplaces and several claw-foot tubs round out the amenities. A full breakfast is served.

Once you've parked at Adams Street Common, most of what you'll want to see in downtown Tallahassee is a short stroll away.

Simply cross the brick-paved street in front of the Governor's Inn to enjoy a night under the stars at **Andrew's Capital Grill and Bar**, which serves lunch and dinner Monday through Saturday and brunch on Sunday. The Spinach and Gorgonzola Salad is very good. Andrew's offers a wide assortment of specialty sandwiches, soups, and pasta dishes.

Around the corner, the award-winning **Andrew's Second Act**, part of the same complex as Andrew's Capital Grill and Bar, serves brunch on Sunday, lunch Monday through Friday, and dinner Monday through Saturday in an upscale setting.

Tallahassee boasts two major universities. **Florida A & M** was founded in 1887 to provide higher education for Florida's black citizens. The **Black Archives Research Center** at Florida A & M has exhibits on African-American culture and history, while the **Foster Tanner Fine Arts Gallery** displays work by African-American artists. **Florida State University** was established in 1857. It is home to the **Museum of Fine Arts**, which hosts traveling exhibitions and has permanent collections on display. The university is the site of hundreds of cultural activities throughout the year.

Every Saturday morning from March through November, **Ponce de Leon Park**, located between Monroe and Adams Streets, is the site of a downtown marketplace that presents musicians, authors, poets, and regional artists and offers local farm-fresh produce.

Tallahassee reveres its live oaks. It protects them along specially designated canopy roads like Old Bainbridge Road, Meridian Road, Centerville Road, Miccosukee Road, and Old St. Augustine Road, all of which originate within the city.

There's much to see and do outside the city. The city is also proud of its railroad heritage. A mule-drawn rail trolley connecting Tallahassee cotton plantations with the coastal community at St. Marks was Florida's first railroad. Financed by Tallahassee businessmen, it was completed in 1837 and modernized in the 1850s. It was in service for 147 years, making it Florida's longest-operating railroad. In 1984, some 16 miles of the old railway bed were bought and converted as part of a rails-to-trails program. Today, the **Tallahassee-St. Marks Historic Railroad State Trail** is popular with cyclists, joggers, and skaters. Pets must be on leashes and well behaved. An adjacent trail is available for horseback riding.

Diners come from far and wide to enjoy a taste of Old Florida at **Nicholson's Family Farmhouse**, located north of Tallahassee in Havana. This home was built in 1828. The surrounding plantation encompassed 3,000 acres at the time of the Civil War. Paul Nicholson, a descendant of the original owner, subsequently purchased the old house and 50 acres and started a restaurant. It proved so popular that he started buying additional houses and moving them here. Nicholson's presently seats 650 diners in five different buildings. Four of the buildings share a kitchen, and the fifth has its own. The specialty here is Midwestern grain-fed beef that's been aged 21 days before being served. The mouth-watering Delmonico is the most popular cut. Nicholson's does not serve alcohol, but guests may request setups. Diners love the 400-year-old live oaks out front presiding over the goings-on, as well as the swings and rockers scattered about. In keeping with the feeling of a family farmhouse, Nicholson's offers wagon rides on Friday and Saturday evenings. It also has an antique and gift shop.

Speaking of antiques, come early if you'd like to browse some of the shops in Havana. **The Cannery**, located on Eighth Avenue, is a renovated canning plant that houses more than 150 dealers. **The Planter's Exchange** on Second Street has antiques and collectibles, along with a tearoom that serves lunch on weekends. Also popular among visitors are the antiquarian bookstore on Seventh Avenue and the shop on Eighth that sells Amish-made furniture of oak and cherry.

Diners claim that **Spring Creek Restaurant**, located about 25 miles south of Tallahassee in a small fishing community, is well worth the drive. This family-owned and -operated establishment serves tempting items like Crab Cakes made from locally harvested blue crabs, Soft-Shell and Stone Crabs in season, and some of the best Hush Puppies you'll find anywhere.

From Tallahassee, head south on FL 363 to visit Wakulla Springs, Natural Bridge, and St. Marks, or follow US 319 south to visit Panacea and Sopchoppy.

All of the following are in Tallahassee and use the 32304 zip code and 850 area code, except where noted.

ACCOMMODATIONS

Calhoun Street Inn—525 N. Calhoun St.; 425-5905

Doubletree Hotel Tallahassee—101 S. Adams St.; 800-222-8733 or 224-5000

Governor's Inn—209 S. Adams St.; 800-342-7717 or 681-6855

ATTRACTIONS

Alfred B. Maclay State Gardens—3540 Thomasville Rd.; 487-4556

Goodwood Plantation—1600 Miccosukee Rd.; 877-4202

Hernando De Soto State Archaeological Site—102 Governor Martin/De Soto Park Dr.; 922-6007

Knott House—301 E. Park Ave.; 922-2459

Lake Jackson Mounds State Archaeological Site—3600 Indian Mounds Rd.; 922-6007

Mary Brogan Museum of Art and Science—350 S. Duval St.; 513-0700

Mission San Luis de Apalachee—2020 Mission Rd.; 487-3711

Museum of Florida History—500 S. Bronough St.; 245-6400

New Capitol—S. Duval St.; 488-6167

Old Capitol Museum—400 S. Monroe St.; 487-1902

Tallahassee Museum of History and Natural Science—3945 Museum Dr.; 576-1636

 CAMPING

Big Oak RV Park—4024 N. Monroe St., 32303; 562-4660

Red and Sam's Fish Camp—5563 N. Monroe St., 32303; 562-3083

 DINING

Andrew's Capital Grill and Bar—208 South Adams St.; 222-3444

Andrew's Second Act—228 S. Adams St.; 222-3444

Chez Pierre—1215 Thomasville Rd.; 222-0936

Kool Beanz Café—921 Thomasville Rd.; 224-2466

Nicholson's Family Farmhouse—200 Coca Cola Ave., Havana, FL 32333; 539-5931

Silver Slipper—531 Silver Slipper Ln.; 386-9366

Spring Creek Restaurant—33 Ben Willis Rd., Crawfordville, FL 32327; 926-3751

 EVENTS

January—Hernando De Soto Winter Encampment

February—Seven Days of Opening Nights

March—Jazz and Blues Festival

March—Springtime Tallahassee

May—Southern Shakespeare Festival

August—Caribbean Carnival

December—Winter Festival

 FOR MORE INFORMATION

Tallahassee Area Convention and Visitor Bureau—106 E. Jefferson St.; 800-628-2866 or 413-9200; www.seetallahassee.com

HIGHLIGHTS

WAKULLA SPRINGS STATE PARK AND LODGE
SAN MARCOS DE APALACHE STATE HISTORIC SITE
ST. MARKS NATIONAL WILDLIFE REFUGE

St. Marks, along with its Wakulla County neighbors Wakulla, Shell Point, Spring Creek, Panacea, and Sopchoppy, provides the perfect antidote to the hustle and bustle of Tallahassee, some 18 miles north. Fortunately for the wildlife and the locals, about 75 percent of Wakulla County is state and national forests, wildlife refuges, and parks.

Four major rivers chart a course through Wakulla County to the Gulf. In the east, the spring-fed Wakulla River is usually crystal clear, while the St. Marks, the Sopchoppy, and the Ochlockonee are blackwater rivers given their characteristic tea color by the dissolved organic material picked up as they drain freshwater swamps and marshes.

As you head south on FL 363 from Tallahassee toward the Gulf coast, you'll drive beside the **Tallahassee-St. Marks Historic Railroad State Trail**, 16 miles of one of Florida's oldest railroads, bought and converted in a rails-to-trails program in 1984. It's popular with cyclists, joggers, and skaters. Cyclists will want to follow the signs at the turnoff from FL 363 to challenge the rolling sand dunes of the ancient shoreline on the 7.5-mile **Munson Hills Off-Road Bicycle Trail**.

Long ago, this was a shallow sea. As glacier melting occurred, sea levels rose and then receded, leaving behind terraces. Over time, five terraces formed. The oldest of them is in northwestern Wakulla County.

About eight miles south of Tallahassee, you'll see the turn for **Natural Bridge State Historic Site**, a place with both Civil War and geological significance. As the St. Marks River winds its way to the Gulf, it disappears beneath the sandy soil near Natural Bridge. The name describes the area between the river's disappearance and its reemergence at St. Marks Spring about 150 feet to the south.

The battle that occurred here during the final weeks of the Civil War is memorialized on six of the battlefield's original 200 acres. A monument commemorates the events in the first week of March 1865. A mere two months later, the Civil War ended and Tallahassee reluctantly received

The lodge and grounds at Wakulla Springs look much as they did when financier Edward Ball brought his friends here during the 1930s.

occupation troops. Governor John Milton, who had called on cadets to defend Tallahassee at Natural Bridge, was already dead of a self-inflicted gunshot wound, his preference to suffering the agony of defeat.

Restrooms and picnic tables are available at the historic site.

About 13 miles south of Tallahassee, you'll come to Wakulla and the turn west to **Wakulla Springs State Park and Lodge**. The first visitors to this area were Paleo-Indians hunting bison and mastodons. *Wakulla* is an Indian word for "strange and mysterious waters." Indeed, this is one of the world's deepest and largest freshwater springs, pumping an average of 250,000 to 400,000 gallons per minute. Divers have gone many, many miles into it at depths of more than 360 feet and still haven't located the source. Wakulla Springs gives rise to the Wakulla River, a venerable waterway blessed with abundant wildlife and bald cypress trees estimated to be 600 years old.

The entire park is a 4,700-acre wildlife sanc-

tuary. We were astounded by the hundreds of birds perched on nearly every available branch or vacant tree root, sitting right alongside hundreds of alligators. The anhinga (or snake bird), the white ibis with its long, curved bill, the yellow-crowned night heron, the limpkin, and the American widgeon with its startling white beak are just a few of the species commonly seen in February, when we visited. Fourteen species of record-breaking fish are also present, but angling and private boating are not allowed inside the park.

Three nature-trail systems introduce guests to the park's cypress wetlands, hardwood hammocks, and upland pine forests. A multiuse trail for hikers, bicyclists, and equestrians winds through 1,300 acres on the north side of the park.

In 1937, financier Edward Ball built a fabulous, 27-room Spanish Mission-style lodge with white stucco walls and a red-tile roof along the Wakulla River. He intended it as a vacation retreat where he and his friends could rest and observe wildlife. It is now listed on the National Register of Historic Places. Upon entering the lobby, you'll note the stone fireplace and cozy furnishings, which look much as they did in Ball's day. The ceiling is decorated with wooden beams hand-painted in intricate, colorful designs. The lodge has a gift shop and a spacious restaurant lined with windows. When we visited, the food in the dining room was very good, but the service was a bit slow at both breakfast and lunch. Remember, you're on Wakulla time. Bring something to read, or wear comfortable shoes for a short stroll around the lovely grounds while your meal is being prepared.

You'll certainly want to take time for the narrated, family-friendly boat ride. The guides we met were knowledgeable and entertaining in equal parts. There's enough action to appeal to all ages. The boat tours operate daily.

If you're bold enough, you can bring your bathing suit and swim, wade, or jump from the observation tower into the 68-degree water within easy sight of lots of alligators. This popular swimming area is apparently safe, unless you venture outside the designated area. Swimmers have lost their lives here when they disregarded the established boundaries between man and beast.

An admission fee is charged to visit the park. The grounds are open daily. The **Welcome Back Songbirds and Spring Nature Festival** takes place here in April. It offers crafts, activities, talks, and walks for all ages.

Finally, you'll reach the Gulf coast community of St. Marks, a tiny fishing village about 30 minutes south of Tallahassee. St. Marks, like most towns in Wakulla County, rarely shows up in glossy magazine ads, mainly because there are no high-rise beach resorts, shopping malls, or theme parks here. But you will find a taste of Florida history at San Marcos de Apalache State Historic Site, great oysters on the locally famous back porch at **Posey's Oyster Bar**, lots of wildlife at St. Marks National Wildlife Refuge, and good fishing in the St. Marks River.

San Marcos de Apalache State Historic Site has exhibits interpreting the site's occupation by Spanish, British, and Confederate soldiers. It also tells the story of the Apalachee Indians, who came here to fish and hunt long before the arrival of the Europeans.

Panfilo de Narvaez was the first European to visit. He and his 300 men arrived in 1527 but stayed only long enough to build ships. Hernando De Soto arrived with 600 men in 1539. He was followed by Franciscan friars from St. Augustine

The boat ride at Wakulla Springs State Park floats past more than 400 alligators in a wonderfully exotic landscape that was the setting for Creature from the Black Lagoon, *two Tarzan films, and the disaster epic* Airport '77.

in 1633. Spanish soldiers built wooden stockades here in 1680, but they were burned and looted by pirates only three years later. The first stone fort was started in 1739 but remained unfinished when the British took control in 1763, following Spain's defeat in the Seven Years' War. The fort was reoccupied by the Spanish in 1787 but was challenged by the infamous pirate Billy Bowlegs. Nine Spanish ships arrived to defend the fort. Bowlegs was eventually captured and sent to Havana in chains. The Spanish fort was briefly commandeered and used as a headquarters by Andrew Jackson in 1818 during the First Seminole War. Some of his men died here and were buried in a cemetery near the fort. In 1857, a sailors' hospital was constructed on the site of the fort by the United States. The fort was reestablished and occupied by Confederate soldiers during the Civil War. The foundation of today's museum and visitor center was built from the ruins of that hospital. The museum is closed Tuesdays, Wednesdays,

Posey's Oyster Bar's back porch is a favorite destination for those in search of fresh oysters and cold beer.

Thanksgiving, Christmas, and New Year's. An admission fee is charged.

A walking tour departs the museum and leads past a pile of stone rubble that was the Spanish fort's outer wall. It passes the moat that connected the Wakulla and St. Marks Rivers at high tide, then arrives at the strategic point of land at the confluence of the two rivers. Today, it's a peaceful spot with a lovely view.

On the third Saturday in May, the manatees are welcomed back to the waters of the Wakulla during the **Humanatee Festival**.

The surrounding town of St. Marks was created by an act of Congress in 1830.

Riverside Café serves breakfast, lunch, and dinner and will rent you a canoe when you've finished. This is one of two spots in town for fresh oysters served raw or steamed. The café also offers Stone Crab Claws in season and an assortment of seafood, steaks, chicken, and vegetarian dishes for dinner.

Down the street, oysters are served on the half shell on the deck overlooking the river at **Posey's**

Oyster Bar. Or you can dress them with horseradish and cocktail sauce if you prefer. Fishermen tie up their boats and climb ashore here, while a steady parade of boats passes up and down the St. Marks River.

While you're in the area, be sure to visit **St. Marks National Wildlife Refuge**, one of the oldest refuges in the nation. The visitor center is open daily. Here, you'll find maps, brochures, and current information on wildlife sightings in the salt marshes, tidal flats, freshwater impoundments, slash-pine flatwoods, and hardwood hammocks that make up the refuge. The hardwood swamps support black bears, otters, wood ducks, and night herons, among other species. Red-cockaded woodpeckers find shelter in the extensive pine woodlands. In all, more than 300 species of birds have been sighted here.

An entrance fee is charged for those traveling beyond the visitor center, in order to generate funds to purchase additional wetlands. Picnic tables, drinking water, and restrooms are available.

The seven-mile drive to the St. Marks Lighthouse passes through portions of the pristine St. Marks National Wildlife Refuge.

The refuge offers hiking along 75 miles of marked trails, game-species hunting in designated areas in the Panacea and Wakulla units from fall to spring, fishing all year in designated areas, boat launching, and crabbing—though you'd better keep an eye out for gators grabbing your bait!

Casual visitors enjoy the seven-mile drive down Lighthouse Road to the historic lighthouse, built in 1831. The light atop the 80-foot tower has been automated since 1960. It remains in operation today under the maintenance of the Coast Guard.

While you're in the refuge, stay on the lookout for one of the nesting pairs of bald eagles sitting in dead trees, tall pines, and oaks. You're most likely to spot wildlife on an early-morning bike ride, while canoeing on one of the refuge's pools or along the shore by the lighthouse. Anglers wade in the area just off the lighthouse. This is also a good place for crabbing. The boat ramp offers easy access for fishing from the flats.

Each October, thousands of monarch butterflies gather for their long journey across the Gulf to wintering grounds in the mountains of Mexico, which inspires naturalists to gather for the **Monarch Butterfly Festival** during the third week of the month. The refuge staff shares its knowledge during sessions about this amazing creature.

Camping is not permitted in the refuge, but a few cabins, a small motel, a marina, and boat rentals are available at **Shell Island Fish Camp** on the St. Marks River. The motel rooms are modern, with two double beds and cable TV, but the two-bedroom cabins are throwbacks complete with screened porches and kitchenettes. The fish camp isn't fancy and isn't supposed to be. It is clean and well kept and has everything an angler needs in its bait-and-tackle store.

Two-bedroom cabins at Shell Island Fish Camp are throwbacks to old-fashioned fish camps.

The other choice for lodging in St. Marks is the **Sweet Magnolia Inn**. Its seven suites have either two double beds and private baths or a queen-sized bed and a Jacuzzi. A generous breakfast is served each morning. The inn also offers a five-course, three-hour dinner cruise aboard the *Seahouse One*. Guests who take the cruise enjoy local delicacies like Blue Crab Cakes, Stuffed Grouper, and Prime Rib.

Drive west on US 98 from St. Marks to visit Panacea, named for the healing powers attributed to a spring that once flowed near town. The waters in the railroad town's spring were popular with travelers in the late 1800s.

Panacea is also home to the **Gulf Specimen Marine Laboratory**. Founded by noted biologist Jack Rudloe, the private, nonprofit lab supplies live fish and invertebrates to colleges and universities in the United States, Canada, and Britain. The main attractions here for most visitors are the various aquariums and touch tanks and the creatures like sea horses, scallops, and starfish that live in them. The touch tanks offer close encounters with

Founded in 1963, the Gulf Specimen Marine Laboratory introduces visitors to marine life found along the Gulf Coast.

living whelks, sand dollars, and crabs. No matter how old you are, watching the tiny hairs undulate across the perfectly symmetrical face of a sand dollar is fascinating. The laboratory gives visitors a sense of the diversity of life along North Florida's fertile coast. It is open daily. An admission fee is charged.

The first weekend in May, 20,000 seafood lovers gather in Panacea for a chance to sample local offerings during the **Blue Crab Festival**. Many of them get a room for the night at **Posey's Motel** or camp in one of the bay-front lots at **Holiday Campground**. The **Harbor House Restaurant** offers seafood and other dishes, along with drinks on the deck.

Located about five miles north of Panacea, Sopchoppy, a tiny community with a huge heart, claims fewer than 300 residents. This is the special kind of place that we hesitate to draw attention to, for fear of changing its character. Writers, craftsmen, artisans, and many other creative people live in or near Sopchoppy, a place Charles Kuralt considered one of his favorites. The

Sopchoppy Worm Gruntin' Festival, featuring a worm-raising technique documented by Kuralt, is an annual event held the first Saturday in April.

Backwoods Pizza, arguably the best place to eat in Sopchoppy, makes gourmet pizzas from scratch and bakes them in a stone oven in a restored 1912 pharmacy building on Municipal Avenue. The owners also operate **Sopchoppy Outfitters**. They'll rent you a kayak, canoe, or bicycle.

Located next door in the historic Ashmore Store, **From the Heart** is a coffee shop, antique store, and meeting place that is the site of monthly jams by the Backwoods Boogie Band. Pickers and grinners are free to sit in with the group. A couple of blocks away is **Mom's Seafood and Steak House**, which packs in the locals for a hearty lunch buffet.

The Sopchoppy River meets the Ochlockonee before entering the bay. The relatively undeveloped Sopchoppy has a canoe trail lined with limestone banks and hardwood forests. **Myron B. Hodge Sopchoppy City Park** offers camping, swimming, and boat-launching facilities.

The Ochlockonee River is the site of a state park where visitors can bike, camp, fish, swim, and paddle a well-known canoe trail that empties into the bay of the same name. The point at the confluence of the Ochlockonee and Dead Rivers is especially scenic. The state park is also the launch site for the **Apalachee Archaeological Boat Trail**, which passes shell middens and other historic sites on the way to the Gulf.

All in all, Wakulla County presents numerous opportunities for birding, hiking, biking, canoeing, kayaking, snorkeling, diving, and fishing.

Among the trails in the area are a portion of the **Florida National Scenic Trail** and the new

Gopher, Frog, and **Alligator** (a colorful name for the Georgia, Florida, and Alabama Railroad) **Trail.**

And don't forget the several boats available for both offshore and charter fishing. Captain Chris Oaks took a group that included Vern on a grouper-fishing outing aboard his 35-foot boat, *Miss Jill.* They departed from **Carroll's Bayside Marina** on Ochlockonee Bay. The Gulf was smooth as they motored an hour and a half to the 50-foot waters where the grouper were waiting. It was December; grouper move to shallow water during the cool months and head for much deeper water in summer. Once Chris dropped anchor, one angler had a six-pound fish in the boat in less than three minutes. Soon, a larger one came in, and then another, until it took a 12-pounder to be the top fish. Vern hooked a 15.7-pound grouper and felt confident it was the winner, since the group needed only one more fish to meet the limit. But the wind was sucked out of his sails within minutes when local angler Don Lesh brought in a 16.1-pounder.

From St. Marks, continue east on US 98 to points south on Florida's Nature Coast.

All of the following are in St. Marks and use the 32355 zip code and 850 area code, except where noted.

A C C O M M O D A T I O N S

Posey's Motel—1168 Coastal Hwy., Panacea, FL 32346; 984-5799

Shell Island Fish Camp and Marina—P.O. Box 115; 925-6226

Sweet Magnolia Inn—P.O. Box 335, 803 Port Leon Dr.; 925-7670

Wakulla Springs Lodge—550 Wakulla Park Dr., Wakulla Springs, FL 32305; 224-5950

A T T R A C T I O N S

Carroll's Bayside Marina—2273 Surf Rd., Ochlockonee Bay, FL 32346; 926-3762

From the Heart—60 Rose St., Sopchoppy, FL 32358; 962-5282

Gulf Specimen Marine Laboratory—P.O. Box 237, Panacea, FL 32346; 984-5297

Natural Bridge State Historic Site—1022 De Soto Park Dr., Tallahassee, FL 32301; 922-6007

Ochlockonee River State Park—P.O. Box 447, Sopchoppy, FL 32358; 962-2771

San Marcos de Apalache State Historic Site—P.O. Box 27, 148 Old Fort Rd.; 925-6216

St. Marks National Wildlife Refuge—P.O. Box 68; 925-6121

United States Forest Service, Wakulla Ranger District—57 Taff Dr., Crawfordville, FL 32327; 926-3561

Wakulla Springs State Park—1 Spring Dr., Wakulla Springs, FL 32305; 922-3632

CAMPING

Holiday Campground—14 Coastal Hwy., Panacea, FL 32346; 984-5757

Ochlockonee River State Park—P.O. Box 447, Sopchoppy, FL 32358; 962-2771

DINING

Alligator Point Marina and Restaurant—1648 Alligator Dr., Alligator Point, FL 32346; 349-2511

Backwoods Pizza—106 Municipal Ave., Sopchoppy, FL 32358; 962-2220

Harbor House Restaurant—107 Mississippi Ave., Panacea, FL 32346; 984-2758

Mom's Seafood and Steak House—2164 Sopchoppy Hwy., Sopchoppy, FL 32358; 984-2655

Posey's Beyond the Bay Restaurant—P.O. Box 294, US 98, Panacea FL 32346; 984-5799

Posey's Oyster Bar—55 Riverside Dr.; 925-6172

Riverside Café—69 Riverside Dr.; 925-5668

Spring Creek Restaurant—33 Ben Willis Rd., Crawfordville, FL 32327; 926-3751

Sweet Magnolia Inn—P.O. Box 335, 803 Port Leon Dr.; 925-7670

Wakulla Springs Restaurant—550 Wakulla Park Dr., Wakulla Springs, FL 32305; 244-5950

EVENTS

March—Battle of Natural Bridge Reenactment

April—Welcome Back Songbirds and Spring Nature Festival at Wakulla Springs State Park and Lodge

April—Sopchoppy Worm Gruntin' Festival

May—Blue Crab Festival at Panacea

May—Humanatee Festival at St. Marks

October—Monarch Butterfly Festival at St. Marks National Wildlife Refuge

December—Wakulla Chivaree

FOR MORE INFORMATION

Wakulla County Tourist Development Council—P.O. Box 67, Panacea, FL 32346; 984-3966; www.wakullacounty.org

8 *Florida's Nature Coast: Dixie, Citrus, Hernando, and Pasco Counties*

HIGHLIGHTS

CANOEING AND KAYAKING

FISHING

NATURAL SPRINGS

The Gulf coast from Wakulla County in the north to Pasco County in the south was once commonly called the Big Bend. In 1995, the state officially designated it Florida's Nature Coast. This string of coastal counties contains a patchwork of rivers that drain cypress, pine, and hardwood forests and marshland into estuaries that eventually empty into the Gulf of Mexico.

The outstanding fishing along the entire Nature Coast provides anglers an abundance of fresh- and saltwater species. Freshwater fishing is popular upstream in the rivers. Gulf-fishing enthusiasts chase a wide range of game-fish species from the surf to offshore. A number of marinas operate along the Gulf coast, and many fishing guides are associated with these marinas. If you're unfamiliar with the area you want to fish, hiring a guide for a half-day trip will help you learn.

The Nature Coast might also be called the Uncongested Coast, because it offers a refreshing change from the crowded beaches of many Florida locales. Unfortunately, the white-sand beaches

Fishing, the Nature Coast's major enticement, is sometimes strenuous, sometimes not.

along the Nature Coast have been damaged by erosion, which is worse here and in the Panhandle than in the rest of Florida. The best beaches, from north to south, are Dekle, Keaton, and Steinhatchee in Taylor County; Horseshoe in Dixie County; Cedar Key and Yankeetown in Levy County; Fort Island Gulf Beach and Crystal River in Citrus County; Pine Island in Hernando County; and Hudson and Anclote in Pascoe County.

These counties are home to 46 springs. Eleven of them are springs of the first magnitude, which means that they issue at least 100 cubic feet of water per second. Wakulla County has the largest, Spring Creek Springs, a submarine spring. Submarine springs are springs that discharge below sea level in a coastal saltwater environment. Submarine springs can sometimes be spotted easily during certain tidal stages, as they boil the surface of the overlying water. These curiosities of nature are found in the United States in Florida, New York, California, and Hawaii, as well as at other sites around the world. Some of the springs along the Nature Coast are not suitable for diving or snorkeling, but many of them provide clear water at 72 degrees.

If you like to chase that little white ball over green grass, you'll be pleased to learn that there are more than 50 golf courses along the Nature Coast.

We love canoeing, as we've found it to be one of the few activities that allow you to quietly photograph wildlife and get some exercise at the same time. Canoe trails abound in Florida. The following are the best along the Nature Coast. For safety's sake, be sure you talk with experienced paddlers before trekking. Some sections of these rivers may be dangerous.

Wakulla River: You can take an easy four-mile trip from FL 365 to the mouth of the St. Marks River. You can paddle upstream as well on the shallow Wakulla. The St. Marks River is navigable but has heavy boat traffic. For additional information, see the chapter covering Wakulla and St. Marks.

You can canoe or kayak many miles of rivers and in the estuaries seeking serenity, fish, or wildlife.

Aucilla River: For a challenging 19-mile run, take a trip down the Aucilla, which runs through Jefferson, Madison, and Taylor Counties. Begin near Lamont on US 27/19.

Steinhatchee River: This river has the second-highest waterfall in the state. Its height varies with rainfall. For additional information, see the Steinhatchee chapter.

Suwannee River: Before selecting a section of this 141-mile canoe trail, you'll need to talk to a couple of outfitters to learn where the dangers lie and which sections suit your expertise.

Withlacoochee River: From near the town of Lacoochee in northeastern Pasco County, this 84-mile river runs north along the borders of Hernando and Citrus Counties to Dunnellon. Just west of Dunnellon, the river becomes Lake Rousseau. Then it becomes a stream again below the dam.

Chassahowitzka River: This scenic river has a number of islands and tributaries to explore. You'll find freshwater springs at its headwaters. **Chassahowitzka River Campground**, operated by the Citrus County Division of Parks and Recreation, has canoes for rent.

Nature Coast Canoe Trail: Begin this popular 17-mile trek on the Salt River off the Crystal River near the Marine Science Center. Follow the markers on the Salt River south to the Homosassa River. From there, the trail goes east on the Homosassa River a few hundred feet to Battle Creek. The southern section of the trail is called the **Michael Byer Memorial Trail**. To explore it, locate the markers at the Homosassa River and Battle Creek, then continue south through Seven Cabbage Cut to the mouth of the Chassahowitzka. This takes you through pristine salt marshes where the wildlife includes ospreys, eagles, a variety of wading birds, manatees, dolphins, and alligators. Be prepared to navigate some difficult areas, and be sure to take water, a compass, insect repellent, sunscreen, and a camera with plenty of film.

For information about Wakulla, Taylor, and Levy Counties, see the chapters on Wakulla and St. Marks, Steinhatchee, and Cedar Key, respectively.

F O R   M O R E   I N F O R M A T I O N :

Citrus County/Homosassa Springs Area Chamber of Commerce—US 19 N., Homosassa Springs, FL 34447; 352-628-2666

Citrus County Tourist Development Council—28 US 19 N.W., Crystal River, FL 34429; 800-537-6667 or 352-795-3149

Dixie County Chamber of Commerce—P.O. Box 547, Cross City, FL 32628; 352-498-5454

Hernando County Tourist Development Council—16110 Aviation Loop Dr., Brooksville, FL 34602; 800-601-4580 or 352-799-7275

Pasco County/Greater Dade City Chamber of Commerce—14112 Eighth St., Dade City, FL 33525; 727-567-3769

Pasco County Office of Tourism—7530 Little Rd. 340, New Port Richey, FL 34654; 800-842-1873 or 727-847-8990

HIGHLIGHTS

STEINHATCHEE LANDING RESORT

FISHING

SCALLOPING

Spanish explorers visited the mouth of the Steinhatchee (Steen-hatch-ee) River in the early 1500s and found a body floating there. They entered the area on maps as Deadman Bay. James A. Stephens, who objected to having a post office named Deadman Bay, changed the name to Stephensville in 1879.

There is another version of the name's origin: Indians found several white men floating in the river. Then again, if that were the case, it seems it would have been Deadmen Bay. But who's counting?

Following a number of spellings ranging from Istenhachee to Stinhatchee to Esteinhatchee, the community took the name of the river in 1931. Steinhatchee, derived from the Indian name Esteen Hatchee, means "River of Man." The mouth of the river is still listed on maps as Deadman Bay. Situated about 90 miles southeast of Tallahassee and about 50 miles west of Gainesville, the town of Steinhatchee is home to about 1,000 residents.

We've visited the area a few times over the years but have yet to see the *Louisa* move. She is a two-masted schooner anchored in the middle of the river.

Does the Louisa *ever move? She seems to always be anchored in the same place in Steinhatchee River year after year.*

Dean Fowler discovered the town's charms in the mid-1980s and decided to build his award-winning **Steinhatchee Landing Resort** on the banks of the river. Here, guests can participate in outdoor activities or kick off their shoes and pile up in a chair on the porch with a book. Twenty-one cottages are available for rent, and five more are on the way; these new cottages are being built

Steinhatchee Landing Resort rests in the middle of bliss, with recreation and relaxation only a few steps in any direction.

in the three styles most prevalent in North Florida—namely, Victorian, Georgian, and the classic shotgun-style, off-the-ground Cracker cottage. The tin roofs, picket fences, narrow, one-way, tree-shaded streets, and wooden walkways were designed to minimize the effects of foot traffic on the natural surroundings and to give the visual impression of a peaceful, rustic village within the village of Steinhatchee.

Not only is a stay at Steinhatchee Landing Resort completely relaxing, it also has all the conveniences of home. Every cottage has a screened porch, a fully equipped kitchen, a washer and dryer, a dishwasher, a microwave, silverware, flatware, glassware, cookware, a VCR, a stereo system, and an outdoor charcoal grill. Guests may use the lighted tennis courts and the river-front swimming pool. Canoes and bicycles are available free of charge for the enjoyment of guests. On a canoe trip along the river, you may see deer, wild boars, ducks, turkeys, and many other birds. You can also enjoy picnicking, hiking the nature trails, fishing, riverboat cruises, scuba diving, and snor-

keling. The resort offers shuttle service to the airports at Cross City, Perry, and Gainesville.

Steinhatchee Landing was chosen "Best Resort of the Year" by readers of *Florida Living* magazine. The rental rates are reasonable by Florida standards.

While you're visiting the resort, ask Dean Fowler to point you toward local sites of interest. He has many good tales about the area and has become a local historian of some note. Be sure to inquire about "the Road to Nowhere"—a road with the straight portions paved and the curves unpaved. Sounds like the perfect place to land an airplane without using an airport, doesn't it? Or you can go looking for the lost Fort Frank Brooke on the banks of the Steinhatchee River. The old fort may be on the resort property, or it may be somewhere between there and Steinhatchee Falls, the second-highest waterfall in the state. One report places it six miles below the falls, where the direction of the river changes from south to southwest. General Zachary Taylor, the man for whom Taylor County

Shooting the Steinhatchee River rapids down Florida's second highest waterfall is better during low water conditions—they get flooded in high water.

was named, ordered the building of Fort Frank Brooke in November 1938 during the Second Seminole War. It was abandoned in June 1840, after the Indian wars moved to South Florida.

Fiddler's Restaurant, the nicest in town, serves delicious seafood, American-style cuisine, and very popular Ribs. The **Bridge End Café**, located at the end of the bridge, is perhaps best known for its hearty breakfasts, but you'll find the food tasty regardless of which meal is being served. Because of its popularity with the locals, we had to wait for sandwiches to go at lunch. At dinner, various seafood, beef, pork, and chicken entrées are offered.

If you'd like to get close to nature, check out Bishop Clark's **Sawgrass Bluff**, a log cabin located back in a marsh beyond the reach of electricity. The cabin is surrounded by water and wildlife within view of the old Confederate salt stills. One of seven different properties that make up **Steinhatchee Outpost**, Sawgrass Bluff is south of Adams Beach, one of the most pristine spots for canoeing, kayaking, and fishing we've ever seen. "Bish," as Bishop Clark is known by his pals, provides accommodations from RV campgrounds to the remote cabin at Beaver Spring Creek, a clear, spring-fed creek that leads canoeists downstream to the takeout at Steinhatchee Falls, a three-foot cascade.

The folks at **Sea Hag Marina** will be happy to arrange a guide, if you'd like to sample the legendary fishing at Steinhatchee. This full-service marina offers a motel, apartments, boat rentals, and a ship's store.

Captain Brian Smith guides out of Steinhatchee. He took us out on a winter morning to catch redfish and speckled trout. Smith knows the area and has the perfect boat to accommodate three

Captain Brian Smith with a couple of clients showing off a sea trout.

or four anglers for a day. He furnishes licenses, bait, tackle, and ice. He stays on top of the fish, too. He also offers offshore fishing trips.

Many species hit beginning in the spring. April, May, and June offer some fantastic fishing for trout, redfish, bluefish, Spanish mackerel, ladyfish, and jack crevalle. These are caught inshore, in the brackish river, and farther out. King mackerel run every spring, too. Grouper, black sea bass, and red snapper can be caught on the bottom in 35- to 55-foot depths. Live bait such as shrimp and pinfish are the most popular with anglers—and with the fish. We had excellent results using Cabela's Living Eye Minnows for saltwater species. Other artificials that work well include topwater plugs, crankbaits, spoons, spinnerbaits, jigs, and a variety of soft plastic grubs.

Summer fishing includes a few more species, such as cobia, tarpon, flounder, and a shark or two.

Steinhatchee is the number-one place in the United States for collecting bay scallops. The season runs from July 1 to Labor Day. All you need is a mask, a snorkel, fins, a mesh bag to hold the scallops, and lots of sunscreen. Danielle Norwood at Sea Hag Marina says, "Scallops seem to prefer areas of bottom covered by the thin, round-bladed type of sea grass more than the flat, broad-bladed turtle grass. Patches of brown algae are also favorite hiding places. Once a few scallops are seen lying on top of the sea grasses, drop the anchor, put up a dive flag, and start collecting."

After scalloping season is over, it's time for trout, redfish, bluefish, and Spanish mackerel to reconvene on the flats.

Grouper fishing is back in full swing in the fall, as is fishing for black sea bass, red snapper, and kingfish. As the water temperature cools in October and November, the "gator" trout move up the Steinhatchee River for the fishingest time of your life. Don't miss the trout run!

While you're in Steinhatchee, you may want to take a day trip to see the manatees at **Manatee Springs State Park** or go diving to explore the vast underwater caverns at Branford, which are both within an hour's drive. Of course, you may prefer to simply kick off your shoes, pile up in a chair on the porch, and listen to the sounds of Florida in its natural state.

All of the following are in Steinhatchee and use the 32359 zip code and 352 area code, except where noted.

ACCOMMODATIONS

Steinhatchee Landing Resort—P.O. Box 789; 800-584-1709 or 498-3513; www.steinhatcheelanding.com

Steinhatchee River Inn—Box 828; 498-4049

ATTRACTIONS

Captain Brian Smith—498-3703; CaptBESmith@att.net

Sea Hag Marina—322 Riverside Drive, P.O. Box 928; 498-3008

CAMPING

Steinhatchee Outpost—P.O. Box 48, Perry, FL 32348; 800-589-1541 or 498-5192

DINING

Bridge End Café—310 10th St.; 498-2002

Fiddler's Restaurant—1306 Riverside Dr.; 498-7427

FOR MORE INFORMATION

Steinhatchee Landing Resort—P.O. Box 789; 800-584-1709 or 498-3513; www.steinhatcheelanding.com

Taylor County Chamber of Commerce—P.O. Box 893, Perry, FL 32348; 800-257-8881 or 850-584-5366

HIGHLIGHTS

ISLAND HOTEL

WALKING AROUND TOWN

CANOEING, KAYAKING, AND FISHING

Cedar Key, about 50 miles southwest of Gainesville via FL 24 and about 50 miles south of Steinhatchee via US 19/98, encompasses 1,000 acres of small islands. This is one of our favorite Nature Coast destinations.

I first visited Cedar Key in the 1960s when I was a sophomore in college, long before meeting Cathy. I remember the Island Hotel, where a couple of elderly gentlemen passed the day whittling on the porch. The most interesting place in town then was the old cemetery east of Gulf Boulevard. I made notes from the headstones, which contained quotes expressing a variety of emotions. Unfortunately, all that remains of those notes are vague memories, but the cemetery is still there waiting for you to explore.

Cedar Key was settled in the early 1840s, during the Second Seminole War. In 1859, the Florida Railroad Company issued a plat for a city of Cedar Key on Way Key, but incorporation waited until 1869. In March 1861, the railroad was completed from Fernandina Beach, an occasion marked by the arrival of the first train on Way Key.

This area played a role in the War Between the States. Confederates controlled Cedar Key in 1861, but the Union blockaded the area the next year, disrupting the port facilities and eventually occupying them. Florida supplied the Confederates with salt, beef, pork, cane syrup, sugar, and cotton. Salt stills were common along the coast. These were large metal vats used for boiling seawater. The residue was bagged for curing meat for the Rebs. Therefore, it was important to the Yankees to destroy the stills. One operation, raided in September 1863, produced 1,500 bushels of salt per day, for which the Confederate government paid $12.50 per bushel.

In the 1870s, the newly named city of Cedar Key began to prosper. New residents were drawn by the sawmills, the stores, the hotels, the steamships, the fishing, the oystering, the boatbuilding operations, and the factory that produced cedar slats for pencils. The community peaked at a population of 2,000 in 1885, the year that Henry Plant's railroad reached Tampa. The new railroad to the deeper harbor at Tampa siphoned off Cedar Key's

The Island Hotel, which has weathered many hurricanes, is still the star attraction of Cedar Key.

prosperity. The area was 500 residents poorer just five years later. Only 700 people remained by 1900. Today, Cedar Key claims a population of 800.

During the War Between the States, the Parsons and Hale General Store—constructed of tabby, or "Florida cement"—became a domicile for Union troops and a warehouse for supplies. After the war, Parsons and Hale reopened. By the 1880s, the proprietors were serving meals and accepting lodgers. A notable guest was America's first ecotourist, the young John Muir, who nearly died of fever here in 1867. After withstanding a devastating hurricane in 1896, the store became the Bay Hotel in 1915. A subsequent owner tried unsuccessfully to raze the building by fire. It ultimately became the **Island Hotel**. Fortunately for visitors, the building has withstood Yankees, hurricanes, arson, and time. It even withstood our anniversary celebration in its **Neptune Bar and Seafood Restaurant**.

Accommodations in the area range from oceanfront condominiums to kitchenette-equipped budget motels built in the 1950s. Among the condominiums are **Island Place**, which offers a pool, a sauna, and Jacuzzis, and **Old Fenimore Mill**, which has Jacuzzis on the balcony overlooking the Gulf. **Cedar Key Bed and Breakfast**, shaded by two giant live oaks at the corner of Third and F Streets, was built in 1880 as housing for employees and guests at the Eagle Cedar Mill. **Cedar Cove Beach and Yacht Club** offers a marina and suites ranging from studio efficiencies to two-bedroom townhouses. **Mermaid's Landing Cottages** invites visitors to relax on the patio beneath the cedar trees, to catch blue crab in traps off the dock, and to bring their pets.

Although Second Street is now lined with an interesting assortment of specialty shops like the **Cedar Keyhole**, a co-op of local artists and craftsmen, the eclectic **Ibis Gallery**, and the delightful

D Street Gallery, the streets are still peaceful enough to remind you of days gone by.

Aquaculture has helped the area rebound economically. Seventy percent of all hard-shell clams in Florida come from here. It takes 18 months to raise a marketable clam. Be sure to order some. They're fresh. Among the excellent choices for dining on Second Street are the **Island Hotel, The Heron**, the **Island Room at Cedar Cove**, and **Cook's Café**. The popular choices on bustling Dock Street include the **Brown Pelican, Seabreeze Restaurant**, and the **Captain's Table**.

Cedar Key State Museum is worth a visit to see the area's history and one of its most complete shell collections. The native vegetation includes the tree Cedar Key was named for.

The area boasts several refuges and preserves you'll want to experience if you're a nature lover.

Cedar Keys National Wildlife Refuge encompasses 800 acres, including a group of restricted-access islands in the Gulf of Mexico. The refuge includes a major seabird rookery and an 1850s lighthouse on Florida's highest coastal elevation. Boats are available at Cedar Key.

Waccassassa Bay State Preserve, a 31,000-acre limited-access preserve between Yankeetown and Cedar Key, offers canoeists and campers access to freshwater and saltwater fishing, photography, and historic-site exploration.

Cedar Key Scrub State Reserve offers a unique scrub habitat on the mainland, a few marked walking trails, and opportunities for bird watching.

Shell Mound Park includes a prehistoric Indian mound and a nature trail. Located off FL 347 on CR 326 outside Cedar Key, it offers camping, picnicking, and a boat ramp.

Lower Suwannee National Refuge is a

Sometimes pleasure paddling among the keys and backwaters rewards you with dolphin sitings.

40,000-acre refuge between Cedar Key and Chiefland. Visitors come here for the nature driving, the hiking trails, the opportunities for wildlife observation and photography, and the access to the Suwannee River.

Manatee Springs State Park offers a first-magnitude spring, 100 campsites, diving, swimming, picnicking, a boat ramp, canoe rentals, and an elevated boardwalk through primordial cypress wetlands to the historic Suwannee River. Riverboat tours are available.

Water is everywhere here, and access is easy thanks to **Cedar Key Kayak Rental**. Although water levels fluctuate, exposing mud flats as the tides recede, we have never had a problem getting back to shore by canoe before dark or before the tide ran out. Once while canoeing, we were charmed by a trio of dolphins and tried unsuccessfully to paddle fast enough to keep up. We fished and explored the beaches of some of the uninhabited islands that make up the Cedar Keys. Cathy usually prefers to paddle while I cast or troll, but on that occasion, she landed a nice speckled trout for dinner. It just doesn't get much better than that.

All of the following are in Cedar Key and use the 32625 zip code and 352 area code, except where noted.

ACCOMMODATIONS

Cedar Cove Beach and Yacht Club—P.O. Box 837; 800-366-5312 or 543-5332

Cedar Key Bed and Breakfast—P.O. Box 700; 800-453-5051 or 543-9000

Island Hotel—P.O Box 460; 800-432-4640 or 543-5111

Island Place Condominiums—P.O. Box 687; 800-780-6522 or 543-5307

Mermaid's Landing Cottages—FL 24; 800-741-9224

Old Fenimore Mill Condominiums—P.O. Box 805; 800-767-8354 or 543-9803

Osprey—P.O. Box 306; 800-890-8327 or 543-9743

Park Place Motel—800-868-7963 or 543-5737

ATTRACTIONS

Cedar Key Kayak Rental—Third St.; 543-9437

Cedar Key Historical Museum—P.O. Box 22; 543-5549

Cedar Key Scrub State Reserve—P.O. Box 187; 543-5567; wbsp@svic.net

Cedar Key State Museum—12231 S.W. 166 Ct.; 543-5350; cksm@svic.net

Cedar Keys National Wildlife Refuge—16450 N.W. 31st Pl., Chiefland, FL 32626; 493-0238

Fishbonz—543-9922

Island Adventures—543-6333

Island Hopper Fishing Guides—543-5904

Lower Suwannee National Refuge—16450 N.W. 31st Pl., Chiefland, FL 32626; 493-0238

Manatee Springs State Park—c/o Suwannee Basin GEOpark, 11650 N.W. 115th St., Chiefland, FL 32626; 493-6072

Nature Coast Expeditions—543-6463

Shell Mound Park—CR 326; 543-6153

Waccassassa Bay State Preserve—(located between Yankeetown and Cedar Key, it is accessible only by boat from Cedar Key); 543-5567

CAMPING

Cedar Key RV Park—P.O. Box 268; 543-5150

Osprey Waterfront RV Hookups—P.O. Box 306; 800-890-8327 or 543-9743

Rainbow Country RV Campground—11951 S.W. Shiloh Rd.; 534-6268

Shell Mound Park—CR 326; 543-6153

Sunset Isle Park—P.O. Box 150; 543-5375

DINING

Brown Pelican—490 Dock St.; 543-5428

Captain's Table—Dock St. (P.O. Box 807); 543-5441

Cooks Café—Second St.; 543-5548

Dock on the Bay—509 Third St.; 543-9143

Island Hotel and Restaurant—373 Second St.; 543-5111

Island Room at Cedar Grove—P.O. Box 716; 543-6520

Seabreeze Restaurant—Dock Street; 543-5738

The Heron—Second St.; 543-5666

EVENTS

April—Sidewalk Art Festival

July—Fourth of July Celebration

October—Seafood Festival

FOR MORE INFORMATION

Cedar Key Area Chamber of Commerce—P.O. Box 610; 543-5600; www.cedarkey.org

11   *Tarpon Springs*

HIGHLIGHTS

SPONGE DOCKS

EPIPHANY CELEBRATION

*H*istoric, charming, and unspoiled, Tarpon Springs is located on Florida's Gulf coast about 15 minutes north of Clearwater. Named for the giant fish found in bayous around town, it could have been named Manatee for the gentle creatures that visit each winter.

Samuel Hope, the area's first landowner, acquired property on the Anclote River in the mid-1860s. Other settlers arrived here just after the War Between the States. They built homes on the banks of the river and in the inland bayous. Within 20 to 30 years, wealthy Northerners were constructing exquisite Victorian homes and luxurious estates along Spring Bayou.

Anson P. K. Stafford, a former governor of the Arizona Territory, brought his family and his sister, Dr. Mary J. Stafford, to Tarpon Springs in the late 19th century. Dr. Stafford, the first woman physician in Florida, opened a practice in her home. The initial section of the **Stafford House** was completed in 1883, four years before Tarpon Springs was incorporated. The home was later enlarged to 10 rooms. Stafford and his sister died in December 1891. The widow Stafford remained in the home until her death in 1931. The Stafford House was placed on the National Register of Historic Places in 1975. The city acquired it in 1994 and is returning it to its 1893 appearance to serve as a cultural and historical resource.

Since the early 1900s, the search for sponges has lured Greek divers to Tarpon Springs and the Gulf of Mexico. The community still feels like a Greek fishing village, complete with working waterfront and shopping district. Downtown is a showcase of historic buildings and homes from the

Tarpon Springs grew to be the world's sponge capital in the 1930s, but tourism ranks first today.

Victorian era. Here is an improbable blend of histories found only in Pinellas County's oldest city.

A Greek named John Cocoris brought sponge divers to Tarpon Springs in late 1905. Many stayed here, establishing family businesses that remain today.

George Billiris, president of the St. Nicholas Boat Line, grew up in Tarpon Springs in a family that made its living in the sponge industry. Billiris became a sponge diver as a teenager. He says, "Divers work from daybreak until dark, and there are usually around 180 working days a year. Boats go out for two or three weeks at a time, year-round. The hands aren't salaried, but work for a share.

"There are two divers who alternate dives, for safety reasons. Safety first, production second. Divers walk on the bottom either quartering the current or headed into it, so the current keeps the field of vision clear. If they go with the current, the disturbed bottom clouds their vision, and they can't see the sponges. It would push the diver along too fast, and they would miss sponges."

Divers wear 172 pounds of gear, including a diving helmet and a weighted belt.

"The helmsman, or pilot, has to follow the diver as he walks, following the air bubbles," Billiris says. "Deck hands tend the diver. Sponges come up in baskets. They are stacked and covered with burlap. Then they are scraped and washed, strung on a line, and stored. The boat doesn't come in until it's full. A boatload of sponges is worth about $12,000.

"We can't supply the demand for sponges. As a sponge merchant, I travel the world not to sell sponges but to explain why we can't meet the market's need."

In the late 1800s, the sponge business was centered in the Bahamas. Then it moved to Key West, and then here. Tarpon Springs was recognized as the "Sponge Capital of the World" during the 1930s. But disaster struck in the form of bacteria that caused a blight. The sponge beds in the Western Hemisphere were wiped out by 1946.

"This was a father-to-son business, and the blight broke the chain. We lost a generation of divers," says Billiris. "In 1959, we discovered the sponges were back, but we had lost our position in the world market. We started over and have now regained our position, with sales of about $12 million a year."

He says there are over 1,400 commercial uses for sponges. "Natural sponges release their contents and get cleaner with use, but synthetic ones do not release all of their contents and get dirtier with use. Some of what goes in a synthetic sponge today will still be there a long time from now."

The **St. Nicholas Boat Line** provides half-hour cruises. Sightseers can watch a diver at work as he looks for sponges. Billiris says, "Tourism is now the number-one business in Tarpon Springs, but it's accidental. It is an outgrowth of what occurs here naturally. Sponge is second."

While Tarpon Springs is not Disney World, and doesn't want to be, it offers lots to do on the water, from visiting the **Sponge Docks** to deep-sea fishing to worshiping the semitropical sun on the beach at **Howard Park**. All the sights and sounds that draw visitors are the by-products of the natural beauty of the area and the day-to-day activities of the sponge trade. Although sponge boats don't come and go with the frequency they once did, the business is alive and well. Boats laden with sponges still return to the docks for auctions attended by wholesalers.

Many of the dozen or so restaurants along the

Dodecanese Boulevard's many shops, restaurants, and its docks draw tourists year-round to Tarpon Springs.

docks grew out of the need to feed the sponge crews, boat captains, and dealers who conduct business here. Incredibly good, authentic Greek cuisine is featured. A full-course Greek lunch at a spot like **Mykonos** is a delicious introduction to this cuisine, from the delicate, flaming, cheese-filled pastry known as Saganaki to the perfectly balanced Garlic, Eggplant, and Caviar Spreads. Even Lima Beans deliver a taste sensation when slow-cooked in onions and olive oil lightly flavored with dill. The lightly floured Kalamari, or fried squid, is tender and tasty, as are the delicately seasoned beef, pork, chicken, and lamb dishes.

During the 1930s and 1940s, shops opened for tourists, who came to observe the booming sponge trade and wanted to take home samples of the prized wool sponges, as well as yellow, wire, grass, and ornamental finger sponges. Some of the original shops remain today, owned by the same

families that started them. They've been joined by a host of specialty shops offering everything from fanciful Caribbean metal sculptures to tropical shirts covered with palm trees and parrots.

While at the Sponge Docks, you can take a cruise on a sponge boat, sightsee your way down the Anclote River to the Gulf of Mexico, go deep-sea fishing, visit a 120,000-gallon saltwater aquarium, or see a live sponge-diving exhibition.

Then there's the historic downtown, with its wealth of antique shops and art galleries. The downtown area is listed on the National Register of Historic Places. The **Cultural Center** on South Pinellas Avenue offers art exhibits in its museum and walking tours and bus tours of the city. At the **Universalist Church** on Grand Boulevard, paintings by George Inness, Jr., a world-renowned landscape artist who lived here, are exhibited from October through May.

The **Epiphany Celebration**, the largest such

religious event in the United States, attracts an average of 40,000 spectators from all over the country. Every year on January 6, boys between the ages of 16 and 19 dive into the waters of Spring Bayou for the wooden cross. Later, the festival moves to the Sponge Docks, where special foods and dancing by costumed groups highlight the festivities.

Among the other colorful events is **Greek Fest**, held in February at St. Nicholas Greek Orthodox Cathedral. St. Nicholas, a replica of St. Sophia Cathedral in Constantinople, boasts 60 tons of Greek marble, 23 stained-glass windows, and glass chandeliers. Built in 1943, it is one of the best-known Greek Orthodox churches in the country. Greek Fest visitors are welcome to sample the food and enjoy the dancing and music.

There's always a big celebration at the Sponge Docks on March 18, **Greek Independence Day**.

And lastly, there's the **Arts and Crafts Festival**, which has drawn appreciative crowds every April for over 25 years. More than 200 artists display their work in Craig Park at Spring Bayou.

Lodging choices range from a four-star resort to condominiums, quaint motels, and bed-and-breakfasts. **Spring Bayou Inn**, a large, comfortable home built around the turn of the 20th century, offers a combination of modern-day conveniences and unique architectural details reflecting the elegance of the past. Guests may relax in their rooms, in a parlor complete with a baby grand piano, or on the spacious wraparound front porch.

Nature lovers have numerous beaches, parks, and trails to explore in the Pinellas County region. Fishing is as popular here as it is in most of Florida. Sports lovers can sit under the lights and cheer for the **Tampa Bay Buccaneers** at Raymond James Stadium or the **Tampa Bay Devil Rays** at Tropicana Field. Professional hockey fans enjoy the **Tampa Bay Lightning**. Major golf events include the **J. C. Penney Golf Classic** at the Westin Innisbrook Resort in Tarpon Springs and the **GTE Suncoast Seniors Classic** at Tampa Palms. The area also offers pari-mutuel sports such as thoroughbred horse racing, dog racing, and jai alai.

All of the following are in Tarpon Springs and use the 34689 zip code and 727 area code, except where noted.

 ### ACCOMMODATIONS

Spring Bayou Inn—32 W. Tarpon Ave.; 938-9333; www.springbayouinn.com

 ### ATTRACTIONS

St. Nicholas Boat Line—693 Dodecanese Blvd.; 942-6425

Tarpon Springs Cultural Center—101 S. Pinellas Ave.; 942-5605

Tarpon Springs Historical Society—160 E. Tarpon Ave.; 938-3711

 ### DINING

Aegean Restaurant—602-604 Athens St.; 939-1032

Mykonos—628 Dodecanese Blvd.; 934-4306

Olympia Café and Deli—543 N. Pinellas Ave.; 939-0929

OPA! Restaurant—614 Athens St.; 934-8444

Plaka Restaurant—769 Dodecanese Blvd.; 934-4752

Santorini Greek Grill—698 Dodecanese Blvd.; 945-9400

Yianni's Restaurant—509-511 Dodecanese Blvd.; 943-2164

 EVENTS

January—Epiphany Celebration

February—Greek Fest

April—Arts and Crafts Festival

May—Taste of Tarpon Springs

September—Peter T. Assimack Memorial Fishing Tournament

December—Lake Tarpon and Bayou Boat Parades

 FOR MORE INFORMATION

Tarpon Springs Chamber of Commerce—11 E. Orange St.; 937-6109; www.tarponsprings.com

12 St. Petersburg-Clearwater-Dunedin-St. Pete Beach

HIGHLIGHTS

SALVADOR DALI MUSEUM

FLORIDA INTERNATIONAL MUSEUM

MUSEUM OF FINE ARTS

ST. PETERSBURG MUSEUM OF HISTORY

DOLPHIN LANDINGS CHARTER

CALADESI ISLAND

St. Petersburg and Clearwater have long been famous for their beaches, their weather, and their wealth of water-related activities. The area enjoys more sunshine than Honolulu. The *Guinness Book of World Records* credits St. Petersburg with the longest run of consecutive sunny days—768 days, from February 9, 1967, to March 17, 1969. In 1910, the *St. Petersburg Evening Independent* began giving away free papers on those occasions when the sun did not shine. By the time the newspaper ceased publication in 1986, the sun had missed shining 295 times—less than four times per year. No other destination in Florida offers award-winning beaches with such a variety of museums, art galleries, and special events. But before we look at today's attractions, let's look back.

The Spanish failed in their efforts to settle the area because they tried to enslave the Indians but couldn't dominate them, and also because there were no riches here. Later, the surrounding waters became a haven for the pirates who raided merchant ships on Florida's east coast and in the Caribbean.

Count Philippe, a surgeon in Napoleon's navy, originally settled in South Carolina after escaping from France. Captured by pirates in the 1830s while exploring Florida's east coast, he won their gratitude by treating a fever epidemic. His reward was stolen treasure and a map describing Old Tampa Bay as "the most beautiful body of water in the world." Philippe established a plantation near Safety Harbor. Using citrus stock he brought from the Bahamas, he cultivated Florida's first grapefruit grove. Today, the former plantation is the site of a park named in his honor.

The Seminole Wars, which started in 1835, hampered further settlement. But they also established Clearwater's roots. In 1841, Fort Harrison was built on Clearwater Harbor. When the wars ended less than a year later, the fort closed and the area was opened to homesteaders. In 1842, James Stevens established a homestead and became known as "the father of Clearwater."

Lieutenant Colonel Robert E. Lee surveyed the area in 1848 for possible coastal defense installations. Lee recommended Mullet Key, a site later used as a military post during both the Civil War and the Spanish-American War. Union forces set up an effective blockade base at Mullet Key and controlled Tampa Bay throughout the Civil War.

In 1875, General John C. Williams of Detroit, Michigan, purchased 1,600 acres in what is now downtown St. Petersburg. After failing as a farmer because his Northern methods weren't suited for this semitropical region, Williams decided to build a city complete with railroad service.

Meanwhile, a small community was growing in the northern part of Pinellas County. Scottish merchants opened a general store and petitioned the government for a post office, to be named Dunedin, a Gaelic word meaning "peaceful rest." The Scots hoped the post office would increase traffic to their store. A wave of Scottish settlers moved to **Dunedin**, which subsequently became a major citrus-producing area and the birthplace of the citrus concentrate industry. Today, the citrus business has all but disappeared, but the community's Scottish heritage is kept alive with the annual **Highland Games** and other festivals.

Before the turn of the 20th century, a Russian immigrant doctor placed the Pinellas County coast in the world's eye as a vacation destination. It was at the April 1885 meeting of the American Medical Society in New Orleans that Dr. Van Bibber presented a paper called "Where Should a Health City Be Built?" At the time, doctors prescribed visits to hot springs and seaside spas as a cure for a variety of ailments. Dr. Bibber concluded that

Dunedin's eclectic shops will keep you browsing for hours.

Point Pinellas was the ideal location for the world's healthiest city. He extolled the benefits of the water and the "delights of a winter climate which has no equal elsewhere."

General Williams's idea of building a city moved closer to reality when he made a land deal with Peter Demens. Originally named Petrovich A. Demensheff, Demens was a Russian immigrant who brought his small-gauge Orange Belt Railroad to the Gulf coast. On the heels of Dr. Bibber's widely publicized report, the new rail service attracted a flood of new residents and helped create the city of Williams's dreams. Demens and Williams differed about a name for the new community. Legend has it that they drew lots and Demens won, naming the city St. Petersburg after his hometown in Russia. Williams constructed the community's first commercial building, the Detroit Hotel, which he named for his hometown.

Henry Plant later purchased the financially troubled Orange Belt and converted it to a standard-gauge railroad. In 1896, Plant built the plush Belleview Hotel near Clearwater, and the area became a playground for the rich. The Biltmore chain bought the property in the 1930s and changed the name to the **Belleview Biltmore**. Today, the hotel is the world's largest occupied wooden structure.

By the 1920s, the St. Petersburg-Clearwater area was an established tourist resort and a secret hideaway for the wealthy and famous.

During World War II, area tourist hotels housed military trainees, and the famous Don CeSar on St. Pete Beach was converted into a military hospital.

The area's history is preserved in several museums.

Let's begin with today's culture at the world-famous **Salvador Dali Museum**. A. Reynolds Morse and Eleanor R. Morse collected the works of Dali over a 45-year period and donated their collection to the people of the state of Florida. Located on the scenic St. Petersburg waterfront, the museum holds the world's most comprehensive collection of works by the Spanish surrealist. The collection includes 94 oils, numerous watercolors, sketches, sculptures, and other art objects—more than 2,500 items in total. Images created by Dali between the ages of 10 and 76

The Salvador Dali Museum displays art from Dali's 66-year career.

are in the collection. His early work reveals a thorough command of traditional European painting. Most Dali novices find it surprising that the artist was so much more than a surrealist. Landscapes, portraits, and still lifes are prominent among his early works. But it's his bizarre imagery that draws crowds of all ages and holds a special fascination for teens. It was after Dali obsessed about the disintegration concept following Hiroshima that some of his most powerful work emerged. Of the 18 so-called master works produced by Dali, six are housed in the St. Petersburg museum.

The city is also home to the **Florida International Museum**, which is noted for hosting traveling exhibits such as "Treasures of the Czars," "Splendors of Ancient Egypt," "Alexander the Great," and "Titanic: The Exhibition." This museum houses the world's largest private collection of John F. Kennedy memorabilia. Galleries re-create the Oval Office and *PT 109*.

The **Museum of Fine Arts**, also in St. Petersburg, is highly respected throughout the Southeast. It is best known for its collection of French impressionist paintings and its European, American, pre-Columbian, and Far Eastern art. Special exhibits feature works on loan from other metropolitan museums.

The **St. Petersburg Museum of History** contains Indian artifacts from the Safety Harbor and Weedon Island sites. It offers exhibits and demonstrations of early pioneer life.

The nearby **Florida Holocaust Museum** is one of the largest such facilities in the United States. Here, the painful story of the Holocaust is told with dignity and without sensationalism, in displays most suitable for grades five and above.

From touch tunnels to laser harps, **Great Explorations** is the best museum in town to get your hands on. This touchy-feely museum invites kids of all ages to enjoy exhibits that entertain while educating.

The **Dunedin Historical Museum** is housed in the original Orange Belt Railroad station, which dates to 1889.

In days gone by, the Pillsbury and Fleishman families and Presidents Hoover and Coolidge came to bask in the opulence of grand St. Petersburg hotels like the Belleview Biltmore, the Renaissance Vinoy, and the Don CeSar. These three are among the six resorts in Florida listed on the National Register of Historic Places.

The second most luxurious way to visit St. Petersburg is to fly in and be chauffeured to the **Renaissance Vinoy Resort** overlooking the brilliant blue Tampa Bay. The most luxurious way is to nestle your own yacht into a slip at the resort's private marina. Holding court on the downtown St. Petersburg waterfront, the Renaissance Vinoy celebrates the best of the old and the new with a seamless combination of sensitive restoration, richly furnished guest rooms, and

exceptional amenities. Built in 1925, the richly colored Mediterranean Revival structure underwent a $93 million restoration and expansion during the 1990s. Master craftsmen returned the hotel to its former glory, from the stencils on the massive cypress beams in the lobby to the frescoes in the dining room. The resort offers special golf and tennis getaway packages, if you've come to play hard. The rest of us enjoy the heated swimming pools, the outdoor spas, and the 5,000-square-foot fitness facility complete with steam rooms, saunas, massage therapists, and personal trainers. If you don't stay here, at least stop in for a memorable lunch or dinner in one of the resort's five restaurants.

For beachcombing, you'll need to head across the causeway to St. Pete Beach, part of a chain of barrier islands. This is the home of another of the area's historic hotel gems, the Gulf-front **Don CeSar Resort**. From beach activities like parasailing and kayaking to golf and tennis privileges, there's something for everyone here.

The Don CeSar Hotel, the pink palace on the Gulf, is one of three remaining luxury hotels from the Golden Era of the 1920s.

The **Tradewinds Resort** properties offer supervised activities for children ages three to 17. Programs vary with the seasons. Those for teens include snorkeling excursions with certified divers.

Much of St. Pete Beach retains an old-fashioned feel. There's a great little shopping district along Corey Avenue and a healthy population of old-fashioned motels and resort marinas scattered among the large resort complexes. Some are on the ocean, while others overlook Boca Ciega Bay, with the shores of St. Petersburg to the east. We stayed at the very comfortable **Bay Street Villas** on the bay. Guests here enjoy the beautiful sunrises across the bay and the boat dock out back, where they can wet a line or watch the brilliant flare climb through the sky as the Space Shuttle lifts off on a clear night.

If cooking is part of what you've come here to escape, you'll be pleased with the dining choices. From surf-side snacks to gourmet dining in elegant resorts and everything in between, Pinellas County boasts a splendid selection of more than 2,300 restaurants. One of the most popular at St. Pete Beach is the **Hurricane**, which offers lighthearted décor, floor-to-ceiling metal palms, and a sunset view. The seafood is great, and the drinks are cold. If you like your Key Lime Pie a little tart, this is the spot for you.

Even if you're not a sailor, we bet you'll enjoy a dolphin cruise. **Dolphin Landings Charter** sails in search of dolphins on Boca Ciega Bay, into the sunset on the Gulf, and to Shell Island, where you can picnic, snorkel, collect shells, or swim, depending on your preference. You have a choice of powerboat or sailboat, but take it from us, when the 42-foot sailboat catches the wind, it feels like you're flying across the water. When you spot

Cathy pilots a Dolphin Landings charter to find dolphins in the Gulf.

your first dolphins gliding through the swells, the day turns magical.

Although Dolphin Landings runs sportfishing cruises, too, much of the local fishing fleet is headquartered a few miles north in the marina at John's Pass. Trips range from half-day excursions for two-pound gray snapper to overnight trips for big grouper, amberjack, and cobia. The equipment you'll need for fishing on the boats, from the bridge, or on the beach is available for rent.

Caladesi Island offers splendid shelling, as well as a quiet walk on the beach.

A short pontoon boat ride will take you a world away from the dazzle of St. Petersburg. **Caladesi Island** is a shell seeker's delight accessible only by boat. One of the few remaining undeveloped barrier islands in Florida, Caladesi has been named one of the top-10 beaches in the United States, based on characteristics including water clarity, cleanliness, respect for the environment, and wildlife. The pontoon boat docks on the bay side of the island in an area surrounded by a mangrove swamp. Once it departs, only the sounds of the surf break the stillness. A three-mile nature trail introduces you to the pristine beach. You can spend your time here swimming, fishing, or picnicking. There's not much to be had in the way of amenities, other than a small ranger station with public restrooms and a snack bar. Except for a single homestead constructed in the late 1800s, Caladesi has remained unchanged except by nature.

A hurricane cut Caladesi Island in two in 1921, creating Honeymoon Island, now a state park as well. Originally settled by the Tocobaga tribe,

Honeymoon Island got its present name in the 1940s. That's when an enterprising entrepreneur named Washburn built 50 palm-thatched bungalows for honeymooners. One couple who applied but did not get to make the trip was Mr. and Mrs. Ronald Reagan. Though the honeymoon haven prospered for only two years, the bonds forged on the island have lasted a lifetime. Not a single divorce has been reported among the 200 couples who came here to celebrate beginning their lives together. As World War II came to dominate American life, the island became a haven for war-weary factory workers. Today, visitors can enjoy bird observation areas, two nature trails, and one of the few remaining virgin stands of Florida slash pine. Shelling is very popular here, as is fishing. Honeymoon Island is easily reached by automobile via the Dunedin Causeway.

Another spot of natural beauty is the 216-acre **Boyd Hill Nature Trail**, which encompasses six trails leading through Florida's various ecosystems. Wildlife abounds here, and there are excellent photo opportunities on every trail. Guided tours are available. The trails are open daily. A small fee is charged.

You'll run out of time before you run out of sunshine, sandy beaches, and interesting things to do in the St. Petersburg area.

All of the following use the 727 area code, except where noted.

 ACCOMMODATIONS

Bay Street Villas and Resort Marina—7201 Bay St., St. Pete Beach, FL 33706; 800-566-8358 or 360-5591

Bayboro House Bed and Breakfast—1719 Beach Dr. S.E., St. Petersburg, FL 33701; 877-823-4955

Belleview Biltmore—25 Belleview Rd., Clearwater, FL 33757; 877-233-9330

Don CeSar Resort—3400 Gulf Blvd., St. Pete Beach, FL 33706; 800-282-1116 or 668-2222

Inn at the Bay Bed and Breakfast—126 Fourth Ave. N.E., St. Petersburg, FL 33701; 888-873-2122 or 822-1700

Lee Manor Inn—342 Third Ave. N., St. Petersburg, FL 33701; 866-219-7260 or 894-3248

Renaissance Vinoy Resort—501 Fifth Ave. N.E., St. Petersburg, FL 33701; 800-HOTEL-1 or 894-1000

Superior Small Lodgings—St. Petersburg/Clearwater CVB, 14450 46th St. North, Suite 108, Clearwater, FL 33762; 888-600-2468

Tradewinds Resort—5600 Gulf Blvd., St. Pete Beach, FL 33706; 572-1212

 ATTRACTIONS

Boyd Hill Nature Trail—1101 Country Club Way S., St. Petersburg, FL 33705; 893-7326

Caladesi Island State Park—1 Causeway Blvd., Dunedin, FL 32528; 469-5942

Dolphin Landings Charter—4737 Gulf Blvd., St. Pete Beach, FL 33706; 367-4488

Dunedin Historical Museum—349 Main St., Dunedin, FL 34697; 736-1166

Florida Holocaust Museum—55 Fifth St. S., St. Petersburg, FL 33701; 820-0100

Florida International Museum—100 Second St. N., St. Petersburg, FL 33701; 800-777-9882

Great Explorations—800 Second Ave. N.E., St. Petersburg, FL 33701; 821-8992

Museum of Fine Arts—255 Beach Dr. N.E., St. Petersburg, FL 33701; 896-2667

Salvador Dali Museum—1000 Third St. S., St. Petersburg, FL 33701; 823-3767

St. Petersburg Museum of History—335 Second Ave. N.E., St. Petersburg, FL 33701; 894-1052

Suncoast Seabird Sanctaury is the largest non-profit wild-bird hospital in the United States. On any given day, you can usually see more than 600 wild birds here.

Suncoast Seabird Sanctuary—18328 Gulf Blvd., Indian Shores, FL 33785; 391-6211

DINING

Bastas Italian Restaurant—1625 Fourth St. S., St. Petersburg, FL 33701; 894-7880

Crab Shack Restaurant—11400 Gandy Blvd., St. Petersburg, FL 33702; 576-7813

El Pass-O Café—1120 Pinellas Bayway, Suite 114, St. Petersburg, FL 33715; 867-6267

Hurricane—807 Gulf Way, St. Pete Beach, FL 33706; 360-9558

Lobster Pot—17814 Gulf Blvd., St. Pete Beach, FL 33708; 391-8592

EVENTS

Every Wednesday—Nature Awareness Walk at Dunedin

January—Florida Clown Day

February—Valentine's Day Optimist Regatta at St. Petersburg

March—Black History Festival at St. Petersburg

March—Downtown Clearwater Art Festival

March—Spring Antiques Fair at Dunedin

April—Regatta and Festival Del Sol Al Sol

April—Highland Games at Dunedin

June—Turtle Walks at Clearwater

September—Florida Birding Festival and Nature Expo at Clearwater

October—Weedon Island Power Paddle Canoe and Kayak

FOR MORE INFORMATION

St. Petersburg-Clearwater Area Convention and Visitors Bureau—St. Petersburg Thunderdome, 1 Stadium Dr., Suite A, St. Petersburg, FL 33705; 877-FLBEACH or 583-7892; www.FloridasBeach.com

13 Tampa

When the first humans set foot in the area that is now Tampa, it had no bay. In fact, the Gulf of Mexico was about 70 miles to the west. The present coastline took shape about 3,000 years ago.

The Spanish were the first Europeans to land on Florida's west coast. Ponce de Leon arrived in 1513.

Panfilo de Narvaez landed at or near Tampa Bay in April 1528, claiming the land for Spain. In 1498, Narvaez had been selected by the governor of Cuba to remove Hernando Cortez from command in Mexico. But Narvaez was subsequently defeated and put in prison. From there, he saw the wealth Cortez sent home to Spain. When he was freed, he went home and convinced the government to allow him to develop *La Florida*. Using his own money for an expedition, he sailed for the west coast of Florida, searching for wealth like that discovered in Mexico and Peru. But he found only Tocobagan Indians. The Indians told

Narvaez to go north, to the Tallahassee Hills. Near starvation, the Spanish killed their horses for food, built forges to transform their metal war implements into saws, axes, and nails, and wove horse manes into rope. The stranded men made rafts to sail west to Mexico. Narvaez's raft turned over when it met a strong river current west of Florida. He did not survive.

Some believe Hernando De Soto arrived in Tampa Bay in 1539. Evidence also points to a De Soto landing farther south in Charlotte Harbor. In either case, De Soto, like Narvaez, didn't fulfill his dream. De Soto traveled in search of riches, believing the same lies the Indians had told Narvaez—that gold was farther north.

A few centuries later, Fort Brooke, built during the Second Seminole War (1835-42), slowly became Tampa. Tampa grew into one of the largest cities around the bay after Henry Plant brought his railroad here in 1884 and built his famous Tampa Bay Hotel in 1891. The unusual-looking,

Henry B. Plant Museum is a must to learn about Tampa's history and to see treasures from the abandoned Moorish hotel.

511-room hotel blended six Middle Eastern minarets, three Byzantine silver domes, and a number of cupolas, crescent moons, and keyhole arches. It became the headquarters for Teddy Roosevelt and his Rough Riders during the Spanish-American War. A list of celebrities came and went.

In 1931, the abandoned Moorish hotel was transformed into the **University of Tampa**. It is now a National Historic Landmark. The univer-

sity's **Henry B. Plant Museum** holds items from the old hotel. A 14-minute video gives visitors an introduction to the man, his transportation empire, and the influence he had on Tampa. The museum's 12 rooms tell the history of his empire, display art objects he accumulated, present furnishings from the old hotel, show how a hotel room looked in 1891, tell about Spanish-American War history, and so much more. The museum is closed Mondays. An admission fee is charged.

The Cuban cigar business also played a part in Tampa's growth. It was one of the largest industries in the area before Plant opened his hotel. In the latter part of the 19th century, Cubans congregated in Ybor (E-bor) City, as did Spaniards, Italians, Germans, and Jews. The varied cultural groups formed their own social clubs. Five of the original six of these remain: El Centro Espanol, L'Unione Italiana, El Circulo Cunbano, Deutch-Amerikanischer Verein, and El Centro Asturiano. Unfortunately, La Union Marti-Maceo fell prey to urban renewal in 1965.

We suggest you begin your exploration of Tampa at the old Ferlita Bakery building at 1818 East Ninth Street, now the **Ybor City State Museum**. Here, you will learn about the political, social, and cultural influences on the Latin Quarter.

Vicente Martinez Ybor left Spain for Havana when he was 14. In 1853, he founded a cigar factory. He moved his business to Key West in 1869, only to find that it had a poor transportation system. In 1885, Ybor negotiated with the Tampa Board of Trade to move to the city. An important factor in his decision was Plant's construction of a railroad into Tampa a year earlier. Ybor was responsible for developing Ybor City by building homes that his workers could purchase.

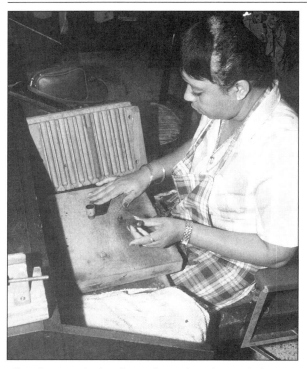

Ybor City was built to house the workers that made the community the largest cigar-producing city in the world.

Recognizing that employees were more likely to stay in Tampa if they owned their homes, he thereby created a stable work force. The city became the largest cigar producer in the world. Within 10 years, cigar companies from Havana, Key West, New York, Chicago, and Philadelphia either moved here or opened businesses in town. Hillsborough County's population and its cattle, citrus, and phosphate-fertilizer industries grew rapidly. Tourism grew. Then came the Depression. Fortunately, Tampa had a stable economy and experienced a rapid recovery. Today, it is the only major Florida city that is not dependent on tourism.

That is not to say that tourists don't flock to Tampa for a taste of its historic buildings, zoos, aquarium, and museums—and for Ybor City. You may want to consider staying in the Ybor City area to be close to its nightclubs, restaurants, shopping, art galleries, music, and history. Ybor City is recognized as the nighttime entertainment center of Florida's west coast.

In recent years, there has been a tremendous revival along Ybor City's colorful Seventh Avenue. If you're traveling west on I-4, take Exit 1, pass the first traffic light at 22nd Street, then turn south (left) on 21st Street. If you're traveling east, take Exit 1 and turn right on 21st Street. Seventh Avenue is six blocks south of the interstate.

You haven't experienced the best that Ybor City has to offer if you haven't been to the original **Columbia Restaurant**, built on Seventh Avenue in 1905. Tampa's oldest restaurant is in its fifth generation of owners. It has a dozen rooms, making it the world's largest Spanish restaurant. It was founded by Casimiro Hernandez, Sr., and named after the song "Columbia, Gem of the Ocean." The restaurant merits a visit just to see its two-story courtyard and its 1936 Don Quixote Room, with its scenes by Sergio de Meza. Flamenco dancing is performed nightly at the restaurant. You'll love the food, too!

For more dining selections, head to downtown Tampa where a smorgasbord of cultures serve you food that ranges in price from expensive to more palatable costs. You can start with good, no, make that the best cuts of beef in town at **Bern's Steak House**.

"We learned early that if you want to be the best at something, you can't worry about the cost or the trouble. We do things differently, and we do them well," is Bern's motto. For more than 40

Just minutes from Tampa, Canoe Escape will put you on the Hillsborough River for a guided or self-guided glide.

years, the Laxer family restaurant has been a Tampa landmark, serving U.S. prime beef, aged 4 to 10 weeks in their coolers. At the end of your meal, you will be given a 65-page dessert menu, so save room.

Le Bordeaux Jazz Bistro is said to have the best French food in the area. The restaurant offers an intimate atmosphere with tableside cabaret singing, as well as a jazz lounge. **Oystercatchers** is the place for seafood. Located next to the 35-acre nature preserve on the shores of Old Tampa Bay, you pick your own fish. Be forewarned: Oystercatcher's is not for the casually dressed. **Roy's Restaurant** serves Euro-Asian cuisine straight from Hawaii. This is an elegant restaurant with a cutting-edge wine list.

We stayed at the **Embassy Suites Hotel** at Fowler Avenue and Spectrum Boulevard. It's convenient to Canoe Escape, the Museum of Science and Industry, the Lowry Park Zoo, and Busch Gardens.

Because hotel and motel chains are easy to locate, in this guide we tend to cover bed-and-breakfasts and special resorts. Although downtown Tampa has plenty of well-known chains, if you're more interested in bed-and-breakfasts or resorts, you might want to stay in outlying areas.

Canoe Escape was at the top of our fun list in Tampa. Joe Faulk and his wife, Jean, began small in 1991 but have since built a large business with many canoes, kayaks, and buses. Joe says he prefers to launch only two or three canoes at a time to provide quiet for his guests on the river, but large groups are welcome also. He offers seven options that range from two hours of paddling to full-day trips. We loved the peacefulness of the Hillsborough River; we found that peacefulness unusual, since the river is so close to the city. We saw our first limpkin, a brown water bird with a strange call. You can expect to see anhingas, white ibises, ospreys, red-shouldered hawks, alligators, Florida red-bellied turtles, peninsula cooters, wild hogs, deer, roseate spoonbills, wood storks, bald eagles, water snakes, and many more species. Be sure to take your camera. The fishing is good, too.

The **Museum of Science and Industry** (MOSI), located at 4801 Fowler Avenue, is the largest

The Museum of Science and Industry is a playground for all ages.

It's as much fun watching the children as it is watching the manatees at Lowry Park Zoo.

science center in the Southeast. It is also the home of the first IMAX dome theater in Florida. Allow three hours or more to enjoy all the exhibits. As you enter, you'll see a diplodocus dinosaur on your left, an airplane overhead, and a high-wire bicycle you can ride above and to your right. As you explore the human body in "The Amazing You," you can step on scales to find out how much water is in you. You can push buttons to see the skies darken, to hear and see thunder and lightning, and to start a fire to learn about the cycle of a forest. You can go back in time to ancient Egypt and learn to write hieroglyphics. You can take a space ride in a simulator—but be prepared to hold on, as it's a bumpy flight. You can get blown away in the hurricane exhibit, where winds measure 74

miles per hour. If you're worried about maintaining your hairdo, do this last. We elected to watch other people get blown away. Then we walked across to the BioWorks Butterfly Gardens. All in all, the museum offers more than 450 hands-on activities for all ages.

From MOSI, go west on Fowler Avenue, turn south (left) on Florida Avenue, and then turn west (right) on Sligh Avenue to reach the **Lowry Park Zoo**. This is another place you'll need several hours to see. The zoo features more than 1,500 animals, many of them rare and endangered, in natural habitats. Among the exhibits is Lorikeet Landing, where you can feed the birds. Children enjoy the petting zoo and the water fountains. We spent a good while watching the manatees and other aquatic species through the windows below water level in the Aquatic Center. The zoo offers daily shows featuring birds of prey and reptiles. The two restaurants on the premises will help you keep up your energy while you try to take it all in.

The zoo is close to **Busch Gardens**, located west on Busch Boulevard. But don't try to experience both in one day unless you have a lot of stamina. Busch Gardens is 335 acres of family adventure. It offers a combination of world-class animal habitats, rides, and live entertainment with an exotic African theme.

In downtown Tampa, we visited the Tampa Bay History Center and the Florida Aquarium.

The **Tampa Bay History Center** is a small but stimulating museum that explores five centuries of regional history, archaeology, and multicultural heritage. It's worth an hour to visit the well laid-out exhibits. Located at 225 South Franklin Street, it is open Tuesday through Saturday.

The **Florida Aquarium**, located at 701 Channelside Drive, is another good place to take your camera. This world-class facility hosts over 10,000 aquatic plants and animals in its Wetlands, Bays and Beaches, Coral Reefs, and Sea Hunt galleries. As you walk the path through the 152,000-square-foot building, you'll pass about 600 species and 5,000 critters. Fishing gear isn't allowed, but we certainly wished we had ours when we saw all those large snook, sea trout, and redfish. The 150-pound politically correct Goliath grouper—formerly known as the jewfish—gave us pause. It was large enough to eat us—and our tackle. Among the residents here are water birds, otters, sharks, Pacific octopuses, and stingrays you can pet. You can take a behind-the-scenes tour, see a dive show, encounter invertebrates and sharks, visit the Dragons Down Under exhibit (where you can see rare sea dragons and seahorses from Australia and beyond), and enjoy the Frights of the Forest exhibit (which has creepy creatures from the world's wet-forest habitats). You may also want to check out **DolphinQuest Eco-Tours**, which lets visitors explore the bay on a 64-foot catamaran. The aquarium is open daily except for Thanksgiving and Christmas.

All of the following are in Tampa and use the 33602 zip code and 813 area code, except where noted.

ACCOMMODATIONS

Don Vicente de Ybor Inn—1915 Republica de Cuba City, 33605; 241-4545

Embassy Suites Hotel—3705 Spectrum Blvd., 33612; 800-EMBASSY or 977-7066

Holiday InnSelect—111 W. Fortune St.; 223-1351

Hyatt Regency—2 Tampa City Center; 800-695-8284 or 225-1234

Raddison Riverwalk—200 N. Ashley; 800-695-8284 or 223-2222

ATTRACTIONS

Busch Gardens—3000 E. Busch Blvd., 33612; 987-5082

Canoe Escape—9335 E. Flower Ave., Thonotosassa, FL 33592; 986-2067

Duck Tours—514 Channelside Dr.; 310-DUCK

Florida Aquarium/DolphinQuest Eco-Tours—701 Channelside Dr.; 800-353-4741 or 273-4000

Henry B. Plant Museum—401 W. Kennedy Blvd., 33606; 254-1891

Light Tackle Fishing Expeditions—12088 Anderson Rd., Suite 137, 33625; 800-972-1930 or 855-0430

Lowry Park Zoo—1101 W. Sligh Ave., 33604; 935-8552

Museum of Science and Industry—4801 E. Fowler Ave., 33617; 800-995-MOSI or 987-6100

Old Hyde Park Village—748 S. Village Cir., 33606; 251-3500

Tampa Bay History Center—225 S. Franklin St., 33602; 228-0097

Ybor City State Museum—1818 E. Ninth Ave., 33605; 247-6323

 CAMPING

Hillsborough River State Park—15402 US 301 N., Thonotosassa, FL 33592; 987-6771

 DINING

Bernini—1702 E. Seventh Ave., Ybor City, FL 33065; 248-0099

Bern's Steak House—1208 S. Howard Ave., 33606; 251-2421

Columbia Restaurant—2117 E. Seventh Ave., Ybor City, FL 33065; 248-4961

Jimmy Mac's Marina Restaurant—5000 W. Gandy Blvd.; 839-3449

Kojak's House of Ribs—2808 Gandy Blvd.; 837-3774

Le Bordeaux Jazz Bistro—1502 S. Howard Ave., 33606; 254-4387

Newk's Lighthouse Café—514 Channelside Dr.; 307-6395

Oystercatchers—6200 W. Courtney Campbell Cswy., 33607; 281-9116.

Roy's Restaurant—4342 Boy Scout Blvd., 33607; 873-7697.

Rumpelmayer's German Restaurant—48112 E. Busch Blvd.; 989-9563

Tony's Ybor Restaurant—2001 22nd St., Ybor City, FL 33605; 247-7283

Wright's Gourmet House—1200 S. Dale Mabry Hwy.; 253-3838

 EVENTS

January—Black Heritage Festival

February—Gasparilla Pirate Fest

February—Ybor City Fiesta Day

February—Florida State Fair

March—Florida Strawberry Festival

March—Gasparilla Festival of the Arts

March—Apollo Beach Manatee Arts Festival

October—NSRA Southeast Street Rod Nationals

November—Ybor City Annual Tampa Cigar Heritage Festival

 FOR MORE INFORMATION

Tampa Bay Convention and Visitors Bureau—400 N. Tampa St., Suite 2800, Tampa, FL 33602; 800-826-8358 or 342-4053; www.visittampabay.com

Just south of Tampa Bay are Ellenton, Palmetto, Bradenton, Anna Maria Island, and Longboat Key.

From I-75, turn west at Exit 43 on to US 301 to reach **Gamble Plantation State Historic Site** in Ellenton. This is the site of the oldest building in Manatee County.

The Second Seminole War ended in 1842, opening the area for settlement and attracting men to large-scale cultivation of sugarcane and its manufacture into sugar. Major Robert Gamble came from Tallahassee. Initially, the acreage he purchased was small for a plantation. But he subsequently increased his holdings until he had nearly 3,500 acres, about 1,500 of them under cultivation. The plantation produced about 1,500 hogsheads, or barrels, of sugar annually.

Gamble built his home of brick and tabby. The outer walls were nearly two feet thick. Eighteen columns supported the roof and the upper verandas, which extended around three sides of the home. A large cistern collected rainwater, to

Gamble Plantation State Historic Site shows how the wealthy lived in the 1800s.

which Gamble added minnows to eat algae and insect larvae, chlorinated water not yet being in use.

In 1856, falling sugar prices and crop losses led him to sell the plantation to two men from Louisiana. The property later came under the ownership of Archibald McNeil, the Confederacy's deputy commissary for the Manatee District. In 1872, Major George Patten purchased the land and mansion for $3,000. Years later, the Pattens abandoned the aging, decaying home to avoid the high cost of maintaining it. They built the nearby white frame house around 1895. By 1920, the abandoned mansion was in ruins. Five years later, the Judah P. Benjamin Chapter of the United Daughters of the Confederacy purchased the property and deeded it to the state of Florida as a historic site.

Visitors can take a tour that includes the **Patten House**, which is the Florida headquarters of the United Daughters of the Confederacy. On our tour, we saw an original Confederate flag with seven stars. There aren't many of those left. The grounds and the picnic pavilion at the rear of the mansion are open each day. The mansion, furnished in period items to give visitors the feel of frontier living, is open Thursday through Monday for scheduled guided tours.

If you're wondering who Judah P. Benjamin

This rare seven-star Confederate flag is on display at Gamble Plantation State Historic Site.

was, he resigned as United States senator from Louisiana to become attorney general, then secretary of war, and finally secretary of state under Jefferson Davis, the president of the Confederacy. Benjamin fled Richmond, Virginia, and a $40,000 bounty for his capture on April 2, 1865. After traveling to Florida under an alias, he stayed at the former Gamble Plantation with McNeil before escaping to Bimini. He then made his way to England, where he became a successful barrister.

From the mansion, go west, then turn south on FL 683, then west on Fourth Street in Bradenton, then north on Main Street to reach the **South Florida Museum and Manatee Aquarium**. This facility suffered a fire before we arrived, and some of the areas were closed for repairs.

You can't miss the mastodon in the first room; this creature reaches to the second floor! You'll learn about the Paleo-Indians, the Timacuan Indians, the Tocobaga tribe of the Tampa area, early European exploration on the Gulf coast, pioneer life, and the space age. We especially enjoyed the Parker Aquarium and the feeding of Snooty, the oldest manatee born in captivity. He seemed to enjoy attention from visitors as he swam in circles and made smooth, playful barrel rolls. Manatees' intelligence is on a par with that of cows. In the wild, they eat only plants—about 125 pounds per day. The grinding wears away their teeth, which are constantly being replaced. They hold their breath between one and three minutes when they're active and from five to 30 minutes when resting or sleeping. They sleep between five and 12 hours a day. Their lungs are about four feet long. They exchange nearly 90 percent of their air with each exhale. It is welcome news that their low numbers have been increasing in recent years. About 3,200 are left in the world.

Drive south on Main, turn east on Manatee Avenue (FL 64), and then turn south on 15th Street East to reach **Manatee Village Historical Park**. This collection of buildings gives visitors a look at life over 100 years ago on the Florida frontier. The historical park contains 10 authentic structures, some of which are listed on the National Register of Historic Places. They come from Florida's original Manatee County, established in 1856, which encompassed more than 5,500 square miles. Today, Manatee, Hardee, Highlands, Okeechobee, Sarasota, De Soto, Charlotte, and Glades Counties occupy that same area.

We stopped first at the **Wiggins Store**, an old general store complete with merchandise of the time. This two-story structure, built in 1903, offered customers the best selection of groceries, dry goods, and gadgets in the area. Customers who traveled far to shop here stayed overnight on the second floor. In the store's Hands-On Room, children of all ages are invited to touch the turn-of-the-20th-century toys, dolls, and other items. Down the brick walk is the Cracker Gothic-style home of the Will Stephens family. The home is an excellent example of rural frame dwellings constructed between 1870 and World War I. Another building at the historical park is the 1860 **Manatee County Courthouse**. The oldest structure of its kind still standing on the South Florida mainland, it is listed in the National Registry of Historic Sites. Visitors also enjoy the one-room schoolhouse used from 1908 to 1929 and the **Fogarty Boat Works** building, which operated from 1866 to 1944. The boat works contains half-hull models, wooden patterns, molds, tools, equipment, and belt-drive machinery.

Manatee Village Historical Park is free to the public. It is open every day.

De Soto National Memorial Park has a small museum, nature trails, and gumbo-limbo trees.

From the historical village, go west through town and north on 75th Street West to visit **De Soto National Memorial Park** on Shaws Point.

Some think that De Soto landed here on May 30, 1539, before trekking north in search of riches. He died three years later of fever and was buried in the Mississippi River. The reason for that burial site was simple: De Soto had told the natives he was a god. If they discovered he had died, they would have learned his lie, which would have meant trouble for the surviving members of the expedition. His second in command then led the party for 16 months. They finally reached Spanish holdings in Mexico.

In addition to memorializing De Soto, the park offers insights into 16th-century life. From December through April, park employees dress in 16th-century costumes and give talks describing the way the Spaniards lived. Staff members demonstrate the use of various weapons of the period and show how food was prepared and preserved for journeys lasting months or even years. In the visitor center, you can watch a 22-minute film about De Soto and the artifacts of the period. Our introduction to gumbo-limbo trees came at the visitor center. They're large trees with peeling bark. Within the park property is a half-mile nature trail that goes out to De Soto Point and passes the ruins of an 1880s tabby house that was part of a pioneer settlement. The park is open daily except for major holidays.

The Bradenton area celebrates De Soto's discovery of Florida's west coast each spring during the month-long **Florida Heritage Festival**, which includes a night parade, sports events, a crafts fair, a plastic-bottle boat regatta, and a reenactment of the 1539 landing at the mouth of the Manatee River.

For dinner, we resolutely recommend **Linger Lodge**. To reach it, take FL 70 from Bradenton and turn south on Braden River Road, which runs into Linger Lodge Road. Owner Frank Gamsky began with a trailer court on the Braden River in

Linger Lodge provides you with a menu full of "Tummy Teasers."

the days when the roads weren't paved. Today, he offers 100 RV sites with hookups for seasonal and long-term customers. Manatee County's most famous raconteur, Frank has been featured on CNN. It's worth going to his restaurant to hear him tell stories of hunting in the Florida mountains and a thousand other off-the-wall quips. Linger Lodge—called Linger Longer Lodge before he took over in 1968—is half taxidermist's shop, half museum, seven-fifths bull, and 100 percent fine restaurant. Frank taught himself how to stuff animals he found dead along the road. The restaurant serves as his exhibit space. Some of the critters he's mounted are more than unusual. You've just got to see them! His love of road kill spills over into the menu. Frank's "Tummy Teaser" choices include Chunk of Skunk, Smidgen of Pigeon, Road Toad à la Mode, and other tasty items. The restaurant offers a daily special called "Guess the Mess." If you guess what it is, you eat it for free. Center Line Bovine, Flat Cat, and the Chicken That Didn't Cross the Road are among the entrées. Or you can ask for the "Pedestrian Menu," which lists foods by their common names. If you want something to go, you can choose from the "Anything Dead on Bread" selections.

While you're in the area, be sure to visit the Gulf islands.

Anna Maria Island contains three municipalities: Anna Maria at the north end, Holmes Beach in the middle, and Bradenton Beach at the south end. Although it was still under construction when we visited the historic district on Anna Maria Island, **BridgeWalk** will be open when you arrive. This two-story building offers everything from studio suites to large, two-bedroom accommodations with full kitchens, fireplaces, whirlpool tubs, and large, screened verandas suitable for outdoor dining. A heated swimming pool, retail shops, and a spa round out the complex, which is within sight of the Gulf and within walking distance of restaurants and shops.

Anna Maria is also home to the **Harrington House**, one of Florida's most highly rated bed-and-breakfast inns. All the guest rooms in this lovingly restored 1925 coquina-block beachfront home have private baths, color cable TV, telephones, and air conditioning. Most have French doors opening to balconies that overlook the heated swimming pool and the Gulf of Mexico. A full island breakfast is served each morning.

We stayed at the **Silver Sands Resort** on **Longboat Key**, south of Anna Maria Island. It was an ideal location. The resort offers one- and two-bedroom apartments, tennis, shuffleboard, a putting green, laundry facilities, grills, beach chairs, umbrellas, and a boat dock.

Fishing opportunities abound on the islands. Of course, there is surf fishing from the beaches. Three hot spots are the passes: Longboat Pass, New Pass, and Big Pass.

Around the Bend Nature Tours offers eco-heritage tours of the coast, guided nature walks, and boat tours. **Ray's Canoe Hideaway** on the Manatee River explores the Singing River by canoe or kayak. It offers easy, year-round paddling fun for those interested in wildlife watching, fishing, picnicking, swimming, sunbathing, hunting fossils, or just finding a quiet moment in nature.

The islands are wonderful places to stay for all kinds of activities—or inactivities. You'll have dining opportunities close to any accommodation you choose. Selecting is the difficult part. Be sure not to miss **Mr. Bones BBQ**!

All of the following are in Bradenton and use the 34206 zip code and 941 area code, except where noted.

ACCOMMODATIONS

Beach Inn—101 66th St., Holmes Beach, FL 34217; 800-823-2247 or 778-9597

BridgeWalk—100 Bridge St., Bradenton Beach, FL 34217; 866-779-2545 or 779-2545

Harrington House Bed and Breakfast—5626 Gulf Dr., Anna Maria Island, FL 34217; 888-828-5566 or 778-5444

Silver Resorts—1301 Gulf Dr., Bradenton Beach, FL 34217; 800-441-7873 or 778-6626

Silver Sands—5841 Gulf of Mexico Dr., Longboat Key, FL 34228; 800-245-3731 or 383-3731

ATTRACTIONS

Around the Bend Nature Tours—1815 Palma Sola Blvd., 34209; 794-8773; www.aroundbend.com

De Soto National Memorial Park—P.O. Box 15390, 34280; 792-0458

Gamble Plantation State Historic Site—3708 Patten Ave., Ellenton, FL 34222; 723-4536

Linger Lodge—7205 Linger Lodge Rd., 34202; 755-2757

Manatee Village Historical Park—604 15th St. E., 34205; 749-7165

Solomon's Castle—4533 Solomon Rd., Ona, FL 33865; 494-6077

South Florida Museum and Manatee Aquarium—201 10th St. W.; 746-4131

 CAMPING

Linger Lodge—7205 Linger Lodge Rd., 34202; 755-2757

Ray's Canoe Hideaway—1247 Hagle Park Rd., 34202; 747-3909; rays.canoe.hideaway@usa.net

 DINING

Linger Lodge—7205 Linger Lodge Rd., 34202; 755-2757

Mar Vista—760 Broadway, Longboat Key, FL 34228; 383-2391

Mr. Bones BBQ—3007 Gulf Dr, 34217; 778-6614

Rod and Reel Pier—875 N. Shore Dr.; 778-1885

Rotten Ralph's—902 S. Bay Blvd.; 778-3953

Sharky's—2519 Gulf Dr. North, Bradenton Beach, FL 34217; 779-9151

Shells—3200 E. Bay Dr., Holmes Beach, FL 34228; 778-5997

 EVENTS

January—Longboat Key Street Art Festival

February—Bradenton Beach Festival

March—Anna Maria Island Springfest

April—Florida Heritage Festival

October—Pumpkin Festival

November—Southeast Nostalgia Fall Nationals

December—WinterFest

 FOR MORE INFORMATION

Bradenton Area Convention and Visitors Bureau—P.O. Box 1000, Bradenton, FL 34206; 800-462-6283 or 729-9177; www.flagulfislands.com

HIGHLIGHTS

CÀ D'ZAN

RINGLING MUSEUM OF ART

MOTE AQUARIUM

RINGLING MUSEUM OF THE CIRCUS

SARASOTA JUNGLE GARDENS

MARIE SELBY BOTANICAL GARDENS

In 1885, the Florida Mortgage and Investment Company promoted Sarasota in Scotland in an effort to get immigrants to come here. The company put the prettiest face possible on Sarasota by promising an abundance of fertile land, plentiful citrus groves, and affordable housing. Scottish families looking for a new start hopped on steamer ships and headed for a new, wonderful life in the United States. When they arrived that December, they were bewildered at seeing what looked like a frontier camp. Main Street still had stumps. Many left, but the optimists among them stayed.

John Hamilton Gillespie, an aristocrat, lawyer, and member of the Queen's Bodyguard for Scotland, was among the optimists. Gillespie is believed to have built the first nine-hole golf course in the United States. He also constructed the De Soto Hotel on Main Street. In 1902, he became Sarasota's first mayor.

Within a couple of decades, Sarasota began attracting wealthy folk.

Bertha Palmer, widow of Chicago developer Potter Palmer, assembled a waterfront winter estate and gardens now known as Historic Spanish Point. What is now Myakka River State Park was Palmer's 30,000-acre ranch, Meadowsweet Pastures. (For information on these two attractions, see the Charlotte Harbor chapter.)

William Selby and his wife, Marie, moved here in the 1920s. Mr. Selby was one of the owners of Texaco Oil Company. They built a Spanish-style home on Sarasota Bay, where Marie began her gardens.

Another wealthy person who came to town in the Roaring Twenties was John Ringling. He and his wife, Mable, built a majestic Venetian-style home named **Cà d'Zan**, which translates from the Venetian dialect as "House of John." They also constructed a museum to house their collection of works by Peter Paul Rubens and other masters of 17th-century Italian and Flemish art. Today, the **Ringling Museum of Art** displays more than 500 years of European artwork. Visitors particularly enjoy the courtyard filled with statues and fountains.

Ringling Museum of Art and its grounds are part of John Ringling's legacy to the city of Sarasota.

Ringling used his circus's elephants to help build the first bridge from the mainland to St. Armands Key. The circus's winter quarters were moved to Sarasota in 1927, giving it the nickname "Circus Town."

Today's Sarasota is recognized as Florida's "Cultural Coast." It is home to a professional symphony, a ballet, an opera, more than 10 theaters, and 30 art galleries. Reservations for accommodations are necessary during the peak season, which runs from February to Easter. The value

Cá d'Zan, John and Mable Ringling's 30-room home on Sarasota Bay, has recently been restored.

season is June through September.

This overview of the area's major attractions starts on Lido Key and St. Armands Key, located west of Sarasota via the Ringling Causeway. You can also reach these keys by driving south on Gulf of Mexico Drive (FL 789) on Longboat Key.

At the northeast end of Lido Key is **Mote Aquarium**. Here, visitors can see a giant squid under glass, take in an exhibit on the Myakka River ecosystem, and enjoy lots of chances to make new acquaintances in the touch tank. The shark tank is also a popular exhibit. We saw some odd-looking creatures here—the walking batfish, the toadfish, the scary-looking green moray eel. We learned that female seahorses deposit eggs into males' brood pouches, where they are fertilized and develop into miniature adults. A large number of sea turtles—2,500 to 3,000—come to the Sarasota area to lay their eggs. Female loggerheads nest every 12 to 15 days during nesting season. Each nest has about 100 eggs, which take 55 days to hatch. The hatchlings usually emerge at night and head toward the brightest spot on the horizon. They swim continuously for up to 24 hours after they enter the ocean in order to reach deeper water. The odds of a hatchling reaching maturity are one in 2,500.

Mote Aquarium is open daily.

Sarasota Bay Explorers is headquartered at the aquarium. Here, you can arrange to cruise the local bays with a marine biologist narrating your trip.

Next to Mote Aquarium is **Pelican Man's Bird Sanctuary**. At this open-air rehabilitation center, you can stroll around looking at pelicans, egrets, owls, herons, hawks, and 30 more species.

The picturesque **St. Armands Circle** on St. Armands Key offers boutiques, sidewalk cafés, and haute cuisine, fulfilling John Ringling's dream of a premier shopping district. You'll also enjoy the

The Mote Aquarium, along with its next-door neighbor the Pelican Man's Bird Sanctuary, are favorite stops on Lido Key.

small park honoring the greats of the Greatest Show on Earth. Charles St. Amand bought 132 acres here in 1893. He paid $21.71. He made his living raising produce and fishing. A misspelling on the deed gave the key its name. Ringling purchased St. Armands Key in 1917.

Just east of St. Armands Circle, **Limetree Beach Resort,** in the heart of world-famous Lido Beach, offers a heated pool, tennis, sailing, bicycling, shuffleboard, volleyball, an exercise room, and a whirlpool spa. Also located on the beachfront is **Sarasota Sands,** which provides tennis facilities, kitchens, and a heated pool.

Dining in the area is topped by the famous **Columbia Restaurant,** which originated in Ybor City (see the Tampa chapter). Their Cuban dishes reached Sarasota in 1959. Just across Ringling Bridge in downtown Sarasota's bustling cultural district is **Mediterraneo Ristoranto,** which serves Northern Italian cuisine.

When you're ready to leave the keys, drive north from Ringling Causeway on US 41, then turn west on Bay Shore Drive, which leads to the

Ringling complex. The complex includes the Ringling Museum of the Circus, Cà d'Zan, and the Ringling Museum of Art.

The Ringling family empire was founded by five of the seven sons of August and Marie Salome Ringling of Baraboo, Wisconsin. The very first Ringling Circus appeared on a Monday afternoon in May 1884 in Baraboo.

P. T. Barnum and James A. Bailey created the Greatest Show on Earth. Bailey acquired full ownership in 1905 and sold a 50 percent interest to the Ringlings. Following Bailey's death in 1906, the Ringlings purchased the circus in October 1907. The Ringling Bros. and Barnum and Bailey Circus became a thrill in every youngster's heart.

Inside the **Ringling Museum of the Circus** are life casts of clowns, costumes, miniature circuses, elaborately carved wagons, and the cannons used to shoot human cannonballs. There's a special tribute to famous animal trainer Gunther Gebel-Williams and one to Emmett Kelly, who created the hobo clown Weary Willie.

The grounds, especially Mable's historic rose garden, warrant a walk-through. You'll see more than 400 species of exotic trees and plants, including huge banyan trees.

Cà d'Zan was undergoing a multimillion-dollar restoration when we were there, so we could only walk around outside. It's an awe-inspiring 30-room mansion on Sarasota Bay.

Sarasota Jungle Gardens is also on Bay Shore Drive. It's one of the oldest attractions in the state and the only zoological park in the area. The jungle trails wind among 240 species of tropical trees, plants, and flowers from all over the world. Visitors enjoy the bird and reptile shows, the "Kiddy Jungle," the 21 animal exhibits, the tropical birds, and the free-roaming flamingos that eat

St. Armands Circle is famous for its upscale dining and shopping.

from your hand. The park is open daily except for Christmas.

To visit **Marie Selby Botanical Gardens**, get back on US 41 and go south past the Flying Fish Fleet and Jack Marina and Restaurant. The gardens will be on your right.

At this tropical oasis on Sarasota Bay, you'll see the world's most spectacular display of rare orchids and bromeliads. The fragrances of some of the orchids nearly made us swoon in ecstasy. If we hadn't had two more weeks on the road, we would have filled our Explorer with orchids and a number of other garden items. You can look, smell, and photograph as you wander about the hibiscus, wildflower, fruit, bamboo, butterfly, mangrove, and other gardens. It's a delightful place. The gift shop is stocked with excellent gardening books. The gardens are open every day except Christmas. Be prepared to be enchanted.

A couple of other local enterprises cater to those with a taste for the outdoors.

Walk on the Wild Side offers eco-tours led by guides who are familiar with Florida's flora, fauna, natural history, and cultural history. The kayaking, canoeing, and hiking excursions are customized to your interests and abilities and offer excellent opportunities for wildlife viewing and photography. Half-day and full-day trips are offered. Lunch is provided on full-day trips.

Enterprise Sailing Charters offers two-, three-, and four-hour tours and romantic sunset sails aboard a 41-foot vessel with three sails. Virtually all passengers consider this the best experience of their vacation. Food, beverages, and memories are included.

All of the following are in Sarasota and use the 34236 zip code and 941 area code, except where noted.

 ACCOMMODATIONS

Cypress Bed and Breakfast Inn—621 Gulfstream Ave. S.; 955-4683

Lido Beach Palms—148 Cleveland Dr., Longboat Key, FL 34236; 383-9505

Limetree Beach Resort—1050 Ben Franklin Dr.; 388-2111

Sarasota Sands—2150 Ben Franklin Dr.; 388-2138

 ATTRACTIONS

Enterprise Sailing Charters—2 Marina Plaza; 951-1833

Marie Selby Botanical Gardens—811 South Palm Ave.; 366-5731

Mote Aquarium—1600 Ken Thompson Pkwy.; 388-4441

Pelican Man's Bird Sanctuary—1708 Ken Thompson Pkwy.; 388-4444

Ringling Museum of Art—5401 Bay Shore Dr., 34243; 359-5700

Ringling Museum of the Circus—5401 Bay Shore Dr., 34243; 359-5700

Sarasota Bay Explorers—1600 Ken Thompson Pkwy.; 388-4200

Sarasota Jungle Gardens—3701 Bay Shore Dr., 34243; 355-5305; www.sarasotajunglegardens.com

Walk on the Wild Side—3434 N. Tamiami Trail, 34243; 351-6500

 CAMPING

Gulf Beach Campground—8862 Midnight Pass Rd., 34242; 349-3839

Pine Shores Trailer Park—6450 S. Tamiami Trail, 34231; 922-1929

Sun-N-Fun RV Resort—7125 Fruitville Rd., 34240; 371-2505

 DINING

Barnacle Bill's Seafood—1526 Main St.; 365-6800

Columbia Restaurant—411 St. Armands Circle; 388-3987

Crab and Fin—420 St. Armands Circle; 388-3964

Fifty's Diner—3737 Bahia Vista St.; 953-4637

Mediterraneo Ristoranto—1970 Main St.; 365-4122

Roessler's Restaurant—2033 Vamo Way; 966-6588

Yoder's Restaurant—3434 Bahia Vista St.; 366-8817

 EVENTS

January—Arts Day Festival

January—Sarasota Film Festival

March—Sarasota Jazz Festival

March—Selby Gardens Spring Plant Fair

September—Colony Stone Crab, Seafood, and Wine Festival

October—St. Armands Art Festival

 FOR MORE INFORMATION

Sarasota Convention and Visitors Bureau—655 N. Tamiami Trail; 800-522-9799 or 955-0991; www.sarasotafl.org

Punta Gorda-Charlotte Harbor-Boca Grande-Venice

HIGHLIGHTS

DON PEDRO ISLAND STATE RECREATION AREA

CAYO COSTA STATE PARK

HISTORIC SPANISH POINTE

MYAKKA RIVER STATE PARK

BABCOCK WILDERNESS ADVENTURES

It's hard to imagine that one of the largest protected marine estuaries in the United States is all but hidden on Florida's Gulf coast about 50 miles south of Sarasota and 25 miles north of Fort Myers. But in the case of Charlotte Harbor, it may be true.

Easygoing Charlotte County is blessed with sandy beaches, 219 miles of coastline, lovely barrier islands, excellent fishing, and breathtaking sunsets. While the bays, sounds, and passes where the Peace and Myakka Rivers merge are the most popular attractions for tourists visiting this area, you will also find golf courses, antique and specialty shops, and plenty of delicious seafood. The area was recently voted one of Florida's small-town gems by *Florida Trend* magazine and made *Money* magazine's list of the best places to live in America.

Punta Gorda is Charlotte County's only incorporated city. The name, which means "Fat Point" or "Broad Point" in Spanish, describes the peninsula on which Punta Gorda sits poking into Charlotte Harbor. The large opening into the harbor is called Boca Grande, Spanish for "Large Mouth."

The Calusa Indians were living and fishing here when Ponce de Leon arrived in 1513. He

The docks at Fishermen's Village in Punta Gorda offer easy access to Charlotte Harbor and the neighboring Gulf of Mexico.

returned in 1521 with two ships and 200 settlers, but the fierce Calusas attacked the fledgling settlement and sent its residents packing. De Leon was wounded during the fight, and gangrene set in. He was in Havana when he eventually died of his wounds. Hernando De Soto came looking for gold in 1539, but he found Juan Ortiz instead. Ortiz was a survivor from an earlier, doomed Spanish expedition. It was an Indian princess who had saved him from death. Researchers have suggested that this story may have been revived 50 years later and applied to British captain John Smith and Pocahontas in Jamestown, Virginia. By the 1700s, the Calusa Indians were extinct, the victims of warfare, of assimilation, and of diseases carried to the New World by the Europeans.

The first white settlers came to the north shore of Charlotte Harbor in the 1860s. When the Florida Internal Improvement Fund offered cheap land, settlers developed a community and built a dock to ship cattle. Few people were willing to endure the hardships of the Florida frontier, so incentives like cheap land had to be offered.

After the arrival of the railroad in 1886, settlers began to depend on income from phosphate, citrus, cigars, turpentine, lumber, and cattle ranching. By the early 1900s, cattle pens were prominent in Punta Gorda, and drinking water was said to be more valuable than gold. On the good side of the tracks, so to speak, the Hotel Punta Gorda catered to wealthy tourists, who berthed their yachts at the hotel's private pier or rode their private rail cars to what was the southern end of the railroad line in the United States at that time. During the Roaring Twenties, Governor Barron Collier bought the hotel and renamed it the Hotel Charlotte Harbor. Unfortunately, the structure that had provided lodging for the likes of Henry

Ford and Thomas Edison burned in 1959.

You can learn all this and much more about the area at the **Florida Adventure Museum**, located on West Retta Esplanade in Punta Gorda.

Or if you're in the mood for some exercise, you can take a historic walking tour of town. The Punta Gorda Historic Walking Tour Guide is available at the Florida Adventure Museum and the Punta Gorda Chamber of Commerce. You'll see several Victorian structures and enjoy the 16 murals that illustrate the history of the area.

One man's foresight is responsible for the absence of waterfront high-rises in Punta Gorda. Colonel Isaac Trabue resolved to preserve the harbor out to the navigable channel when he platted Punta Gorda and planned for public parks in 1885. **Gilchrist Park** is the result. A sidewalk begins outside the **Best Western Waterfront** in Punta Gorda and ambles through Gilchrist Park along the water's edge. It's a great place to walk or jog, and the sunsets are inspirational. The Best Western's **Waterfront Café and Pub** overlooks

Gilchrist Bed and Breakfast has a perfect location for those who want to enjoy a stroll through Gilchrist Park in Punta Gorda.

Charlotte Harbor, as does the hotel's swimming pool. Both are good spots for relaxing. All three meals are served in the café.

You can also enjoy pleasant accommodations at **Gilchrist Bed and Breakfast** on Gilchrist Street. Built in 1941, the house has tongue-and-groove ceilings, a tin roof, lovely gardens, and two guest rooms with queen-sized beds, private baths, and private porches.

You'll want to sample some of the fine restaurants in town while you're visiting.

Smokey's Smoke House Restaurant has been in business for 30 years, so you know it's doing something right. The hot homemade Biscuits and Sausage Gravy are a favorite at breakfast. At lunch, you can get smoked meat sandwiches, burgers, ribs, or chicken. The restaurant is open every day except Monday.

The menu at the **Summer Mood Café** includes gourmet sandwiches, soups, and salads. The art displayed on the walls is for sale.

The back deck of **Harpoon Harry's** in Fishermen's Village is a popular meeting place for cold beer, raw oysters, steamed seafood pots, and sandwiches. The restaurant is open daily for lunch and dinner.

Fishermen's Village started out as the Maud Street City Docks in 1929. Today, it's filled with interesting clothing, gift, and specialty shops. Fishermen's Village also offers 47 two-bedroom condominium villas with complete kitchens, lofts, balconies, and waterfront views. Guests enjoy the use of tennis courts and the heated swimming pool.

Visitors to the area can enjoy a host of charter-fishing excursions and sightseeing cruises. The **King Fisher Fleet** docks at Fishermen's Village. Ralph Allen, the owner and captain, offers deep-sea and back-bay fishing trips. He holds three world records for fishing. There are more than 100 species to catch, and something is biting all year long. The peak season is from December to April, but Vern had one of the best fishing days he's ever enjoyed one early October, when he landed the "grand slam"—redfish, sea trout, snook, and tarpon—with Captain Ralph. Each spring, the sea turns white when 40,000 to 60,000 tarpon concentrate at the mouth of the estuary at Boca Grande Pass. The largest tarpon taken on Captain Ralph's boat so far weighed 180 pounds. He'll get all the tackle together that you'll need, so come as you are.

The King Fisher Fleet also offers a variety of regularly scheduled sightseeing cruises. For example, the Out Island Day Cruise to Cabbage Key begins with a two-and-a-half-hour narrated cruise on the Charlotte Harbor aquatic preserve from the mouth of the Peace River down the length of the harbor, on to the Intracoastal Waterway, and among the islands of Pine Island Sound. Sightseers take lunch at the historic Cabbage Key Inn, built in 1938 on top of a Calusa Indian shell midden accessible today only by boat. The fleet's wildlife-viewing cruise stops for lunch at a waterfront restaurant located at Burnt Store Marina on the eastern shore of Charlotte Harbor. Naturalists from Charlotte Harbor Environmental Center (CHEC), a nonprofit organization, narrate a nature cruise inland up the Peace River.

CHEC offers classes and conservation information, maintains nearly four miles of nature trails and the **Discovery Museum** off Burnt Store Road, and manages **Cedar Point Park** and the **Amberjack Slough**, which offer access to nature from daybreak to sunset. A short wading trip with a dip net at **Ponce de Leon Park** in the company of Monica Dorken, CHEC educator, showed us that this is a healthy estuary teeming with marine life of every shape, size, and description.

You'll have another chance to see wildlife at the 65,000-acre **Babcock/Webb Wildlife Management Area**, which offers fishing, camping, and hunting.

Across the Collier Bridge, the waterfront **Harbour Inn** on the famed Tamiami Trail in Port Charlotte has its own antique mall and tearoom. There are resorts, campgrounds, motels, and condominium rentals in the area to suit almost every style and budget.

Breakers Restaurant and Brew Pub overlooks the harbor in Port Charlotte. It offers microbrewed beers, wine, a full bar, delicious Crab Dip, grouper, tuna, shrimp, chicken, steaks, and seafood.

While you're on this side of the harbor, consider driving to Placida for a **Grande Tours** kayak tour. You can join Captain Marian Schneider on a dolphin tour, on which you can use a hydrophone to listen to the dolphins. Grande Tours offers guided tours, kayak launching, and backcountry adventures, along with limited accommodations including a bunkhouse if you're traveling with a bedroll and an apartment if you're not. If you haven't kayaked before, Grande Tours offers a two-hour class that includes an introduction to basic paddling skills, followed by a one-hour paddling tour. We paddled with Ed Engel and Captain Jack Taylor down Coral Creek to Gasparilla Sound, part of Charlotte Harbor Estuary. They introduced us to kayaking trails through some of the mangrove forests there. It's also possible to paddle over to **Don Pedro Island State Recreation Area**, part of a seven-mile-long island accessible by water only. Docks, picnic tables, grills, and a restroom are available for daytime use. Man-

groves line the bay side overlooking the Intracoastal Waterway. Swimming, shelling, and sunbathing are popular activities along the mile of white-sand beaches, sand dunes, and sea oats on the Gulf side.

Palm Island Resort offers two miles of unspoiled beach along the northern end of the island. A car ferry is available for resort guests. If you make more than one round trip per day, it will cost you an additional $23, but most visitors find little reason to leave once they discover Palm Island. The resort has two-story condominiums containing either four or eight attractively decorated units. All are on pilings, so even the first floor has a view of the water. Four pools with hot tubs, two restaurants, two bars, and a general store are within the resort. The **Rum Bay Restaurant** serves appetizers like Conch Fritters, Crab Cakes, and Blackened Tuna Bits on a skewer. The dinner menu features salads, seafood, steaks, pasta, and chicken dishes. Specialty drinks include the signature Rum Bay Smash, a concoction of rum,

The wonderfully isolated Palm Island Resort occupies the northern end of a glistening white barrier island accessible only by boat or ferry.

The Boca Grande Lighthouse, or Port Boca Grande Lighthouse as it's also known, was accessible only by water until the Boca Grande Causeway was built from Placida in 1958.

cream of coconut, and tropical juices. Breakfast is served on weekends. This family-friendly resort offers Saturday-morning nature programs, kids' activities in the morning and afternoon, and a resident pirate who puts in appearances on cue. The resort's recreation department has bicycles, kayaks, and boogie boards for rent. There are 11 tennis courts, a pro shop, and a tennis pro for lessons; there is no charge for court time. If you bring your boat, you can put in on the mainland side, leave your trailer parked on the mainland, and rent a slip on the island. The closest marina is **Palm Island Marina** on the mainland. The resort will also arrange fishing charters.

A trip to **Cayo Costa State Park** is popular with experienced paddlers who launch their own kayaks or rent from Grande Tours. Situated on an eight-mile-long barrier island with a completely undeveloped beach, Cayo Costa is accessible only by boat, which accounts for its being one of the

least-visited state parks in Florida. The park service maintains a picnic area with shelters, restrooms, and outdoor showers in a grove of shade-providing pine trees. If kayaking is not your style, you can make arrangements for the ferry at Bokeelia on Pine Island or through the King Fisher Fleet from Punta Gorda. A tram transports visitors from the marina and park office to tent sites and cabins along the beach. You must bring your own provisions, as no stores, hotels, or condominiums are anywhere in sight.

Follow FL 771 over the toll causeway to visit the lighthouses at Gasparilla and Boca Grande. Named for Jose Gaspar, a Spanish naval officer turned pirate whose very existence is in question, Gasparilla Island is six miles long. Portions of it are in Charlotte County and portions in its more glamorous neighbor, Lee County, home of Fort Myers and the fashionable resorts on Sanibel and Captiva Islands. Gasparilla Island is accessible from the Fort Myers side by boat only. The first lighthouse you'll reach, traveling north to south, is the Entrance Range Rear Lighthouse, known locally as the **Gasparilla Lighthouse**. It's next to Boca Grande's only public beach and tops out at 105 feet above sea level, making it considerably taller than its companion, the **Port Boca Grande Lighthouse**, a lovely white frame cottage with a bright red roof and a light in the cupola. The Port Boca Grande Lighthouse sits at the southern end of Gasparilla Island, where it has guarded the entrance to Charlotte Harbor since December 31, 1890. Boca Grande has a quaint downtown area with shops to browse, restaurants, vacation home rentals, and classic accommodations like the elegant **Gasparilla Inn**.

North of Charlotte Harbor on the way to Sarasota, the community of Osprey and its **Historic Spanish Point** beckon. Historic Spanish Point is an environmental, archaeological, and historical site overlooking Little Sarasota Bay. It is home to a burial mound, or midden, that dates to the Archaic period, which lasted from around 300 to 1000 A.D. It is one of the largest and best-preserved early shell middens in Florida. The story of citrus cultivation on Spanish Point is told at a packing house used to prepare and ship oranges, limes, and lemons. A recording describes how workers wash the fruit with detergent and seawater, then lay it on shelves for the skin to dry and cure, making it tougher for shipping. Visiting the archaeology exhibits, the pioneer homestead, and the formal gardens takes about two hours. The visitor center is located close to the entrance off US 41 in a refurbished 1927 school. Here, you can get a brochure and see when the next tour begins. Historic Spanish Point is open daily.

Continue north to visit Venice, a small town

This peaceful chapel adjacent to the Pioneer Cemetery is one of the buildings preserved at Historic Spanish Point.

with several nice public beaches known for their abundance of sharks' teeth. Downtown, you'll find several interesting shops and restaurants. Built in 1926, the **Banyan House Historic Bed and Breakfast** is a Mediterranean-style two-story inn with guest rooms and suites featuring attractive, airy décor, private baths, and cable television. Some suites have private balconies. All guests have access to the courtyard, pool, and spa.

East of Osprey and north of Port Charlotte is

Although beaches are appealing to many, a kayak trip through the mangrove forests at Myakka River State Park provides a stunning introduction to this most important South Florida habitat.

one of Florida's largest and finest treasures, **Myakka River State Park**. Start your exploration at the visitor center, where exhibits and several short films introduce the river and the 28,850-acre park, one of Florida's first state parks. The Myakka River, designated a Wild and Scenic River, is 66 miles long. About a fifth of it runs through the park. Birders and nature lovers are astonished at the thousands of creatures here, from colorful insects to wood storks. More than 250 species of birds have been recorded at Myakka. Visitors may rent canoes to explore the river and lake. There's an easy launch from a boat ramp on Upper Myakka Lake. The park also offers nearly 40 miles of hiking trails, airboats, sightseeing trams that run through the backwoods, and a fantastic elevated boardwalk. The facilities include five cabins, a 76-site campground, and several small primitive campgrounds.

East of Charlotte Harbor, you can see Florida up close and natural at the 90,000-acre **Crescent B**, a working cattle ranch. Here, **Babcock Wil-**

derness **Adventures** offers swamp buggy eco-tours if you're feeling lazy and off-road mountain bikes if you're not. You don't have to be an expert mountain biker, but the experience will be more enjoyable if you're in reasonably good shape. On the nine-mile off-road bike tour, you'll encounter lots of alligators and bison, once native to Florida. You may see the shaggy bison rubbing against pine trees to soothe their itchy hides. In addition to serving as bison scratching posts, the pines have also been used to harvest turpentine. You may see panthers, alligators, sandhill cranes, Osceola turkeys, and lots of wading birds whether you're biking or riding the swamp buggy, a sort of canvas-topped truck/bus combination on oversized wheels. A field full of roseate spoonbills greeted us as we drove the 2.3-mile-long driveway. As you enter the concession and gift shop area, you'll spot the shack that was built for the movie *Just Cause*, filmed here in 1994. The alligators kept stunt doubles busy filling in for the stars when the script called for slogging through the swamp. You'll be

Herds of bison graze at Babcock Wilderness Adventure's Crescent B, a working ranch that also serves as a wildlife habitat.

well advised to keep a watchful eye out as well. It's best to call ahead to arrange a tour.

Drive south of Charlotte Harbor on US 41 or I-75 to visit Fort Myers, the twin islands of Sanibel and Captiva, and the fabulous J. N. "Ding" Darling National Wildlife Refuge.

All of the following are in Punta Gorda and use the 33950 zip code and 941 area code, except where noted.

ACCOMMODATIONS

Banyan House Historic Bed and Breakfast—519 Harbor Dr., Venice, FL 34285; 484-1385

Best Western Waterfront—300 Retta Esplanade; 800-525-1022 or 639-1165

Cayo Costa State Park—c/o Barrier Islands Geopark, P.O. Box 1150, Boca Grande, FL 33921; 964-0375

Fishermen's Village—1200 W. Retta Esplanade; 800-639-0020

Gasparilla Inn—500 Palm Ave., Boca Grande, FL 33921; 964-2201

Gilchrist Bed and Breakfast—115 Gilchrist St.; 575-4129

Harbour Inn—5000 Tamiami Trail (US 41), Charlotte Harbor, FL 33980; 625-6126

Holiday Inn Harborside—33 Tamiami Trail; 877-639-9399 or 636-2167

Myakka River State Park—13207 FL 72, Sarasota, FL 34241; 361-6511

Palm Island Resort—7092 Placida Rd., Cape Haze, FL 33946; 800-824-5412

ATTRACTIONS

Babcock/Webb Wildlife Management Area—29200 Tuckers Grade, Punta Gorda, FL 33955; 575-5768

Babcock Wilderness Adventures—8000 FL 31, Punta Gorda, FL 33982; 800-500-5583

Cayo Costa State Park—c/o Barrier Islands Geopark, P.O. Box 1150, Boca Grande, FL 33921; 964-0375

Don Pedro Island State Recreation Area—c/o Barrier Islands Geopark, P.O. Box 1150, Boca Grande, FL 33921; 964-0375

Florida Adventure Museum—260 W. Retta Esplanade; 639-3777

Grande Tours—12575 Placida Rd., Placida, FL 33946; 697-8825

Historic Spanish Point—337 N. Tamiami Trail, Osprey, FL 34229; 966-5214

King Fisher Fleet, Fishermen's Village—1200 Retta Esplanade; 639-0969

Myakka River State Park—13207 FL 72, Sarasota, FL 34241; 361-6511

CAMPING

Babcock/Webb Wildlife Management Area—29200 Tuckers Grade, Punta Gorda, FL 33955; 575-5768

Cayo Costa State Park, c/o Barrier Islands Geopark—P.O. Box 1150, Boca Grande, FL 33921; 964-0375

Myakka River State Park—13207 FL 72, Sarasota, FL 34241; 361-6511

 DINING

Amimoto—2705 Tamiami Trail; 505-1515

Breakers Restaurant and Brew Pub—23241 Bayshore Dr., Port Charlotte, FL 33980; 743-2800

Harbour Tea Room—500 Tamiami Trail (US 41), Port Charlotte, FL 33980; 629-5996

Harpoon Harry's, Fishermen's Village—1200 W. Retta Esplanade; 637-1177

Shells Seafood Restaurant—1900 Tamiami Trail, Port Charlotte, FL 33948; 766-7200

Smokey's Smoke House Restaurant—415 Cooper St.; 639-2000

Summer Mood Café—122 Nesbit St.; 575-9113

 EVENTS

January—Sullivan Street Winter Craft Fair

March—Peace River Seafood Festival and Boat Show

March—Charlotte Harbor Nature Festival

July—Kids' Fishing Day

 FOR MORE INFORMATION:

Charlotte County Visitors Bureau—1600 Tamiami Trail, Suite 100, Port Charlotte, FL 33948; 888-478-7352 or 743-1900; www.pureflorida.com

HIGHLIGHTS

TARPON FISHING AT BOCA GRANDE

EDISON AND FORD WINTER ESTATES

SHELLING AT SANIBEL ISLAND

J. N. "DING" DARLING NATIONAL WILDLIFE REFUGE

LOVERS KEY STATE RECREATION AREA

KORESHAN STATE HISTORIC SITE

Situated on Florida's southwestern Gulf coast at the mouth of the Caloosahatchee River, Fort Myers is surrounded by miles of the most beautiful beaches in the country and thousands of acres of protected natural areas, much to the delight of bird watchers, nature lovers, and wildlife enthusiasts. Fort Myers is called the "City of Palms" because of the royal palms along its avenues. Its most famous citizen, Thomas Alva Edison, imported and planted the first of the 1,800 majestic royal palms that now line McGregor Boulevard.

Fort Myers is the county seat of Lee County, though it is not the largest city. That honor falls to Cape Coral, which boasts a population of about 102,000 and more canals than Venice, Italy. Fort Myers has a population of approximately 45,000. Its downtown area includes boutiques, restaurants, cafés, nightclubs, shops, museums, and historic sites.

Easily accessible via the Sanibel Causeway near the end of McGregor Boulevard and arguably the best known of Florida's many spectacular barrier islands, Sanibel is a magnet for nature lovers, as is its quieter neighbor, Captiva. Among the more than 100 islands in the area are many accessible only by boat, like Cayo Costa, Cabbage Key, Useppa Island, North Captiva, and Mound Key. Others like Estero Island (the home of Fort Myers Beach) and Pine Island are linked to the mainland by bridges. Since it has no sandy beaches—and thus no hordes of tourists—Pine Island is particularly appealing to fishermen. It is also becoming known as something of an artists' colony. Pine Island is the site of **Mangomania**, an annual celebration honoring the tropical fruits grown here.

To learn more about the area's colorful history, begin your visit with a trip to the **Fort Myers Historical Museum** in the historic Atlantic Coast Line train depot. Inside, you'll find exhibits on prehistoric Florida, the Spanish explorers, and early Fort Myers. The museum is open Tuesday through Saturday. An admission fee is charged. Outside, the Esperanza, the longest and one of the last private Pullman rail cars, offers a glimpse into the luxury of the railroad's heyday.

The southwestern tip of Florida was the hunting and fishing ground of the Calusa Indians from 1200 B.C. to 1600 A.D. Some historians say they were the most violent and aggressive tribe in North America. Their origin remains a mystery, though some believe they came from Mexico and Central America to escape the Aztec invasion of their homeland. The Calusas processed fish for trade as early as 200 A.D., leaving behind huge piles of shells, known as middens. They inhabited the area south of Sarasota on the Gulf coast and Cape Canaveral on the Atlantic coast.

Other than shipwreck survivors, Juan Ponce de Leon and his men are believed to have been the first Europeans to see Florida's west coast. On May 24, 1513, they landed somewhere near Fort Myers, probably at Punta Gorda on the western shore of Charlotte Harbor, but perhaps at Punta Rassa near Fort Myers.

Fort Myers was the site of one of the first forts along the Caloosahatchee River. Constructed in 1841 and originally named Fort Harvie, it was reactivated and renamed Fort Myers to honor Colonel Abraham Myers in 1850. Fort Myers played an important part in the Third Seminole War— or the Billy Bowlegs War, as the final conflict with the Seminole is also known. After Billy Bowlegs surrendered to the army at Fort Myers, the fort was abandoned.

Following the removal of the vast majority of Seminoles, cattle raising boomed along the Caloosahatchee. According to Charlton W. Tebeau in *A History of Florida*, Jacob Summerlin emerged as Florida's first cattle baron during that time. His cows grazed from Fort Meade on the Peace River to Fort Myers on the Caloosahatchee.

During the Civil War, Fort Myers was used to hold cattle destined for sale to the Union as provisions for the gunboats patrolling the Gulf off Sanibel Island. The fort was abandoned after the war ended. Most of its 50 buildings were dismantled and salvaged for materials.

The first settlers arrived in 1866, taking up residence in the dilapidated remains of the fort. Jacob Summerlin's cowmen drove herds along McGregor Boulevard to Punta Rassa. There, they loaded them on boats bound for the lucrative markets in Cuba. Summerlin lived at Bartow near Orlando but built a home for his cowmen at Punta Rassa in 1874. It was located near the present tollbooth for the Sanibel Causeway.

Commercial fishing attracted early settlers, many of whom lived in fish cabins built on pilings along this portion of the coast. Supplies were brought in and fish collected by "run boats" from the Punta Gorda Fish Company.

The first tarpon landed by a sportfisherman was caught in the 1880s. Wealthy Northern sportsmen soon followed, seeking the "silver king." They're still coming today. Located 15 miles away as the crow flies, Boca Grande is the tarpon fishing capital of the world, drawing anglers like the George Bushes every year.

A Fort Myers building boom began in 1898. The **Murphy-Burroughs Home** led the way in the creation of a "Millionaire's Row." The Georgian Revival mansion is open for tours Tuesday through Friday from October 15 to May 15 and Friday only from June 1 to November 30.

In 1898, the whole town—which consisted of 347 residents—turned out when Thomas Edison lit up the Royal Palm Hotel, along with 10 streetlights. Each February, Fort Myers turns out again to celebrate its most famous resident with three weeks of events called, appropriately enough, the **Edison Festival of Light**.

Edison visited Fort Myers for the first time in the company of his business partner, Ezra Gilliland, on March 20, 1885. They loved what they saw, purchasing waterfront acreage along the Caloosahatchee River within 24 hours of their arrival.

While his contemporaries were building imposing mansions on Florida's east coast, Edison designed and constructed an inviting home to suit the climate. It had wide verandas, floor-to-ceiling doors, and windows to catch the breezes. The home was built in sections in Fairfield, Maine, and sent on sailing schooners to Fort Myers. This was probably the first example of prefabricated housing in the United States.

Edison had only three months of formal education and, according to one of his teachers, was not an exceptional student. From the time he was a young man, he was also nearly totally deaf. Nonetheless, Edison would hold 1,093 patents during his lifetime, obtaining at least one patent every year for 65 consecutive years. He was the

The deep friendship of Thomas Edison and Henry Ford was evidenced by Ford's purchase of Mangoes, an estate home adjoining Edison's.

first to record sound, the first to produce a movie—a three-second film called *The Sneeze*—the first to develop the electric light, and the first to generate electricity. He arguably had more influence on people all over the world than anyone else in the past 1,000 years.

During nearly 45 years of wintering here, Edison entertained many well-known houseguests, including Harvey Firestone and Henry Ford. Ford and Edison met in New York in 1896 at a convention of the Detroit Edison Illuminating Company and became great friends. Today, Edison's and Ford's neighboring winter estates, Edison's laboratory, a museum filled with memorabilia of both men, and Edison's beautiful gardens are open for tours daily except for Thanksgiving and Christmas. Botany was one of Edison's great passions, as evidenced by the hundreds of varieties of plants here. Although the gardens were originally filled with plants intended for experimentation, Mrs. Mina Edison added roses, orchids, and bromeliads. The banyan tree brought back from Calcutta in 1925

Thomas Edison wintered here in "Seminole Lodge" overlooking the Caloosahatchee River.

as a four-foot seedling by Harvey Firestone now has aerial roots more than 400 feet in circumference, the largest in the continental United States. The tree this specimen came from in India is more than 1,000 years old and covers 15 acres. Henry Ford purchased the house next door in 1916. A fence with a gate that always remained open—the "Friendship Gate"—separates the two homes. At the end of your tour, you can cruise along the Caloosahatchee River on one of the four replicas of Edison's electric boats. A fee is charged for tours of the estates and for the cruise.

Another attraction in Fort Myers is the **Imaginarium Hands-on Museum and Aquarium**. A giant "Pipe-O-Saurus" and a colorful awning announce more than 60 indoor and outdoor exhibits for the curious of all ages. Here, you can explore the simulated effects of a thunderstorm, make your predictions in a TV studio for wannabe weather forecasters, and gain an understanding of the forces of nature in a hurricane experience that will blow you—or at least your hairdo—away. Visitors enjoy the three 900-gallon aquariums, the touch tanks, the video presentations at the Theater in the Tank, and the educational computer games about explorers, trade, finance, and cultural experiences. Both the Imaginarium and the Figment of the Imaginarium Museum Store are open daily. An admission fee is charged.

The **Calusa Nature Center and Planetarium** has exhibits on the natural history of southwestern Florida, boardwalks through 105 subtropical acres, and astronomy and laser shows. The center is open daily. An admission fee is charged.

For a journey through a 2,200-acre wetland ecosystem, visit the **Six Mile Cypress Slough Preserve**. A 1.2-mile boardwalk winds past subtropical ferns, showy bromeliads, and an assortment of wading birds. The preserve is open daily. A parking fee is charged, but seasonal guided walks are free.

From November through March, **Manatee Park** is the home of the West Indian manatee, thanks to its warm waters. Year-round, visitors to the park can learn about the endangered West Indian manatee and the plants and butterflies native to southwestern Florida. The park offers plantings, walking tours, and workshops. Volunteer interpretive naturalists assist visitors with questions. The park has manatee viewing areas, picnic areas, a nonmotorized boat launch and a fishing deck on the Orange River, and kayak rentals. It is open daily. A parking fee is charged.

A local institution for more than 60 years, the **Shell Factory** offers millions of shells and shell-related gifts. It is also an old-fashioned entertainment complex featuring bumper boats, miniature golf, a video arcade, and a railroad museum. At the Pearl Pavilion, visitors can harvest pearls from Japanese oysters and select mountings.

The public and semiprivate golf courses scattered throughout Lee County include some of the finest greens in the state. The winter weather is perfect, but the crowds and the rates drop in summer.

If you're a fan of the great American pastime, you'll be pleased to learn that Fort Myers is home to the spring-training camps of both the Minnesota Twins and the Boston Red Sox.

World-class tarpon fishing is king here, but inshore fishing for snook, redfish, spotted seatrout, sheepshead, and mangrove snapper is popular year-round. Offshore guides offer angling opportunities for grouper, shark, cobia, blackfin tuna, bonito, barracuda, and Spanish and king mackerel. Freshwater species include bass, crappie, bluegill, shellcracker, catfish, and Oscar.

Many charter boats offer fishing, shelling, and nature-based trips.

It's well worth the 15-mile drive down McGregor Boulevard to the Sanibel Causeway to visit Sanibel and Captiva Islands. At various points along the way, you'll see cars parked and their drivers enjoying the sun and sand. The boat launches at both ends of the causeway are suitable for small boats. Anglers wade out and cast into the surf or line up along the rock piles at bridge abutments. That's just for starters. It gets even better.

As you cross the end of the causeway, you'll notice a visitor center on the right before you reach Periwinkle Way, one of the most heavily traveled roads on Sanibel. This is a good spot to obtain maps, directions, and information about lodgings. At present, there are no traffic lights or streetlights on Sanibel or Captiva, but there are lots of interesting inns, rental homes, shops, and restaurants to suit every taste and budget.

At the stop sign, turn left, or south, to visit Lighthouse Beach at the southeast end of Sanibel. A wooded nature trail leads to the base of the historic **Sanibel Lighthouse** and its popular fishing pier. Lighthouse Beach extends around the point from the bay to the Gulf. The lighthouse and the two frame cottages joined to it by a stairway were completed in 1884. The light guided ships carrying cattle from Punta Rassa to markets in Key West and Havana until the Spanish-American War broke out in 1898. These are the oldest surviving buildings on Sanibel.

The island offers a wide range of lodging choices.

We enjoyed the **Sanibel Inn's** beachfront location, its modern amenities, the lovely landscaping on its eight acres (including butterfly and hummingbird gardens), and its overall environ-

The lighthouse at Sanibel Island was accessible only by boat or ferry until the Sanibel Causeway was completed in 1963.

mental friendliness, as evidenced by the recycling bin in our room, the light-blocking curtains in accord with sea-turtle protection guidelines, and the eco-friendly children's discovery programs. Each room has attractive furnishings, a refrigerator, a microwave, a coffee maker, and a private screened balcony. Although 96 rooms are offered, the resort has a secluded feel. Add a heated pool with a Gulf view, scrumptious on-site breakfasts and dinners at the **Portofino Restaurant**, and

The Sanibel Inn maintains lush landscaping and open areas to enhance enjoyment of the natural beauty of its Gulf-front location.

bicycle and sea kayak rentals, and you'll find everything you need for a great Sanibel getaway.

When the Reverend George Barnes's boat ran aground on Sanibel Island in the 1880s, he thought God had led him to paradise. Over time, the church and home he built evolved into an island inn. Today, the **Casa Ybel Resort** offers 114 luxurious one- and two-bedroom suites, beachfront dining in the **Thistle Lodge** (a Victorian mansion built by Dr. Barnes for his daughter), and a host of recreational activities for children and adults. This resort has won high praise from *Condé Nast Traveler*.

We had no problem locating delicious food on Sanibel. We started with a tasty breakfast at the **Sanibel Café**. It was so good that we would have returned for lunch and dinner had we not decided to try the tasty Clam Chowder, Swamp Cabbage Salad, Calamari, and Shrimp and Lobster Wontons at **Gilligan's**.

Gulfside Park, off Casa Ybel Road, is great for families. Thanks to its central location, it is protected from currents, and the shelling is usu-

ally first-rate. The large number of shells on Sanibel is attributed to the shape of the island and the lack of an offshore reef. Sanibel sits in the Gulf in an east-west direction. When cold winds from the north or northwest blow across the island, they push surface water away from the land. Bottom currents in the direction of the land then replace the surface waters, thus uprooting live shells and bringing them ashore, often in vast numbers. No live mollusks may be collected at any time on Sanibel, though visitors routinely employ the "Sanibel stoop" to collect some of the hundreds of varieties of shells littering the beaches.

You can learn more about shells and see samples from around the world at the **Bailey-Matthews Shell Museum**. From tourist cameos and carrier shells to tridacna, the oldest shell in the world, the story of shells is told here. Special emphasis is placed on the shells of Sanibel and Captiva, so this is a good place to figure out what you've discovered on the beach at low tide. Maybe you'll find the rarest of them all, the elusive brown speckled junonia. The museum's gift shop has dishes with sea themes, picture frames, and lots of books about shells. The museum is open Tuesday through Sunday. An admission fee is charged.

Tarpon Bay Beach, located in Sanibel's mid-island area, is popular with visitors. A guided kayak trip with **Tarpon Bay Recreation** is the perfect way to learn about this watery world. Our guide, Dan Underhill, cautioned first-time kayakers, "If you fall out of the kayak, do one thing before you panic—stand up! The water is very shallow." The paddling is easy enough for beginners to feel comfortable here. No collecting of either shells or live mollusks is allowed at Tarpon Bay, but you'll collect memories that will last a lifetime.

Tarpon Bay offers canoe and kayak access to the mangrove forest, one of the most productive ecosystems on earth.

Approximately 65 percent of Sanibel Island is protected within the boundaries of **J. N. "Ding" Darling National Wildlife Refuge**. The 6,000-acre refuge is named for Pulitzer Prize-winning cartoonist and environmentalist Jay Norwood "Ding" Darling. Trails 10 to 12 feet wide have been cut through the native mangrove forests in parts of the refuge. Most of the bay-side trees we encountered on the **Commodore Creek Canoe Trail** were red mangroves, easily identified by their arching prop roots, which spread outward from the trunk in all directions. These trees have developed large root systems to deal with the lack of oxygen in the soil. Red mangrove forests have been described as "forests that walk" because it looks as if the trees are walking on the surface of the water. Their extensive root systems slow water and act as a filtration system, trapping and cycling organic materials and nutrients. They also provide protection for young fish, crustaceans, and shellfish. Birds nest in the

branches and fish among the roots. From root to crown, a mangrove forest is one of the most productive ecosystems in the world.

The main entrance to the wildlife refuge is on the right as you head toward Captiva on the Sanibel-Captiva Road. The bird watching at the refuge is legendary, though visitation is heavy. Nearly 300 bird species, 50 types of reptiles and amphibians, and 32 species of mammals have been seen here. The best time for birders to visit is at low tide.

The refuge's visitor center, located near the entrance, is open daily. It offers interesting exhibits, lots of information about current sightings, and restrooms. The refuge has hiking trails and canoe trails. Its five-mile scenic drive is open Saturday through Thursday. A fee is charged to drive, bicycle, or walk it.

To visit Captiva, cross the small bridge at Blind Pass. Stephen "Dr. Beach" Leatherman named Captiva the most romantic beach two years in a row. It's easy to understand why, once you've seen the fabulous sunsets and the long, unbroken expanse of white, sandy beach.

Jose Gaspar, a pirate believed by many historians to be fictitious, supposedly roamed the seas of southwestern Florida, made his base on Sanibel, and kept women captives on Captiva.

Without doubt, the best-known accommodation on Captiva is the 'Tween Waters Inn. It takes its name from its location between Pine Island Sound and the Gulf of Mexico. The inn has been a work in progress since 1926, when it started with a single cottage. Famous guests here have included Charles and Anne Morrow Lindbergh, who wrote *Gift From the Sea* while staying at Captiva. Through the years, the inn has evolved to offer cottages, rooms, and suites with bay or Gulf views. Breakfast and dinner are served in the inn's award-winning **Old Captiva House Restaurant**. The **Crow's Nest Lounge** offers live entertainment, cool drinks, and casual dining. For lunch at 'Tween Waters, you'll need to head to **The Canoe and The Kayak**, a bay-side deli-restaurant-market. The inn's marina offers canoe and boat rentals. Guests have use of the tennis courts, the Olympic-sized swimming pool, and the fitness center—that is, if they can release themselves from the "Captiva crouch," a posture assumed by Captiva shelling enthusiasts.

The **Bubble Room Restaurant** on Captiva offers delicious food and a lighthearted décor with 1930s and 1940s memorabilia. **R. C. Otter's Island Eats** has casual, outside dining. Other popular dining choices include the **Mucky Duck** and the **Green Flash**.

Several interesting barrier islands north of Captiva are accessible only by boat.

'Tween Waters Inn is situated on Captiva Island, across the road from the Gulf and overlooking Pine Island Sound.

One of them is Cabbage Key, a 100-acre island without a single paved road or automobile anywhere in sight. The main house here, now the **Cabbage Key Inn and Restaurant**, was built in the 1930s on top of a 38-foot-high shell mound by the son of playwright and novelist Mary Roberts Rinehart. The historic restaurant is a favorite spot for boaters. It is claimed by many to be the inspiration for Jimmy Buffet's "Cheeseburger in Paradise." In addition to Cheeseburgers, the restaurant serves breakfast and dinner daily. An area fisherman started the tradition of taping a dollar bill to the wall in the bar, so he'd have enough for a drink in case the fishing was poor. Since then, thousands of folks have signed their dollars and taped them on just about every available surface, including the walls. The inn's marina offers berthings, charter services, fishing guides, and boat rentals. It's a good idea to call ahead, since it can get pretty busy, especially on weekends. The seven air-conditioned cottages have one, two, or three bedrooms and look like they are straight from the 1930s. Some have kitchens. The six guest rooms in the inn have private baths, air conditioning, and Old Florida décor. Some have fireplaces. You don't come here for luxury. You come for the ambiance.

According to legend, Useppa Island was named for Joseffa de Mayorga, a Mexican princess held captive by pirate Jose Gaspar. Her name became Useppa in the local dialect. Eight miles north of Captiva and two miles south of Boca Grande Pass, Useppa Island was the private retreat of millionaire Barron Collier. In the early 1900s, he built a mansion for himself and cottages for his famous guests, who included the Rockefellers, the Rothschilds, Herbert Hoover, and Zane Grey. Although Useppa remains a private club and residential community, you may find lodging at the historic **Collier Inn** at the Useppa Island Club in suites with wooden flooring, modern amenities, and antique furnishings or in one of the cottage rooms or suites decorated in 1920s Old Florida style. A continental breakfast is served daily, and a full breakfast is available on weekends. The lunch and dinner menus vary, but fresh seafood, hand-cut meats, and freshly baked breads, pies, and cakes are always served. Guests can swim in the pool or the Gulf, play tennis or croquet, sail, or take a fishing trip. **Captiva Cruises** has a luncheon cruise to Useppa that includes a visit to the **Useppa Island Museum**, where visitors can learn about the island's fascinating history. Useppa's marina has sailboats, kayaks, and canoes available for island guests and berthings for craft up to 120 feet long.

The barrier islands south of Fort Myers include Fort Myers Beach on Estero Island, which is easily accessible by auto, and Lovers Key.

With its T-shirt and trinket shops, wave-runner rentals, miniature golf courses, restaurants, and clubs, Fort Myers Beach holds a special attraction for the young crowd. Fort Myers Beach offers a bustling waterfront and accommodations that are generally less pricey than Sanibel or Captiva.

Located south of Fort Myers Beach, **Lovers Key Beach Club and Resort** offers one- and two-bedroom suites with fully equipped kitchens, high-speed internet access, and televisions in the living room and bedroom. Many of the suites have lovely whirlpool tubs. The resort's lagoon-style pool overlooks Estero Bay. There's also a pool-side grill.

Located between Fort Myers Beach and Bonita Beach on FL 865, **Lovers Key State Recreation Area** is Florida's newest state park and a great spot to spend a day at the beach. The park offers more than 700 acres on four islands, five miles of hiking trails, three miles of canoe trails, and trams that run regularly from the main parking lot to the beach for those interested in swimming, shelling, and sunbathing. The concession at the main parking lot offers food and drinks, canoe and kayak rentals, and an assortment of guided tours. This is a good spot for fishing and birding. It's not unusual to spot dolphins and manatees. One of the recreation area's islands, Black Island, is the takeout spot for a canoe trail that begins seven miles upstream at **Koreshan State Historic Site**.

The Koreshan settlement was the dream of Dr. Cyrus Teed. Following a life-altering "illumination," he changed his name to Koresh and founded the Koreshan Unity, a religion that believed that man lived on the inside surface of the earth and looked inward on gases containing the sun, moon, stars, and planets. In 1892, he established a cooperative community in the wilds of Florida along the banks of the Estero River. He envisioned that it would become a city of 10 million ardent followers. The settlement's numbers

The Koreshan Unity practiced celibacy, communal owner-ship, and gender equality more than 100 years ago in an isolated utopian settlement in southwest Florida.

reached a peak at almost 250. In 1961, the four surviving members of the Koreshan Unity deeded 305 acres of their holdings to the state of Florida. Several of the original buildings, including Teed's home, have been restored and are now part of Koreshan State Historic Site.

The 60-site campground is usually packed from the first cold snap in December until the insects return in full force in April. This is also a popular area for wildlife viewing while canoeing the Estero River, which has been designated a Florida Canoe Trail. If you're not traveling with your own canoe, you may rent one at the ranger station and paddle three miles down to Estero Bay. From that point, it's about another mile to Mound Key, a shell midden that has been desig-nated a State Archaeological Site. If you'd like to stretch your legs, check out the trail that crosses the island.

Continue south on US 41 to visit Naples, Marco Island, and Everglades City.

All of the following are in Fort Myers and use the 33901 zip code and 239 area code, except where noted.

ACCOMMODATIONS

Cabbage Key Inn and Restaurant—P.O. Box 200, Pineland, FL 33945; 283-2278

Casa Ybel Resort—2255 Gulf Dr., Sanibel Island, FL 33957; 800-276-4753 or 472-3145

Lovers Key Beach Club and Resort—8771 Estero Blvd., Fort Myers Beach, FL 33931; 677-798-4879 or 765-1040

Sanibel Inn—937 E. Gulf Dr., Sanibel Island, FL 33957; 800-449-1833 or 472-3181

Song of the Sea—863 E. Gulf Dr., Sanibel Island, FL 33957; 800-965-7772 or 481-3636

'Tween Waters Inn—15951 Captiva Rd., Captiva Island, FL 33924; 800-223-5865, 866-893-3646, or 472-5161

Useppa Island Club—P.O. Box 640, Bokeelia, FL 33922; 888-735-6335 or 283-5255

ATTRACTIONS

Bailey-Matthews Shell Museum—3075 Sanibel-Captiva Rd., Sanibel Island, FL 33957; 395-2233

Calusa Nature Center and Planetarium—3450 Ortiz Ave., 275-3435

Captiva Cruises—P.O. Box 580, Captiva Island, FL 33924; 472-5300

Edison-Ford Winter Estates—2350 McGregor Blvd.; 334-3614

Fort Myers Historical Museum—2300 Peck St.; 332-5955

Imaginarium Hands-on Museum and Aquarium—2000 Cranford Ave.; 337-3332

J. N. "Ding" Darling National Wildlife Refuge—1 Wildlife Dr., Sanibel Island, FL 33957; 472-1100

Koreshan State Park—3850 Corkscrew Rd., Estero, FL 33928; 992-0311

Lovers Key Recreation Area—8700 Estero Blvd., Ft. Myers Beach, FL 33931; 463-4588

Manatee Park—FL 80 (1.5 miles east of I-75 off exit 25); 694-3537

Murphy-Burroughs Home—2505 First St.; 332-6125

Sanibel Historical Museum Village—800 Dunlop Rd., Sanibel Island, FL 33957; 472-4648

Shell Factory—2787 N. Tamiami Trail, 33903; 888-743-5571

Six Mile Cypress Slough Preserve—7751 Penzance Crossing; 432-2004

Tarpon Bay Recreation—900 Tarpon Bay Rd., Sanibel Island, FL 33957; 472-8900

Useppa Island Club—P.O. Box 640, Bokeelia, FL 33922; 888-735-6335 or 283-5255

CAMPING

Cayo Costa State Park—c/o Barrier Islands Geopark, P.O. Box 1150, Boca Grande, FL 33921; 964-0375

Fort Myers/Pine Island KOA—5120 Stringfellow Rd., St. James City, FL 33956; 800-562-8505 or 283-2415

Koreshan State Park—3850 Corkscrew Rd., Estero, FL 33928; 992-0311

DINING

Bubble Room—15001 Captiva Dr., Captiva Island, FL 33924; 472-5558

Gilligan's—2163 Periwinkle Way, Sanibel Island, FL 33957; 472-0606

Green Flash—15183 Captiva Dr., Captiva Island, FL 33924; 472-3337

Lighthouse Café—362 Periwinkle Way, Sanibel Island, FL 33957; 472-0303

McT's Shrimphouse and Tavern—1523 Periwinkle Way, Sanibel Island, FL 33957; 472-3161

Mucky Duck—Andy Rosse Ln. S.W., Captiva Island, FL 33924; 472-3434

Old Captiva House Restaurant—15951 Captiva Rd., Captiva Island, FL 33924; 472-5161

R. C. Otter's Island Eats—Andy Rosse Ln., Captiva Island, FL 33924; 395-1142

Sanibel Café—2007 Periwinkle Way (in Tahitian Gardens), Sanibel Island, FL 33957; 472-5323

Sunshine Café—Captiva Village Sq., Captiva Island, FL 33924; 472-6200

The Canoe and Kayak at 'Tween Waters Inn—15951 Captiva Rd., Captiva Island, FL 33924; 472-5161

Thistle Lodge at Casa Ybel Resort—2255 W. Gulf Dr., Sanibel Island, FL 33957; 472-3145

E V E N T S

February—Edison Festival of Light

March—Sanibel Shell Fair and Craft Show

March—Sanibel Music Festival

July—Mangomania

November—American Sandsculpting Festival

F O R   M O R E   I N F O R M A T I O N :

Lee Island Coast Visitor and Convention Bureau—(mailing address: 2180 W. First St., Suite 100); 888-231-6933 or 338-3500; www.LeeIslandCoast.com

HIGHLIGHTS

CORKSCREW SWAMP SANCTUARY

TEN THOUSAND ISLANDS

EVERGLADES NATIONAL PARK

SMALLWOOD STORE MUSEUM

FAKAHATCHEE STRAND STATE PRESERVE

BIG CYPRESS NATIONAL PRESERVE

The first thing you'll notice when you enter downtown Naples is the sun-drenched streets lined with colorful sidewalk cafés, shops, and art galleries. Things have certainly changed since the days when Seminole Indians set up stands to sell their crafts on Fifth Avenue and a lady who lived above the first commercial building along Fifth pitched her table scraps to the alligators outside.

The seven miles of firm, pinkish white beach made a popular gathering place for Victorian travelers. In 1888, an avid "seabather" proclaimed that the swimming at Naples was "healthful and unequaled." The Naples Hotel became a favorite winter resort for the rich and famous.

Naples lies about 1,000 miles south of its European counterpart. Some say the city got its name from ambitious Florida real-estate developers who compared the bay in southwestern Florida favorably to the Italian bay.

Barron Gift Collier arrived in 1911 and was so taken with the area that he purchased more than a million acres between Naples and Everglades City, believing he could transform the swamps into prime real estate.

Travel got a little easier in 1918 when the first shell road into the area, a portion of the Tamiami Trail between Naples and Fort Myers, was completed. It got a lot easier when the trail, hailed as the greatest road built in the 20th century, was completed from Naples to Miami about 10 years

The streets of Naples are lined with fashionable shops, chic restaurants, and elegant hotels.

later. The Tamiami Trail made it unnecessary to travel north to Jacksonville in order to reach Miami from Naples.

Start your explorations at the visitor center on Fifth Avenue South, one of the main streets in Naples. Here, you'll discover information about this cosmopolitan city and its hidden and not-so-hidden charms.

To find your way in Old Naples—a National Historic District that contains the city's historic core and many examples of classic Florida architecture—remember that the numbered avenues run east and west and the numbered streets run north and south. You might also consider taking a ride around town courtesy of **Naples Trolley Tours**, which offers narrated tours that cover the city's history, attractions, shopping, and dining. Best of all, you can get off when you come to a spot you want to explore, get on the next trolley, and continue your tour.

Fifth Avenue South goes all the way to the beach. It is lined with classical and contemporary art galleries, antique shops, gourmet restaurants, cafés, and boutiques. The **Inn on Fifth** is an elegant downtown hotel with 87 large, well-appointed rooms including several suites. The amenities include a heated rooftop pool, a full-service spa and salon, a fitness center, and two restaurants, the **Grill on Fifth** and the casual **McCabe's Irish Pub**.

Or you might try Third Street South, which offers a revitalized shopping village in what was once the business district of Old Naples. It has cafés, restaurants, galleries, and gift and specialty shops that sell everything from fashion apparel and fine jewelry to books and toys. You could easily spend a day on Third Street South and still not explore every nook and cranny.

Before you give up on gift ideas, visit the **Teddy Bear Museum** on Pine Ridge Road. Here, thousands of the cuddly bears are on exhibit, but another thousand or so can come home with you from the gift shop. It's open daily except Tuesday.

A few blocks away, the historic **Naples Fishing Pier and Beach** is the focal point of Old Naples at sunset. The original pier in Naples was destroyed by a hurricane in 1910. The present pier replaced the one destroyed by Hurricane Donna in 1960. No fee is charged to stroll its 1,000-foot length, but you may have a dickens of a time finding a legal spot to park in time to see the sunset on busy weekends. Though they're not the boisterous affairs celebrated in Key West, sunsets are still savored here.

Within easy walking distance of the pier is the only bed-and-breakfast in Naples, the **Inn by the Sea**. The 1937 guesthouse, listed on the National Register of Historic Places, remains true to its Old Naples roots. The inn's three guest rooms and two suites have private baths, pine floors, tin ceilings, ceiling fans, and classic furnishings. Breakfasts include homemade muffins and breads, French Toast, quiche, fresh fruit, cereals, yogurts, and beverages.

Also in the vicinity is **Palm Cottage**, built in 1895. This is one of the oldest buildings in Naples. Built as a winter home using tabby—made of crushed seashells, lime, and sand—it is open for tours.

If you want to stay at the beach, you'll need to drive north along Gulf Shore Boulevard.

For both beach activities and golf, check out the **Naples Beach Hotel and Golf Club**. This 125-acre resort includes six buildings offering 318 rooms overlooking the Gulf or the 18-hole golf course, a spa, a free "Beach Klub for Kids," and a restaurant called **HB's on the Gulf**. At HB's, appetizers like Florida Fishcakes—a delicious concoction of grouper, snapper, and scallops topped with Lobster Sauce—prepare the way for a tempting array of entrées.

The **Edgewater Beach Hotel** is an all-suite beachfront resort. Each of its one- and two-bedroom suites has a full-sized refrigerator, a microwave, and a sink. The **Crystal Parrot** on the sixth floor is a great place to have dinner and watch the sunset.

A bit farther north along the beach is the **Vanderbilt Beach Resort**, which offers a variety of lodging choices, the **Turtle Club Restaurant**, a heated pool overlooking Vanderbilt Beach, bayside docks, and a private boat ramp for guests.

If you want to really pull out the stops, try the **Ritz-Carlton Naples** overlooking Pelican Bay. This Mobile Five-Star resort has 495 rooms and suites, two pools, a large spa named the best hotel spa in the United States by readers of *Travel and Leisure*, and seven award-winning restaurants including the **Dining Room**, the only AAA Five Diamond restaurant in southwestern Florida. Even the lobby is furnished with museum-quality antiques. If golf is your priority, you'll be pleased to learn that the **Ritz-Carlton Golf Resort Naples** is located down the street.

Staying in Naples is expensive, but you can find mid-priced hotels along US 41 a five-minute drive from the beach. Rates are lowest from May through December.

At the other end of the price spectrum is **Tin City**, a funky, fun waterside shopping spot in a 1920s clam-shelling and oyster-processing plant overlooking Naples Bay. Tin City has restaurants and shops selling everything from Grateful Dead T-shirts to hammocks and nautical gifts. While

you're here, you can have lunch or dinner at the **Riverwalk Fish and Ale House** or **Bill's Pier on Fifth** or even arrange a sightseeing cruise or a fishing trip.

Across the water, the open-air **Waterfront Café** is a great spot for a casual lunch. Its assortment of appetizers includes Sautéed Mussels and Calamari. The café also offers soups, salads including the popular Grilled Tuna and Spinach Salad, sandwiches, fish, seafood, steaks, chops, and chicken. It serves breakfast on Sunday and lunch and dinner daily.

The **Collier County Museum**, tucked away in the Collier County Government Center, tells much of the history of Naples and Collier County in interesting exhibits. The story begins with the prehistoric animal population in southwestern Florida, which peaked about 10,000 years ago during the last Ice Age, otherwise known as the Pleistocene Epoch. It may be hard to imagine as you travel the prosperous streets of Naples today, but the fossil record includes remains of ancient land mammals including mammoths, mastodons, herds of camels, horses, bison, fierce saber cats with nine-inch fangs, lions, giant armadillos, rhinoceroses, huge dire wolves, ground sloths, and short-faced bears that grew to nearly twice the size of today's grizzlies.

A highly developed Indian civilization flourished along the lower Gulf coast. The Calusas lived here until the 1700s, followed by the Seminoles, a tribe gradually formed from small bands of Creek Indians who found their way to Florida and were joined by refugees from Florida tribes and escaped black slaves. This coalition of blacks and Indians was unique in American history and succeeded for many years, despite tremendous opposition. Outnumbered and outgunned, the

Seminoles resisted removal by the United States government in three major clashes known as the Seminole Wars. The few Seminoles who remained in southwestern Florida after 1855 escaped to Big Cypress Swamp and the Everglades.

By the late 1880s, trading posts had become an important source of supplies for the few settlers and Seminoles living on the southwestern Florida frontier. Alligator hides were an important item, usually taken salted and rolled to be traded. Between 1880 and 1894, Florida hunters killed an estimated 2.5 million alligators for their hides.

The museum tells the stories of trailblazers like the Memphis-born Barron Gift Collier, the man for whom the county is named, and of South Florida's plume hunters. Outside the museum is a fine example of the buggies used to haul cypress out of the swamps during the 1920s. The **Craighead Native Garden**, part of the museum grounds, has more than 150 varieties of plants and trees. The museum is open Monday through Saturday except for national and county holidays. Donations are accepted.

Located in the heart of town, the **Conservancy of Southwest Florida Nature Center** clings to the last vestige of Naples in its natural state. Natural-history exhibits, nature trails, and 13 acres along the mangrove-lined Gordon River introduce visitors to South Florida habitats. The gift store on the premises offers nature-based books and other items of interest. The conservancy conducts specially scheduled day trips, bike tours, canoe and kayak clinics, guided canoe and boat trips, and eco-mini-vacations called Green Getaways. It also has an animal rehabilitation center where hundreds of orphaned, injured, and sick birds and other animals are treated before being returned to the wild.

The Conservancy of Southwest Florida Nature Center is the headquarters for beginning your exploration of the natural side of Collier County.

In north Naples, you'll find the 166-acre **Delnor-Wiggins State Pass Recreation Area**, an oceanfront refuge for nesting loggerhead turtles during the summer. This 1.2-mile stretch of award-winning beach gets heavy use from swimmers, sunbathers, beachcombers, and boaters.

Fortunately for nature lovers, some of the most pristine areas to be found anywhere in Florida, including the western portion of Everglades National Park, are only a short drive from the glitz of downtown Naples.

Corkscrew Swamp Sanctuary, 30 miles northeast of Naples, was established to protect the largest remaining bald cypress forest in North America. This 11,000-acre sanctuary is owned and managed by the National Audubon Society. The bald cypresses found here are nearly 600 years old and reach heights of up to 130 feet and circumferences of 25 feet.

In sparing the cypress forest, important territory was also saved for native plants and birds including little blue herons, swallow-tailed kites, the ever-shy limpkins, and great egrets, once hunted to near-extinction for their showy white plumes, which were used to adorn ladies' hats. Corkscrew is particularly well known for the colony of nesting wood storks that gathers here each winter, reputed to be the largest in the United States.

A visitor information center, environmentally friendly restrooms, and a 2.25-mile boardwalk with interpretive displays are available for visitors to Corkscrew. Fortunately, you won't have to fight off as many mosquitoes as you might expect. Mosquito fish inhabit the waters here. With a stout little body up to an inch and a half long and a big appetite for mosquito larvae, they're nature's own mosquito-control system. In general, the mosquito population in most parts of southwestern Florida declines significantly from the first cold snap in December or January through March or April. But you'd better bring insect repellent along with your sunscreen and drinking water, just to be safe.

The 9,200-acre **Rookery Bay National Estuarine Research Reserve**, located south of Naples, protects countless plant and animal species in 12 habitat communities. Its red, black, and white mangrove forests serve as important storm breaks and erosion controls. Red and black mangroves usually grow close to water. Red mangroves are easily identified by the extensive salt-excluding prop roots extending from the trunk and larger branches into the water. Most of the red mangroves at Rookery Bay are 40 to 100 years old, the older mangrove forests having succumbed to hurricanes in 1918 and 1960. Hundreds of finger-like projections called pneumatophores extend upward from the roots of black mangroves. They allow oxygen to diffuse into the roots during low tide. Black mangroves have adapted to the salin-

ity of this environment by excreting excess salt through their leaves. White mangroves are typically found above the high-tide mark.

The **Briggs Nature Center** on Shell Island Road is the reserve's interpretive facility. It offers an observation deck, two nature trails, and a half-mile boardwalk with interpretive signs. Naturalist-led boat tours may be arranged by reservation from April through December. A boat ramp, a canoe rental facility, and guided canoe trips are also available. Scheduling a sunset cruise to the major roosting areas is a special treat for birders.

The 6,423 acres of **Collier-Seminole State Park** were left as a gift by Barron Collier. The vast majority of the acreage is undisturbed mangrove swamp, but a rare stand of native royal palms is also protected within the park. The campground here has 137 sites (including a tent-camping area), electrical hookups, restrooms, showers, and a dump station. The marina has a boat launch, or you can rent a canoe at the ranger station to explore the park's 12.5-mile canoe trail. If that sounds like too much work, or if the mosquitoes are especially wicked, you can sit back and enjoy the view aboard one of the park's tour boats. The visitor center is a reconstruction of a Seminole War-era blockhouse. But one of the most interesting man-made exhibits in the park is a huge walking dredge used to build the Tamiami Trail through the Everglades. The dredge moved along scooping out a huge canal, then used the dredged material to construct the roadbed.

Located about 20 miles south of Naples, Marco Island is the largest and most developed of southwestern Florida's Ten Thousand Islands, a wild, beautiful area of mangrove islands on the Gulf coast that forms the western edge of Everglades National Park. Evidence of occupation by

Calusa Indians was unearthed in a famous archaeological dig on Marco Island in 1895 and 1896. Nets, tools, wooden masks, and boxes were discovered, as was the beautiful carving known as the *Key Marco Cat*, now displayed at the Smithsonian Institution.

Today, towering condominiums and oceanfront resorts like the **Marco Island Marriott Resort and Golf Club**, the **Hilton Marco Island Beach Resort**, and the **Radisson Suite Beach Resort** line much of the island's Gulf frontage. The Marriott offers guided bicycle tours and a sailing trip to secret shelling islands. But the island has not been entirely taken over by major resorts. Here and there, you'll find an oasis like the fishing village of Goodland, located on the southeast side of the island.

The main attraction for visitors, other than Goodland's laid-back attitude and uncongested streets, is a visit to **Stan's Idle Hour Seafood Restaurant**. Stan's is open daily for lunch and dinner from November through April and on weekends the rest of the year. The live entertainment here ranges from fish-cleaning contests and fashion shows to the annual **Men's Legs Contest**, a fundraiser for the American Cancer Society, and the **Mullet Festival**, a three-day event featuring fried and smoked mullet and the crowning of the annual Buzzard Lope Queen and Princess.

You'll find no shortage of dining opportunities on Marco Island. The **Café De Marco**, an award-winning bistro, specializes in fresh seafood but also offers selections like Rack of Lamb, Filet Mignon, and chicken dishes. It's open for dinner daily from November to April and is closed Sundays the rest of the year. Located in the refurbished home of Captain Bill Collier, the son of one of Marco Island's earliest settlers, **Marek's**

Collier House Restaurant is the place to go for fine dining and an extensive wine list.

The 31-acre **Tigertail Beach Park**, located on the southwest side of Marco, is open to the public daily. It offers concessions, showers, restrooms, a playground, and unspoiled views of the sand and sea.

We strongly suggest that those searching for the beauty of the Everglades head to Everglades City, since this is the heart of the area. Everglades National Park, the Ten Thousand Islands, Big Cypress, and Fakahatchee are all nearby. Thankfully, there's not a high-rise or a national motel franchise anywhere in sight at Everglades City, a tiny fishing village that was once the center of Barron Collier's dream for southwestern Florida.

Men like W. S. Allen and George W. Storter were in Everglades City long before Barron Collier. In fact, Storter's home was the foundation for the **Rod and Gun Club**. He sold it to Collier in 1922. Collier transformed the classic building overlooking the Barron River into an exclusive club for his wealthy and influential guests. The three-story clapboard lodge and its dining room are still open today.

Barron Collier was born in Memphis, Tennessee, in 1873 and made his first million dollars in advertising by the age of 26. From the time of his inaugural vacation to southwestern Florida in 1911, when he bought the Useppa Inn near Fort Myers, until 1928, when the Tamiami Trail (now US 41) was finished, Collier amassed over a million acres. As he explained it, "I was fascinated with Florida and swept off my feet by what I saw and felt."

In 1923, there wasn't a single mile of paved road in Collier County when Collier made a personal pledge to the Florida legislature to finish the

The Museum of the Everglades has exhibits and photos illustrating the history of Everglades City and the construction of the Tamiami Trail

Tamiami Trail. He sank more than a million dollars of his own money into the endeavor before the state highway department took over in 1926. Much of the remainder of the proposed route through the Everglades ran over a bed of limestone rock. It took about 2.6 million sticks of dynamite to blast out the 31-mile stretch from Carnestown to the Dade County line. The 273-mile trail officially opened on April 26, 1928, at a total cost of $8 million.

You can learn about Barron Collier, the Tamiami Trail, and the history of Everglades City at the **Museum of the Everglades**. The building that houses the museum was constructed as a laundry for workers on the Tamiami Trail. It is now listed on the National Register of Historic Places. The museum is open Tuesday through Saturday except for holidays. Donations are accepted.

The two-story building across the road is a refurbished 1923 bank building also listed on the National Register. Today, it houses **On the Banks of the Everglades**, a bed-and-breakfast inn. The

rooms on the first floor have shared baths, while the second-floor efficiency suites have kitchens and private baths.

We thoroughly enjoyed our stay at the other bed-and-breakfast in town, the **Ivey House**. Owner David Harraden paddled the Everglades for the first time in 1978. As he put it, "The beauty of the Everglades seeps in—the longer you sit in it, the greater its appeal." After a decade of providing overnight canoe adventures into the Everglades, David purchased the Ivey House. Originally a recreation center for workers who built the Tamiami Trail, it was converted to a boarding-house after the trail was completed. David transformed the Ivey House into a bed-and-breakfast in 1989 while continuing to offer guided canoe trips with his **North American Canoe Tours**, (NACT).

Today, NACT continues to offer equipment rentals, shuttle services, and, best of all, overnight guided paddle trips that explore mangrove tunnels and venture to beautiful, isolated beaches offering some of the best seashell collecting in Florida. The trips are of varying levels of difficulty. Some are easy half-day paddles, like the one we took with Dave in Big Cypress. The most strenuous is the eight-day, 98-mile Wilderness Waterway trip. The more decadent trips have boat tows, deck chairs, and coolers of cold beer, but still let you experience camping in this vast, quiet wilderness. You'll learn a lot about yourself and the area. This is, after all, the Everglades—or what's left of the Everglades. It's about as wild as it gets. The birding is best from December through March, when the mosquito population is at its lowest, but you'll still need tent netting. Fortunately, you can get about everything you need from Dave, except the yearning to go.

Behind the façade of the newest addition to the Ivey House Inn is a screened courtyard centered around a lovely, thoroughly refreshing swimming pool.

In May 2001, the property welcomed a major addition, the lovely **Ivey House Inn**. It's clear that the owners put a lot of thought into the design. The 17 rooms are comfortable and attractively furnished with two queen-sized beds, private baths, small refrigerators, televisions, and phones. And the screened courtyard with its sparkling-clear swimming pool and landscaped waterfall is nothing short of wonderful. Having a laundry room tucked securely inside the inn is a bonus, especially when you can toss in a load and head for the pool.

We went out with David for a motorboat tour through enough of the beautiful Ten Thousand Islands to understand how very easy it would be to get lost if you wandered far from the main channel. It's about six miles from the dock at Everglades City to the Gulf. Along the way, we passed crabbers going to collect their stone-crab traps. Baited with pigs' feet and snouts, the traps rest on the clear bottom in about 30 feet of water. They're collected every five days once the season opens

in mid-October. There are a couple of places in town where you can get crabs fresh from the boat.

Better yet, you can pay a visit to the **Oyster House Restaurant** and get them chilled, cracked, and ready to dip in melted butter or Mustard Sauce. If stone crabs aren't in season, there are lots of other good choices, including grouper, the especially delectable scamp, oysters served raw, steamed, or fried, alligator, frog legs, blue-crab claws, and Hush Puppies good enough to melt in your mouth. Add a cold draft beer, and you've got a meal to remember. The restaurant will even prepare your own cleaned catch. For those who insist, the Oyster House also serves tasty steaks and chicken breasts.

While you're out this way, stop by the **Everglades National Park Gulf Coast Visitor Center**, the park's western saltwater gateway. This is a good place to begin an exploration of the Ten Thousand Islands area. The visitor center offers maps and information on fishing, boating, and canoeing the 99-mile **Wilderness Waterway**, as well as information on guided boat tours through the mangrove bays and estuaries bordering the sawgrass prairies in the vast, federally protected wilderness. The center is open daily.

Continue on US 29 past the turnoff to Everglades National Park to visit Chokoloskee and the historic **Smallwood Store Museum**. Settlement in the Chokoloskee Bay area by plume, hide, and fur hunters started in the late 19th century. In 1906, Ted Smallwood started a trading post that was the only business on the island for many years. It also served as the local post office. The doors shut in 1982, but Ted's granddaughter later reopened the place as a museum. Original goods from the store are exhibited inside.

This area gained a measure of notoriety with

Smallwood's Store was for many years the community center for early settlers and an important source of trade for the Seminoles living in Southwest Florida.

Peter Matthiessen's 1990 publication of *Killing Mister Watson*, in which he retells a tale of frontier justice in a lawless land.

If you want to concentrate on fishing while you're here, Captain Gary Thompson is the man to see. He guides clients in search of snook, tarpon, redfish, trout, and cobia. A fourth-generation Everglades native, he also does historical, birding, and wild orchid tours. Several other experienced local guides are available as well.

Fakahatchee Strand State Preserve near Copeland is the main drainage slough of the southwestern part of Big Cypress Swamp. The preserve shelters the wood stork, the black bear, the Everglades mink, and the extremely rare Florida panther. This linear swamp, also known as a strand, has the largest concentration and variety of wild orchids in North America. An exhibit at the visitor center has photos of some of the many orchids that grow here, including several that are

quite rare. For those who want to see the orchids for themselves, swamp walks are conducted on the third Saturday of the month from November to February. You should call ahead for reservations, because the walks are limited to about 15 people.

Along US 41 between Everglades City and Miccosukee, you'll see signs for **Big Cypress National Preserve**, which encompasses 729,000 acres of wild country. Visitors here enjoy camping, hiking 31 miles of **Florida National Scenic Trail**, paddling the **Turner River Canoe Trail**, biking, driving along the Turner River Road and a 26-mile, one-lane loop road, hunting, fishing, and trapping according to game-management regulations. Off-road vehicles like swamp buggies and airboats are allowed in many areas. The visitor center, located near the Tamiami Trail, offers information on such things as the precautions to take during hunting season, off-road vehicle permits, and access to Florida National Scenic Trail.

The **Miccosukee Indian Reservation** is north of US 41. Here, you can enjoy demonstrations and exhibits of woodcarving, beadwork, doll making, and basket weaving. The reservation's museum contains exhibits, films, photos, and paintings.

Along the way to the reservation, you'll see several signs advertising airboat rides in the Everglades. The noise an airboat makes is tremendous, but its ability to skim over grass and water is unparalleled. Rides depart continuously from Miccosukee.

Once you reach the **Shark Valley Visitor Center** of Everglades National Park on US 41, much stricter national park regulations are in effect. Airboats and swamp buggies are forbidden At the visitor center, you can walk, bike, or take a two-hour guided tram ride that tells the story of the Everglades and its ecology on the way to the 65-foot observation tower at the halfway point.

For more on Everglades National Park, see the chapters covering the Everglades and the Keys.

Continue on US 41 and turn south on FL 997 to visit Homestead, the Everglades, and the Keys.

All of the following are in Naples and use the 34102 zip code and 941 area code, except where noted. The 941 area code changes to 239 in 2003.

 ACCOMMODATIONS

Edgewater Beach Hotel—1901 Gulf Shore Blvd. N.; 800-821-0196 or 262-6511

Everglades Cozy Cabins—805 Copeland Ave. at Glades Haven Marina, Everglades City, FL 34139; 695-2746

Hilton Marco Island Beach Resort—560 S. Collier Blvd., Marco Island, FL 34145; 800-443-4550 or 394-5000

Inn by the Sea—287 11th Ave. S.; 800-584-1268 or 649-4124

Inn on Fifth—699 Fifth Ave. S.; 888-403-8770 or 403-8777

Ivey House—107 Camelia St., Everglades City, FL 34139; 695-4666 or 695-3299; www.iveyhouse.com

Lemon Tree Inn—250 Ninth St.; 888-800-LEMO or 262-1414

Marco Island Marriott Resort and Golf Club—400 S. Collier Blvd., Marco Island, FL 34145; 800-438-4373 or 394-2511

Naples Beach Hotel and Golf Club—851 Gulf Shore Blvd.; 800-237-7600 or 261-2222

On the Banks of the Everglades—201 W. Broadway, Everglades City, FL 34139; 888-431-1977 or 695-3151

Radisson Suite Beach Resort—600 S. Collier Blvd., Marco Island, FL 34145; 800-333-3333 or 394-4100

Ritz-Carlton Naples—280 Vanderbilt Beach Rd.; 800-241-3333 or 598-3300

Rod and Gun Club—P.O. Box 190, Everglades City, FL 34139; 695-2101

Vanderbilt Beach Resort—9225 Gulf Shore Dr. N.; 800-243-9076 or 597-3144

 ATTRACTIONS

Big Cypress National Preserve—HCR 61, Box 11, Ochopee, FL 34141; 695-4111

Briggs Nature Center, Rookery Bay National Estuarine Research Reserve—401 Shell Island Rd.; 775-8569

Collier County Museum—Collier County Government Center, 3301 Tamiami Trail E.; 774-8476

Collier-Seminole State Park—20200 E. Tamiami Trail; 394-3397

Conservancy of Southwest Florida Nature Center—1450 Merrihue Dr.; 262-0304

Corkscrew Swamp Sanctuary—375 Sanctuary Rd.; 348-9151

Delnor-Wiggins State Pass Recreation Area—11100 Gulfshore Dr., 34108; 597-6196

Everglades National Park, Gulf Coast Visitor Center—P.O. Box 119, Everglades City, FL 34139; 695-3311 or 695-2591

Everglades National Park, Shark Valley Visitor Center—36000 SW Eighth St. (US 41), Miami FL 33194; 305-221-8776 or 305-221-8455

Fakahatchee Strand State Preserve—P.O. Box 548, Copeland, FL 33926; 695-4593

Marco Island Trolley—P.O. Box 1935, Marco Island, FL 34146; 394-1600

Miccosukee Indian Reservation—P.O. Box 440021, Miami, FL 33144; 305-223-8380

Museum of the Everglades—105 W. Broadway, Everglades City, FL 34139; 695-0008

Naples Trolley Tours—1010 Sixth Ave. S.; 800-592-0848 or 262-7300

North American Canoe Tours—P.O. Box 5038, Everglades City, FL 34139; 695-4666 or 695-3299; www.evergladesadventures.com

Palm Cottage—137 12th Ave. S.; 261-8164

Smallwood Store Museum—360 Maimie St., Chokoloskee Island, FL 33925; 695-2989

Teddy Bear Museum—2511 Pine Ridge Rd.; 598-2711

Thompson's Guide Service—Everglades City; 695-4102; www.thompsonguideservice.com

 CAMPING

Collier-Seminole State Park—20200 E. Tamiami Trail; 394-3397

 DINING

Bistro 821—821 Fifth Ave. S.; 434-7061

Café De Marco—244 Palm St., Marco Island, FL 34145; 394-6262

Marek's Collier House Restaurant—1121 Bald Eagle Dr., Marco Island, FL 34145; 642-9948

Maxwell's on the Bay—4300 Gulf Shore Blvd.; 263-1662

Oyster House Restaurant—901 Copeland Ave., Everglades City, FL 34139; 695-2073

Stan's Idle Hour Seafood Restaurant—221 W. Goodland Dr., Goodland, FL 34140; 877-387-2582 or 394-3041

Waterfront Café—US 41 (Tamiami Trail); 775-8115

 EVENTS

January-February—Mullet Festival

February—Native American and Pioneer Heritage Days

February—Everglades Seafood Festival

November—Old Florida Festival

 FOR MORE INFORMATION

Tourism Alliance of Collier County—5395 Park Central Court, Naples, FL 34109; 800-688-3600; www.classicflorida.com

Naples Area Chamber of Commerce—895 Fifth Ave. S.; 262-6141; www.naples-florida.com

*I*n Gainesville, you're in the heart of outdoor opportunities. A hiker came through here in 1774 and called this area "the great Alachua savanna." That was naturalist William Bartram describing what is today **Paynes Prairie State Preserve**. Human occupation of the savanna dates back to 10,000 B.C. The wide plain was home to prehistoric Indians, Timucuans, Seminoles, and later the largest cattle ranch in Spanish Florida.

Paynes Prairie is a 21,000-acre preserve about 10 miles south of Gainesville. To reach it, take the Micanopy exit from I-75 about 10 miles south of Gainesville and follow US 441 to the main entrance. It was named for a Seminole chief, King Payne. Its savanna remains one of the most significant natural areas in Florida. The basin was formed when the underlying limestone dissolved and the terrain settled. Today, it is covered by marsh and wet prairie vegetation with areas of open water. In 1891, the basin flooded enough to become a temporary lake but did no lasting harm.

Recreation here includes biking, hiking, horse-

William Bartram described 10,000-year-old Paynes Prairie as the "great Alachua savanna."

back riding, camping, canoeing, boating, fishing, and picnicking.

Another natural place worth a visit is **Devil's Millhopper State Geological Site**, located on CR 232 (Millhopper Road) northwest of Gainesville. Your first stop should be the interpretive center, where you'll learn how the sinkhole was formed. A short video explains how the sinkhole got its name and tells the Indian legend of the sink. A half-mile nature trail begins at the interpretive center and makes a circuit around the sink. It's only a short walk to the boardwalk and its 232 steps down into the hole.

Devil's Millhopper is the state park system's only geological site. During the 1800s, farmers ground grain in gristmills. The top of the mill was a hopper that fed into the grinder—hence millhopper. The fossilized bones and teeth from ancient animals that were found at the bottom were said to be what the devil put in the millhopper.

The 117-foot-deep cavity has a bottom 500 feet in diameter. As you descend, you'll enjoy the sight of lush vegetation and the sound of water rolling down the slopes. Rainwater seeps through the surrounding soil and drains to a layer of limestone. Clay beneath the stone prevents further downward movement, causing the water to flow along the limestone layer until it spills from springs around the sink. About 12 springs collect in a natural drain that eventually flows to the Gulf of Mexico. Among the bottom's lush vegetation are rare plant species that can adapt to varying amounts of sunlight and moisture. The 63-acre park is also home to animals including the gopher tortoise.

A little over three miles west of Devil's Millhopper on CR 232 is **San Felasco Hammock State Preserve**. San Felasco was purchased in 1974 under Florida's Environmentally Endangered Lands Program because of its diversity of plant communities and geological features, but joggers and hikers have taken it for their own. When we were here, a car with Arizona plates let out four joggers—this place has widespread popularity.

The preserve was used by Indians for thousands of years—at least since 8000 B.C. Fox Pond, just outside the southeast corner of the preserve, is a late-17th-century Spanish-Potano mission site. Potano was the name of the Indian culture living in the area, and San Felasco is believed to be the mission site of San Francisco de Potano. Mispronunciation of San Francisco by Indians and early settlers led to the preserve's present name.

At least 18 biological communities exist in the 6,900-acre preserve. The preserve contains rare plants, champion trees, and a representative of almost every major forest type in North Florida. The diversity of plant communities at San Felasco reflects the karst topography of northwestern Alachua County, which includes rolling hills, bluffs, springs, stream valleys, and numerous sinkholes.

Visitors can take a self-guided walk. On Saturdays from October to April, they can also enjoy ranger-led hikes and horseback rides, both of which can be arranged as overnight trips. Contact the rangers at Devil's Millhopper for more information.

Cyclists and hikers can take advantage of the 13 miles of off-road bike trails that snake through 2,000 acres in the preserve's northernmost section. The one-mile loop serves beginners, while the 4.2-mile loop is appropriate for intermediate cyclists. Advanced riders can tackle a trail measuring eight strenuous miles. The trailhead is behind Progress Corporate Park, located off US 441 just south of Alachua. Turn on to Progress Drive and continue straight. As at the Millhopper Road entrance, you'll reach a two-dollar self-pay station. The preserve is open daily.

The **Gainesville-Hawthorne State Trail** is a 16-mile trail built on an old railroad bed. Its 10-foot-wide paved surface and adjacent equestrian path are open to everyone from skaters to people in wheelchairs. To reach it, go east on University Avenue, south on CR 20, and then right on S.E. 15th Street. Beginning at Boulware Springs (3300 15th Street S.E.), the trail carries you past streams, marshes, hammocks, and prairie and through small towns to historic Hawthorne. Picnic tables and restrooms are spaced along the way.

Look for the offshoot trail, **La Chua Trail.** It's said to be excellent for wildlife viewing. It's for foot traffic only. If you make the three-mile round trip, you'll enjoy views of wet prairie and marsh habitat including Alachua Sink and Alachua Lake. To reach La Chua Trail, continue on 15th Street S.E. past Boulware Springs to Camp Ranch Road and park near the trailhead. Or you can park at Boulware Springs and hike or bike the 1.4 miles to the turnoff for La Chua Trail.

One of the top attractions in Gainesville is the **Florida Museum of Natural History**, located at 34th Street S.W. and Hull Road. The nearby **Samuel P. Harn Museum of Art** and the **Curtis M. Phillips Center for the Performing Arts** complete the cultural plaza on the western edge of the University of Florida campus.

As you enter the central gallery of the Florida Museum of Natural History, you'll be greeted by a 12-foot tall, 16,000-year-old mammoth. Only the tusks and a few foot bones are not original to the great animal, which was recovered from the Aucilla River. The Bones-to-Stones Room, one of six display rooms, explains how fossils are formed and excavated. The cute horse standing about two feet at the shoulder is the only skeleton of its kind. It's about 18 million years old. A walk through the museum's cave will introduce you to rock formations and life underground. You'll walk out of the cave into a forest, where you'll see life from the floor to the canopy. After that, you'll enter an exhibit on village life in northwest Florida in 860 A.D. The museum's Fossil Plant Garden is landscaped with modern species of plants whose fossilized ancestors lived million of years ago.

Southwest of Gainesville are some attractions that are well worth the drive.

Fred Bear Archery and Museum is located just off I-75; turn south off Archer Road on to Fred Bear Drive. The museum is a tribute to the accomplishments of Fred Bear, the founder of Bear Archery. During his 50-year archery career, Bear traveled the world to promote wildlife management and the sport of bow hunting. As a member of the Explorer's Club and the Safari Club International, Bear killed many big-game animals and earned six world records. All of his trophies and the world's largest private collection of archery artifacts are now housed in the museum. Note the elephant mount as you go upstairs to the museum. Fred Bear killed it with one arrow. You can tour the factory and watch the process of creating bows that propel arrows more than 200 miles per hour.

Farther out Archer Road, turn north on 58th Drive S.W. to reach **Kanapaha Botanical Gardens.** It'll take you about two hours to tour all the gardens in the 62-acre facility. Kanapaha is a cultural, educational, and recreational resource for the community. The state's most diverse botanical garden, it features rare and unusual plants from around the world. Two miles of paved, wheelchair-accessible walkways weave through the Herb Garden, the Bamboo Garden, the Hummingbird Garden, the Rock Garden, the Bog Garden, the Sunken Garden, and nine more. The colors are at their best from June through September.

Drive west on Archer Road, then turn north on Tower Road. After about a mile, turn right on

41st Place S.W. at the sign for the veterans' memorial known as **A Walk Through Time**. Here, one foot traveled equals one year of American history. Visitors start at 1775 with the American Revolution and end at Desert Storm. On the granite columns are red bricks representing American casualties in various wars. Each brick symbolizes 1,000 deaths. The War Between the States and World War II cost the most lives. Desert Storm has only a sliver of a brick.

Since there are so many things to see and do, you'll need a place to stay in Gainesville. Laurel Oak Inn and Magnolia Plantation Bed and Breakfast are within walking distance of downtown and some good restaurants.

Monta Burt and his wife, Peggy, took a run-down, apartment building for college students and returned it to its original 1885 Queen Anne glory when they created **Laurel Oak Inn**. After two years of work, they opened in the fall of 2001. The colorful inn has front and back porches, a lovely, spacious yard, and large laurel oak trees. Rich wood glows in the living and dining rooms. The bedrooms have comfortable feather beds and fireplaces, while the bathrooms have air-jet tubs or showers. One of the five rooms is wheelchair accessible. TVs and phones are available on request; a large TV sits in the morning room. Monta prepares a full, gratifying breakfast.

Next door is **Magnolia Plantation Bed and Breakfast**. Cindy and Joe Montalo restored this 1885 French Second Empire Victorian mansion and opened their inn in 1991. Since then, it has received many honors. The inn was named "Best Bed and Breakfast in Florida" by *Florida Living* magazine and "Most Romantic Bed and Breakfast in Florida" by the *Most Romantic Escapes in Florida* guidebook. Cindy's recipes have been featured in a va-

A Walk Through Time represents a linear timeline of American history. On the granite columns are red bricks representing American casualties in various wars

riety of cookbooks. Articles on the inn have appeared in *Southern Living*, *Victorian Decorating Ideas*, *Florida Living*, and the *Orlando Sentinel*.

Gainesville's restaurants appeal to every taste, from Cuban to barbecue. **Café Tropical** and **Emiliano's Café** offer Caribbean fare. **Grill Masters** and **Northwest Grille** serve pasta dishes, steaks, and seafood. **Copper Monkey** is noted for its steaks and burgers.

The beautiful Laurel Oak Inn was once a run-down apartment building.

Just south of Paynes Prairie on US 441 lies the quaint community of Micanopy. Here, you'll find the lifestyle that faded from most cities back in the 1950s. If the town looks familiar, it's because *Doc Hollywood* was filmed here.

Founded in 1821 and named for Chief Micanopy of the Seminoles, Micanopy is believed to be the oldest inland town in Florida.

Thrasher Warehouse, home of the **Micanopy Historical Society Museum**, is one of 39 local sites listed on the National Register of Historic Places. Constructed around 1890, the warehouse retains the original cashier's cage, some of the original pipes that carried carbide gas to the brass light fixtures, a large Coca-Cola sign painted in the 1920s, old photographs, memorabilia, and artifacts. When you leave, you'll feel like the world hasn't changed so much after all. Small donations are suggested for admission.

Micanopy's two dozen or so antique shops, four restaurants, and two bed-and-breakfasts belie the sleepy country atmosphere. The streets of this cozy town host a hubbub of activity on weekends.

From Micanopy, we suggest you go west on CR 346, turn south at CR 325, and go over **Cross Creek** to the home of Marjorie Kinnan Rawlings, who moved here with her husband, Charles, in 1928. The author immediately felt affection for their home and acreage at Cross Creek. "When I came to the Creek, I knew the old grove and the farmhouse at once as home," she wrote.

Her cracker farmhouse and orange grove are now a state historic site. The home, tended by park rangers and volunteers, has been preserved so that nothing much has changed since she died in 1953. The eight-room house—comprised of three separate structures connected by a bathroom, screened porches, and open porches—was 40 years old when she moved in. The Cracker-style architecture—characterized by tall ceilings, an abundance of windows, and screened doors to take advantage of breezes—was well suited to the hot Florida climate.

She said of the citrus grove that surrounded her house, "Enchantment lies in different things for each of us. For me, it is in this: to step out of

Cross Creek is where Marjorie Kinnan Rawlings typed the Yearling *and other novels.*

the bright sunlight into the shade of orange trees; to walk under the arched canopy of their jadelike leaves; to see the long aisles of lichened trunks stretch ahead in a geometric rhythm; to feel the mystery of a seclusion that yet has shafts of light striking through it. This is the essence of an ancient and secret magic."

Divorced from Charles in 1933, she stayed at Cross Creek alone through the Great Depression. In 1941, she married Norton Baskin and divided her time between here and their St. Augustine home. She and Baskin bought the Warden Castle and operated it as a hotel. It later became the Ripley's Believe It or Not! Museum. She continued to write until her death at age 57.

Tours are given Thursday through Sunday. An admission is charged for the house, but you can roam the grounds for free.

Go south from Cross Creek to join US 301, which will take you into Ocala and Silver Springs.

All of the following are in Gainesville and use the 32601 zip code and 352 area code, except where noted.

ACCOMMODATIONS

Herlong Mansion Bed and Breakfast—402 Cholokka Blvd. N.E., Micanopy, FL 32671; 466-3322

Laurel Oak Inn—221 7th St. S.E.; 373-4535; www.laureloakinn.com

Magnolia Plantation Bed and Breakfast—309 7th St. S.E.; 375-6653

Shady Oak Bed and Breakfast—203 Cholokka Blvd. N.E., Micanopy, FL 32671; 466-3476

Sweetwater Branch Inn Bed and Breakfast—625 E. University Ave.; 800-595-7760 or 373-6760

ATTRACTIONS

Bikes and More—2133 Sixth St. N.W.; 373-6574

Devil's Millhopper State Geological Site—4732 Millhopper Rd., 32653; 955-2208

Florida Museum of Natural History—S.W. 34th St. and Hull Rd., 32611; 846-2000

Florida National Scenic Trail Association—5415 13th St. S.W., 32608; 800-343-1882 or 378-8823

Fred Bear Archery and Museum—I-75 at Archer Rd., 32608; 376-2411

Kanapaha Botanical Gardens—4700 58th Dr. S.W., 32608; 372-4981

Marjorie Kinnan Rawlings State Historic Site—CR 325, Cross Creek (mailing address Route 3, Box 92, Hawthorn); 466-3672

Micanopy Historical Society Museum—P.O. Box 462, Micanopy, FL 32667; 466-3200

Paynes Prairie State Preserve—100 Savannah Blvd., Micanopy, FL 32667; 466-3397 or 466-4100

Recycled Bicycles—805 W. University Ave.; 362-4890

Samuel P. Harn Museum of Art—34th St. S.W. at Hull Rd., 32611; 392-9826

San Felasco Hammock State Preserve—4732 Millhopper Rd., 32653; 955-2208

Spin Cycle—309 13th St. N.W.; 373-3355

 CAMPING

Blue Springs—Blue Springs Park, 7450 N.E. 60th St., High Springs, FL 32643; 386-454-1369

Paynes Prairie State Preserve—100 Savannah Blvd., Micanopy, FL 32667; 466-3397 or 466-4100

Traveler's Campground—17701 April Blvd., Alachua, FL 32615; 386-462-2505

 DINING

Café Tropical—2441 43rd St. N.W.; 375-7500

Copper Monkey—5109 39th Ave. N.W.; 377-7665

Cuban Express—101 23rd Ave. N.E.; 381-0074

David's BBQ—5121-A 39th Ave. N.W.; 373-2002

Emiliano's Café—7 First Ave. S.E.; 375-7381

Grill Masters Restaurant—7750 W. Newberry Rd., 32606; 333-3108

La Tienda Latina—2404 13th St. S.W.; 367-0022

Northwest Grille—5115 N.W. 39th Ave., 32606; 376-0500

 EVENTS

February—Paynes Prairie Primitive Arts Festival

March—Gatornationals

April—Farm and Forest Festival

May—Fifth Avenue Arts Festival

June—Black Music Celebration

September—Possum Creek Fall Festival

 FOR MORE INFORMATION

Alachua County Visitors and Convention Bureau—30 E. University Ave.; 374-5260; www.visitgainesville.net

Gainesville Area Chamber of Commerce—300 E. University, Ave.; 334-7100

HIGHLIGHTS

HORSE FARMS
OCALA NATIONAL FOREST

*Y*ou know about Silver Springs and its famous glass-bottomed boats, which have been an international attraction for decades, but do you know why this area ranks with Lexington, Kentucky; Newmarket, England; and Chantilly, France?

First, some background on Marion County and its county seat, Ocala.

Some say the name Ocala means "spring," while others say it derives from a Timucuan Indian term meaning "fair land" or "big hammock"— take your pick.

Following the Indian Removal Act in 1830, Fort King, located near 36th Avenue S.E. and Fort King Street in Ocala, was the center of events that led to the Second Seminole Indian War in 1835. In an effort to control the Seminoles, white settlers were offered 160 acres to move to Florida. Many came from South Carolina, home of Revolutionary War hero Francis Marion, "the Swamp Fox." The county was named Marion in his honor in 1844. Two years later, the county seat was named Ocala.

Between 1871 and 1875, Marion County's citrus industry began to grow. The discovery of phosphate prompted another land boom. A fire destroyed four blocks of downtown Ocala in 1881, including the courthouse, five hotels, and all of the principal businesses. When brick structures replaced the wooden ones, Ocala became known as Brick City. By 1890, it was one of the largest towns in Florida, and Silver Springs had become an international tourist attraction.

The rich year-round pastures led to the growth of the thoroughbred industry here. The first thoroughbred farm, Rosemere, was established in 1935. In 1956, a local product named Needles won the Kentucky Derby and the Belmont Stakes, putting Marion County on the horse-racing map. Marion County boasts more than 1,000 farms and training centers, including approximately 450 thoroughbred farms. It is home to more than 40 different horse breeds. Marion County has more horses and ponies than any other county in the nation. It is in the company of Lexington, Kentucky; Newmarket, England; and Chantilly, France, as major thoroughbred centers. The Florida thoroughbred industry has produced 41 North American champions, 18 Breeders' Cup

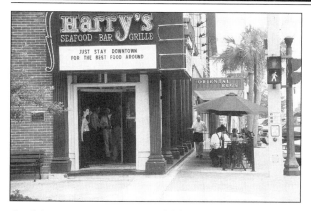

Ocala's town square is surrounded by shops and restaurants.

champions, and six Kentucky Derby winners. Some of the horse farms open for tours are **Adena Springs South** (620-2343), **Ocala Stud Farm** (237-2171), **Young's Paso Fino** (867-5305), and **Ocala Breeders' Sales Company and Training Center** (237-2154).

The **Ocala Historic District** encompasses numerous well-preserved structures built from the 1880s through the 1930s. It catalogs the development of Ocala's finest residential area from the opening of the railroad era through the boom of the 1920s.

The **Tuscawilla Park Historic District** is a residential area northeast of historic downtown Ocala. This area developed primarily between 1880 and 1920. It is significant for its association with many of Ocala's prominent businessmen, politicians, and civic leaders, particularly members of the Jewish community. The oldest existing building in Florida designated as a synagogue is here; it dates to 1888. The district also contains some old residential buildings. Most are frame vernacular, but you'll also see examples of the Second Empire, Queen Anne, Colonial Revival, Gothic Revival, Spanish Revival,

Georgian Revival, Carpenter Revival, Carpenter Gothic, and Bungalow styles.

The **Appleton Fine Arts Museum** houses permanent collections of antiquities; European paintings, sculpture, and decorative arts; and Pre-Columbian, West African, and Asian art. The Edith Marie Appleton Wing has a 22,000-square-foot gallery for traveling exhibitions, making this one of the largest art museums in Florida.

If fine arts aren't racy enough for you, you can visit the **Don Garlits Museum of Drag Racing**. It contains the cars of Shirley Muldowney, Dean Moore, Tom McEwen, and Art Matone, as well as antique and restored cars. Located 15 minutes south of Ocala at I-75 and CR 67, it's open daily except Christmas.

If you'd like a leisurely and in-depth look at local waters and wildlife, **Captain Tom's Custom Charter** offers freshwater pontoon sightseeing and fishing trips on the Ocklawaha and Silver Rivers. Captain Tom also offers ecology trips. His boats have canopy tops for shade, and he customizes his service to fit the interests of guests, be it fishing, bird-watching, moonlight cruises, dinner cruises, picnics, or photography jaunts.

Opportunities for fishing, boating, swimming, and other watersports abound in a region that encompasses hundreds of freshwater springs, lakes, and the Silver, Rainbow, Ocklawaha, and Withlacoochee Rivers. The pure waters of the springs and spring-fed lakes and rivers are a dream come true for folks who enjoy snorkeling and diving.

Ocala National Forest receives more visitors than any other national forest in Florida. The forest includes palms, large live oaks, and scrubby sand pines. The sand-pine scrub ecosystem here is the largest continuous forest of its type in the world. The sand pine is the only tree capable of growing to a usable timber size in this forest's dry, sandy soil.

Nearly three-quarters of Ocala National Forest's 383,000 acres are in eastern Marion County. The forest offers unique ecological sites, trails, springs, hundreds of campsites, and horseback trails that are part of the Florida National Scenic Trail. Among the attractions here are Salt Springs, Salt Springs Trail, Fore Lake Recreational Area, Juniper Springs Recreational Area, Silver Glen Springs, Lake Eaton, Lake Eaton Sinkhole, and Mill Dam Recreation Area, to name just a few.

Marked hiking trails are located throughout the forest.

The two **Lake Eaton Sinkhole Trails** (measuring 1 mile and 1.7 miles round-trip) go by an 80-foot sink that's 450 feet in diameter. An observation deck lets you look down into the sinkhole.

Lake Eaton Loop Trail (2.1 miles round-trip) allows hikers to explore the sand-pine scrub forest and gives access to Lake Eaton's west bank from FR 79.

Salt Springs Trail goes from the parking lot on CR 19 to Salt Springs Run. The distance is 1 mile by the northern path and 1.1 miles by the southern path (2 miles round-trip). Salt Springs Run flows four miles from the spring to Lake George, a wide spot in the St. Johns River. The water at the spring tastes salty and stays at 74 degrees year-round.

Fore Lake Recreation Area is a day-use and camping area that is open year-round. It has a sandy beach along the 77-acre Fore Lake. Visitors can fish and boat in small, non-gasoline-powered craft. There's a fishing pier at the southeast corner of the lake.

Mill Dam Recreation Area is one of the most picturesque day-use areas in Ocala National For-

est. Built by the Civilian Conservation Corps (CCC) in the 1930s, the area is open from April 1 through September 30. The 170-acre lake has a 300-foot sandy beach and is popular with swimmers. Anglers may use the boat ramp located south of the day-use area.

The CCC also built **Juniper Springs Recreation Area** in the 1930s. Juniper Springs and nearby Fern Hammock Springs send about 13 million gallons of 72-degree water daily into Juniper Creek, which flows through the Juniper Wilderness.

Contact Ocala National Forest for information on campgrounds and other recreational opportunities.

Also east of Ocala is **Silver River State Park**, named for the river that flows through it. The park's 5,000 acres contain 14 distinct plant communities, nearly 20 miles of river frontage, and many springs. Nearby Silver Springs is the headwater of the Silver River, which flows into the Oklawaha River on its way to the St. Johns River.

The 0.75-mile **River Trail** leads from the parking area to the Silver River. Be sure to bring your camera, as you'll have an excellent view of the river.

Sink Hole Trail is a combination of three trails totaling 3.5 miles. It takes hikers through a mixed forest, a hardwood hammock, a scrub community, and a sand-hill community. Interpretive signs, benches, and picnic tables are located along the way.

Silver River Museum and Environmental Education Center is located on the shore of the river within the park. It features exhibits on Florida history, natural history, geology, archaeology, paleontology, and ecology. The museum has a replica of a Florida Cracker village.

Silver Springs isn't just a lot of water; various shops and restaurants abound.

The park is open to the public every day of the year. Campsites and cabins are available.

For those interested in motorsports, the **Ocala Speedway**, just north of town, offers racing every Saturday night. **Hardrock Cycle Park**, located on Gainesville Road N.W., offers mountain-bike trails, motocross tracks, and even camping.

Those needing a place to stay in Ocala can choose from major hotels and motels, as well a couple of bed-and-breakfasts. **The Seven Sisters** is an 1880s eight-room Queen Anne that offers private baths, a full breakfast, and afternoon tea. **Heritage Country Inn** has six rooms with private baths. Both of these bed-and-breakfasts have received a Triple Diamond rating from AAA.

Silver Springs is located just a few miles east of Ocala on CR 40. This is the site of the world's largest artesian spring. More than 550 million gallons of water gush to the surface daily.

The famous Silver Springs glass-bottomed boats got their start in 1878, when someone had the idea to use a glass panel to patch a hole in a dugout canoe, and so invented a new category of watercraft. In time, these vessels drew a stream of visitors to the clear springs. They've evolved from that first wooden canoe into a fleet of motorized boats carrying dozens of people at a time on half-hour excursions. You pass over schools of fish and see some of the springs that feed the river. You'll be amazed by the underwater views of fish and eelgrass swaying in the strong currents roiling up from the limestone depths.

Over the decades, other attractions have been added. If you plan carefully, you can enjoy the entire 350-acre park in one day. Take your camera and plenty of film.

Lost River Voyages is a riverboat venture through undeveloped wetlands for a look at Florida

Silver Springs' first glass-bottom boat was the outgrowth of a creative repair job on a canoe.

the way 16th-century explorers might have seen it. The tour turns around at a rehabilitation facility where injured owls, eagles, and vultures reside.

The **Jungle Cruises** boats ply a canal past habitats for monkeys, Barbary sheep, antelope, gazelles, llamas, ostriches, and more.

On the **Jeep Safari**, guides drive a jungle route where zebras, two-toed sloths, and several species of deer dwell. The ride also splashes through a three-foot-deep, well-stocked alligator pit.

World of Bears, Panther Prowl, Wings of the Springs, Big Gator Lagoon, Doolittle's Petting Zoo, and **Kids Ahoy! Playland** are among the other attractions at Silver Springs.

The **Twin Oaks Mansion Concert Stage** features country-and-western, rock-'n'-roll, bluegrass, Cajun, big-band, and gospel headliners.

At the **Historical Showcase**, visitors enjoy exhibits that detail Hollywood's love of Silver Springs. Among the many movies made at Silver Springs were six Tarzan films, *The Yearling, Rebel Without a Cause, Thunderball,* and *Moonraker.* Segments of the television series *Sea Hunt* and *Mutual of Omaha's Wild Kingdom* have been filmed here, as have commercials and nature documentaries.

Wild Waters is a nine-acre water park adjacent to Silver Springs. Its highlights include a wave pool, water cannons, and lots of slides. The Twin Twister is a pair of 60-foot-tall tower slides.

Visitors to these attractions have easy access to gift shops, snack bars, and cafés. The parks are open daily from March to Labor Day and Thursday to Sunday from September to February.

All of the following are in Ocala and use the 34470 zip code and 352 area code, except where noted.

ACCOMMODATIONS

Heritage Country Inn—14343 FL 40 W., 34481; 489-0023

Rosslor Manor—P.O. Box 687, Silver Springs, FL 34489; 236-4219

Seven Sisters Inn—820 Fort King St. S.E., 34471; 867-1170

ATTRACTIONS

Appleton Museum of Art—4333 Silver Springs Blvd. N.E.; 236-7100

Captain Tom's Custom Charter—P.O. Box 1836, Silver Springs, FL 34489; 546-4823

Don Garlits Museum of Drag Racing—13700 S.W. 16th Ave., Ocala, FL 34473; 352-245-8661

Marion County Museum of History—307 Terrace S.E., 34471; 629-2773

Ocala National Forest—Lake George Ranger District, 17147 E. FL 40, Silver Springs, FL 34488; 625-2520

Ocala Speedway—9050 Gainesville Rd; 622-9400

Silver River Museum and Environmental Education Center—1445 N.E. 58th Ave.; 236-7148 or 236-5401

Silver River State Park—1425 58th Ave. N.E., 34470; 236-1827

Silver Springs—5656 E. Silver Springs Blvd., Silver Springs, FL 34488; 236-2121

CAMPING

Ocala KOA—3200 38th Ave. S.W., 34474; 237-2138

Ocala National Forest—Lake George Ranger District, 17147 E. FL 40, Silver Springs, FL 34488; 625-2520

Rainbow Springs State Campground—18185 S.W. 94th St., Dunnellon, FL 34432; 352-489-5201

DINING

Bella Luna Café—3425 College Rd. S.W.; 237-9155

Charlie Horse Restaurant—2426 Silver Springs Blvd.; 622-4050

Fred Fleming's Famous BBQ—2415 College Rd. S.W.; 861-8300

Harry's Seafood Bar and Grille—24th First Ave. S.E.; 840-0900

Kotobuki Steak House—2463 27th Ave. S.W.; 237-3900

Semolina's International Pastas—3500 W. College Rd.; 873-8059

EVENTS

June—Powell Memorial 125 Late Model Celebrity Race, Ocala

July—Ocala Sturgis Rally

August—Ocali Fest

September—Corvette Show, Ocala

October—Oktoberfest, Silver Springs

October—Antique Car Show, Silver Springs

November—White Buffalo Society Native American Festival, Silver Springs

November—Championship Ocala Scottish Games and Irish Feis

FOR MORE INFORMATION

Ocala/Marion County Chamber of Commerce—110 E. Silver Springs Blvd; 629-8051; www.ocalacc.com

Silver Springs—5656 E. Silver Springs Blvd., Silver Springs, FL 34488; 236-2121; www.silversprings.com

DeLand-Lake Helen-Cassadaga-De Leon Springs-Barberville

HIGHLIGHTS

HENRY A. DELAND HOUSE MUSEUM

SKYDIVE DELAND

BLUE SPRING STATE PARK

ST. JOHNS RIVER

LAKE WOODRUFF NATIONAL WILDLIFE REFUGE

You'll find a variety of outdoor possibilities in western Volusia County, away from the crowded beaches and famous central Florida amusement parks. This is St. Johns River country. It offers myriad opportunities to fish, canoe, camp, water-ski, watch wildlife—maybe even see the elusive Florida panther—visit museums, and lounge in whirlpools. And if you want fast action, you can take a flying leap at Skydive DeLand.

DeLand, an appealing community of about 35,000 people, takes pride in its national Mainstreet Award. It is about thirty minutes from the Atlantic coast and the bustle of Daytona Beach. You'll find an eclectic assortment of ethnic restaurants from Cuban to Vietnamese, along with a selection of antique and specialty shops. The broad mix of accommodations ranges from national hotel and motel chains to fish camps. DeLand is home to Stetson University—and yes, it's the Stetson of hat fame.

A good place to start is the **Henry A. DeLand House Museum**, built in 1886 at 137 West Michigan Avenue. Originally a one-and-a-half-story structure, it was built on land purchased from Henry DeLand, the founding father of the city. In 1893, John B. Stetson, the hat manufacturer and benefactor of the university that bears his name, purchased the home for faculty housing. Ten years later, Dr. Charles Farriss purchased the home. He made significant changes by raising the roof and adding the second floor and the Greek Revival portico. One interesting feature is the firewood trolley located by the wood-burning fireplaces, which allowed logs to be pulled back and forth between the rooms to feed the fires as needed. The dining-room table was made by gun-stock workers at the Remington small-arms factory. If you're a history buff, you'll enjoy the extensive collection of period photographs of western Volusia County displayed on the walls. The artifacts and memorabilia in the cabinets and cupboards trace the development of DeLand and the surrounding area.

The **African American Museum of the Arts**, located at 325 South Clara Avenue, is the only museum in the area devoted primarily to African-American and Caribbean-American culture and art. This one-story facility houses a revolving gallery featuring works of both established and emerging artists. Six major exhibitions are displayed annually. The museum also is home to a permanent collection of more than 150 artifacts, including sculptures and masks, from the countries of Africa. The museum is open Wednesday through Saturday. Admission is free, though donations are accepted.

The **Gillespie Museum of Minerals** was established at Stetson University in 1958. It is recognized as one of the finest mineral collections in the United States. The museum offers displays relating to a variety of earth-science topics. Among them are exhibits of petrified dinosaur bones and fluorescent minerals in a special darkroom.

If museums are a little tame for you, there are opportunities for thrills in DeLand, too. Patrons of **Skydive DeLand** have made more than one million jumps. Those bold enough to take the plunge have included Tom Cruise and Nicole Kidman, and now, Cathy says, "my weak-brained, adrenaline-junkie husband." After a brief training session, I exited a plane at 13,500 feet attached to my highly trained tandem-skydive partner, Pablo Iragorri. The minute-long, 8,000-foot free fall was breathtaking—and I can't wait to go again! I came home delighted with the obligatory "Been there, done that" T-shirt and the video, which came courtesy of skydiving videographer Rick Power, who stopped counting his jumps in the vicinity of 20,000. As soon as you work up the courage, you, too, can combine the thrill of falling with the exhilaration of flying.

Vern bids adieu before going into the wild blue at Skydive DeLand.

Southeast of DeLand are the enchanting towns of Lake Helen and Cassadaga.

Clauser's Bed and Breakfast Inn in Lake Helen is popular with folks visiting Cassadaga or just coming to enjoy the spacious rooms, the gazebo complete with a hot tub, and the wonderful hospitality. People find their way to this peaceful setting beneath the huge live oak trees year after year. The Victorian home offers guest rooms and a delicious breakfast each morning, but you'll want to get up a little early for a cup of coffee on the screened porch. Expect to be greeted by the household cat or to catch a glimpse of its rival, the neighborhood raccoon, depending on how early you rise. A well-planned addition offers more guest rooms and a gathering room out back beyond the hot tub. Clauser's is a splendid central location for exploring Cassadaga, the Atlantic beaches, DeLand, and De Leon Springs.

Cassadaga is the remnant of a spiritualist community founded in 1894. Its 57 acres are protected as a historic district on the National Register. The turn-of-the-century homes along the tree-lined

The old and the new inns of Clauser's Bed and Breakfast Inn are separated by a marvelous hot tub inside a gazebo.

streets are occupied by spiritual counselors, who come here to live, work, and study. They are granted lifetime leases on the land their homes rest upon.

Guests may experience spiritual healings during church services or during a special healing center a half-hour before church. There's a special night of mini-readings on the first Monday of each month. Or you can make arrangements for a private reading when you arrive.

Cassadaga welcomes the curious, along with believers. Falling into the first category, Cathy found her reading to be a thoroughly enjoyable experience. As they say here, they have nothing to prove or defend. If getting a reading works for you, you're encouraged to carry your spiritual counselor's words with you. This was literally true in Cathy's case. She brought a tape recording of her reading home, courtesy of the Reverend Jerry Frederich.

Blue Spring State Park, south of DeLand off US 17/92 in Orange City, is more than a scenic area for fishing, canoeing, and swimming. Indeed, it plays a vital role in the survival of the manatee.

These graceful giant mammals gather here from November through March upon leaving the colder waters of the St. Johns River for the 72-degree spring. Segregated swimming areas keep the bathers from the manatee refuge zone.

Anglers will find an abundance of bluegill, largemouth bass, shellcracker, and crappie (locally called speckled perch). A concession stand offers snacks, camping supplies, and limited groceries. Canoe rentals are available. Most facilities and activities are wheelchair accessible.

Hontoon Island State Park is accessible only by private boat or by a passenger ferry that operates free of charge. There is a park fee once you land on the island. A parking area is provided on the mainland.

The picnic area is located near the boat basin, overlooking the St. Johns River. A self-guided trail begins at the ranger station and follows Hontoon Dead River to the large Indian mound at the southwest corner of the island. Allow two hours for your walk. Located within walking distance of the river is a campground set in a pine forest. Primitive camping is available to registered backpackers. The sites are at the end of a four-mile hiking trail that winds through shaded hammocks and flatwoods. Six rental cabins are also available. A boat ramp and docks are provided on the St. Johns River for boaters and canoeists. Docks are provided for day-use. Overnight dockage is also available.

Hontoon Landing Resort and Marina on the St. Johns River gives you the choice of staying in a waterfront lodge or in a houseboat equipped with a television, a VCR, and all the conveniences of home—except your pets. Small rental boats are available, as are short- and long-term boat slips.

Holly Bluff Marina rents houseboats and lets you keep pets with you. It's just north of Hontoon State Park and three miles from Blue Spring State Park. Each boat is equipped with a generator to power the air conditioner and other electric appliances. Houseboats are easy to drive, and no special license is required. A trained instructor will teach you how to operate the boat.

Captains Rick and Ron Rawlins own **Highland Park Fish Camp** on the St. Johns River. Rick says the fishing is wonderful along the river and its tributaries. The very best times for bass are December and January. February and November are the next-best months, followed by September and October. Bass spawn from January to March. Wild river shiners and shad are among the best baits for bass. The largemouth black bass reigns as king in most of Florida's 3 million acres of fresh water, which provide some of the best bass fishing in the nation. Anglers spend more than $500 million annually on largemouth bass fishing in the Sunshine State. But bass aren't the only game-fish species worth a try. Rick says crappie are eager eaters year-round. Bluegill and shellcracker also top the anglers' hit parade.

When Rick and I went to net shad for bait, we had about 30 alligators for company. A fishing trip here is thus a wildlife viewing experience, too. Be sure to take a camera. Rick saw his first wild panther while fishing.

Highland Park Fish Camp has every thing you need—cabins, RV and tent sites, boat rentals and storage, a fishing shop, groceries, and fishing guides.

If you get your kicks from horses and horse racing, head to **Spring Garden Ranch Training Center**, where world-renowned winners come for the winter. This is the largest training center for Standard-bred horses in the United States. Quali-

At the Old Spanish Sugar Mill you can make your own breakfast before heading out for adventures in Valousia County.

fying races are held every Tuesday from January 1 to May 1, but there's no betting. The restaurant on the premises is open daily during the winter season, when the racehorses exercise in the mornings. The restaurant operates on a seasonal basis during the rest of the year.

De Leon Springs is located about nine miles north of DeLand. Famed Spanish explorer Juan Ponce de Leon didn't find the Fountain of Youth he sought here during the early 1500s. The surrounding country was part of a plantation known as Spring Garden when the United States acquired Florida from Spain in 1821. John James Audubon came to visit in 1832 and sketched some of the birds he saw. By 1872, the owner of the spring added a pier and bathhouses.

Today's visitors find a great deal to enjoy in the place named in Ponce de Leon's honor. People come to swim, scuba-dive, fish, canoe, and otherwise sample the sparkling waters at **De Leon Springs State Recreation Area** today.

While you're in town, be sure to visit the **Old**

Lake Woodruff National Wildlife Refuge affords you opportunities to add to your bird count if you're a birder.

Spanish Sugar Mill, now a rustic restaurant with a view of the springs. As you walk to your table, you'll notice an electric griddle built into its center, where you can cook your own pancakes from the restaurant's special five-grain flour batter. Fresh fruit toppings, bacon, eggs, and vegetarian sausage round out the menu. The small gift shop is stocked with souvenirs, taste treats, and a good sampling of Florida books.

De Leon Springs provides access to the 22,500-acre **Lake Woodruff National Wildlife Refuge**. The refuge contains three impoundments, marshes, swamps, and uplands. As you'd expect, there's no shortage of gators, large and small, in these waters. There's also an eagle colony, reported to be the second-largest in the country. You'll have a good chance for sighting black-necked stilts; limpkins; great, little blue, green, and tricolored herons; glossy ibises; and sandhill cranes. According to refuge manager Henry Sansing, this is the home of the second-largest roosting colony of swallow-tailed kites in Florida. Six miles of hiking trails provide good access to

the refuge. An observation tower offers visitors a bird's-eye view.

The **Pioneer Settlement for the Creative Arts**, located 15 miles north of DeLand at the junction of US 17 and FL 40 at Barberville, is an Old Florida settlement featuring a turpentine still, a log cabin, a blacksmith's shop, a woodwright's shop, a pottery shed, a post-and-beam barn, and gardens in season. We enjoyed this stop very much. The old schoolhouse contains artifacts, relics, and artwork. The settlement offers popular hands-on educational programs for 25,000 children annually. It also provides adult workshops and has a year-round calendar of festivals celebrating early Florida pioneer life. It is open year-round but is closed Sundays and major holidays.

All of the following are in DeLand and use the 32720 zip code and 386 area code, except where noted.

 A C C O M M O D A T I O N S

Clauser's Bed and Breakfast Inn—201 E. Kicklighter Rd., Lake Helen, FL 32744; 800-220-0310 or 228-0310; www.clauserinn

DeLand Country Inn Bed and Breakfast—228 W. Howry Ave.; 736-4244

Eastwood Bed and Breakfast—442 E. New York Ave.; 800-613-8424 or 736-9902

Highland Park Fish Camp—2640 W. Highland Park Rd.; 800-525-3477 or 734-2334

Pioneer Settlement for the Creative Arts is a quaint village featuring demonstrations of life in the late 1800s and early 1900s.

Holly Bluff Marina—2280 Hontoon Rd.; 800-237-5105 or 822-9992

Hontoon Landing Resort and Marina—2317 River Ridge Rd.; 800-248-2474 or 734-2474

ATTRACTIONS

African American Museum of the Arts—325 S. Clara Ave., 32721; 736-4004

Blue Spring State Park—2100 W. French Ave., Orange City, FL 32763; 775-3663

Cassadaga Spiritualist Camp—P.O. Box 319, Cassadaga, FL 32706; 228-2880

De Leon Springs State Recreation Area—601 Ponce de Leon Blvd. 32130; 985-4212

Gillespie Museum of Minerals, Stetson University—234 E. Michigan Ave.; 822-7330

Henry A. DeLand House Museum—137 W. Michigan Ave.; 740-6813

Highland Park Fish Camp—2640 W. Highland Park Rd.; 800-525-3477 or 734-2334

Hontoon Island State Park—2309 River Ridge Rd.; 736-5309

Lake Woodruff National Wildlife Refuge—4490 Grand Ave., De Leon Springs, FL 32130; 985-4673

Pioneer Settlement for the Creative Arts—1776 Lightfoot Ln., Barberville, FL 32105; 749-2959

Rivertown Antique Mall—114 S. Woodland Blvd.; 738-5111

Safari River Tours (De Leon Springs State Park)—601 Ponce de Leon Blvd.; 668-1002

Skydive DeLand—1600 Flightline Blvd., 32724; 738-3539

Spring Garden Ranch Training Center—900 Spring Garden Rd., De Leon Springs, FL 32130; 985-5654

St. Johns River Cruise—2100 N. French Ave., Orange City, FL 32763; 330-1612

 CAMPING

Blue Spring State Park—2100 W. French Ave., Orange City, FL 32763; 775-3663

De Leon Springs State Park—601 Ponce de Leon Blvd., De Leon Springs, FL 32130; 985-4212

Gemini Springs Park—37 Dirksen Dr., DeBary, FL 32713; 668-3810

Highland Park Fish Camp—2640 W. Highland Park Rd.; 800-525-3477 or 734-2334

Hontoon Island State Park—2309 River Ridge Rd.; 736-5309

 DINING

Allgoods Little New Orleans—100 N. Woodland Blvd.; 943-8833

Artisan Restaurant—215 N. Woodland Blvd.; 736-3484

Christo's and Eleni's Italian Restaurant—803 W. New York Ave.; 734-5705

Harry's Restaurant (Best Western/Deltona Inn)—481 Deltona Blvd.; 860-3000

Holiday House Restaurant—704 N. Woodland Blvd.; 734-6319

Hunter's Restaurant—202 N. Woodland Blvd.; 736-7957

JC's Lobster Pot—2888 W. New York Ave.; 734-7459

Karling's Inn—4640 US 17 N., De Leon Springs; 985-5535

Le Jardin—103 W. Indiana Ave.; 740-0303

Main Street Grill—100 E. New York Ave.; 740-9535

Old Spanish Sugar Mill and Restaurant—De Leon Springs State Park, 106 Ponce de Leon Blvd., De Leon Springs, FL 32130; 985-5644

Yesterday's Restaurant—145 N. Woodland Blvd.; 734-1917

E V E N T S

January—Mardi Gras on Main Street and Dog Parade, DeLand

January—Railroad Show, DeLand

March—Antique Bottle and Insulator Show, DeLand

March—Antique and Classic Motorcycle Auction, DeLand

April—Cracker Day, DeLand

May—Wild Game Feast, DeLand

August—A Day in the History of De Leon Springs

August—Neighbor Day Celebration, Pioneer Settlement for the Creative Arts, Barberville

September—River Town Craft Show, DeLand

November—Fall Festival of the Arts, DeLand

December—St. Johns River Christmas Boat Parade, DeLand

December—Christmas Tour of Historic Homes, DeLand and Lake Helen

F O R   M O R E   I N F O R M A T I O N

St. Johns River Country Visitor's Bureau—101 N. Woodland Blvd., Suite A-308; 800-749-4350 or 734-0575; www.stjohnsrivercountry.com

Sleepy little Mount Dora has a population of less than 10,000. It awoke one year with the new distinction of being called the "New England of the South," which attracted a throng of shoppers and gawkers. Founded in 1874 on the gently sloping lakeside hills amid ancient oak trees and 19th-century clapboard houses, Mount Dora has maintained its laid-back country charm while hosting as many as 300,000 visitors.

It lies about 20 miles northwest of Orlando on US 441. In 1880, postmaster R. C. Tremain christened the place Royellou in honor of his three children, Roy, Ella, and Louis. Three years later, Mount Dora became the name.

Within walking distance of downtown are parks, playgrounds, a fishing dock, a boat ramp, and picnic pavilions. Various historic buildings have been combined into a self-guided tour. The oldest structure, established in 1883, is the 87-room **Lakeside Inn**. The 1893 home of the first mayor, J. P. Donnelly, and the **Mount Dora Area Chamber of Commerce**, located in the 1915 railroad depot, are both listed on the National Register of Historic Places.

You'll find plenty of fascinating artifacts in the art galleries and antique shops of Mount Dora. The annual art festival is a huge draw, as is **Renninger's Florida Twin Markets**, a 115-acre flea market with a vast assortment of antiques and collectibles.

If you want to take time away from shopping, you can swim, fish, boat, water-ski, windsurf, and play racquetball, tennis, golf, shuffleboard, and croquet. If you enjoy fierce competition, grab a

Lawn bowling is very popular among the residents of Mount Dora.

The Cannonball takes you around Mount Dora's country-side and lake.

bowling ball for some championship-level lawn bowling at Evans Park.

An excellent way to get acquainted with Mount Dora is aboard the **Mount Dora Road Trolley**. This hour-long tour is rich in local history. The trolley makes runs Monday through Saturday. Sunday runs are added from June to September. A special lunch tour is also available.

Or you can take an hour-long tour aboard the **Cannonball**, a Baldwin locomotive that has enjoyed a career in the movies. The Cannonball chugs from Mount Dora to Tavares and back while guests see the sites and hear about the history of the area. It operates Tuesday through Sunday.

All in all, Mount Dora is a shopper's dream where a great many shops are clustered in just a few blocks. And the local bed-and-breakfasts are more than eager to provide you a comfortable place to rest your tootsies.

All of the following are in Mount Dora and use the 32757 zip code and 352 area code.

 ACCOMMODATIONS

Christopher's Inn Bed and Breakfast—539 Liberty Ave.; 888-398-9436 or 383-2244

Coconut Cottage Inn—1027 McDonald St.; 383-2627

Darst Victorian Manor—495 Old US 441; 383-4050

Dora Way—1123 Dora Way; 735-5994

Emerald Hill Inn—27751 Lake Jem Rd.; 383-2777

Farnsworth House—1029 E. Fifth Ave.; 888-770-8355 or 735-1894

Gazebo Guest Cottages Bed and Breakfast—106 E. Third Ave.; 735-5203

Magnolia Inn—347 E. Third Ave.; 800-776-2112 or 735-3800

Mount Dora Historic Inn—221 E. Fourth Ave.; 800-927-6344 or 735-1212

Nelson Manor—1355 N. Donnelly St.; 735-5288

Simpson's—441 N. Donnelly St.; 383-2087

 ATTRACTIONS

Mount Dora Road Trolley—Fourth Ave. at Alexander St.; 357-9123

The Cannonball—150 W. Third Ave.; 735-4667

Rusty Anchor Water Tours—400 W. Fourth Ave.; 383-3933

CAMPING

Woods-N-Water Trails RV—135 N. Bay Rd.; 735-1009

DINING

Cecile's French Corner—237 W. Fourth Ave.; 383-7100

Goblin Market—331-B Donnelly St.; 735-0059

Greenhouse Restaurant—3725 W. Old US 441; 735-2800

Palm Tree Grille—351 Donnelly St.; 735-1936

Shiraz Bistro—301 N. Baker St.; 735-5227

Windsor Rose English Tea Room—144 W. Fourth Ave.; 735-2551

EVENTS

Third weekend in January, February, and November—Renninger's Antique Extravaganza

February—Arts Festival

February—Festival of Exotic Cars

March—Antique Boat Festival

April—Sailing Regatta

October—Bicycle Festival

FOR MORE INFORMATION

Mount Dora Chamber of Commerce—341 Alexander St.; 383-2165; www.mountdora.com

Orlando has many layers of entertainment. Everyone knows of Walt Disney World, SeaWorld, and Universal. They're the trump card in the city's deck, but there is so much more. It is the "so much more" we'll concentrate on in this chapter, though we still won't be able to cover it all. You'll need several days to visit the Mouse. You'll be wise to add a few more to experience the other sites.

The city is in the middle of the state, about 60 miles west of Cape Canaveral. While stories abound about how it got its name, it was probably named for Orlando Reeves, an American soldier during the Seminole War in 1835. Reeves, at his post on the banks of what is now known as Lake Eola, sounded the alarm of an Indian raid and was killed by an arrow. It is said that the soldiers who stayed to make their homes here named the town for him.

By 1860, Orlando had become a lawless town of gunfighters and rustlers, along with some cotton growers. Orlando grew in the middle of a cotton field. The War Between the States caused devastation to the cotton growers, since most of the pickers were gone. A hurricane in 1871 ruined what was left of the cotton business.

The town survived on cattle and citrus farming until the freeze of 1894-95, which damaged 95 percent of the citrus trees. The farms took 15 years to recover. The citrus industry peaked here in the 1950s with 80,000 acres of producing trees.

There is no mistaking the entrances to the multitude of theme parks around Orlando. Here you see the entrance to SeaWorld.

In 1956, many miles of citrus groves were purchased for a missile factory—today's Lockheed Martin. And then in the 1960s, Disney quietly bought up farmland for what was to become the world's largest theme park and the planet's most popular man-made attraction. The park spurred all kinds of growth and brought in other attractions to satisfy the hordes of Disney tourists and reach out for a share of the tourists' dollars. This feeding frenzy couldn't be sated, thereby transforming Orlando into a large, modern, and successful city.

No matter your lodging needs, Orlando can meet them. The city has more than 105,000 guest rooms, from moderately priced hotels to all-suite properties to bed-and-breakfasts to theme resort lodgings. About 4,300 restaurants cater to tourists and locals. Orlando draws more than 43 million visitors annually, and visitors spend more than $20 billion. *Ka-ching!*

We began our tour of the city at the **Mennello Museum of American Folk Art**. The museum opened in 1998 on the banks of a lake in Loch Haven Park. Its focus is on preserving, exhibiting, and interpreting its permanent collection of paintings by Earl Cunningham. The Cunningham collection, donated by Marilyn and Michael Mennello of Winter Park, was opened to the public in 1998. The museum also offers special exhibitions, publications, and programs that celebrate traditional and contemporary American folk artists.

Earl Cunningham was born in Edgecomb, Maine, near Boothbay Harbor, in 1893. His love of the ocean defined both his life and his painting. He left home at 13 and supported himself as a tinker. He later became a seaman, traveled the East Coast, and worked as a chicken farmer in Georgia. He painted many of his works during that time.

In 1949, Cunningham settled in St. Augustine, where he opened a curio shop called The Over-Fork Gallery. He continued to paint, primarily landscapes of places he knew from Nova Scotia to Florida. He produced 450 works in his lifetime, 50 of which reside permanently in the museum. He advertised his paintings as "Not For Sale" and often refused to sell them, since he wanted to keep them together as a family. He was a bit of a nut.

A recluse, he eventually committed suicide. Since his death in 1977, Cunningham's work has received a great deal of attention and secured him a place as a major 20th-century American folk artist.

Close by is the **Orlando Museum of Art**.

And next door on Princeton Street is the **Orlando Science Center**, which offers 207,000 square feet of hands-on and interactive exhibits for all ages. Some of the favorites here are TechWorks, which reveals the secrets behind lasers; ShowBiz Science, which explains special effects and the latest in computer-generated imaging for the movies; BodyZone, which shows what your body does to food and what food does to your body; and Cosmic Tourist, which gives guests a tour of our solar system and details the inner workings of the earth.

The Henry P. Leu Gardens is primarily known for its camellia collection, which encompasses more than 2,000 specimens. You can take a 20-minute guided tour of the Leu House Museum. The restored late-19th-century home began as a Florida farmhouse. It is now listed on the National Register of Historic Places.

The property was originally deeded to David and Angeline Mizell in 1855. Their son, John Thomas Mizell, erected the farmhouse—a two-story frame structure with five rooms—in 1888.

Leu Gardens is primarily known for its camellia collection of over 2,000 specimens.

Duncan Clarkston Pell of New York purchased several parcels here in 1902, eventually putting together most of the current acreage. In 1906, John H. Woodward became the third owner of the property. It was he who completed the house as it stands today. After his wife's death in 1928, the estate went into trust. The home was rented out until 1936, when Harry P. Leu bought it.

Leu, a wealthy businessman, and his wife, Mary Jane, traveled the world and brought back exotic plants and 240 varieties of camellias. Leu had an intense interest in flowers and trees and beautifying Orlando. He was known as "the Johnny Appleseed of central Florida" because he gave away so many plants. During one of his trips, Leu discovered the Sasanqua camellia, which does not grow well in Florida. But after 10 years of cultivation and development, he achieved a pattern of success with his Snow on the Mountain, Cleopatra, and Rosa Sasanqua varieties, among others.

In 1961, the Leus deeded their property to the city with the stipulation that it remain a botanical garden.

The **Cultural Corridor** and the **Downtown Arts District** comprise a geographic area in downtown Orlando created to promote the arts, local artists, and the economic development of the downtown area. The district includes theaters, galleries, and artists' studios. For the lengthy list, contact the Orlando/Orange County Convention and Visitors Bureau.

A relatively new museum at 511 West South Street focuses on the contributions that Floridians of African-American descent have made to the fields of jazz and entertainment. The **Wells' Built Museum of African American History** contains artifacts and memorabilia such as instruments, musical scores, costumes, playbills, recordings, photographs, and other material from jazz pioneers. It is open Monday through Friday.

Though there are thousands of rooms in and around Orlando, you'll find few bed-and-breakfasts. **The Courtyard at Lake Lucerne**, tucked in an intimate garden setting within walking distance of shops and restaurants, is a collection of four historic homes from different eras. Guest rooms and suites are available in settings ranging from a grand 1893 painted lady to an Art Deco home. The painted lady, the **Dr. Phillips House**, is considered the crown jewel. This splendidly restored home has six of the loveliest rooms in the city; the rooms include king- or queen-sized beds and marble baths with whirlpools. The **Norment-Parry**, built in 1883, is the eldest sister. Four of her six lavishly furnished bedrooms have sitting rooms in the Victorian tradition; antiques are displayed throughout. The Southern-style sister is the **I. W. Phillips House**, which has the grace of Old Florida. It offers three suites, two with double tubs; a whirlpool is in the honeymoon suite. The sassy sister, **The Wellborn**, flaunts the popular Art Deco

The Norment-Parry is one of a quartet of affectionately re-stored inns in the Courtyard at Lake Lucerne near down-town Orlando.

style. All 15 uniquely decorated one-bedroom suites have a living room and a bath. Some come with an equipped kitchen. The honeymoon suite has a double whirlpool bath.

The one-of-a-kind **Holiday Inn Family Suites Resort** offers unmatched accommodations for families. First, it's imaginative. Second, it's de-signed for children of all ages. Although it is very close to Walt Disney World, it is a one-stop des-tination on 24 acres. Rooms range from Kidsuites and Cinemasuites to Sweetheart and Classic two-bedroom suites. Your day begins with a free break-fast and, when you're ready, a free shuttle to Disney. Kids have their own check-in where they receive a welcome bag of goodies. They also have their own train for rides around the property. The East Building has 500 suites, a zero-depth entry to a pool that will remind you of a water park, Ping-Pong, two whirlpools, a nine-hole miniature-golf course, and much more. The West Building has 300 adult-oriented suites, a lap pool, two whirlpools, Ping-Pong, and shuffleboard. Room

service is available. Between the two buildings are the LocoMotion Game Room, the Crossing (which offers family entertainment every night), the **Club Dining Car**, a general store, **Foodland Express**, a fitness center, and the **Carbooze Bar and Lounge**.

For an evening of upscale dining and accom-modations, try the **Walt Disney World Swan and Dolphin Hotel**. This resort in the center of Disney World offers luxurious rooms plus 14 restaurants ranging from the popular **Shula's Steakhouse** to the grand **Palio's**, an award-winning Italian bis-tro. No matter what your style, it's offered here: Japanese, American, Italian, steaks, seafood, burgers, sandwiches, Disney Character Dining, and a cafeteria open 24 hours a day. Guests can also enjoy tennis, beach volleyball, miniature golf, swimming pools, health clubs, and the rest of Disney. Adults can grab some time to themselves by sending the children to Camp Dolphin, a su-pervised program of arts, crafts, movies, and ar-cade games offered daily in the afternoon and evening.

Once inside a large theme park like this one at Universal Studios, it takes days to experience all the rides.

Looking for a place to shop? **Universal Studios CityWalk** is a 30-acre dining, shopping, and entertainment area featuring specialty shops, nightclubs, theaters, and theme restaurants. At **Universal Studios**, you can "ride the movies." At Universal's Islands of Adventure, you'll come to expect the unexpected in the five distinct island settings. **Old Town** is a retail and entertainment destination offering a wide variety of merchandise and fun for the whole family. Located at 5770 West Irlo Bronson Highway, it includes eight restaurants, 75 shops, and 15 amusement-park rides. **Pointe*Orlando**, located on International Drive, is a combination of more than 70 shopping, dining, and entertainment venues along open-air promenades.

Orlando's world-famous theme parks and family attractions offer everything from magic acts to roller coasters.

For a special treat for all of the family, you can swim with dolphins at **Discovery Cove**, located across from SeaWorld. Interacting with a bottlenose dolphin is just one of the several ex-periences that will stay with you for a lifetime. Besides its well-known dolphins, sharks, and polar bears, **SeaWorld** also offers rides.

Walt Disney World put Orlando on the major-attractions map. Cirque du Soliel, Disney-Quest, Animal Kingdom, Epcot, the Magic Kingdom, Disney-MGM Studios, Pleasure Island, Downtown Disney, and much more will keep you busy for days and days.

And lest you outdoorsmen forget, you're in the middle of lake country. Largemouth bass are teeming, even big'uns. Guides offer half-day and all-day trips for those looking for a lunker.

All of the following are in Orlando and use the 32821 zip code and 407 area code, except where noted.

ACCOMMODATIONS

Courtyard at Lake Lucerne—211 N. Lucerne Circle E., 32801; 800-444-5289 or 648-5188

Holiday Inn Family Suites Resort—14500 Continental Gateway; 800-387-KIDS or 387-KIDS; www.hifamilysuites.com

Maggie's Bed and Breakfast—314 E. Anderson St.; 425-9175

Swan and Dolphin Hotel—1200 Epcot Blvd., Lake Buena Vista, FL 32830; 934-3000

Things Worth Remembering Bed and Breakfast—2603 Coventry Ln., 34761; 800-484-3585 or 291-2127

Downtown Disney is a tiny part of 80,000 acres of entertainment, shopping, dining, and lodgings.

Thurston House Bed and Breakfast—851 Lake Ave., 32751; 800-843-2721 or 539-1911

Veranda Bed and Breakfast—115 N. Summerlin Ave., 32801; 800-420-6822 or 849-0321

 ATTRACTIONS

Discovery Cove—6000 Discovery Cove Way; 877-4-DISCOVERY

Guinness World Records Experience—8437 International Dr.; 248-8891

Harry P. Leu Gardens—1920 N. Forest Ave., 32803; 246-2620

Masters of Magic Show—8815 International Dr., 32819; 352-3456

Mennello Museum of American Folk Art—900 E. Princeton St., 32803; 246-4329

Old Town—5770 W. Irlo Bronson Hwy., 34747; 396-4888

Orange County Regional History Center—65 E. Central Blvd.; 897-6350

Orlando Museum of Art—2416 N. Mills Ave.; 896-4231

Orlando Science Center—777 E. Princeton St., 32803; 800-672-4386 or 514-2000

Pointe*Orlando—9101 International Dr., 32819; 248-2838

Ripley's Believe It or Not Odditorium—8201 International Dr., 32819; 363-4418

SAK Comedy Lab—398 W. Amelia St.; 648-0001

SeaWorld—7007 SeaWorld Dr.; 351-3600

Skycoaster of Orlando—5905 International Dr., 32819; 248-8449

Southern Ballet Theater—1111 N. Orange Ave.; 426-1733

Splashing Tail Charters—P.O. Box 720732, 32872; 739-0965

Universal Studios—1000 Universal Studios Plaza; 800-363-8000

Walt Disney World—3100 Bonnet Creek Dr., Lake Buena Vista FL 32830; 824-4321

Wells' Built Museum of African American History—511 W. South St.; 297-5790

Wet 'n' Wild—6200 International Dr., 32819; 800-992-9453 or 351-9453

 CAMPING

Disney's Fort Wilderness Resort and Campground—4510 N. Fort Wilderness Trail, Lake Buena Vista, FL 32830; 407-824-2900

DINING

Holiday Inn Family Suites Resort—14500 Continental Gateway; 800-387-KIDS or 387-KIDS

Livingston Street Café—400 W. Livingston St.; 843-6664

Palio's—Walt Disney World Swan Hotel, 1200 Epcot Resorts Blvd., Lake Buena Vista, FL 32830; 934-1609

Pirates Dinner Adventure—6400 Carrier Dr., 32819; 248-0590

Shula's Steakhouse—Walt Disney World Dolphin Hotel, 1500 Epcot Resorts Blvd., Lake Buena Vista, FL 32830; 934-4000

Sleuths Mystery Dinner Shows—7508 Universal Blvd., 32810; 363-1985

Walt Disney World Swan and Dolphin—1200 Epcot Blvd., Lake Buena Vista, 32830; 934-3000

EVENTS

First Saturday of each month—Downtown Arts Market

January—Zora Neale Hurston Festival of the Arts and Humanities

January—Camellia Show

April—Spring Band Concert

May—Spring Moon Stroll

September—Crealde Benefit

October—Fall Moon Stroll

November—Valencia Film Festival

November—Commemoration of Kristallnacht (Night of the Broken Glass)

FOR MORE INFORMATION

Orlando/Orange County Convention and Visitors Bureau—6700 Forum Dr., Suite 100; 800-551-0181 or 363-5872; or www.orlandoinfo.com

HIGHLIGHTS

FOREVER FLORIDA

GATORLAND

REPTILE WORLD SERPENTARIUM

FISHING

MEDIEVAL TIMES

Florida's many faces range from attractions designed to electrify and exhilarate you to quiet resorts for leisurely lounging like a lazy lizard. In between are as many faces as Medusa had snakes—more about that later.

Kissimmee puts you in the middle of Florida's range of attractions. Though the focus here is on heritage touring and eco-tourism, the town is just a jump away from Disney World, SeaWorld, Universal, and all those adrenaline junkie hangouts, and 40 miles from the coast. We found good lodging prices, great fishing, and, most importantly, a natural face in Kissimmee and St. Cloud.

Located in central Florida 10 minutes south of the Mouse, Kissimmee and St. Cloud offer visitors a glimpse into what remains of the "real Florida" in this part of the state. The towns have supported preservation efforts that offer visitors the chance to discover for themselves some of the area's remaining natural treasures.

A large part of the heritage around here is connected to the "cow-hunters," as Florida cowboys were known. These Cracker cowboys rounded up cattle that had been living in the wild since the Spanish conquistadors lost them back in the 1500s. By the time settlers and cow-hunters showed up, there were lots of wild cattle to be herded from the cypress swamps. Because the alligators were so thick, the cow-hunters would sacrifice the weaker cows to the hungry reptiles, crack their rawhide whips, and hustle the rest of the herd down the path before the gators came back for more.

Turn south off US 192 on to Bass Road to visit the **Osceola County Historical Society and Pioneer Enrichment Center**. Here, you'll find a small museum on 12 acres. You'll also see what kind of house these tough early Florida Crackers, who supposedly got their names from the whips they cracked, lived in. If you've always thought that all the real cowboys were out west, you'll have to admit that these guys truly qualified. The Crackers were herding cattle before the West was young. Even their dogs were tough, thinking nothing of plunging through the undergrowth, grabbing the massive, reticent cows by the nose, ear, or tail, and dragging them out.

The **Kissimmee Sports Arena**, also south of US 192, opens every Friday night for a rodeo. Visitors are invited to a banquet hall to tap their toes to a live band after the bull riding, barrel racing, and bronco busting ends.

The **Silver Spurs Rodeo**, ranked among the top and largest rodeos east of the Mississippi, is more than half-century old. Cowboys come to Kissimmee in February and October to try for the $100,000 purse.

Until the 1940s, cattle drives stopped traffic on US 192, the main thoroughfare—now nearing a half-dozen lanes—that runs between Kissimmee and Disney World. Speaking of Disney, as folks around here often do, Kissimmee might be called "Disney South"—way south. The Nature Conservancy owns and operates the 12,000-acre **Disney Wilderness Preserve**, located 12 miles south of Kissimmee. To reach it, go down Pleasant Hill Road (CR 531), located a half-mile west of Poinciana Boulevard. Turn on to Old Pleasant Hill Road. The entrance is a half-mile south on Scrub Jay Trail. Disney purchased the land for a theme park it never developed. It later donated the property to the Nature Conservancy.

You can search for wildflowers under the tall longleaf pines, or hike through a hammock of live oaks draped with Spanish moss on self-guided interpretive nature trails, or discover the tracks of bobcats and white-tailed deer, or listen to the waves gently lapping the shoreline of Lake Russell, or watch birds. Guide-led trail walks are offered on the first Saturday of the month from October to April. Some visitors like to take an off-road buggy tour to observe the native pine flatwoods and wetlands. The tours are offered on Sundays from September to June and on select Saturdays from January to March. The preserve opens daily except for major holidays.

While you're in the area, don't miss **Forever Florida**. This attraction began as a 1,200-acre cattle ranch more than 30 years ago. Since then, it has evolved into a 4,700-acre wilderness preserve, working cattle ranch, and petting zoo. Tours of the vast acreage take you down dusty trails on horseback, on a bike, or in an open-air Cracker coach with seats ten feet off the ground. Guides describe the nine ecosystems full of increasingly rare plant and animal species, from the Osceola turkey to the secretive Florida panther and wild hog. You can reach Forever Florida by going east from St. Cloud to Holopaw, turning south on US 441. You'll see it on the east (left) side of the highway after 7.5 miles.

For a close view of the local reptiles, try the renowned Gatorland, just north of Kissimmee on US 441, or Reptile World Serpentarium, located on US 192 in St. Cloud.

Gatorland has been a popular roadside attraction since 1947. We expected to see lots of big

When you see this gator mouth at Gatorland, be sure to go in and see the rest.

This gator's mouth moves quickly to claim wieners tossed in by visitors at Gatorland.

reptiles behind the gaping jaws of the giant green gator menacing the entrance at Gatorland. What we didn't expect to find were so many birds perched in the trees above them. It looked like a perilous choice of domicile at best. But as we soon learned, the gators extend the birds protection from all the other predators waiting to rob their nests. Of course, the gators don't do this from any sense of altruism. Rather, they exact a price from time to time. From tricolored herons to egrets, birds filled the trees, panting and fanning themselves in the heat. An elevated walkway lets you walk beside the birds, an excellent opportunity for photographers without an expensive, high-powered lens.

At Gatorland, you can feed the large reptiles. Tossing a handful of wieners gets the gators moving and allows you to take some action shots of them competing for food. Most of the time, they just loll about.

Reptile World Serpentarium occupies a white concrete-block building on US 192 in St. Cloud. Although George VanHorn works with glass be-

tween him and his audience, the action is still almost too close for comfort. Seeing a big, writhing, striking snake resist George's efforts to pin it at the neck, grab it by the head, and get it to bite the edge of a collecting flask to release its venom is enough to get you on your feet. Though he's been bitten many times, George says he has loved the work since he was a boy. The venom he collects is processed and shipped to research laboratories throughout the world.

We sat outside watching through the large glass windows as he prepared to milk an eight-foot king cobra. This snake got loose, its hood fully flared. George grabbed its tail and lifted it onto the table, where it struck a hand towel, wasting its venom. We jumped up, kicking over the

Looking for a nice place to hang around? Try Reptile World Serpentarium.

Boggy Creek Airboat Rides offer an exciting way to look at the Everglades.

bench we were sitting on, even though the glass wall was between us and the action. You don't get that kind of rush from a roller coaster.

You can see George milk the venom of cobras and other poisonous snakes from Tuesday through Sunday. You can also view more than 60 species from the reptile kingdom.

If you're in the mood for another kind of adrenaline fix, you can fly a World War II fighter-trainer at **Warbird Adventures**. Yes, you fly the plane. Whether you want an aerobatic adventure or a smooth sightseeing flight, you take the controls in the front seat, and an instructor teaches you everything about flying a piece of history. To reach Warbird Adventures, go north from US 192 to North Hoagland Boulevard.

Next door is the **Flying Tigers Warbird Restoration Museum**. Here, you can see restored World War II aircraft and vintage aircraft. Call and ask for a guided tour. It's a very interesting visit.

The Kissimmee area offers world-class largemouth bass fishing. Anglers can avoid the crowded hotels and motels lined up along US 192 between

Kissimmee and Disney World and stay at the **East Lake Fish Camp** along the shores of Lake Toho.

Here you'll find outfitters like the guys at **Boggy Creek Airboat Rides**, who'll take you for a closer look at Florida's wildlife than you ever imagined possible. A night tour of East Lake Tohopekaliga is just the thing to remind you that you're not in Kansas anymore, and that it's not Toto that all those sets of shining eyes are attached to. Daily airboat and parasail rides are offered for those who don't want to go out there at night. If you're worried about gators seeing you as bait being trolled along as you begin or end a parasail ride, be reassured. Your feet never touch the water with the rig they use. You take off and land from a platform on the back of the boat.

In case you're having trouble wrapping your tongue around all those syllables, Tohopekaliga—pronounced "Toe-hoe-pa-ka-lie-ga"—is popularly known as "Toho" among anglers. It is part of the Kissimmee chain of lakes, headwaters of the Everglades.

Pro angler Terry Segraves shows us what a little Lake Toho largemouth bass looks like. It lacked one pound of being a ten-pound bass.

Pro bass angler Terry Segraves lives in Kissimmee and fishes the Kissimmee chain year-round. The morning we fished together was hot and still, and it was only May. At dawn, we were photographing Terry with a nine-pound large-mouth bass. Nine-pounders aren't caught every day here, but they aren't rare by any means.

The lakes near Terry are East Toho, Cypress, Hatchineha, and Kissimmee. Thirty miles farther south is Okeechobee. These lakes average about eight feet in depth and have plenty of aquatic plants, islands, and alligators. Terry says the best season on Toho is the fall, when the bass are bulking up for their spawn, which occurs around January. But bass hit all year long in the Kissimmee chain.

Accommodations abound in Kissimmee and St. Cloud because the towns are so close to Disney and the other attractions. We stayed at **Wonder-land Inn** on South Orange Blossom Trail in Kissimmee, which boasts a AAA Three-Diamond rating. The inn opened in 1999. Owner Rosemarie O'Shaughnessy is more than delightful. Guests enjoy the country-garden setting and the 11 artistically appointed rooms with refrigerators and private baths; some have kitchenettes. The continental breakfast is elegant. The inn can arrange for "Romance on the Water," "Equestrian Florida Adventure," "Eagle Watching," "Sunrise Balloon Flight," and other special outings. An unusual bonus is the white squirrels on the property.

Medieval Times, located on US 192, or Irlo Bronson Memorial Highway, gives exciting dining a new slant. You enter a castle to enjoy a four-course medieval banquet while watching audacious knights on horses competing in tournament games such as jousting and sword fighting. There's much pageantry before the contest, including some amazing Andalusian horse feats. The jousting and

Talk about your unusual monuments. Look at this one in downtown Kissimmee composed of rocks from various states.

sword fights are real—choreographed, but real. The knights charge at full speed down the arena with lances lowered, and when they hit, splinters fly and a knight falls. The tournament eliminates all but two, who joust and then swing their swords, maces, or bolas. Sparks fly when they hit. The victorious knight parades around the arena displaying the winning colors. And the meal and tournament aren't all. This is a medieval fantasy world where you can spend hours. We were thoroughly entertained.

Or if you'd rather get off the main drag, you can head down Broadway to the real town of Kissimmee, where the dining is saner, if not better.

If you have time, take a walk around the downtown area. Kissimmee has the oldest continuously operating courthouse in the state. The old hanging tree lives on, too. At the very least, you should check out the Monument of the States, put together from rocks from around the country. It's fun and funky.

Be sure to contact the Kissimmee-St. Cloud Convention and Visitors Bureau for its *Guide to Eco-Heritage and Outdoor Recreation* booklet, as well as other tourist information.

All of the following are in Kissimmee and use the 34742 zip code and 407 area code, except where noted.

ACCOMMODATIONS

Wonderland Inn—3601 S. Orange Blossom Trail, 34746; 877-847-2477 or 847-2477

ATTRACTIONS

Boggy Creek Airboat Rides East—3702 Big Bass Rd., 34744; 348-4676

Boggy Creek Airboat Rides West—2001 E. Southport Rd., 34746; 933-5822

Capt. Bob's Lunker Bass Guide Service—4050 O'Berry Rd., 34746; 888-847-642 or 931-3118

Champion Pro Guide Services—2317 Emperor Dr., 34744; 888-715-7661 or 935-9344

Disney Wilderness Preserve—2700 Scrub Jay Trail, 34759; 935-0002

Florida Fishmasters Pro-Guide—3325 13th St., St. Cloud, FL 34769; 800-424-5090 or 892-5962

Flying Tigers Warbird Restoration Museum—231 N. Hoagland Blvd.; 933-1942

Forever Florida—4755 N. Kenansville Rd., St. Cloud, FL 34773; 888-957-9794

Gatorland—14501 S. Orange Blossom Trail, Orlando, FL 32837; 800-393-JAWS or 855-5496

Jay's Bass Bustin' Guide Service—2151 Underwood Ave., St. Cloud, FL 34771; 892-9582

Kissimmee Sports Arena—958 S. Hoagland Blvd., 34741; 933-0020

Osceola County Historical Society and Pioneer Enrichment Center—750 N. Bass Rd.; 396-8644

Reptile World Serpentarium—5705 E. Irlo Bronson Memorial Hwy., St. Cloud, FL 34771; 892-6905

Warbird Adventures—233 N. Hoagland Blvd., 34741; 870-7366

WayFun Kayak Adventures—1670 Sundance Dr., St. Cloud, FL 34771; 957-0071

CAMPING

Canoe Creek Campground—4101 Canoe Creek Rd., St. Cloud, FL 34772; 800-453-5268 or 892-7010

East Lake Fish Camp—3705 Big Bass Rd., 34744; 800-621-3848 or 348-2040

Floridian RV Resort—5150 Boggy Creek Rd., St. Cloud, FL 34771; 892-5171

Gator RV Resort—5755 E. Irlo Bronson Memorial Hwy., St. Cloud, FL 34771; 888-252-0020 or 892-8662

Great Oak RV Resort—4440 Yowell Rd., 34746; 396-9092

Kissimmee Campground and Mobile Home Park—2643 Alligator Ln., 34746; 396-6851

Kissimmee/Orlando KOA—4771 W. Irlo Bronson Memorial Hwy., 34746; 800-562-7791 or 396-2400

Lake Toho Resort and Red's Fish Camp—4715 Kissimmee Park Rd., St. Cloud, FL 34772; 892-8795

Merry 'D' Sanctuary—4261 Pleasant Hill Rd., 34746; 800-208-3434 or 870-0719

Orange Grove Campground—2425 Old Vineland Rd., 34746; 800-322-6746 or 396-6655

Osceola Mobile Park—2660 N. Orange Blossom Trail #80, 34744; 847-4690

Ponderosa RV Park—1983 Boggy Creek Rd., 34744; 847-6002

Richardson's Fish Camp—1550 Scotty's Rd., 34744; 846-6540

Sherwood Forest RV Resort—5300 W. Irlo Bronson Memorial Hwy., 34746; 800-548-9981 or 396-7431

Southport Park—2001 E. Southport Rd., 34746; 933-5822

DINING

Arabian Nights Dinner Theater—6225 W. Irlo Bronson Hwy.; 396-1787

Black Angus—2001 W. Vine St.; 846-7117

Capone's Dinner and Show—4740 US 192 W.; 397-2378

Cattleman's Steakhouse—2948 Old Vineland Rd.; 397-1888

Fat Boys Bar-B-Q—1606 W. Vine St.; 847-7098

Fat Boys Bar-B-Q—2912 13th Street, St. Cloud, FL; 892-4400

Lucky Duck Café—2791 Poinciana Blvd.; 396-8300

Medieval Times—4510 Irlo Bronson Memorial Hwy.; 239-8666

E V E N T S

January—Kissimmee Sunshine Regional Chili Cookoff

March—Battle at Narcoossee Mill

April—St. Cloud Spring Fling and Florida State Offshore Boat Championships

April—Jazzfest Kissimmee

October—Silver Spurs Rodeo

October—Kissimmee-St. Cloud Anglers Challenge

October—Fall Festival

November—Anglers Challenge Lake Toho Pro-Am

December—St. Cloud Art Festival

December—Anglers Challenge Big Fish Open

F O R   M O R E   I N F O R M A T I O N

Kissimmee-St. Cloud Convention and Visitors Bureau— P.O. Box 422007; 800-327-9159 or 847-5000; www.floridakiss.com

FANTASY OF FLIGHT

CYPRESS GARDENS

CHALET SUZANNE

BOK TOWER AND GARDENS

FISHING

Polk County, sitting in the center of the state among so many lakes, presents the outdoor enthusiast with many opportunities to fish, canoe, and photograph wildlife. There are a couple of attractions that draw millions here and are familiar names to most people: Bok Tower and Cypress Gardens. We'll introduce you to some other places we're sure you'll like.

Polk is the fourth-largest county in the state, and the interesting places are spread out. Let's start in the northern part of the county along I-4.

Our first stop is at **Fantasy of Flight** in Polk City, located about halfway between Orlando and Tampa. Here, you'll find a large collection of vintage and one-of-a-kind aircraft. Outside a large restoration hangar is an airfield containing two of the only remaining airworthy B26s in the world and a Short Sunderland, the largest operational flying boat in existence. It was used for antisubmarine patrols in World War II. Fantasy of Flight takes visitors back to World War I, aviation's golden era during the 1920s and 1930s, and World War II. Among its attractions are the Ford Tri-Motor featured in *Indiana Jones and the Temple of Doom*, a replica of the *Spirit of St. Louis*, a Japanese Zero, a Corsair F4U, a B-24J Liberator, and a P-51 Mustang.

You can see the history of aviation in one of the hangars at Fantasy of Flight.

From Polk City, go southwest on I-4 and turn south to Lakeland.

You'll find a superb place to stay at the **Terrace Hotel**, a fastidiously restored, elegant hotel a couple of blocks off the town square. The restaurant and bar are appealing in looks and taste. You're close to other restaurants, antique shopping, and a couple of notable attractions.

At **Florida Southern College** on Lake Hollingsworth Drive is the largest collection of Frank Lloyd Wright architecture in the world. A self-guided tour directs you to the 12 completed "Child of the Sun" structures, including a chapel, seminar buildings, and a library. In true Frank Lloyd Wright style, part of one of the buildings caved in during construction and had to be repaired. Wright's use of native materials, topography, and environment are inspirational, if difficult to maintain. To hurry the formation of a patina on the copper being used in construction, he had the workmen urinate on it. A dean of the college once called Wright to tell him the roof was leaking on his desk. Wright, not one to suffer criticism, told the dean to move his desk and hung up.

You'll find interesting displays at the **Frank Lloyd Wright Visitor Center**. You can pick up a walking-tour guide at the visitor center Tuesday through Sunday. The campus is open year-round, but some buildings may be locked when school is not in session.

From the campus, you can stroll to the **Polk Museum of Art**, located in Lakeland's downtown historic district. A free admission policy has been in effect since the museum opened in 1966. It houses nine galleries on two floors, including an outdoor sculpture garden and a permanent gallery that is home to an extensive Pre-Columbian art collection. The museum's two main galleries display traveling exhibits of historic and contemporary work. Upstairs are the museum's collection and student works.

Next, we'll head east to Cypress Gardens, located south of Winter Haven. From Lakeland, go south on US 98 and turn east on CR 540. Next door to Cypress Gardens is the **Central Florida Visitors and Convention Bureau**, the place to get maps, brochures, and other information about what the county has to offer.

Cypress Gardens is a 200-acre tropical theme park noted for its beautiful plants and flowers and its world-famous water-skiing shows. Florida's first theme park, it opened in 1936. It contains 8,000 species of plants from 90 countries. Some 400,000 annuals are added seasonally each year. The gardens are in full bloom during March and April but are beautiful year-round. During our tour with horticulturist Joe Freeman, we learned that the gardens were laid out through the viewfinder of a camera, in order to plan color from top to bottom. The original gardens showcase bougainvillea, orchids, gardenias, 26 different types of

A ride in Cypress Gardens takes you sky-high for a 360-degree view of the gardens, lakes, and countryside.

bananas, 30 different types of palms, and thousands of other brilliantly colored plants along the edge of canals and Lake Eloise.

You can cruise Lake Eloise on a paddle-wheel boat, watch European circus acts and professional ice-skating shows, or grab the nearest bench and enjoy the surroundings. The butterfly conservatory shows off 30 to 50 species, most from Florida and South America. Butterflies usually live only about two weeks, depending on nectar sources.

We witnessed several water-skiing world records the day we visited. Many were daredevil efforts. After setting a record, one of the acrobatic skiers, Steve Bates, thanked Winter Haven Hospital, Advil, and workmen's comp.

The park is open daily. Plan on spending a full day here.

From Cypress Gardens, go east on CR 540, turn south on US 27, and then head east on Chalet Suzanne Road to **Chalet Suzanne**.

This is the site of a famous Florida boom/bust/boom story. Carl and Bertha Hinshaw moved to Lake of the Hills during the boom days of the 1920s to develop a lovely upscale community with J. L. Kraft. But soon after construction began, the Great Depression hit. Kraft pulled out of the deal. Then Carl died of pneumonia, leaving Bertha with the property, no money, and two children to support.

She put out a sign offering lodging to tourists. The first family showed up a few weeks later. They enjoyed their stay so much that they decided to come back and to tell their friends. A short time later, Mr. and Mrs. Duncan Hines were touring Florida and discovered Chalet Suzanne. They subsequently listed the place in a Christmas-card catalog of wonderful places to stay and dine on the way to and from Florida. That cata-

Chalet Suzanne's Romaine Soup is so good it went to the moon.

log eventually became *Adventures in Good Eating*, one of the first travel/leisure books in the United States.

The Hinshaw family still owns the resort and its Mobile Four-Star restaurant, along with a soup cannery that began in Carl Junior's garage when guests pleaded to take home his signature Romaine Soup. The soup was so good that *Apollo 15* pilot James Irwin requested it for a moon mission. Romaine Soup is served with every meal. Thirteen unique gourmet soups and three sauces developed by Carl Hinshaw, Jr., are sold nationwide and shipped directly from the cannery.

Chalet Suzanne is listed on the National Register of Historic Places. It has five dining rooms, 30 guest rooms, a landing strip for airplanes, a gift shop, the Ceramic Salon, the Antiques Chapel, and the soup cannery. It has been selected by Uncle Ben's Rice as one of the top 10 country inns and has been a Florida Trend Golden Spoon Winner for 30 consecutive years.

Our next destination is **Bok Tower and Gardens**. Go east on Chalet Suzanne Road, turn south

Bok Tower and Gardens were a gift to the people of the United States from Netherlands-born Pulitzer-prize-winner Edward Bok.

on CR 17, and then drive east on Burns Avenue (CR 17A).

Editor and Pulitzer Prize-winning author Edward William Bok was born in the Netherlands in 1863 and came to the United States at age six. In 1886, he founded the Bok Syndicate Press, which led to his editorship of *Ladies' Home Journal* in 1889. Under his management, the magazine became one of the most successful and influential

in the United States. After 30 years as editor, he retired in 1919. A year later, he published *The Americanization of Edward Bok*, which won the Gold Medal of the Academy of Political and Social Science and the Pulitzer Prize for best autobiography. A noted philanthropist, he created the American Foundation—later known as the Bok Tower Gardens Foundation—in 1925. He died in Lake Wales in 1930.

Bok Tower and Gardens, a National Historic Landmark, was his gift to the American people. In 1928, he created a 205-foot carillon tower constructed of Georgia marble and St. Augustine coquina. It stands along Lake Wales Ridge on top of Iron Mountain, 324 feet above sea level. Within the tower are 60 bronze bells weighing from half a pound to 12 tons. Recitals are given daily. Frederick Law Olmstead, the famous landscape designer of New York's Central Park and the gardens of the Biltmore Estate in Asheville, North Carolina, designed the serene 157-acre woodland gardens surrounding Bok Tower.

While you're here, you might enjoy touring neighboring **Pinewood Estate**. A word of warning: don't be alarmed at the extreme friendliness of the squirrels. They seem to get a kick out of running up your legs and sitting on your shoulder until you feed them. This is a wildlife sanctuary and an excellent place to get close-up pictures of many critters, including swans in the reflecting pool.

Pinewood Estate, a 20-room Mediterranean Revival villa completed in 1929, lies on eight acres adjacent to Bok Tower and Gardens. First called El Retiro, this was the winter home of C. Austin Buck, vice president of Bethlehem Steel. The house was situated to give views through the surrounding pine trees. Pinewood changed hands several times over the years before the Bok Tower Gardens Foundation acquired it in 1970. Guided tours are offered daily from October through mid-May. A six-week special event called Christmas at Pinewood starts annually the day after Thanksgiving.

If you prefer to spend your time with nature, you might want to pay a visit to **Lake Kissimmee State Park**, located in the northeastern portion of the county. Here, you'll have the opportunity to see more than 50 species of endangered, threatened, and rare animals. Nine distinctive plant communities are found in the park.

Bird watchers will be pleased to discover the 42-acre **Audubon Nature Center** in Winter Haven. From the trails at the nature center, you can observe more than 140 species of birds, 15 species of mammals, 21 species of reptiles, 10 species of amphibians, 26 species of butterflies, 12 species of dragonflies, and 150 species of plants. Among the birds at the center are green-backed herons, red-tailed hawks, red-bellied woodpeckers, and bald eagles.

You'll find nearly 40 percent of Florida's native vertebrate wildlife (excluding saltwater fish) represented in the **Green Swamp Wildlife Management Area**, which occupies parts of Lake, Polk, and Sumter Counties. This place has suffered few intrusions from the industrialized world, leaving the habitat truly natural and undisturbed. The diverse vegetation allows for an abundant wildlife community. Within the Green Swamp, you may canoe or fish in five rivers, bike abandoned railroad corridors that have been converted to cycling trails, or simply sit back and take your pleasure.

Tiger Creek Preserve is a 4,500-acre wilderness located east of Lake Wales. Alligators and such rare creatures as the flat-footed scrub lizard and the friendly scrub jay roam freely. The preserve has hardwood swamps and hammocks, sand pines, scrub oak, pine flatwoods, pygmy fringe trees, and sand hills. This is strictly a nature preserve and therefore has no picnic or restroom facilities.

Now, if it's fishing you want, the area's 600 freshwater lakes ought to tell you you're in the right place. As Captain Reno Alley, owner of **Memory Makin' Guides**, says, "We make fishing dreams come true."

And that's true. We fished with Alley for less than five hours, and we boated more than 100 pounds of Florida-strain largemouth bass. We met Alley before dawn at Walk-in-Water Lake (Lake Weohyakapka). Before the sun was up, we landed a five-pounder—first cast, too!

His busiest season is January through March, when the big boys bite. Alley averages hauling in a 10-pounder every three days. If you prefer using artificial baits, March and April are the best months.

All of the following use the 863 area code, except where noted.

 ACCOMMODATIONS

Chalet Suzanne—3800 Chalet Suzanne Dr., Lake Wales, FL 33859; 800-433-6011 or 676-6011

G. V. Tillman House Bed and Breakfast—301 E. Sessoms Ave., Lake Wales, FL 33853; 800-488-3315 or 676-5499

Highland Park Hills Country Inn—1650 S. Highland Park Dr., Lake Wales, FL 33853; 888-676-8281 or 676-8281

Noah's Ark—312 Ridge Manor Dr., Lake Wales, FL 33853; 800-346-1613 or 941-676-1613

Terrace Hotel—329 E. Main St., Lakeland, FL 33801; 888-644-8400 or 688-0800

 ATTRACTIONS

Audubon Nature Center—115 Lameraux Rd., Winter Haven, FL 33884; 324-7304

Bok Tower and Gardens—1151 Tower Blvd., Lake Wales, FL 33853; 676-1408

Cypress Gardens— P.O. Box 1, Cypress Gardens, FL 33884; 676-1408

Fantasy of Flight—1400 Broadway Blvd., Polk City, FL 33868; 984-3500

Frank Lloyd Wright Visitor Center—111 Lake Hollingsworth Dr., Lakeland, FL 33801; 680-4110

Lake Kissimmee State Park—14248 Camp Mack Rd., Lake Wales, FL 33853; 696-1112

Memory Makin' Guides—800-749-CAST or 635-6499

Polk Museum of Art—800 E. Palmetto St., Lakeland, FL 33801; 688-7743

Tiger Creek Preserve—225 E. Stuart Ave., Lake Wales, FL 33853; 678-1551

 CAMPING

A-OK Campground—6925 Thornhill Rd., Winter Haven, FL 33880; 294-9091

Bullock's Landing—1011 Thompson Nursery Rd., Lake Wales, FL 33853; 676-0000

Camp 'n Aire Campground—3531 US 27 N., Lake Wales, FL 33853; 638-1015

Cherry Pocket Fishing Resort—3100 Canal Rd., Lake Wales, FL 33853; 439-2031

East Haven RV Park—4320 Dundee Rd. (CR 542),Winter Haven, FL 33884; 324-2624

Grape Hammock Fish Camp—1400 Grape Hammock Rd., Lake Wales, FL 33853; 692-1500

Holiday Travel Park of Cypress Gardens—7400 Cypress Gardens Blvd., Winter Haven, FL 33884; 800-858-7275 or 324-7400

Lake Wales Campground—3430 US 27 S., Lake Wales, FL 33853; 638-9011

Peace Creek RV Park—7000 US 27 N., Lake Wales, FL 33853; 439-5205

Thomas Landing—3952 Sam Keen Rd., Lake Wales, FL 33853; 692-1121

DINING

Antiquarian Restaurant and Bay Street Gallery—211 Bay St., Lakeland, FL 33801; 682-1059

Chalet Suzanne—3800 Chalet Suzanne Dr., Lake Wales, FL 33859; 800-433-6011

Harry's Seafood Bar and Grille—101 N. Kentucky Ave., Lakeland, FL 33801; 686-2228

LekaricA Restaurant—1650 S. Highland Park Dr., Lake Wales, FL 33853; 888-676-8281 or 676-8281

Terrace Hotel—329 E. Main St., Lakeland, FL 33801; 888-644-8400 or 688-0800

EVENTS

January—Florida Citrus Festival, Winter Haven

January—Camellia Celebration, Bok Tower and Gardens

April—Sun 'n Fun Fly-In, Lakeland

May—Spring Flower Festival, Cypress Gardens

October—Pioneer Days, Lake Wales

November—Festival of Trees, Winter Haven

December—Garden of Lights, Cypress Gardens

FOR MORE INFORMATION

Central Florida Visitors and Convention Bureau—P.O. Box 61, Cypress Gardens, FL 33884; 800-828-7655 or 298-7565; www.sunsational.org

HIGHLIGHTS

AMELIA ISLAND MUSEUM OF HISTORY

FORT CLINCH STATE PARK

FERNANDINA BEACH'S HISTORIC DISTRICT

AMELIA ISLAND PLANTATION

It's not large—two miles by 13 miles, about the size of Manhattan—but Amelia Island has much to offer. Its long, rich history reaches back to the colonization of the New World. Today, it provides visitors with deluxe accommodations, dining, and relaxation. Visitors are sure to enjoy the delightful guided walking tour of Fernandina Beach, the island's only city.

Let's start by getting you there. If you are going to Amelia Island from the west, travel I-10 to Baldwin, turn north on US 310, and take FL A1A to the island and Fernandina Beach. From I-95, take Exit 129, turn east on to FL A1A, travel 15 miles, and cross the Intracoastal Waterway on to Amelia Island. As they say around here, Amelia Island is easy to get to but hard to leave.

Your first stop should be the **Amelia Island Museum of History**, located at 233 South Third Street in Fernandina Beach. Here, you'll get a feel for what transformed this once-turbulent island into a serene, dignified community touted as "the Rest of Florida." The museum is housed in a renovated 1935 county jail, where 35 docents and 135

volunteers keep Amelia Island's history alive. It is open Monday through Friday. If you have a couple of hours to learn more about the town, ask for a conducted walking tour of the historic district. This adds depth and appreciation for what this city and island have gone through, taking you up Historic Centre Street and into the Silk Stocking District presenting many great historical figures who influenced the architecture and business here. These tours can be modified for children.

Amelia is sometimes called "the Island of Eight Flags." In the museum, you'll hear about the eight flags that flew over the island. Indeed, this is the only place in the United States to undergo eight occupations. It is said the French visited, the Spanish developed, the English named, and the Americans tamed the island.

The French visited from 1562 to 1565. The first recorded European in the area, Jean Ribault, landed May 3, 1562, and named the place the Isle de Mai.

The Spanish landed in 1565. Pedro Menendez defeated the French and founded St. Augustine that year. The Spanish dominion lasted until 1763, during which the island was called Santa Maria, after the Santa Maria Mission.

The English destroyed the colony and mission in 1702. James Oglethorpe renamed the island for the daughter of King George II, Princess Amelia. Oglethorpe established a fort, only to abandon it in 1742.

From 1763 to 1783, the island became known as Egmont for John Percival, the earl of Egmont. He never set foot on the island but owned it under a land grant.

American forces invaded in 1777 and 1778. After the Revolution, under the Second Treaty of Paris, Britain ceded Florida back to Spain. In 1811, the Spanish post here received the name Fernandina in honor of King Ferdinand VII of Spain.

The Spanish experienced three breaks in their ownership.

The first came on March 17, 1812, when the patriots of St. Mary's, Georgia, overthrew them and raised a flag that read, *"Salus Populi Lex Suprema,"* ("the safety of the people is the supreme law"). It flew for one day before being replaced by the United States flag. The Spanish acquired the help of Seminole Indians and freed slaves to retake the island and raise their flag again on May 16, 1813.

Spain completed construction of the wood-and-earth Fort San Carlos on a bluff on the northwestern end of the island in 1816. It was captured in June 1817 by Sir Gregor MacGregor, a Scottish-born general turned South American soldier of fortune, who raised his Green Cross of Florida—a green St. George cross on a white field. Only one shot was fired during the takeover, and it was an accident. MacGregor and most of his men left in September 1817 to continue fighting the Spanish.

Pirate Luis Aury sailed into Fernandina Harbor two days after MacGregor's departure and raised the Mexican flag over Fort San Carlos on September 21. It happened to be the only flag he had handy, and it waved only a short time also.

Without a shot being fired, United States troops landed in December 1817 and held the island in trust for Spain until 1821, when Spain ceded Florida to the United States. The Stars and Stripes was hoisted up the fort's pole.

In 1847, the fort was rebuilt and named for General Duncan Lamont Clinch, an important figure in Florida's Seminole Wars of the 1830s.

Rebs occupied it when the War Between the States began in 1861. General Robert E. Lee ordered withdrawal the following year, leaving the fort to the Yankees, who were sailing in with 28 gunboats. Old Glory was the eighth flag to fly over the island.

Operations at the fort were severely reduced following the Civil War. Eventually, it was abandoned. In 1898, the fort was reactivated for several months during the Spanish-American War, after which it was abandoned again until 1926, when it was sold. In 1935, the state of Florida purchased the forsaken fort and 256 surrounding acres. The Civilian Conservation Corps constructed buildings and developed a park here, which was opened to the public in 1938. The Coast Guard used the fort during World War II.

Today, the 1,121-acre **Fort Clinch State Park**, located east of downtown, has 8,400 feet of shoreline along the sound and 4,000 feet of Atlantic coast. The western side is an extensive estuarine marsh system. The park offers picnicking, camping, saltwater fishing, shelling, hiking, nature study, and interpretive programs. The fort has cannons, jail cells, a blacksmith shop, and a hospital.

Fort Clinch endured several abandonments and reconstructions to become a center for re-enactments and a state park used by campers, hikers, bikers, and anglers.

Reenactments are held the first weekend of every month. The park offers Amelia Island's only camping facility. Sixty-two family campsites are located in different areas, from shaded hammocks to near the beach. The fort and visitor center are open daily. Pets are permitted in designated areas only. Guide dogs for the deaf and blind are welcome.

While you're in town, be sure to check out the waterfront. Fernandina has the deepest natural harbor in the southeastern United States—17 feet at low tide. Spanish galleons displaced about 15 feet of water and had a life expectancy of about five years because worms and mollusks ate through the wood. The Spanish learned that the rivers here contain tannic acid, which cleansed the hulls and added a few years of life to the vessels, which took two and a half years to build. In the 1800s, there were as many as 400 ships here at one time. A little girl wrote in her diary that she walked from gangplank to gangplank on the ships from Fernandina to Cumberland Island, more than a mile away.

In the 1850s, the town of Fernandina was moved south about a mile to become the terminus for Florida's first cross-state railroad. The new site allowed for a shorter railroad trestle to be built over the Amelia River. Organized by Senator David Levy Yulee, the railroad ran 114 miles from Fernandina to Cedar Key. The efforts of Yulee, the first Jewish United States senator, gained Florida admission to the union as the 27th state. In January 1861, it became the third state to adopt the Ordinance of Secession. Yulee served in the Confederate Congress from 1861 to 1865.

Fernandina Beach's historic district retains the evidence of the town's greatest period of prosperity, which ran from 1875 to 1900. Northern tourists flocked here via steamers to stay in two elegant hotels. The shipping of lumber, phosphate, indigo, and naval stores boomed.

Following the turn of the 20th century, tourism went south after Fernandina Beach declined an offer from Henry Flagler to build one of his hotels here. Bypassing Amelia Island, Flagler built hotels south along the Atlantic coast, taking tourism with him.

The long decline left Fernandina Beach too poor to tear down its old buildings. This was not thought to be a blessing until the last couple of decades, when the town's second golden period began. Today, Fernandina Beach is richly blessed with a 50-block historic district with more than 250 structures on the National Register.

Joe Anderson, docent with the Amelia Island Museum of History, gave us the grand tour of Fernandina Beach. Pointing out a water fountain in front of the chamber of commerce at the end of Centre Street near the docks, he said Mrs. W. B. C. Duryee, wife of Union commandant at Fort Clinch, gave the fountain to the city to be

When Mrs. W.B.C. Duryee gave this fountain to the city, it was meant only for horses and dogs because she didn't like people.

used by horses and dogs. She preferred the company of animals to that of humans—and the people of Amelia Island preferred the company of animals to her. The fountain, which gained a human water spigot some years later, still functions today.

What is now Centre Street served as an Indian path 4,000 years ago. Today, the street connects the river with the Atlantic and is the focus of down-

town. Streets north and south of Centre are alphabetical. For example, the streets south of Centre are named for trees—Ash, Beech, Cedar, etc.

You can pick up a brochure for a walking or driving tour of Fernandina Beach at the **Depot of Florida**, which houses the chamber of commerce. The brochures, though not as informative as the Amelia Island Museum of History's docent tour, will take you to a number of historic buildings.

One of the highlights is the **Palace Saloon**, Florida's oldest. Built in 1878, this former haunt of the Vanderbilts, DuPonts, Rockefellers, and Carnegies still serves its Potent Pirate's Punch and other spirits from a 40-foot hand-carved mahogany bar designed by Adolphus Busch of Anheuser-Busch fame. A well-known bartender, Uncle Charlie, worked here from about 1900 to his death in 1960. He challenged patrons to land quarters on the décolletage of either of the two carved ladies' busts in the bar. At the end of the night, he would sweep up his quarters. His ghost is reported to protect the quarters he missed col-

Fernandina Beach's Centre Street is a step back in time and step in the right direction. It's lined with unique boutiques, fine dining, and history.

lecting from behind the bar.

During Prohibition, it took more than two years to deplete the Palace's supply of spirits. It became the first hard-liquor bar in Florida to sell Coca-Cola.

Carnegie heir Florence Nightingale "Floss" Carnegie Perkins tried unsuccessfully to buy the murals on the walls to the left as you enter the saloon for a home on nearby Cumberland Island, Georgia. It is reported she left in a tiff when denied her desires. She also visited the local jail asking to see where the prisoners were held. She commented that the décor was awful. She offered to have the rooms painted and furnished. The sheriff accepted her generosity. She then asked if he knew why she was doing this. He didn't. She explained that her son was intermittently arrested for staying too long at the Palace Saloon, and she wanted him to be comfortable on such occasions.

The grand Victorian homes in the historic district are adorned with opulent turrets, gables, bays, gingerbread, and fish-scale decorations. The buildings along Centre Street house an eclectic collection of antique, curio, gift, book, clothing, and specialty stores. A walk along the street provides a taste of today mixed with the flavor of yesterday. **Ship's Lantern** and **Corner Copia** have a sidewalk aquarium. The fish look up for handouts that signs say you should not give.

The island has a superb array of restaurants that will please any palate. From intimate to waterfront, from rustic to brick courtyards, the settings are as varied as the food. We had a splendid feast at **Horizon's Continental Cuisine**, located at Eighth and Ash Streets. Salads that make a meal, rare tuna, and fine beef left us with no room for dessert. Horizon's is open Monday through Saturday.

Outdoor activities are as varied as the restaurants.

Golfers can swing atop bluffs overlooking the Atlantic or from the marshes along the Intracoastal Waterway.

Forty tennis courts are available day and night. **Amelia Island Plantation** holds the Bausch & Lomb Women's Tennis Championships each April.

Jogging along the beach will give your legs a stretch. Bird-watching will keep your eyes very busy. Opportunities for kayaking, horseback riding, sailing, and aerial tours also abound.

Fishermen ply the Amelia River, Cumberland Sound, and the Atlantic Ocean for speckled trout, striped bass, redfish, drum, sheepshead, flounder, whiting, Spanish mackerel, dolphin, kingfish, grouper, tuna, and pompano.

We fished Egan Creek for sea trout, redfish, and flounder with Captain Ben Evans, owner of **Hot Ticket Charters**, and Pat McSweeney, both from Jacksonville. In sheltered waters, Captain Ben uses his flats skiff. Back in the rivers and creeks, he uses casting lures, live bait, and fly rod. When using his larger boat, he fishes primarily with bait for black drum, cobia, large sharks, tarpon, barracuda jacks, king mackerel, Spanish mackerel, bluefish, whiting, sea bass, sheepshead, and dozens of other species, depending on the season. Captain Ben is a lifelong fisherman and naturalist. His first home was here on Amelia Island, where he learned to fish as a boy. He has a Coast Guard Offshore Masters License. He enjoys teaching adults and kids the art of fishing and enjoying nature. He offers customized nature tours based on what you want to see. Dolphins, wild horses, alligators, and birds are just a few of the possibilities. Your trip could include historical mansions, a sunset cruise, or beachcombing on deserted islands. Allow at least an hour and a half for your tour. Longer trips might include a tour all the way around Cumberland or Amelia Island.

Fletcher Avenue, running parallel to the Atlantic Ocean, provides access to the beaches. There are nearly 30 access points, each marked with signs.

People walking on the Atlantic beaches sometimes find Megalodon teeth, especially after the intermittent dredging of the submarine channel to Kings Bay Naval Base, north of the island. These teeth, as large as your hand, came from the mouth of the world's largest shark, ancestor of the great white shark. Modern sharks shed about 30,000 teeth in their lifetime. Shark teeth can be found inland where the seas ran high between glaciations.

The **Amelia Island Lighthouse**, the oldest structure on the island, is located east of Fernandina Beach. It sits 107 feet above sea level. The lighthouse was built in 1838 using materials salvaged from the discontinued Cumberland Island Lighthouse, about three miles north in Georgia. A new cupola was added in 1881, raising the height of the tower to 58 feet. Located at the mouth of the St. Marys River, the tower is in a residential area. Unfortunately, the only way to get near it is through private property. It is not open to the public, and its future is in debate.

You'll find an abundance of places to stay on the island.

The **Fairbanks House Bed and Breakfast** is unique even among Fernandina's historic Victorians. Guests at this 1885 creation of famed architect Robert Schuyler are surrounded by luxury. Its grounds cover an entire acre in the heart of the 50-block historic district. Listed on the National Register of Historic Places, the four-story Italianate villa is adorned with dormers, bay windows, massive chimneys, balustrade balconies,

Much of Fernandina's rich history is told through the architecture of places such as the Fairbanks House Bed and Breakfast, which was built during the island's first Golden Years.

porches, and a fifteen-foot tower. Legend has it that one of the Fairbanks descendants stood in the tower and watched the 1901 Jacksonville fire 50 miles away. Under the 12-foot ceilings are polished heart-of-pine floors, a carved Honduran mahogany staircase, Eastlake furniture, and French and English antiques. Each of the inn's guest rooms, suites, and cottages has a private bath. Guests love the queen- and king-sized canopy or four-poster beds and the "magic" electric fireplaces that burn with no heat for romantic viewing and heat when there's a chill. Cable television and telephones are provided in each room. The inn's three cottages are favorites of guests for their genteel country charm. This 10-room, 8,000-square-foot mansion, once called "Fairbanks' Folly" because of its opulent excesses, is operated by Bill and Theresa Hamilton. Wait until you taste Theresa's breakfasts! She calls the inn "Camp Fairbanks" because it's where you camp when you return from your outings. Theresa or Bill will make reservations for you on the Voyager Ventures schooner or other attractions. Bicycles are at the ready for you to peddle around town.

Florida House Inn, the state's oldest surviving tourist hotel, was built in 1857. This authentically restored Florida Vernacular estate epitomizes Amelia Island's golden age of tourism. Among its guests were General Ulysses S. Grant, the Carnegies, the Rockefellers, and Jose Marti, who plotted the Cuban War for Independence (1895-98) from his suite. An eavesdropper heard and reported the scheme, which led to the demise of the revolution. Originally, the inn had 25 rooms and no plumbing. It has since been renovated to 14 rooms and one suite, all with private baths. All meals are served boardinghouse style, just like the old days, when guests sat together at long tables.

Among the 10 bed-and-breakfasts on the island are the **Bailey House**, an 1895 Queen Anne; the **Hoyt House**, a 1905 replica of the Rockefellers' Jekyll Island cottage; the **Amelia Island Williams House**, built in 1856; and **Elizabeth Pointe Lodge**, a Nantucket-style house on the Atlantic.

The **Ritz-Carlton**, one of the island's most luxurious hotels, is a AAA Five-Diamond resort. This oceanfront retreat has 449 guest rooms, including several spacious suites and such amenities as twice-daily maid service, plush terry robes, and balconies with breathtaking ocean views. Guests can swim in either the outdoor or the indoor pool, relish a workout in the fitness center, or indulge themselves at the spa.

The new **Hampton Inn and Suites**, located just across the road from the marina, has 122 rooms. The lobby features a winding staircase, a fireplace, trays of homemade cookies, and a comfortable sitting area. Guests enjoy a complimentary buffet breakfast. The amenities include a gift shop and an exercise room. Some rooms offer whirlpools, fireplaces, and balconies. The inn is conveniently located within walking distance of shops, restaurants, taverns, and historical attractions.

Amelia Island Plantation, a AAA Four-Diamond resort on the southern end of Amelia Island, offers 660 guest accommodations ranging from deluxe hotel rooms to oceanfront penthouses. Opportunities for recreation here include 54 holes of championship golf, an award-winning tennis program, seven miles of nature trails, biking, basketball, nature programs for children and adults, and a 200-yard boardwalk over the salt marsh. The 1,350-acre property overlooks the Atlantic on the east and the Intracoastal Waterway on the west. Included in that acreage is Drummond Point Park, an ideal site for birders and Walkers Landing, which features a midden, or Indian shell mound, used centuries ago as a waste site or burial ground.

All in all, there is much to see and do on

Amelia Island Plantation, known for its luxury lodging, fine dining, and championship golfing, also offers nature programs for its guests.

Amelia Island. Plan to spend several days visiting the highlights. But be forewarned that some people fall in love with the island and stay much longer.

From Amelia Island, FL A1A leads south toward Jacksonville.

All of the following are in Fernandina Beach and use the 32034 zip code and 904 area code, except where noted.

ACCOMMODATIONS

Addison House—614 Ash St.; 800-943-1604 or 277-1604

Amelia House Bed, Breakfast, and Sail—222 N. Fifth St.; 800-980-3629 or 321-1717

Amelia Island Plantation—3000 First Coast Hwy., 32035; 800-874-6878 or 491-6917

Amelia Island Williams House—103 S. Ninth St.; 800-414-9257 or 277-2328

Ash Street Inn—102 S. Seventh St.; 800-277-6660 or 277-4941

Bailey House Victorian Bed and Breakfast—28 S. Seventh St.; 800-251-5390 or 261-5390

Elizabeth Pointe Lodge—98 S. Fletcher Ave.; 800-772-3359 or 277-4851

Fairbanks House Bed and Breakfast—227 S. Seventh St.; 888-891-9882 or 277-0500; www.fairbankshouse.com

Florida House Inn and Restaurant—20 S. Third St., Amelia Island, FL 32034; 800-258-3301 or 261-3300

Hampton Inn and Suites—19 S. Second St.; 491-4911

Hoyt House Bed and Breakfast—804 Atlantic Ave.; 800-432-2085 or 277-4300

Ritz-Carlton—4750 Amelia Island Pkwy.; 277-1100

1735 House—584 S. Fletcher Ave.; 800-872-8531 or 261-4148

ATTRACTIONS

Amelia Island Museum of History—233 S. Third St.; 261-7378

Amelia Island Plantation—3000 First Coast Hwy., 32035; 800-874-6878 or 491-6917

Amelia River Cruises and Charters—2206 Florida Ave.; 261-9972

Fort Clinch State Park—2601 Atlantic Ave.; 277-7274

Hot Ticket Charters—1507 S.R. 13 N., Jacksonville, FL 32259; 287-3973; www.hotticketcharters.com

Kayak Amelia—888-30-KAYAK or 321-0697; www.kayakamelia.com

Kelly Seahorse Ranch—7800 First Coast Hwy., Amelia Island State Recreation Area; 941-5166

Palace Saloon—Centre and Second Street; 261-9068

Peterbrooke Chocolatier—316-B Centre St.; 261-2802

Voyager Ventures—One Front St.; 321-1244

 CAMPING

Fort Clinch State Park—2601 Atlantic Ave.; 277-7274

 DINING

Amelia Inn/The Verandah—Amelia Island Plantation, 3000 First Coast Hwy.; 491-6917; www.aipfl.com

Beech Street Grill—801 Beech St.; 277-3662

Brett's—One Front St. at foot of Centre St.; 261-2660

Centre Street Café—316 Centre St.; 277-6600

1878 Tavern Grille—12 N. Second St.; 321-5668

Florida House Inn—22 S. Third St., Amelia Island, FL 32034; 261-3300

Golden Grouper—201 Alachua St.; 261-0013

Grill and Cafe—Ritz-Carlton, 4750 Amelia Island Pkwy.; 277-1100

Horizon's Continental Cuisine—803 Ash St. (corner of Eighth and Ash); 321-2430

T-Ray's Burger Station—202 S. Eighth St.; 261-6310

 EVENTS

First weekend of each month—Fort Clinch reenactments

March—Concours d'Elégance

April—Bausch & Lomb Women's Tennis Championship

May—Isle of Eight Flags Shrimp Festival

August—Youth Fishing Tour

November—Victorian Seaside Holidays

December—Holiday Tour of Historic Treasures

 FOR MORE INFORMATION

Amelia Island Chamber of Commerce and Visitor Center—P.O. Box 472; 800-2amelia or 261-3248; www.ameliaisland.org

Amelia Island Tourist Development Council—102 Centre St.; 800-2amelia or 277-0717; www.ameliaisland.org

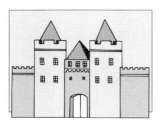

Jacksonville came very close to being the oldest city in America, instead of St. Augustine. You'll learn why a little later.

If you're heading south from Amelia Island via FL A1A, stop by **BEAKS**—the Bird Emergency Aid and Kare Sanctuary—on Big Talbot Island. All species of wild birds are taken in here for care and rehabilitation. About 2,000 are brought here each year. Eagles, wood storks, pelicans, and turkeys are among the large species, but songbirds are brought here, too. You can walk around the grounds to see birds in large cages, behind fencing, and free. A free-range turkey strutted and flirted with his reflection in our chrome bumper and followed our Explorer from the compound. The education programs at BEAKS attract 6,000 people annually. The sanctuary is open daily for tours by individuals and groups.

Anglers should note the boat ramp after crossing the Nassau Sound bridge on to Big Talbot Island. The ramp offers easy access to the Intra-

coastal Waterway and the Atlantic Ocean. Additional parking is provided for those who want to fish from the bridge.

Just south of BEAKS along FL A1A are **Big Talbot Island State Park** and **Little Talbot Island State Park**. They offer a wealth of recreational opportunities in an unspoiled environment of beaches, dunes, coastal hammocks, and marshland.

One mile past Nassau Sound is an area known as The Bluffs, a splendid place for photographers to get some dramatic shots. Picnickers may take advantage of the tables at The Bluffs or farther south at Wayside, west of the unimproved boat ramp at Simpson Creek. Grills are available at The Bluffs picnic area.

For those who enjoy hiking, Big Talbot Island has five marked trails where it is not uncommon to see raccoons, opossums, and gopher tortoises. The shy bobcat can sometimes be spotted.

South of Big Talbot is the 2,500-acre Little Talbot, one the few remaining undeveloped barrier islands in Florida. The state park has a 4.1-mile hiking trail, more than five miles of beaches, plenty of parking, dune walkovers, and beach bathhouses. The Little Talbot campground serves the state parks on both Big Talbot and Little Talbot. A portion of the campground is on a coastal hammock on the western side of the island, while other sites are along Myrtle Creek, a tidal marsh. Forty of the sites come equipped with water and electric hookups. A nature trail, a boat ramp, a playground, two bathhouses with showers, and canoe and bicycle rentals round out the amenities. Saturday programs and ranger-guided walks are offered seasonally.

Before visiting the area, it is a good idea to acquire a map of the area or to contact the Jacksonville Convention and Visitors Bureau for a copy of its tour planner. You're going to need it to see how to reach the numerous rich sites covered here.

If you're still heading south on FL A1A, you'll cross the Fort George River on to Fort George Island. Fort George Island boasts the longest record of civilization in Duval County. Immense shell mounds document Indian habitation reaching back 7,000 years. Oysters were a large part of the Indians' diet, and the discarded shells accumulated over time to form enormous middens.

"They be all naked and of goodly stature, mighty, faire and as well shapen . . . as any people in all the worlde, very gentill, curtious and of a good nature. . . . The men be of tawny collour, hawke nosed and of a pleasant countenance. . . . The wemen be well favored and modest." This description came from French explorer Jean Ribault when he first encountered the Timucuan tribe of Chief Saturiwa at the mouth of the St. Johns River in 1562. The Timucuan culture had not changed for more than 1,000 years. The tribe

inhabited central and North Florida and southeastern Georgia. Timucua was the common language spoken.

What is known of Timucuan culture is derived from historical and archaeological research. Besides collecting shellfish and fishing, the Timucuans hunted and gathered in the forests and swamps and planted maize, squash, and beans. French colonist Jacques le Moyne's sketches of Timucuan ceremonies and customs gave many Europeans their first view of Native Americans. These are commonly seen in museums in Florida and history books. A Franciscan priest translated a set of catechisms and confessionals from Spanish into Timucuan in 1612, the first translation involving a Native American language.

Florida tribes did not long survive contact with Europeans. After driving out the French, Spain imposed tribute on the Timucuans and forced them into missions. Ravaged by European diseases and attacks by other Indians, the Timucuan population rapidly disintegrated from the tens of thousands to only about 550 in 1698. No known Native Americans today call themselves Timucuans.

Jacksonville, the site of the first European settlement in Florida, was never a Spanish stronghold. In 1562, Jean Ribault and a group of settlers, mostly Huguenots who wanted to escape religious persecution, came ashore and claimed the land for France. They later established Fort Caroline at the mouth of the St. Johns River on the southern bank. Citing a previous claim to Florida made during the 1513 voyage of Ponce de Leon, Spain quickly dispatched soldiers to rid the land of the French interlopers.

In the mid-1500s, France, emerging from feudalism, desired to become an empire like Spain, which was the world's leading power and had a

The largest city in land area in the United States, Jacksonville provides a smorgasbord of opportunities for its visitors.

foothold in the Americas. France wanted to partake of the riches Spain had looted from the New World. France's first attempt at a claim in North America was at La Caroline, a settlement near the mouth of the St. Johns River in Florida. The settlement, intended to be a commercial venture, became partly a religious colony because of the growing persecution of French Protestants (Huguenots) in France. Admiral Gaspard de Coligny proposed to the Crown that the colony also be a refuge for Huguenots.

An expedition led by Jean Ribault left France in February 1562. He erected a monument at the River of May (the St. Johns River), then headed north, leaving a small garrison at Charlesfort near Port Royal Sound, and finally sailed home. Within months, the situation of his men became desperate, and they returned to France.

Admiral Coligny urged another attempt in April 1564. He favored a permanent settlement of 200 soldiers and artisans, as well as a few women. Led by René de Goulaine de Laudonnière, who had accompanied Ribault on his previous

expedition, the colonists reached the River of May on June 22. With help from the Indians, they began building a village and fort on the river's south bank, naming the area La Caroline, after their king, Charles IX.

Today, the reconstructed Fort Caroline is part of the 46,000-acre **Timucuan Ecological and Historic Preserve**, which runs from the southern bank of the Nassau River south to the St. Johns River. A small area containing **Fort Caroline National Memorial** and the **Ribault Monument** is on the southern bank of the St. Johns River northeast of Jacksonville off Fort Caroline Road.

The Timucuans helped the French adapt to local conditions by sharing food and helping them build a village and Fort Caroline. Relations turned unpleasant the following spring when the colonists were close to starvation. Conditions became even worse when mutinous colonists sailed off on their own. The Spanish learned of the presence of the French colony when they captured some of the mutineers. Meanwhile, the

Had Fort Caroline, within the 46,000-acre Timucuan Ecological and Historic Preserve, succeeded, Jacksonville would be the oldest city in America.

remaining colonists at Fort Caroline, having failed to find the riches they believed were in this part of the New World, prepared to leave Florida in August 1565. But Ribault arrived in the nick of time with a relief expedition of 600 soldiers, settlers (including women and children), and supplies.

On learning of Ribault's return to Florida, Philip II of Spain sent Admiral Pedro Menendez to rout the French. Initially repulsed off the coast, Menendez established a base south at San Augustin (St. Augustine). Ribault prepared to sail south to attack the Spanish, but the Timucuan chief read the weather signs and warned him not to go by water. Ribault rebuked the words of the savage and sailed south.

Park Ranger Craig Morris says Ribault missed two opportunities to defeat Menendez. First, Ribault didn't go by land. Second, he sailed safely to San Augustin and demanded that Menendez surrender. When Menendez declined, Ribault did not dispatch his troops, but waited at the mouth of the harbor for two days. On the morning of the third day, a hurricane arrived, beaching his ships far to the south of San Augustin.

Not one to miss an opportunity, Menendez marched north with 500 soldiers to attack the weakly guarded colony at Fort Caroline. Early on the morning of September 20, his troops massacred 140 settlers, sparing about 60 women and children. Forty to 50 others escaped and sailed for France.

Menendez then marched south to shipwrecked Frenchmen, Ribault among them. The French threw themselves on his mercy, but Menendez considered them heretics and enemies of his king. At a place later named Matanzas—meaning "massacre" or "slaughters"—Menendez's men put the sword to about 350 men. A few musicians quickly switched to Catholicism and were spared.

French revenge came in April 1568, when Dominique de Gourgues attacked and burned Fort Caroline. He then returned to France.

According to Ranger Norris, had Ribault taken advantage of the chief's warning and gone by land or pursued Menendez quickly at San Augustin, St. Augustine would not be America's oldest city. Jacksonville would hold that title. It shows that one man's decision can change history. Norris also maintains that the Huguenots were the first to come to the New World seeking religious freedom—a foreshadowing of the Pilgrims.

You can drive to Fort Caroline or arrive by boat using the new dock. Golf carts are available for those who need to ride to visit the exhibits and sites.

The present-day fort was modeled after Le Moyne's drawings. The original site is unknown.

Spain rebuilt Fort Caroline and renamed it San Mateo, only to abandon it the next year. France never strongly challenged Spanish claims in North America again. Spain controlled Florida for the next two centuries.

It was at the end of that time, in 1736, that General James Oglethorpe, founder of the Georgia Colony, built Fort Saint Georges on what is now Fort George Island, located north of the mouth of the St. Johns River. The fort no longer exists, and its location is unknown. Mount Cornelia, a series of remnant dunes rising 65 feet above sea level, is a possible site. To learn more about Fort George Island and its former inhabitants, take the 4.4-mile self-guided Saturiwa Trail tour. Guidebooks are available at the ranger station on the island.

Kingsley Plantation on the Ft. George River was an interesting experiment in liberalizing slave conditions.

Also on Fort George Island is the **Kingsley Plantation**, tucked away amid the towering, moss-laden oaks. The oldest plantation in Florida, it is now a federal park inside the 40,000-acre Timucuan Preserve. Turn west off FL A1A at the sign and follow the road three miles to the plantation.

Early in the 19th century, many people came to Spanish Florida. Pioneers like Zephaniah Kingsley sought to make their fortunes by purchasing land and establishing plantations. Others were forced to come here to work on those plantations, their labor enriching the men who owned them. Some of the enslaved later became free landowners who struggled to keep their footing in a dangerous time. All of these people played a part in the history of Kingsley Plantation.

In 1814, Zephaniah Kingsley moved to Fort George Island, bringing a wife and three children, with a fourth to be born at Fort George. His wife, Anna Madgigine Jai, was from Senegal, West Africa. She had been purchased by Kingsley as a slave, then set free in 1811. She actively partici-

pated in plantation management, acquiring her own land and slaves. The enslaved work force of about 60 at the Fort George plantation produced sea-island cotton, citrus, sugarcane, and corn. Kingsley continued to acquire property in North Florida. He eventually possessed over 200 slaves and more than 32,000 acres, including four major plantation complexes.

The United States purchased Florida from Spain in 1821. The Spanish had relatively liberal policies regarding issues of race. American territorial law brought many changes. At a time when many slaveholders feared slave rebellions, oppressive laws were enacted. Conditions for Florida's black population, free and enslaved, deteriorated. Kingsley was against the restrictive laws, arguing that more humane treatment would ensure peace and the perpetuation of slavery. In 1828, he published his opinions in *A Treatise on The Patriarchal, or Co-operative System of Society As It Exists in Some Governments . . . Under the Name of Slavery.*

To escape what Kingsley called a "spirit of intolerant prejudice," Anna Jai and their sons moved to Haiti in 1837. There, Kingsley established a colony for his family and some of his former slaves. In 1839, he sold Fort George Island to his nephew Kingsley Beatty Gibbs. Zephaniah Kingsley died in New York City in 1843.

Kingsley's residence on the bank of the Fort George River may have been constructed as early as 1798. The unusual floor plan consists of a two-story central area with foursquare corner rooms. The visitor center is in the front room, and historical exhibits are in other rooms. You can see sea-island cotton growing in the garden and learn about the cultivation of plantation crops. The barn, located to the left as you walk to the residence, is built of tabby; an oyster-shell concrete used in many Florida structures. Both tabby brick and poured tabby were used in the construction of the barn.

When you enter the plantation, your first stop is the slave quarters. Ruins of 23 tabby cabins stand as reminders of the enslaved men, women, and children who once lived and worked on the plantation. One cabin has been restored to its original appearance. Slaves worked on a task system. A worker had to hoe half an acre, pick 90 to 100 pounds of cotton, gin 20 to 30 pounds, split 100 feet of rails, square 100 feet of timber, make a quarter-acre of beds and furrows, or dig 600 feet of ditch. After completing his job, the remainder of the day was his.

The Spanish had little interest in developing the Jacksonville area, since their base of operations was St. Augustine. During the two and a half centuries of Spanish colonial rule, Jacksonville was farmland and fields. By 1816, settlers built the community of Cow Ford, so named because it was where cattlemen moved their livestock across the St. Johns River to the St. Augustine market. Today, the ford area is at the intersection of Bay and Liberty in downtown Jacksonville.

Florida became an United States territory in 1821. More settlers arrived, which stimulated Cow Ford's growth. In 1822, the town was officially founded and renamed for Andrew Jackson, the territory's provisional governor. River pilots and fishermen settled the area north of Jacksonville Beach. Now called Mayport, it was known as Hazard in the early 1800s.

By 1882, residents of Jacksonville were coming to the beaches by steamboat down the St. Johns River to enjoy the ocean air. A band of Jacksonville businessmen built a summer resort at the beach to attract tourists. A railroad surveyor set up housekeeping with his family in a tent on the beach and erected another tent as a store. He established a post office and named the town Ruby, after his oldest daughter. From a tent city in 1884, Jacksonville Beach grew into a business, resort, and residential community. By June 1885, the Jacksonville and Atlantic Railway Company ran from South Jacksonville to the beach. Crowds of beachgoers arrived with tents. Soon, Ruby became a tent city. The next year, the town was renamed Pablo Beach, after the San Pablo River. It wasn't long before luxury hotels were constructed and new residences filled the area. Pablo Beach became the chosen resort of people from Jacksonville and southern Georgia. Its location on the Atlantic Ocean near historical and entertainment attractions makes it a great place to stay while exploring the "First Coast" today.

In 1901, a fire ravaged Jacksonville, destroying thousands of buildings. It took years for the city to rebuild. In the early decades of the 20th century, Jacksonville became the East Coast capital for filmmaking. Meanwhile, at the beaches, the boardwalk era was born. Dance pavilions, shooting galleries, boxing and wrestling matches, and restaurants offered new entertainments to the many visitors. Later, auto racing and horse racing on the beach came into vogue. In 1925, Pablo Beach changed its name to Jacksonville Beach at the request of the city of Jacksonville.

Today, Jacksonville is the largest city in the United States by land area. More than a million souls make their home here. Mix together historical landmarks, renovated old neighborhoods, skyscrapers, and the ambiance of the Old South, and you have a sophisticated, thriving metropolis.

While you're in town, be sure to visit the

The Museum of Science and History is a "must do" in Jacksonville for learning history and meeting this bony friend.

excellent Currents of Time exhibit at the **Museum of Science and History** (MOSH), located at 1025 Museum Circle. The exhibit takes you through the past 12,000 years of Jacksonville-area history. It offers many details about the Indian cultures, the Battle of Thomas Creek during the American Revolution, the Seminole Wars, the War Between the States, the 1901 fire and how it started, the moviemaking business, the eight German saboteurs here during World War II, and much, much more. MOSH entertains all ages with its exhibit on whales, dolphins, and manatees and its Prehistoric Park, which contains a full-sized allosaurus skeleton measuring 39 feet. The Alexander Brest Planetarium transports visitors through the universe. Kids Space introduces children five and younger to science. You'll also find an exhibit on sunken treasure and Jacksonville's Jaguar Hall of Fame. Allow several hours to take it all in.

The **Cummer Museum of Art and Gardens**, located at 829 Riverside Avenue, is the largest fine-arts museum in northeastern Florida. It was founded in 1958 when Jacksonville resident Ninah

Holden Cummer created an endowment to build a museum on the site of her family home. Her collection of paintings by European and American masters formed the nucleus of the museum's permanent collection, which also includes ancient, medieval, Renaissance, Baroque, Rococo, 19th-century, impressionist, and modern paintings and sculptures. Pre-Columbian ceramics and Japanese prints are part of the collection. In 1965, the museum received the Constance and Ralph Wark collection of Meissen porcelain. It is one of the two foremost collections of Meissen in the world. One of the most outstanding additions is Thomas Moran's painting *Ponce de Leon in Florida*, acquired in 1996. Also recently acquired is *The Generosity of Scipio* by 17th-century Dutch artist Jan Steen.

The Cummer has one of the finest formal gardens in the Southeast. More than two and a half acres of formal English and Italian gardens lie along the St. Johns River. Visitors can walk under the wisteria arbors or find an open bench near a fountain or a reflecting pool to pause and enjoy the beauty of the flowers or the Cummer live oak, which has a canopy measuring more than 175 feet. The Italian garden has just undergone a restoration, returning it to the original splendor Mrs. Cummer envisioned in 1931.

This museum and gardens are open daily.

The **Ritz Theatre and LaVilla Museum**, located at 829 North Davis Street, celebrates the rich legacy of the African-American community known as LaVilla, which thrived in Jacksonville for more than 100 years. The stories and legends of LaVilla, once called "the Harlem of the South," live on within the walls of the newly reconstructed 32,000-square-foot museum and theater.

The facade of the old Ritz from 1929 remains, but the inside is new. The stage productions are fresh and exciting and appeal to a diverse audience. The 400-seat theater features a state-of-the-art sound system and a 30-by-40-foot stage. It is constantly filled with musical programs, theatrical productions, movies, and multimedia events.

The museum houses a permanent exhibit of the history of African-Americans in northeastern Florida. It replicates scenes of everyday life in the first half of the 20th century and documents the past with photographs and artifacts. Of special interest is *Lift Ev'ry Voice and Sing*, an animatronic presentation featuring native sons James Weldon Johnson and John Rosamond Johnson. Throughout the year, the dramatically lit gallery features a wide variety of exhibits of fine art, folk art, local art, and history. You may be particularly interested, as we were, in the exhibit called "Portraits by Weems: Visual Storyteller, 1929-1979." Ellie Lee Weems moved to Jacksonville in 1929, opened a studio, and began a 50-year black-and-white photographic history of the African-American community.

The museum is open Tuesday through Sunday. It will take you two or three hours to devour the artifacts and history.

The waterfront area is the focal point of Jacksonville. The **Riverwalk** is a 1.2-mile wooden boardwalk bordering the St. Johns River. It's a pleasant place to stroll, to shop, or just to rest on one of the benches and watch the riverboats cruise past. Seafood fests, parties, parades, and craft exhibitions take place on the Riverwalk. Water taxis are available from the Riverwalk to Jacksonville Landing.

As for shopping, the avenues on the south side and **Regency Square** in Arlington feature more than 100 nationally known retailers and several major department stores.

Avondale, one of the country's largest National Historic Districts, caters to the upscale shopper with a bounty of specialty boutiques, fine galleries, and gourmet eateries.

San Marco Square, fashioned after St. Mark's Square in Venice, revolves around a water fountain capped with three enormous bronze lions and a gazebo. An open-air produce market adds hustle and bustle to streets lined with fine-dining establishments and boutiques specializing in the finest tobacco, designer clothing, precious artwork, and gifts.

A festive marketplace atmosphere prevails at **Jacksonville Landing** on the north bank of the St. Johns River. A stroll through the landing's shops uncovers novelty and gift items, name-brand apparel, antiques, toys, and locally fashioned accessories.

Antique and arts-and-crafts enthusiasts may think they've landed in paradise. Hundreds of thousands of square feet of antique malls and quaint beach-side boutiques offer the finest collectibles, period pieces, restored furnishings, original artwork, and more. Twelve blocks from the shore on Beach Boulevard sits Beach Plaza, home to **Worth Antiques Gallery**, one of the largest galleries of its kind on the East Coast. More than 50,000 square feet burst with reasonably priced, quality merchandise. **Max's at Worth**, a restaurant inside the gallery, is a favorite resting spot for veteran scavengers.

The **Budweiser Brewery** is across the Trout River on the north side of Jacksonville at 111 Busch Drive. Eberhard Anheuser was originally a soap manufacturer. He took over a failing brewery in St. Louis and spent the next 20 years making it grow. Along came Adolphus Busch, who married Eberhard's daughter, Lilly. It was Busch who transformed the local brewery into an industry giant, becoming the real founder of Anheuser-Busch. His secret was pasteurization. Anheuser-Busch's process allowed its beer to be shipped unrefrigerated, which gave it a considerable advantage over breweries that had to keep their beer cold and deliver it close to the plant.

During Prohibition, Anheuser-Busch Brewing changed its name to Anheuser-Busch, Inc., and made soft drinks, ice cream, and malt syrup—anything to save the company while waiting out the dry years between 1920 and 1933. It first used Clydesdales—its worldwide symbols today—in April 1933.

Jacksonville's plant makes seven brands and more than 8 million barrels of beer a year. Together, the 12 Anheuser-Busch breweries yield about 105 million barrels per year. A barrel holds 31 gallons. You may be surprised to learn that the company brews 51 brands of beer and four non-alcoholic brands.

The plant offers tours six days a week. Fifty thousand people take the tour annually. It begins with a video showing the brewing steps. You walk down a long hall that overlooks most of the process from beginning to end. The tour is wheelchair accessible. You may sample a couple of the tasty products if you're over 21. Otherwise, you may sip a soft drink in the hospitality room at the end of the hour-long tour.

While you're on this side of town, be sure to visit the nearby **Jacksonville Zoological Gardens**, located off Heckscher Drive, south of Busch Drive. It displays animals such as warthogs, kudus, cheetahs, rhinos, elephants, leopards, lions, and monkeys in natural settings, as if they roam the plains of East Africa. The great-apes exhibit features five species of primates housed in an in-

novative natural enclosure. The meerkats exhibit houses a family of lively little creatures.

There is something comforting about the charm, warmth, and hospitality of a quality bed-and-breakfast. There are many hotels and motels in Jacksonville and along the local beaches, but we prefer a comfy bed-and-breakfast. Fortunately there are some excellent choices in the area.

In town are the **Cleary-Dickert House** and the **Plantation Manor Inn**. At Jacksonville Beach are Pelican Path Bed and Breakfast, **Ruby Inn by the Sea, Fig Tree Inn Bed and Breakfast**, and **Sabal Palm Inn**.

We especially enjoyed staying at **Pelican Path Bed and Breakfast** on the Atlantic Ocean because the owners, Joan and Tom Hubbard, instantly seemed like old friends. Conversations over breakfast were lively and made us happily delay getting on with our book research.

San Francisco was the inspiration for the architecture. The bay windows on the second

The Pelican Path Bed and Breakfast in Jacksonville Beach offers an amenity found at no other inn. Since the innkeepers are certified in personality-preference testing, they'll offer you interpretations.

floor provide an ocean view from all the guest rooms and add to the light and spaciousness of the rooms. All guest rooms have a private bath, a television with a VCR, a refrigerator, a coffee maker, a hair dryer, and a telephone. The ocean-front rooms have spa tubs, king-sized beds, and private balconies. The inn provides a full break-fast overlooking the beach, bicycles for guest use, easy access to shopping, dining, and other attrac-tions, on-site parking, and a smoke-free environ-ment. It is proud of its AAA Triple-Diamond rating.

Joan Hubbard is a Florida-licensed marriage and family therapist, and Joan and Tom are certi-fied Myers-Briggs Type Indicator (MBTI) practi-tioners. They offer a "Communicating for Real Understanding" program for couples visiting their bed-and-breakfast. The program plus some won-derful, relaxed beach time are sure to revitalize couples' relationships, giving them promise of a better way to communicate for real understand-ing. The "Seniors Weekend" program looks at what types of plans seniors have made, evaluates how successful these are in terms of current com-fort, and compares them to what others with their preference type are enjoying.

Jacksonville Beach, located on a barrier island, has all the amenities of a large beach resort and the hospitality of a hometown. Here, you'll find miles of uncrowded white-sand beaches.

If you're an angler, you have the Intracoastal Waterway, the St. Johns River, and the Atlantic Ocean to choose from.

If you're a golfer, you have the 18-hole mu-nicipal golf course, nearby public courses, and two famous resort courses. The local beaches are home to more than 20 golf courses maintained year-round. You can also explore the new **World Golf Hall of Fame** at nearby **World Golf Village**.

At the **Sea Walk Pavilion**, visitors enjoy con-certs or festivals nearly every weekend from April through October.

The beaches are known for their many great restaurants. You can dine on the oceanfront or along the Intracoastal Waterway and top off the evening with live music and entertainment at lo-cal nightspots.

If shopping is your idea of fun, the local art galleries and antique shops will keep you busy.

Adventure Landing in Jacksonville Beach is the area's largest amusement park. It features min-iature golf courses, batting cages, a go-cart track, a multilevel laser-tag arena, and Shipwreck Island, an interactive water park complete with a 65-foot Caribbean play village with 12 slides, a wave pool, and more than 200 nozzles to spray and squirt you and your friends.

From Jacksonville Beach, you can drop down FL A1A to St. Augustine or go southwest to Gainesville via US 301. If you travel US 301, be sure not to exceed the speed limit; AAA notes that there are a few towns that make a lot of money from passing out tickets. One local convention and visitors' bureau warned us to be especially aware of Lawty and Waldo. We were legal all the way between the two. Be careful.

All of the following are in Jacksonville and use the 32202 zip code and 904 area code, ex-cept where noted.

ACCOMMODATIONS

Cleary-Dickert House—1804 Copeland St., 32204; 387-4762

Fig Tree Inn Bed and Breakfast—185 S. Fourth Ave., Jacksonville Beach, 32250; 246-8855

Pelican Path Bed and Breakfast—11 N. 19th Ave., Jacksonville Beach, FL 32250; 888-749-1177 or 249-1177; www.pelicanpath.com

Plantation Manor Inn—1630 Copeland St., 32204; 384-4630

Ruby Inn by the Sea—802 Second St., Jacksonville Beach, FL 32250; 241-4577

Sabal Palm Inn—115 S. Fifth Ave., Jacksonville Beach, FL 32250; 241-4545

 ATTRACTIONS

Adventure Landing—1944 Beach Blvd., 32250; 246-4386

Alhambra Dinner Theatre—12000 Beach Blvd.; 800-688-SHOW or 641-1212

BEAKS—12084 Houston Ave., Big Talbot Island, FL 32226; 901-251-BIRD

Big and Little Talbot Island State Parks—12157 Heckscher Dr., 32226; 251-2320

Budweiser Brewery Tour—111 Busch Dr., 32218; 800-765-1055 or 751-8116

Cummer Museum of Art and Gardens—829 Riverside Ave., 32204; 356-6857

Fort Caroline National Memorial—12713 Mt. Pleasant Rd.; 641-7155

Hot Ticket Charters—1507 CR 13 N., 32259; 904-287-3973; www.hotticketcharters.com

Jacksonville Landing—2 Independent Dr.; 352-1188

Jacksonville Zoological Gardens—8605 Zoo Pkwy., 32218; 757-4463

Kayak Adventures—413 Second St., 32250; 888-333-2480 or 249-6200

Kingsley Plantation—11676 Palmetto Ave., 32226; 251-3537

Museum of Science and History—1025 Museum Cir., 32207; 396-7062

Ritz Theatre and LaVilla Museum—829 N. Davis St.; 632-5555

Timucuan Ecological and Historic Preserve—12713 Ft. Caroline Rd., 32225; 641-3798

World Golf Hall of Fame—1 World Golf Place, St. Augustine, FL 32092; 940-4000

Worth Antiques Gallery—1316 Beach Blvd., Jacksonville Beach, FL 32250; 247-2211

Camping

Big and Little Talbot Island State Parks—12157 Heckscher Dr., 32226; 251-2320

 Dining

Chart House—1501 River Place Blvd.; 398-3353

Dave and Buster's—7025 Salisbury Rd.; 269-1525

Harry's Seafood Bar and Grille—1018 N. Third St., Jacksonville Beach, FL; 249-7911

Island Grille—981 N. First St., Jacksonville Beach, FL; 241-1881

Matthew's Restaurant—2107 Hendricks Ave.; 396-5222

River City Brewing Co.—835 Museum Dr.; 398-2299

Seven Bridges Grille and Brewery—9735 Gate Pkwy.; 997-1999

Sticky Fingers Restaurant and Bar—363 Atlantic Blvd., Atlantic Beach, FL 32266; 241-RIBS

Wine Cellar—1314 Prudential Dr.; 398-8989

 Events

February—Scottish Highland Games

April—Springing the Blues Festival

April—Riverside Avondale Historic Home Tour

April—Jacksonville Jazz Festival

April—Beaches Festival Weekend

May—Mug Races, St. Johns River

June—Fiesta Playera

July—Great Atlantic Seafood Festival, Jacksonville Beach

September—Riverside Arts Festival

October—Jacksonville Agricultural Fair

November—Sea and Sky Spectacular

December—Festival of Trees, Cummer Museum of Art and Gardens

 For more information

Jacksonville and the Beaches Convention and Visitors Bureau—201 E. Adams St.; 800-733-2668 or 798-9111; www.jaxcvb.com

HIGHLIGHTS

CASTILLO DE SAN MARCOS

FORT MATANZAS NATIONAL MONUMENT

HARBOR SHUTTLE

FOUNTAIN OF YOUTH NATIONAL ARCHAEOLOGICAL PARK

RIPLEY'S BELIEVE IT OR NOT! MUSEUM

ST. GEORGE STREET

SPANISH QUARTER VILLAGE

MEMORIAL PRESBYTERIAN CHURCH

OLDEST HOUSE

ST. AUGUSTINE ALLIGATOR FARM

ST. AUGUSTINE LIGHTHOUSE AND MUSEUM

History stretches back farther here than in any other continuously occupied city in the United States, so it makes sense that you'll need a good deal of time for your explorations. That's what we found after running and gunning for three days—we simply needed more time to see it all. We'd advise you to investigate St. Augustine at a leisurely pace and enjoy it thoroughly.

St. Augustine was founded before the English colonized Jamestown, Virginia, and 55 years before the Pilgrims landed at Plymouth Rock, Massachusetts. There are more than 85 historic sites and attractions here. We'll show you some of the sites and mention many others worth your attention. St. Augustine's fascinating history at-

tracts millions of visitors annually.

Juan Ponce de Leon was probably not as gullible as some history books state. You've probably read that he came in search of the Fountain of Youth. Actually, his job, as a seasoned explorer, was to claim and explore land along the Atlantic coast for Spain.

Although he is given credit for being the first European to "discover" Florida, several maps drawn before his arrival in April 1513 show an unmistakable Florida peninsula. According to *The Oldest City: St. Augustine Saga of Survival*, edited by Jean Parker Waterbury, the more likely candidates for being the first are John and Sebastian Cabot, Amerigo Vespucci, and maybe some unrecorded slave traders. If slave traders preceded Ponce de Leon, that would explain the hostility of the Indians at the arrival of the Spanish newcomers.

He sighted land on April 2. When he saw the delightfully verdant landscape, he named the place La Florida; the word *florido* translates as "flowery" or "flowering." Where he landed is not known, but it is thought to have been somewhere between the mouth of the St. Johns River and Cape Canaveral. Soon thereafter, he sailed south.

In 1562, Jean Ribault claimed the land for France. Citing a previous claim to Florida made by Ponce de Leon, Spain dispatched soldiers to rid the land of the French interlopers. Ribault's first effort at colonization failed.

In April 1564, René de Goulaine de Laudonnière, who had accompanied Ribault on his previous expedition, sailed up the River of May (the St. John's River) to begin building Fort Caroline, the first European settlement in Florida. By coincidence, Pedro Menéndez de Aviles saw Florida's shore the same day. He had been sent to roust the French from Spanish soil. Menéndez was sailing north to seek the French when he made note of a harbor and named it San August'n. After a brief encounter of nothing more than name-calling, the French ships sailed eastward, and the Spanish sailed south to San August'n to retake possession of Florida.

The city of St. Augustine began with the offloading of cargo. The Timucuan Indians looked on. Today, a large cross at the mission of Nombre de Dios off San Marco Avenue marks the landing site.

Menéndez still had to fulfill his mandate to rid Florida of the French. He marched north and attacked Fort Caroline on September 20, sparing only the women and children. Later, he learned from some Indians survivors that the French fleet was stranded south of there. The French "Lutherens" were found on Anastasia Island, across an inlet from the settlement. When Menéndez informed the French of the outcome of the battle at Fort Caroline, they pleaded for ships to return to France. It's claimed that Menéndez said, "Give up your arms and surrender to my mercy. I will treat you as God directs me to." Hiding most of his men behind the dunes, Menéndez ferried 127 French prisoners, 10 at a time, across the inlet. Their hands bound, they were marched toward St. Augustine. At a point Menéndez had marked, his soldiers killed them.

We've heard and read several versions of this story. Another version is that when each group arrived on the opposite shore, it was taken behind the sand dunes, where the men were given a chance to denounce their heretic religion. When they refused, their throats were cut.

In all, 16 were spared: four artisans who were needed in St. Augustine, some impressed sailors from Breton, and some Catholics.

Two weeks later, the scene was repeated. This time, the Spanish killed 134 Frenchmen, Ribault among them. Those spared were a dozen musicians and four Catholics. The inlet was subsequently named Matanzas, Spanish for "slaughter" or "massacre."

Within three months, Menéndez rid Florida of the French, after which the Spanish continued their control of the coast.

In 1586, Sir Francis Drake sacked and burned the settlement. In 1668, English pirate Robert Searles ravaged the town.

In view of the threat from the English, who were set on colonization, Queen Mariana of Spain authorized the construction of a stone fortification. The **Castillo de San Marcos** was built between 1672 and 1695 of coquina, a shell quarried on Anastasia Island that had the unique quality of absorbing cannonballs, rather than shattering under their impact. This, the nation's oldest masonry fortress, has never been conquered. It's on San Marco Avenue. You can't miss it. Boat tours can take you by the fort. A tour of the inside will give you an appreciation of what it took to build such a strong structure using primitive tools. You'll note the diamond-shaped bastion at each corner of the fort. The walls and entrance could be protected by gunfire from the bastions.

A related military site is **Fort Matanzas National Monument**, located on Rattlesnake Island, 14 miles south of St. Augustine via FL A1A. Attacked in 1740 by James Oglethorpe of Georgia, the Spanish were under siege for 27 days. They sent small boats down Matanzas Inlet to meet their supply ships on the coast. When they got back to St. Augustine, they realized that the enemy could do likewise. They therefore began construction of Fort Matanzas, which was completed in

Fort Matanzas on Rattlesnake Island protected the southern approach to St. Augustine.

1742. The fort protected the southern approach to the city. Today, the fort may be reached only by boat. It is worth your time to watch the video at the visitor center before crossing the river. The fort is open daily except Christmas. There is no fee to enter the park or to ride the wheelchair-accessible ferry to Rattlesnake Island. Birders love the island, where a great many migrating species may be seen from February through April and during September and October. As many as 202 species can be counted here.

Though St. Augustine has a population of only 12,000 people, it draws more than a million visitors annually. Knowledgeable tour guides can lead you through the centuries via horse and carriage, trolleys, river cruises, and walking tours. The tours provide historically accurate information accented with anecdotes and tales that are a colorful part of the city's history. **Old Town Trolley Tours** has 20 stops. You can get off to dine, shop, or sightsee, then get back on board. Your ticket is good for three days on the orange and green cars. **Harbor Shuttle** offers narrated historic maritime tours, water-taxi service, and themed cruises. This is an excellent way to see the city and learn about it from the water. Harbor Shuttle also offers a Pirate Treasure Hunt on Conch Island.

Let's start our exploration of St. Augustine at the **Florida Heritage Museum and Old Jail**, located at 167 San Marco Avenue. The Old Jail, listed on the National Register of Historic Places, was completed in 1891. It held prisoners for more than 60 years. This is one of the few remaining 19th-century confinement facilities in Florida. You can tour the sheriff's living quarters, the cells, the maximum-security area, and the gallows. You can also see a collection of guns used in crimes.

Next door is the **Old Florida Museum**. Here,

you'll see exhibits that cover the period from pre-European to pioneer times. This hands-on museum lets you write with a quill pen, use an old corn mill, drill holes with a colonial pump drill, work on a dugout canoe, play old-time games, and much more.

Look east from the Old Jail and you'll see a towering, bronze-colored cross on the west bank of Matanzas Bay. Next to it lies the mission of **Nombre de Dios**, site of the first Catholic mass said in what is now the United States.

Between the Old Jail and the tall cross is **Fountain of Youth National Archaeological Park**, where archaeological discoveries are open to your viewing. These include the site of the first Christian Indian burials in North America, Timucua Indian hut foundations and relics, and evidence that Pedro Menéndez's colony occupied the site during the 16th century. The Spanish became convinced that there surely must be something in the water to produce the vigor of the Timucuans. The Indians often reached heights approaching seven feet and lived into their 60s, unlike the Spanish, who were just over five feet and died nearly two decades earlier, on average. While you're here, be sure to get a sip of the water, just in case.

Next, stop in the Howard Johnson's parking lot to visit with the **Old Senator**, a 600-year-old live oak. It's 600 feet from the Fountain of Youth.

Farther down San Marco Avenue are the **Old City Gates**, which open on to St. George Street, now a pedestrian mall through the oldest part of town.

Before going back in time, look across the street from the gates at the **Ripley's Believe It or Not! Museum**. The museum features artifacts and oddities from the Robert Ripley collection:

shrunken heads from the Amazon, the Iron Maiden of Nuremberg, the world's largest moving Erector Set model, a prehistoric shark jaw, a model of the tallest man who ever lived, and hundreds of other curiosities.

The museum occupies Castle Warden, built in 1887 by William G. Warden. One of the first poured-concrete structures in the United States, this was Warden's winter home. He, Henry Flagler, and John D. Rockefeller were partners in Standard Oil. Legend has it that Warden built the residence so he could watch Flagler go broke building his railroad connecting St. Augustine to New York. The home became a hotel in early 1942. It was owned and operated by author Marjorie Kinnan Rawlings and her husband, Norton Baskin, until 1946. Ripley tried to buy the building several times before he died in 1949. His heirs purchased it later that year and opened the museum in 1950, on his 57th birthday.

The **Huguenot Cemetery** is located at Orange Street near the Old City Gates. This is where all the Protestants from this once predominantly Catholic town were buried. The yellow-fever epidemic of 1821 killed Catholics and Protestants alike, but the town had no place to bury Protestants. It was unthinkable to integrate the dead. The city council obtained a half-acre of land that was subsequently acquired by the local Presbyterians in 1832. The word *Huguenot* in the cemetery's name probably refers to the members of the 1564 French expedition that established Fort Caroline.

Now, let's visit old St. Augustine and its 144 blocks of historic houses, many of them listed on the National Register of Historic Places. The city's architecture spans several centuries and ranges from coquina and tabby cottages to the early-20th-century structures capped by towers, turrets,

Enter the 1700s by visiting the six-acre Spanish Quarter Village, a replica of early St. Augustine life.

and terra-cotta roofs. The heart of the city is the 11 pedestrian-only blocks of the historic district. St. George Street, the main thoroughfare, is lined by 18th-century historic landmarks mixed with galleries and boutiques.

You'll get a picture of 18th-century life in the **Spanish Quarter Village**. This living-history museum features settlers clad in 1740s-style britches and bonnets. They're busy spinning and woodworking. You'll also find soldiers who'll tell you of life long ago. You'll see demonstrations by the leather maker and the blacksmith. The smith had to be paid in cash, since he had to pay cash for the valuable metal he used. If a house burned, people searched the ruins to retrieve nails and other metal objects. Most tradesmen were paid by barter. Since candle makers had to import beeswax, only the church and the well-to-do could afford beeswax candles. Common people used tallow candles that were smoky and smelled bad, so they generally went to bed at sunset.

In 1740, there were 2,000 people in St. Augustine. Each of the 40 taverns, many run by the

widows of soldiers, had a specialty—the best paella in town, the best bakery, etc. Customers drank wine, sherry, and brandy. Beer didn't last long in this climate. Taverns were also segregated by class—one for soldiers, another for officers, and another for merchants. If you were able-bodied and free, you were in the militia. Everyone walked around armed or kept a weapon nearby, since residents never knew when they might be attacked. They used charcoal for cooking because it produced little smoke. Charcoal was also put in braziers and used to warm the houses.

Many of the buildings in the Spanish Quarter Village are reconstructions on the original foundations, but some are original. Your ticket here is good for two days. Allow a minimum of an hour for a quick visit.

The **Oldest Wooden Schoolhouse**, located near the Old City Gates, was built more than 200 years ago, when Florida was under Spanish rule. It was made of red cedar and cypress and put together with wooden pegs and handmade nails. The schoolmaster lived upstairs over the small classroom. Artifacts and copies of the books the pupils studied are exhibited today.

The **Oldest Store Museum**, a general store that operated from 1835 to 1960, contains more than 100,000 items that remain from the original stock. Many were found in the attic. Bikes, tools, guns, household goods, medicines, and hardware are all on display. A Model-T truck, a Conestoga wagon, and a steam tractor are among the collection.

Go south on St. George to King Street, then turn right on King to see Henry Flagler's $2 million resort, the Ponce de Leon Hotel. Featuring Tiffany stained glass, gold-leaf Maynard murals, and electricity by Thomas Edison, it was the most lavish hotel of its day. Today, it is part of **Flagler College**.

Henry Flagler built the Memorial Presbyterian Church in 1889 in memory of his daughter. Flagler is interred here.

What was once a grand sister hotel across King Street is now the **Lightner Museum**. The former Hotel Alcazar, built in 1888, houses ornate collections of antiques, natural-science items, artifacts from the 19th century, and one of the world's most impressive cut-glass displays.

Also in this neighborhood is another Flagler building that is even more impressive. Go west on King Street and turn north on Sevilla Street to visit the Venetian Renaissance Revival **Memorial Presbyterian Church**. Flagler built the church in 1889 in memory of his daughter, Jenny. It was constructed without regard to expense in order to meet Flagler's goal of being finished within the year. From the towering 100-foot-high dome to the heavy wooden pews, all was completed on schedule except for the stained-glass windows, which took 12 years to finish. Unlike the former Ponce de Leon Hotel, the stained glass in the church was not produced by Tiffany, but by a German named Schlotterman, who worked closely with Tiffany. Flagler purposefully omitted a church bell, perhaps in the belief that the pealing would disturb his guests at the hotel. Flagler is entombed in the round mausoleum to the left of the entrance.

We need to make one more stop before heading across the Bridge of Lions on St. Francis Street. The Gonzalez-Alvarez House, known as "the **Oldest House**," is one of the country's best-documented homes. Although the settlement was repeatedly raided and razed by the English and pirates, Europeans and Americans have continuously occupied the site of the Oldest House since the early 1600s.

You'll find many splendid places to dine. Incredibly fresh seafood is served straight from the docks in more than 150 eateries on the beaches of Anastasia Island and in St. Augustine. Options range from waterfront shrimp shacks to gourmet bistros and turn-of-the-century Victorian mansions. The area's strong Minorcan heritage inspires spicy dishes and savory specialties such as Pilau and sauces from the datil pepper.

Many local accommodations are within the budget of most vacationers. There are more than 7,000 guest rooms, suites, and villas in St. Augustine and along the beaches of Anastasia Island. The

The Gonzalez-Alvarez House, the oldest house in the nation's oldest city, has been occupied since the early 1600s.

28 Victorian and colonial bed-and-breakfasts and lodges in the historic district offer more than 160 guest rooms. Or if you like the outdoors, there are RV parks and three state parks for roughing it.

Now, let's cross the magnificent **Bridge of Lions** to Anastasia Island and its 24 miles of beaches. We'd be remiss not to tell you the real name of the span—it's the Henry Flagler Memorial Bridge, built in 1927. You'll note the beasts carved of Carrara marble.

Anastasia State Recreation Area is a 1,700-acre bird sanctuary with five miles of beaches, lagoon waterways, wildlife, and sand dunes.

Faver-Dykes State Park, located at the southern tip of St. Johns County, is a 752-acre forest for endangered bald eagles and wood storks. It boasts trails and camping areas along its meandering marshes.

Guana River State Park in nearby Ponte Vedra Beach is a pristine 2,200-acre preserve with a five-mile strand, an ancient Spanish well, and 2,000-year-old Indian shell bluffs.

The Atlantic's waves are sprinkled with water enthusiasts who are busy sailing, windsurfing, scuba diving, and body surfing. Surf and jetty casters reel in black drum, bluefish, redfish, sea trout, snook, and Spanish mackerel. Pier angling is available at **Lighthouse Pier, Vilano Beach Pier**, and the **St. Johns County Pier** at St. Augustine Beach. Common catches are sheepshead, flounder, trout, black drum, and redfish. Farther out, private and charter boats carry deep-sea anglers to marlin, kingfish, sailfish, dolphin, and wahoo.

We stayed on Anastasia Island at **Beacher's Lodge**, located right on the Atlantic. It's close to our next attractions, the St. Augustine Alligator Farm and the St. Augustine Lighthouse.

The **St. Augustine Alligator Farm**, located on

The St. Augustine Alligator Farm is home to 2,700 gators and crocs, and the only place in the world where you can see all 23 crocodilian species in one place.

FL A1A, began in 1893 and is one of the oldest attractions in Florida. Here, you'll see all 23 species of crocodiles—2,700 alligators and crocodiles in all, including rare white alligators. Plan on spending several hours and catching a couple of the shows. One tidbit we learned is that alligators lose their teeth and grow new ones throughout their lives. They have 700 to 800 teeth in a lifetime. And their tails are not defensive weapons—during the show, you'll learn what they're used for. Alligator feedings take place twice daily. They are usually served nutrias, rodents imported to Louisiana that are now a nuisance. You cannot feed the alligators, but you may feed the other animals. Also on the premises is a rookery that is part of the Florida Birding Trail. It is home to hundreds of egret, ibises, herons, and other wading birds. The farm is home to many exotic and endangered animals. It is open every day.

Our next-to-last stop was a real treat because we learned that running a lighthouse involved a lot more than we thought. Looking through the keeper's logs showed us their many duties: going out to rescue people from sinking ships, repairing glass that ducks crashed into, putting up netting to prevent it from happening again, etc. The work went on and on like that for years.

The **St. Augustine Lighthouse** replaced a Spanish watchtower made of coquina. Fires were built on top of the watchtower to mark its location for the Spanish fleet.

No two lighthouses are painted the same, nor do any have the same flashing-light pattern. Thus, they may be distinguished day or night. The St. Augustine Lighthouse is painted with a black and white spiral, and the light flashes every 30 seconds. The top of the lighthouse is 165 feet above sea level. Weather permitting, you may climb the steps inside the lighthouse, stroll around the observation deck, and look into the lens room. Children must be seven years old and four feet tall. In case you're wondering about taking the elevator, there isn't one.

The first lighthouse on the site was approximately 500 yards northeast of the current one. It fell into the ocean in 1880. Construction on the present lighthouse began in 1871 and was completed in 1874. Its 219 steps lead to the first-order Fresnel lens. The Fresnel recipe for glass was destroyed by Hitler's men in World War II and has not been duplicated. In 1955, the lighthouse

At the St. Augustine Lighthouse you're only 219 steps from a panorama of the Atlantic beaches and the story of the intricate working of lighthouse life.

was automated, and lamplighters—men who tended the light but did not live on-site—replaced the keepers. This is a functioning, Coast Guard-maintained lighthouse and an active aid to navigation. In February, you may see migrating right whales from the top of the lighthouse.

You'll notice a building attached to the base of the tower. It's the oil house. To the left of the entrance was the keeper's office. Lighthouse keepers were required to keep detailed records. To the right of the entrance is the fuel storage room.

Originally, lard oil was used because whale oil was already expensive and scarce in 1874. Later, a brick storage building was built on the grounds when kerosene replaced lard as the fuel. In winter, the keepers heated the oil to a liquid state, then rushed up the steps to pour it into the reservoir before it congealed again. Once you walk the steps, think about having to run them with a 30-pound bucket of oil.

The keeper's quarters, a two-story brick duplex, was gutted by fire in 1970. The Junior Service League of St. Augustine restored the structure and opened it as a museum. One side of the keeper's quarters has been restored to its Victorian appearance. The basement has exhibits. You'll also find a gift shop with books and lots of model lighthouses. The house and the tower are listed on the National Register of Historic Places.

Our last stop has plenty of sea life to see. Go south on FL A1A beyond the Matanzas Inlet bridge. **Marineland** opened its doors to visitors in 1938. The world's first oceanarium, it became Florida's most popular attraction in the 1950s, earning a spot on the National Register of Historic Places. Some areas were being remodeled when we visited.

You'll see dolphins, sea lions, penguins, flamingos, and other wildlife. The daily programs and presentations make this a matchless experience. The Dolphin Encounter program allows you to enter the water with dolphins. Guests attend a presentation about dolphins and what it takes to work with these graceful mammals. Then they suit up and get in with them. Availability is limited, so be sure to make reservations. If you like to snorkel or scuba-dive, you can jump in the 450,000-gallon Rectangular Oceanarium, where you'll get to rub fins with stingrays, sea turtles, and a plenitude of fish. If you prefer to stay dry, you can

walk around the top and look down on the sea creatures, or go downstairs and look through the glass windows. Marineland's original attraction, it contains more than 500 fish, representing 50 species. The observation glass was especially formulated to allow filming of underwater scenes for Hollywood productions.

All of the following are in St. Augustine and use the 32084 zip code and 904 area code, except where noted.

 ## ACCOMMODATIONS

Beacher's Lodge—6970 FL A1A S., 32080; 800-527-8849 or 471-8849

Casa De La Paz—22 Avenida Menéndez; 800-929-2915 or 829-2915

Casa Monica Hotel—95 Cordova St.; 800-648-1888 or 827-1888

Casablanca Inn—27 Avenida Menéndez; 800-826-2626 or 829-0928

St. Francis Inn—279 St. George St.; 800-824-6062 or 824-6068

 ## ATTRACTIONS

Castillo de San Marcos—1 S. Castillo Dr.; 829-6506

Florida Heritage Museum and Old Jail—167 San Marco Ave.; 800-397-4071 or 829-3800

Fort Matanzas National Monument—8635 FL A1A S., 32086; 471-0116

Fountain of Youth National Archaeological Park—11 Magnolia Ave.; 800-356-8222 or 829-3168

Ghostly Encounter—One King St.; 800-597-7177 or 827-0807

Ghosts Tours—6 Granada St.; 888-461-1009 or 461-1009

Guana River State Park—2690 S. Ponte Vedra Blvd., Ponte Vedra Beach, FL 32082; 825-5071

Harbor Shuttle—264 St. George St. #3; 823-3094

Lightner Museum—75 King St., 32085; 824-2874

Marineland—9600 Ocean Shore Blvd., Marineland, FL 32080; 888-279-9194 or 460-1275

Memorial Presbyterian Church—32 Sevilla St.; 829-6451

Nombre de Dios—27 Ocean Ave.; 824-2809

Old Florida Museum—254 San Marco Ave.; 800-813-3208 or 824-8874

Old Town Trolley Tours—167 San Marco Ave.; 829-3800

Oldest House—14 St. Francis St.; 424-2872

Oldest Store Museum—4 Artillery Ln.; 829-9729

Porter's Wax Museum—17 King St.; 584-4781

Ripley's Believe It or Not! Museum—19 San Marco Ave.; 824-1606

Spanish Quarter Village—P.O. Box 210, 32085; 825-5033

St. Augustine Alligator Farm—999 Anastasia Blvd., 32080; 824-3337

St. Augustine Lighthouse and Museum—81 Lighthouse Ave.; 829-0745

CAMPING

Anastasia State Park—1340-A FL A1A S., 32084; 461-2033

Devil's Elbow Fish Camp—7507 FL A1A S., 32086; 471-0398

Faver-Dykes State Park—1000 Faver Dykes Rd., 32086; 794-0997

North Beach Camp Resort—4125 Coastal Hwy., 32095; 824-8309

Ocean Grove RV Resort—4225 FL A1A S., 32084; 471-3414

Pacetti Marina and RV Park—6550 FL 13 N.; 284-5356

Peppertree RV Resort—4825 FL A1A S., 32084; 800-325-2267 or 471-5263

Shamrock Campground—3575 US 1 S., 32086; 797-2270

St. Augustine Beach KOA—525 W. Pope Rd., 32084; 471-3113

St. Johns RV Park—2495 FL 207, 32086; 824-9840

Stagecoach RV Park—2711 CR 208, 32093; 824-2319

 DINING

A1A Ale Works—1 King St.; 829-2977

Barnacle Bill's Seafood House—14 W. Castillo Dr.; 824-3663

Columbia—98 St. George St.; 824-3341

Florida Cracker Café—81 St. George St.; 829-0397

Fusion Point—237 San Marco Ave.; 823-1444

Harry's—46 Avenida Menéndez; 824-7765

La Parisienne Restaurant—Seaside Plaza, 60 Hypolita St.; 829-0055

Mi Casa Café—69 St. George St.; 824-9317

95 Cordova—95 Cordova St.; 810-6810

Oasis—4000 FL A1A at Ocean Trace Rd., St. Augustine Beach, FL; 471-3424

O'Steen's Restaurant—205 Anastasia Blvd.; 829-6974

 EVENTS

January—Winterfest

February—Menéndez Day

March—Spring Arts and Crafts Show

April—Sawgrass Jazz and Blues Festival

Palm Sunday—Blessing of the Fleet

May—Gamble Rogers Folk Festival

June—Spanish Night Watch

June—Drake's Raid

Summer—Minorcan Festival

September—Founder's Day

November—Colonial Folk Arts and Crafts Fair

December—British Grand Illumination

 FOR MORE INFORMATION

St. Johns County Visitors and Convention Bureau—88 Riberia St., Suite 400; 800-418-7529 or 829-1711; www.visitoldcity.com

HIGHLIGHTS

DAYTONA INTERNATIONAL SPEEDWAY

MUSEUM OF ARTS AND SCIENCES

HALIFAX HISTORICAL MUSEUM

SUGAR MILL BOTANICAL GARDENS

PONCE INLET LIGHTHOUSE

When you hear the name Daytona Beach, you probably think of two things—racing and great beaches. The racing tradition at this Atlantic-coast city between St. Augustine and Cape Canaveral began on the hard-packed sands of Ormond Beach in 1902. Credit is given to oil billionaire John D. Rockefeller because he spent his winters in Ormond Beach. His presence attracted other affluent people, Ransom E. Olds, the founder of Oldsmobile, among them. Local legend maintains that Olds asked one of his friends, Alexander Winton, if he had ever sped down the beach. Winton, who owned a sports car called "the Bullet," took Olds's comment as a challenge to race. The race between them ended in a tie, but it didn't end Winton's fascination with speed. He returned in 1903 with "the Bullet No. 2" to set a land-speed record of 68 miles per hour.

Races were held on the shores of Ormond Beach and Daytona Beach from 1904 to 1935. A new land-speed record was set 15 times. Sir Malcolm Campbell broke his world record five times at Daytona Beach between 1928 and 1935.

His most famous run occurred in 1935, when he tried to achieve a speed at 300 miles per hour. Campbell's official speed of 276.82 miles per hour was his last run at Daytona Beach. That year also marked the end of the beach speed runs.

This history is celebrated at the **Boardwalk** amusement area, where the Speeding Through Time exhibit features over 30 granite plaques.

Daytona grew from two cars racing along the beach to the home of NASCAR and Daytona International Speedway.

Memorabilia from the early days of racing can be found at the Halifax Historical Museum, located at 252 South Beach Street.

In the early 1940s, Bill France began a career as a race promoter. He and 18 other members of the racing industry formed the National Association of Stock Car Racing (NASCAR) on December 14, 1947. The following year, a new four-mile stretch of beach track near Ponce Inlet incorporated a paved portion of FL A1A. Today, you can see the original first turn at **Oceandocks**, an open-air seafood restaurant, and beach racing artifacts and videos at the Ponce Inlet Lighthouse Museum, located at the southern end of the peninsula.

Crowds congregated for a decade to see the beach races, but France had a vision of a track designed for stock-car racing. In 1959 came the completion of a high-banked 2.5-mile track known as Daytona International Speedway. The first Daytona 500 was run on February 22, 1959, in front of 41,000 spectators. The race had an ending similar to the one run by Olds and Winton in 1902. Initially, it was judged too close to call. Johnny Beauchamp claimed victory that day, but three days later, after newsreels were reviewed, Lee Petty was named the first Daytona 500 winner.

Now, more than 200,000 race fans attend the Daytona 500, held each February. Other races include the Pepsi 400 in July, motorcycle races in March and October, and go-carts races the week after Christmas.

Daytona USA is a year-round attraction dedicated to auto racing. It features a historic walk of fame that chronicles events in racing and the evolution of speed. Sir Malcolm Campbell's restored Bluebird V is on display, as is the current winning Daytona 500 car. You can watch a 15-minute film,

participate in a do-it-yourself pit stop, play racing-themed video games, and race in the computer simulators before a screen of track. I had fun doing this, but Cathy rode with a friend who wiped out and raced in the wrong direction half the time. It feels very real—so real that you have to attend a short class before firing your engine. You can also take a narrated tour into the infield, but I suggest not doing that while cars are running, since you won't be able to hear anything. But you can certainly get some good photos from the inside fence. And take earplugs!

Daytona Beach's largest tourist event is **Bike Week**, held the first week in March. More than 400,000 motorcyclists make an annual pilgrimage. Motorcycle gangs are strongly discouraged from attending. **Biketoberfest**, held in October, is another event that attracts motorcycle enthusiasts. Known for its family-oriented activities, it draws about 60,000 motorcyclists.

Among Daytona's many good restaurants is one that out-kitsches them all. *Kitsch* is defined as shoddy or cheap artistic or literary material. **Buca di Beppo** (which translates as "Joe's Basement") is all that and a whole lot more. It's the most entertaining and interesting restaurant we've ever experienced. Don't get the wrong idea—it serves excellent food in servings larger than you can eat. In fact, your meal comes with a take-home box. The scrumptious Italian dishes are served family-style. The servers are half the fun, and the kitsch on the walls completes the humorous mayhem. One word of advice: Be sure to go in the restroom.

At the other end of the spectrum is the elegant atmosphere at the **Clocktower Restaurant** at the Adam's Mark. The **Adam's Mark Resort**, the Ocean Walk Resort, and the surrounding attractions and shops make up **Ocean Walk Village**,

This photo of the Ocean Walk Resort gives guests a great view of the Atlantic, its beaches, and the mirthful Lazy River tube ride.

a $200 million oceanside district to be completed around the end of 2002.

We stayed at the **Ocean Walk Resort**, located at 300 North Atlantic Avenue. This 300-unit luxury resort had just opened. We spent time relaxing in the whirlpool and splashing in the Lazy River, a rush of water that pushes oversized tubes around a narrow, walled course. Golfers can practice at the indoor training center before hitting some of the nearby championship links. The traffic-free Atlantic beach is only a few yards away, and two amusement parks are close by. I got a bang from the reverse bungee slingshot.

Adventure Landing Park is located across from the resort on Earl Street. It offers five acres of rides, water slides, miniature golf, a two-level go-cart track, and an interactive arcade with more than 300 games. It's a kid's paradise.

The **Museum of Arts and Sciences** is located adjacent to the **Tuscawilla Nature Preserve** at 1040 Museum Boulevard, west of Nova Road. Exhibits at the museum include a 130,000-year-old, 13-foot-tall giant sloth, African ritual art, and Chinese art.

Of special interest is the largest collection of Cuban art in the free world. The collection encompasses cigar-making equipment, service medals from the Spanish-American War, and photos of tourists in Havana in 1912. All in all, 500 years of relations between Cuba and Florida are represented. Fulgencio Batista was a major donor to the museum. Batista was elected president of Cuba in 1940 and left office in 1944. He lived on the Halifax River in Daytona Beach throughout the 1940s and 1950s. He returned to Cuba in 1952, but polls indicated he couldn't win the election, so he led a military coup to seize control. On January 1, 1959, he left Cuba, but President Eisenhower refused him admission to the United States. He subsequently lived in the Dominican Republic, Portugal, and Spain, where he died in 1973.

You'll also want to check out the **Root Family Museum**, part of the Museum of Arts and Sciences. The Root family designed the Coca-Cola "Mae West" bottle. You'll see glass bottles representing the changing trends in bottling over the decades. Also displayed are a range of early Coke

The Museum of Arts and Sciences houses several museums including Fulgencio Batista's collection of Cuban art and the Root family's large Coca-Cola vending-machine collection.

vending machines, a 1925 Model-T route truck, and much more. This is the second-largest collection of Coca-Cola memorabilia in the world.

Two railroad cars are displayed as part of the newest permanent exhibit at the Museum of Arts and Sciences. The Root family traveled throughout the country in these railroad cars, known as "Dell Rapids" and "Silver Holly." Dell Rapids, built in 1948, is one of six cars of its type ever made. This observation-parlor car features a lounge area with windows across the ceiling and down and around the car's end. You'll have to walk through these cars to believe the opulence. And you'll find it hard to believe that they were piles of tattered, rusty junk before restoration.

Due north of the museum at 640 Mary McLeod Bethune Boulevard is the two-story **Mary McLeod Bethune Home**, where you will find a good deal of African-American history. Dr. Bethune was a famous civil-rights leader and educator and the founder of Bethune-Cookman Col-

lege. Her home preserves her legacy in numerous citations, plaques, artifacts, and photographs. Bethune played a major role in developing the national desegregation movement and was the highest-ranking appointee to President Franklin Roosevelt's "Negro Cabinet."

Beginning with just $1.50 and five young pupils, Bethune, a daughter of freed slaves from South Carolina, opened the doors to the Daytona Literary and Industrial School for Training Negro Girls in 1904. The school later merged with Jacksonville's Cookman College in the mid-1920s.

Bethune was laid to rest behind her home. The home and grave site are open for viewing year-round.

Daytona Beach is recognized as the site of the first racially integrated game in major-league baseball history. This historic contest featured the Brooklyn Dodgers and the Montreal Royals, a Dodgers farm team. In early 1946, Hall of Fame legend Jackie Robinson, then with the Montreal Royals, was forbidden to play in neighboring Florida cities because of rigid segregation laws. On March 17, thanks to the combined efforts of Dr. Bethune, the publisher of the local newspaper, and the general manager of the Dodgers, Robinson played in Daytona Beach. His historic feat led to the end of the color barrier in major-league baseball.

The place where Robinson made history was renamed **Jackie Robinson Ballpark**. At the entrance stands a bronze statue of Robinson with two children. It was dedicated by his wife, Rachel, on September 15, 1990. Located in the heart of Daytona Beach's historic downtown waterfront area, the ballpark is home to the Florida State League's Daytona Beach Cubs, an affiliate of the Chicago Cubs.

While you're in town, be sure to visit the

Halifax Historical Museum at 252 South Beach Street—but make sure you have a couple of hours to spend. Cathy took enough notes on Indian and Spanish history to make a small book. The museum features Indian and Spanish artifacts found at nearby plantations, automobile-racing memorabilia from the early years, and a wide range of artifacts from antique typewriters to surfboards. It's open Tuesday through Saturday. An admission fee is charged.

If you drive south on Nova Road (CR 5A) from the Museum of Arts and Sciences, turn left on Herbert Street, and go left on Old Sugarmill Road, you'll come to **Sugar Mill Botanical Gardens**. Here, you'll see two rarities in addition to the botanical gardens. One of them is the remains of Florida's first attraction, the Bongoland theme park; fifty-year-old dinosaur statues still haunt the premises. The other is the ruins of the Dunlawton Plantation sugar mill, listed on the National Register of Historic Places. You'll see a rare collection of iron boiling kettles, pistons, a steam furnace, and the gears of a sugarcane press. The mill, used to process sugar, molasses, and rum, was destroyed during the Seminole Indian War of 1835.

There is no admission charge for the gardens, which provide a wholesome family environment where you can stroll the trails and learn more about the extensive flora and fauna native to Florida.

We welcomed the boat ride from Port Orange to Ponce Inlet via **Sunny Daze and Starry Nites River Cruises**. We boarded at 4009 Halifax Drive under the Dunlawton Avenue Bridge and learned about the Halifax River from Captain Mark Sheets's narration. The leisurely trip provided us plenty of opportunities to see and photograph an assortment of wildlife that included pelicans, her-

Sugar Mill Botanical Gardens has a rare collection of sugar cane processing items, botanical gardens, and remnants of Florida's first roadside attraction, Bongoland theme park.

ons, egrets, and dolphins. Though we saw no manatees on our trip, they're often present.

We got off the boat at the southern end of the peninsula and walked a short distance to the **Ponce Inlet Lighthouse**. Author Stephen Crane once shipwrecked near here, and he and his companions used the old Mosquito Inlet Lighthouse to steer to shore. Crane's classic story "The Open Boat" grew from that 1897 event.

The first lighthouse here, built in 1835 on the New Smyrna side, was never put to use because a storm undermined the foundation, causing the tower to lean. A year later, the lighthouse toppled into the ocean. The present structure is 175 feet tall. It was begun in 1883 and completed in 1887. The light from its first-order Fresnel lens shone 19 miles. The lighthouse, which still operates today, rests on a foundation 12 feet deep and 45 feet wide. The lower wall of the rust-red cone is solid brick eight feet thick. The structure was renamed the Ponce de Leon Inlet Lighthouse in 1926, probably because the people encouraging tourism thought the word *mosquito* was not particularly seductive. Some 203 steps lead to the top. Those who make the climb are rewarded with a panoramic view of Ponce Inlet, the Halifax River, and the surrounding area. We watched surfers ride waves at the mouth of the inlet.

Other buildings around the lighthouse house maritime artifacts, educational exhibits, a rare Fresnel Lens exhibit, and photos and video of the Daytona Beach races held on the nearby sands.

The lighthouse is open seven days a week. A gift shop is on the premises.

While you're here, see if you find **Inlet Harbor Marina and Restaurant** as delightful as we did.

From May 1 through October 31, the area beaches host spawning sea turtles. They come out of the surf at night to lay their eggs in the sand, after which they return to the sea. Two months later, baby turtles emerge from the nests and crawl to the ocean. To protect these vulnerable babies, rules are in place that prohibit beach driving and limit beachfront lighting at night.

The fishing in and around Daytona Beach is spectacular. Marlins and blues are found in the Gulf Stream. Closer to shore, sailfish, dolphin, king mackerel, wahoo, and tuna are caught trolling. On the bottom around the reefs, grouper and red snapper are the most-sought species, while the king-sized jack crevalle and amberjack threaten to bust anglers' tackle. A fleet of nearly 25 off-shore craft, including both private charter and party boats, sails daily. Most boats leave from the docks at Ponce Inlet.

Surf fishing here is a year-round sport. It requires only medium-weight tackle and shrimp or mullet for bait. Pompano, whiting, bluefish, redfish, flounder, and jack crevalle thrive in the 23-

mile fishing area. Many varieties of fish are caught from the **Main Street Pier** in the heart of Daytona Beach and the **Sunglow Pier** at the southern end of the beach. There is a daily pier charge. Monthly and seasonal passes are available.

Tomoka State Park, located at 2099 North Beach Street in Ormond Beach, was once the site of the Timucuan Indian village of Nocorocco. It became the Mount Oswald Plantation in 1766. Today, the 1,540-acre park offers camping, fishing, nature trails, picnic areas, a boat launch, and canoe rentals.

Canoeing and kayaking enthusiasts may paddle a few area canoe trails that are part of the Florida Recreational Trail System. The **Spruce Creek Trail** begins 10 miles west of New Smyrna Beach at the Moody Bridge, one mile south of the Port Orange interchange on I-95. It then flows five miles upstream and nine miles downstream. The **Tomoka River Trail** begins on CR 40 one mile west of I-95 and flows for 13 miles. The **Bulow Creek Trail** begins at Bulow Plantation Ruins State Historic Site north of Ormond Beach and flows for 13 miles.

All of the following are in Daytona Beach and use the 32114 zip code and 386 area code, except where noted.

 A CCOMMODATIONS

Adam's Mark Resort—100 N. Atlantic Ave., 32118; 800-444-ADAM or 254-8200

Coquina Inn Bed and Breakfast—544 S. Palmetto Ave.; 800-805-7533 or 254-4969

Live Oak Inn Bed and Breakfast—448 S. Beach St.; 800-881-4667or 252-4667

Ocean Walk Resort—300 N. Atlantic Ave., 32118; 800-649-3566 or 323-4800

 ATTRACTIONS

Adventure Landing Park—601 Earl St.; 258-0071

Daytona Beach River Cruise—351 Basin St., Halifax Harbor Marina; 248-1441

Daytona International Speedway—1801 W. International Speedway Blvd.; 947-6800

Florida Coastal Cruises—P.O. Box 1227, New Smyrna Beach, FL 32170; 800-881-BOAT or 428-0201

Halifax Historical Museum—252 S. Beach St.; 255-6976

Mary McLeod Bethune Home—640 Mary McLeod Bethune Blvd.; 255-1401

Museum of Arts and Sciences—1040 Museum Blvd.; 255-0285

Ponce Inlet Lighthouse—4931 S. Peninsula Dr., Ponce Inlet, FL; 761-1821

Sugar Mill Botanical Gardens—950 Old Sugar Mill Rd., Port Orange, FL; 767-1735

Sunny Daze and Starry Nites River Cruises—4009 Halifax Dr. (at Aunt Catfish's Restaurant), 32129, Port Orange, FL; 253-1796

 CAMPING

Daytona Beach Campground—4601 Clyde Morris Blvd., 32119; 761-2663

Harris Village and RV Park—1080 US 1 N., Ormond Beach, FL 32174; 673-0494

International RV Park and Campground—3175 W. International Speedway Blvd.; 239-0249

Ocean Village Camper Resort—2162 Ocean Shore Blvd., Ormond Beach, FL 32176; 441-1808

Rose Bay Travel Park—5200 S. Nova Rd.; 767-4308

Seaside RV Park on the Ocean—1047 Ocean Shore Blvd., Ormond Beach, FL 32176; 441-0900

Sunshine Holiday Camper Resort—1701 N. US 1, Ormond Beach, FL 32174; 672-3045

Tomoka State Park—2099 N. Beach St., Ormond Beach, FL 32174; 800-326-3521 or 676-4050

 DINING

Barnacles Restaurant—869 S. Atlantic Ave.; 673-1070

Buca di Beppo—2514 W. International Speedway Blvd.; 253-6253

Clocktower Restaurant—Adam's Mark Resort, 100 N. Atlantic Ave.; 254-8200

Inlet Harbor Marina and Restaurant—133 Inlet Harbor Rd., Ponce Inlet, FL; 767-5590

Knickers—1000 Champions Dr.; 274-5742

 EVENTS

January—Winterfest Weekend

February—Daytona 500

March—Bike Week

May—Greater Daytona Beach Striking Fish Tournament

July—Pepsi 400

October—Biketoberfest

November—Birthplace of Speed Weekend Celebration

November—Greek Festival

December—World Karting Association Finals

 FOR MORE INFORMATION

Daytona Beach Area Convention and Visitors Bureau—126 E. Orange Ave.; 800-854-1234 or 255-0415; www.daytonabeach.com or www.daytonabeachcvb.org

30

Florida's Space Coast: Merritt Island-Titusville-Cocoa-Port Canaveral-Cocoa Beach-Melbourne

HIGHLIGHTS

KENNEDY SPACE CENTER VISITOR COMPLEX

MERRITT ISLAND NATIONAL WILDLIFE REFUGE

ASTRONAUT HALL OF FAME

COCOA BEACH PIER

RON JON SURF SHOP

BREVARD ZOO

You already know that Florida's Space Coast got its name from the space industry and that it is home to the Kennedy Space Center. But it also has many other worthwhile enticements, from Canaveral National Seashore to the Ron Jon Surf Shop. Brevard County stretches 72 miles north to south and 25 miles east to west. It includes Titusville, Merritt Island, Port Canaveral, Cape Canaveral, Cocoa Beach, Melbourne, and other cites offering museums, cruises, fishing, and golf.

What has 8,000 times more horsepower than all the cars in the Daytona 500 and weighs 6.2 million pounds? It's the 363-foot-long, 160 million horsepower Saturn V rocket. Want to see one? It's at the **Kennedy Space Center Visitor Complex**, located east on FL 405 across Indian River Lagoon from Titusville. Be prepared to stay all day, because there is much to see and do. Among the attractions are the space shuttle *Ex-*

plorer, the Rocket Garden, the Space Walk of Honor, the Launch Status Center, an exhibit on early space exploration, two IMAX theaters, seven places to eat, and two Space Shops. The best tour is that of the Apollo/Saturn V Center, where you'll learn about the history of American rocketry and see the launch of a Saturn V on a giant screen. It's exciting! Then you get to see the actual rocket on its side.

Also, this is the only place on earth where you can meet an astronaut and ask questions. This program is aimed at inspiring children to strive for excellence. Want more? Monday through Friday, you can dine with an astronaut, too. Time is limited, so each guest has the opportunity to get autographs, chat, and take pictures.

The visitor complex is open every day except Christmas.

Leaving the Kennedy Space Center, you'll

These five F-1 engines that power the Saturn V rockets are on display at the Kennedy Space Center. They have a perfect safety record; not one has ever failed.

notice **Merritt Island National Wildlife Refuge** on your left before you cross the bridge heading toward Titusville. Merritt Island's 140,000 acres harbor more federally endangered species than any other refuge in the United States. This is one of the top birding sites along Florida's Atlantic coast. One of the most popular features of the refuge is its one-way driving loop. The **Black Point Wildlife Drive** showcases wading birds, waterfowl,

shorebirds, gulls, and terns. Vast scrub lands cover most of the interior of the refuge. Migratory birds frequent the upland hammocks during spring and fall.

East of Merritt Island National Wildlife Refuge is **Canaveral National Seashore**. Here, you'll pass through scrublands populated by Florida scrub jays, which can usually be seen near the pay station. Of great interest to birders are the pelagic birds seen in fall and winter—boobies, shearwaters, storm petrels, Northern gannets, and jaegers. During fall, watch for migrating raptors. Merlins and peregrine falcons are seen here regularly.

When you reach Titusville, be sure to stop at the **Astronaut Hall of Fame**. Here, you can explore the world's largest collection of astronaut artifacts. You'll also see tributes to the heroes of the Mercury, Gemini, and Apollo programs. You can suit up, strap down, and blast off to experience the sensations of astronaut training aboard simulators like the G-Force Trainer, which is sure to put you tight in your seat. You can feel what it's like to walk on the moon, to ride a rover across the rocky Martian terrain, and to guide a space shuttle to a smooth landing. This taste of space is open daily except for Christmas.

A good way to get a perspective of the area while you're in Titusville is to contact **Space Coast Nature Tours**. This company will take you on a cruise in Indian River Lagoon, where you'll see eagles, dolphins, and alligators and enjoy views of NASA's space-shuttle assembly building and launch pads. Your guide is sure to offer interesting facts about the diverse history of the area.

From Titusville, go south on US 1 to the quaint little village of Cocoa. It's said that when trying to come up with a name for the growing community, a Mrs. James, who served meals to

The town named for a box of cocoa was first known for its citrus flavors.

travelers, looked on her shelves and saw a box of cocoa. She said, "Cocoa's a good name," and so it was. The name stuck.

The burgeoning citrus industry increased the population of Cocoa in the late 1880s. Then came the land boom of 1919 and the construction of bridges east to the new city of Cocoa Beach. The boom went bust in 1926. The next period of growth came courtesy of Patrick Air Force Base south of Cocoa Beach. It became a missile testing area, and the Space Coast grew. In 1975, Cocoa decided to recreate its old downtown and call it **Olde Cocoa Village**.

A walk around the village makes for a pleasant day of looking in shops and galleries. Be sure to scrutinize the large mural on Brevard Avenue. The walls of the Bank of America building were painted to depict historical scenes. The faces of the people in the mural were initially left blank. Citizens subsequently made donations to have their likenesses filled in. The **Porcher** (por-CHAY) **House**, located at 434 Delannoy Avenue, is listed on the National Register of Historic Places. It was

built in 1916 by Edward Porcher, who invented citrus-handling equipment. His wife, who was very fond of card games, had a heart, spade, diamond, and club carved into the coquina high on the front of the house. The city purchased the house in 1987 and restored it. You can tour it Monday through Friday. Also on Delannoy Avenue is **Travis Hardware**, a business that has been in the same family for more than 100 years. The character of the original 1885 building is preserved in the sliding ladders, tin ceiling, and skylights. The store was expanded in 1907.

The *Cocoa Belle*, a 90-foot sternwheeler, offers lunch and dinner cruises out of Cocoa. It leaves **Whitley Marina** for two- to three-hour runs in the Indian River. Dance cruises float away every Friday and Saturday evening.

Our next stop is Port Canaveral, located to the east via FL 528. Here, you'll find cruise ships galore, along with opportunities for fishing, swimming, manatee watching, picnicking, and camping.

From the opening of Disney World in 1971, Port Canaveral served the cruise industry as a port

Port Canaveral offers a wide variety of water sports and is the largest cruise-ship port in the United States.

of call for cruise ships. In 1982, Scandinavian World Cruises established Port Canaveral as its home port. In 1995, it became the home port for Disney Cruise Lines. In a short span, Port Canaveral grew into one of the largest cruise ports in the world. It became the busiest cruise port in the Western Hemisphere in 2000, offering berths for **Carnival Cruise Lines, Disney Cruise Lines, Royal Caribbean International, Sterling Casino Lines**, and **SunCruz Casino**. A great variety of cruise choices is available for adults or families with children—everything from gaming cruises that last part of a day to cruises to the Bahamas and the eastern Caribbean that stretch from three days to a week.

Visitors can also enjoy biking, swimming, surfing, sailing, snorkeling, diving, and sailboarding. Port Canaveral has developed more recreational facilities than all other ports in Florida combined.

Nearby **Jetty Park** encompasses 35 acres and is one of the most popular parks in Brevard County. It offers excellent fishing and camping facilities. **Port's End Park** is a four-acre park featuring a boat ramp and an observation tower for watching ships in the harbor. **Central Park** is a 10-acre facility featuring three launching ramps. These are just a few of the 126 parks in the county.

If you head south down FL A1A to Cocoa Beach, be sure to ride the **Cocoa Beach Trolley**, which will cost you only a dollar. This coastal community has some of the best restaurants and accommodations in the area. We stayed on the southern end of town at **Crawford's Cocoa Cabanas**. The cabanas are on the ocean. The one-bedroom versions sleep six and include a big-screen TV, a fully equipped kitchen, a picnic table, a grill, and laundry facilities. **Bernard's Surf, Fischer's, Gregory's Steak and Seafood, Lobster Shanty,**

Ron DiMenna began selling surfboards in New Jersey. Two years later he opened this Ron Jon Surf Shop in Cocoa Beach.

The Mango Tree, and many other restaurants can satisfy your dining desires while you're in Cocoa Beach.

Cocoa Beach Pier is one of the best places on the Space Coast to view a shuttle launch. More than 800 feet long, the pier offers four restaurants and the **Mai Tiki Bar**. You can shop at specialty stores, play volleyball in the sand, or fish from the eastern end of the pier for a fee.

Who hasn't seen the billboards for **Ron Jon**

Surf Shop scattered up and down the eastern seaboard? The shop in Cocoa Beach encompasses 52,000 square feet. Billed as a psychedelic palace of sand and surf, it is an out-of-this-world experience. The company began in 1963 with 3,000 square feet in a strip shopping mall. Don't worry about hours; the place never closes. The store offers a complete line of watersports equipment. Customers can rent beach bikes, surfboards, bodyboards, Jet-Skis, and surf gear. A scuba-diving training facility is on the premises.

Depending on the level of security at **Patrick Air Force Base**, you may not be able to go south down FL A1A to reach Melbourne from Cocoa Beach. Presently—and subject to change—RVs and covered trucks are not allowed to use FL A1A, pickups must stop for inspection, and cars must slow down through the inspection point. You may have to drive north, then go west on FL 520, then head south on US 1 to reach Melbourne.

While most of the city is located on the mainland, a small portion is on a barrier island. The Indian River Lagoon separates the two. Melbourne is ranked one of the most popular places in the nation for retirees.

The **Brevard Zoo**, located at the north end of town, should be your first stop. This is a magnificent community project constructed completely by volunteers. Unique to the Brevard Zoo is Paws On, a one-of-a-kind interactive environmental adventure where children and adults learn about animals through play and hands-on exhibits. At the zoo, you can walk into the mouth of a full-size replica of a right whale, tunnel through a giant soil cube, dig for dinosaur bones, and sit on a stegosaurus skeleton. More than 413 animals representing 126 species from around the world reside in naturalistic settings. Elevated boardwalks

This little guy at Brevard Zoo in Melbourne likes to be petted and will follow you around.

guide visitors through a lush tropical hammock past a variety of animals native to Latin America and Florida, including jaguars, llamas, rheas, giant anteaters, tapirs, monkeys, exotic birds, alligators, crocodiles, river otters, bald eagles, and red wolves. The recently opened Australia exhibit features an aviary containing cockatoos, lorikeets, budgerigars, and laughing kookaburras, along with an outback habitat of red kangaroos, emus, and wallabies. An admission fee is charged.

Andretti Thrill Park has five tracks to test your driving skills, a water thrill ride, a championship miniature-golf course, kiddie rides, the Rio Grande Express Railroad, laser tag, slot-car racing, and an arcade area. It's open daily year-round.

Florida's Space Coast offers some of the best fishing in the country. Few places in the world have the variety of species found here, from largemouth bass and crappie on the St. Johns River to redfish, trout, and snook in Indian River Lagoon to billfish offshore in the Atlantic.

Golfers will be glad to know there are 22 public courses in the county.

All of the following use the 321 area code, except where noted.

ACCOMMODATIONS

Anthony's on the Beach—3499 S. Atlantic Ave., Cocoa Beach, FL 32931; 800-301-1338 or 783-9892

Crawford's Cocoa Cabanas—1901 S. Atlantic Ave., Cocoa Beach, FL 32931; 799-0307

Indian River House Bed and Breakfast—3113 Indian River Dr., Cocoa, FL 32922; 631-5660

Inn at Cocoa Beach—4300 Ocean Beach Blvd., Cocoa Beach, FL 32931; 800-343-5307 or 799-3460

Royal Oak Resort and Golf Club—2150 Country Club Dr., Titusville, FL 32780; 800-884-2150 or 269-4500

South Beach Inn—1701 S. Atlantic Ave., Cocoa Beach, FL 32931; 800-548-4244 or 784-3333

Surfside Suites—176 S. Atlantic Ave., Cocoa Beach, FL 32931; 784-1182

Wisteria Inn—1924 Catterton Dr., Melbourne, FL 32901; 727-0717

ATTRACTIONS

Andretti Thrill Park—3960 S. Babcock St., Melbourne, FL 32901; 956-6706

Astronaut Hall of Fame—6225 Vectorspace Blvd., Titusville, FL 32780; 269-6100

Brevard Museum of History and Natural Science—2201 Michigan Ave., Cocoa, FL 32926; 632-1830

Brevard Zoo—8225 N. Wickham Rd., Melbourne, FL 32940; 243-WILD

Canaveral National Seashore—308 Julia St., Titusville, FL 32796; 267-1110

Captain John Kumiski Fishing Guide Service—284 Clearview Rd., Chuluota, FL 32766; 407-977-5207

Jetty Park—400 E. Jetty Rd., Cape Canaveral, FL 32920; 783-7111

Kennedy Space Center—SR 405, Merritt Island, 32899; 449-4444

Lone Cabbage Fish Camp—SR 520 (at St. Johns River Bridge), Cocoa, FL 32926; 632-4199

Merritt Island National Wildlife Refuge—P.O. Box 6504, Titusville, FL 32782; 861-0667

Museum of Art and Science—1463 Highland Ave., Melbourne, FL 32935; 242-0737

Porcher House—434 Delannoy Ave., Cocoa, FL 32922; 639-3500

Ron Jon Surf Shop—4151 N. Atlantic Ave., Cocoa Beach, FL 32931; 799-8888

Space Coast Nature Tours—30 N. Holiday Ln., Titusville, FL 32796; 267-4551

Valiant Air Command Warbird Museum—6600 Tico Rd., Titusville, FL 32780; 268-1941

 CAMPING

Cape Kennedy KOA Kampground—4513 W. Main St. (FL 46), Mims, FL 32754; 800-KOA-3365 or 269-7361

Casa Loma Estates—6560 N. Harbor City Blvd., Melbourne, FL 32940; 254-2656

Forest Village—8701 Meadowlark Dr., Cocoa, FL 32926; 631-0305

Jetty Park Campground—400 E. Jetty Rd., Cape Canaveral, FL 32920; 783-7111

Long Point Park and Campground—700 Long Point Rd., Melbourne Beach, FL 32951; 952-4532

Manatee Hammock Park—7275 US 1 S., Titusville, FL 32780; 264-5083

Oak Mobile Home and RV Park—915 Florida Ave., Cocoa, FL 32922; 632-2299

Outdoor Resorts of America—3000 FL A1A S., Melbourne Beach, FL 32951; 800-752-4052 or 724-2600

Sebastian Inlet State Recreation Area—9700 FL A1A, Melbourne Beach, FL 32951; 984-4852 or 589-9659

Tingley's Marina and RV Park—2750 Tingley Dr., Merritt Island, FL 32953; 452-0504

Wickham Park—2500 Parkway Dr., Melbourne, FL 32935; 255-4307

 DINING

Bernard's Surf—2 S. Atlantic Ave., Cocoa Beach, FL 32931; 783-2401

Bonefish Willy's—2459 Pineapple Ave., Melbourne, FL 32935; 253-8888

Cocoa Belle—Whitney Marina at Hubert Humphrey Bridge, Cocoa, FL 32922; 632-6262

Fischer's—2 S. Atlantic Ave., Cocoa Beach, FL 32931; 783-2401

Gregory's Steak and Seafood—900 N. Atlantic Ave., Cocoa Beach, FL 32931; 799-2557

Grills—Sunrise Marina, Port Canaveral, FL 32920; 868-2226

Lobster Shanty—2200 S. Orlando Ave., Cocoa Beach, FL 32931; 783-1350

Mango Tree—118 N. Atlantic Ave., Cocoa Beach, FL 32931; 799-0513

Royal China—1275 FL A1A N., Cocoa Beach, FL 32931; 784-8008

EVENTS

February—Jambalaya Jam in Melbourne

February—Grant Seafood Festival in Melbourne

March—Greek Festival in Melbourne

March—TICO Warbird Air Show in Titusville

March—St. Patrick's Day in Cocoa Village

June—Sebastian Inlet Sea Turtle Walks in Melbourne

August—Fais Das-Dos Cajun Festival and Craft Show in Melbourne

September—Family Salsa Festival in Melbourne

October—Boo at the Zoo in Melbourne

October—Oktoberfest in Melbourne

November—Space Coast Birding and Wildlife Festival at Merritt Island National Wildlife Refuge

December—Festival of Trees in Melbourne

FOR MORE INFORMATION

Space Coast Office of Tourism—8810 Astronaut Blvd., Suite 102, Cape Canaveral, FL 32920; 800-93-OCEAN or 868-1126; www.space-coast.com

31

Fort Pierce-Port St. Lucie-Lake Okeechobee

HIGHLIGHTS

FROGMAN MUSEUM

DOLPHIN WATCH AND WILDLIFE ECO TOURS

SAVANNAS STATE PRESERVE

SMITHSONIAN MARINE ECOSYSTEMS

ST. LUCIE COUNTY HISTORICAL MUSEUM

LAKE OKEECHOBEE

ROLAND MARTIN LAKESIDE RESORT

St. Lucie County includes two incorporated municipalities: Fort Pierce and Port St. Lucie. This area remains in a more natural state than any other part of the Treasure Coast.

Lieutenant Colonel Benjamin Kendrick Pierce came here in 1837 to establish a fort for the army during the Seminole War. After the Seminoles left for the Everglades in 1842, Fort Pierce began to develop as a permanent settlement. Today, the area is primarily agricultural, though tourism is burgeoning. It boasts a friendly lifestyle and the safest beaches in Florida. Eco-tourism, fishing, diving, and golf are drawing more and more people.

Fishing is the most popular sport in this area. You can find channel bass, snook, redfish, tarpon, and sea trout in the Indian River and the St. Lucie River. You can cast the surf and go offshore fishing. **North Jetty Park** has a protected beach that is popular among families with small children.

South Jetty Park, located on the south side of Fort Pierce Inlet, has restrooms, a 1,200-foot fishing jetty (the longest in Florida), and picnic shelters with grills. The miles of canals in St. Lucie County are famous for largemouth bass and bream. The chain of lakes that extends from Jensen Beach to Fort Pierce, known as the Savannas, is renowned for its bass.

The lobstering off St. Lucie County's shoreline is excellent because of Fort Pierce Inlet's breeding area. In-shore reefs ranging from 12 to 35 feet in depth offer excellent diving and trapping opportunities during lobster season, which runs from August through March. Record catches for the Treasure Coast have been taken here.

Diving is another popular sport here. From snorkeling to scuba-diving deepwater wrecks, St. Lucie County offers dive excursions for every level. The 1715 wreck of the Spanish Treasure

Fleet gave this area its name—the Treasure Coast. There are 11 dive sites between Fort Pierce and Port St. Lucie. Some wrecks are easily accessible, lying as close as 200 yards off the beach.

The UDT/SEAL Museum—popularly known as the **Frogman Museum**—is located on North Hutchinson Island in Fort Pierce, the same beach where the first United States Navy Frogmen trained for D-Day in 1943. This is the only museum dedicated to these elite men. You'll see equipment, weapons, diving gear, demolition apparatus, parachutes, rubber rafts, uniforms, photographs, and memorabilia from their missions from every era.

For those in the mood for a touring excursion, **Dolphin Watch and Wildlife Eco Tours** offers cruises through one of the country's most pristine ecosystems, the Indian River Lagoon. Dolphins, birds, and other wildlife can be seen roaming the river. The two-hour narrated trip starts with a tour through **Fort Pierce Inlet State Park** and continues to **Jack Island Wildlife Preserve**. Tours depart from the **Fort Pierce City Marina**. Reservations are recommended.

Savannas Recreation Area is home to the last freshwater lagoon system in the state. It offers fishing, boat ramps, hiking, nature trails, bird watching, canoe rentals, and camping. It covers 550 acres and encompasses five distinct biological communities. It's south of Fort Pierce at 1400 East Midway Road, between US 1 and Indian River Drive.

Savannas State Preserve, located east of Port St. Lucie, provides a glimpse of the largest remaining freshwater marsh on the east coast of Florida. It offers a multiuse trail for hiking, bicycling, and horseback riding. This area is ideal for wildlife viewing and canoeing. Guided canoe and walk-

ing trips are conducted from November through April.

The **Smithsonian Marine Ecosystems** exhibit, located at 420 Seaway Drive, next to the St. Lucie County Historical Museum in Fort Pierce, shows how marine ecosystems work and the role humans play in their preservation. The exhibit's 2,000-gallon Caribbean coral reef is home to hundreds of plants and animals. The reef illustrates the dynamic features of natural ecosystems in miniature.

The **St. Lucie County Historical Museum** is devoted to local history. Visitors here can see a re-creation of Seminole Indian encampments. The Galleon Room contains items from the wrecked 1715 Treasure Fleet. Among the other exhibits are a restored 1919 fire engine, a 1907 settler's home, a general store, and photo collections.

About 35 miles west of Fort Pierce is Lake Okeechobee. This shallow lake encompasses 730 square miles and offers excellent fishing, boating, and bird watching.

Fishing is an important part of Lake Okeechobee's tourism industry and several communities offer resorts, fishing guides, and marinas. The Roland Martin Lakeside Resort is pictured here.

Work started on the giant levee that encircles the lake in 1930, following two devastating hurricanes. On September 18, 1926, a storm hit Miami Beach, drove inland, and crumbled a portion of the five-foot earthen dike along the southern edge of Lake Okeechobee. Hundreds died and thousands were injured and left homeless. But the worst was yet to come. Two years later, a hurricane hit Palm Beach before reaching Lake Okeechobee. Much of the lake still had a natural shoreline at that time. The storm blew water northward, flooding the town of Okeechobee. Then the winds on the backside of the storm blocked the only escape routes as a wall of water roared over the towns of Belle Glade, Clewiston, and Pahokee on the southern shore. Nearly 2,000 people were killed. Out of the devastation came a network of flood-control canals and a 30- to 40-foot-tall levee—known as the Herbert Hoover Dike—that rings the lake. That construction dramatically changed South Florida and the Everglades, into which Lake Okeechobee drained.

Today, several small communities line the shores of the lake. Among them is Okeechobee, the county seat of Okeechobee County. Incorporated in 1915, Okeechobee has about 5,000 year-round residents. During winter and spring, many Northerners come to town to enjoy the mild weather, the fishing, and the wildlife.

Crappie fishing around Okeechobee is best from November to March and bream fishing from March to July. Largemouth bass and catfish are also taken from these fertile waters. **Okeechobee Fishing Headquarters** is home to the Lake Okeechobee Guide Association, which will gladly set you up with an experienced guide. Owner Greg Maclean is a Bassmaster Tournament winner.

Recreational boating is popular as well. Boat-ers can follow the St. Lucie Canal on the east, the centrally located Lake Okeechobee, and the Caloosahatchee River on the west to travel from the Atlantic to the Gulf. Airboats scoot across the lake. Several Okeechobee companies offer guided tours. The Kissimmee River enters the lake at Okeechobee, providing a little over 30 percent of the lake's inflow.

Lodging choices around Okeechobee include modern motels, lakeside fish camps, and RV parks including the **Okeechobee KOA Kampground Resort and Golf Course**, the largest KOA in North America.

Located north of town, **Kissimmee Prairie State Preserve** is a 75-square-mile remnant of the vast prairies that once covered Florida from Orlando to Okeechobee and nearly from the Gulf to the Atlantic. One of the last remaining dry prairies in Florida, it is home to the rare caracaras and Florida grasshopper sparrows. The preserve is accessible by foot, bicycle, or horse.

Clewiston, in Hendry County on the southwest shore of Lake Okeechobeee, was originally a campsite for Native Americans who came to fish. The first permanent development began in 1920, when Tampa banker Alonzo Clewis and his two Philadelphia partners purchased land, laid a railroad connecting Clewiston with the Atlantic Coast Line, and hired a company to begin dredging a drainage district. Within a few years, they planted sugarcane. The crop proved so abundant that Clewiston became known as "America's Sweetest Town." Sugarcane farming is still the main industry in the area. Huge citrus groves also thrive here. Hendry County produces more citrus than any other county in Florida.

Three marinas are located inside the locks at Clewiston. Fishing is intensely popular here. Just

The Clewiston Inn is on the National Register of Historic Places.

ask famed pro bass angler Roland Martin. His **Roland Martin Lakeside Resort** has 130 covered slips, a guide service, boat rentals, and a marina store that sells everything from tackle to sunscreen. He also offers an RV park with full hookups, motel rooms, efficiencies, bungalows, and condominiums.

The United States Sugar Corporation built the **Clewiston Inn** in 1938 to host company executives and visiting dignitaries, including President Herbert Hoover. It was also a favorite of the British Royal Air Force pilots who trained nearby during World War II. The inn has 47 rooms, including suites and efficiencies, a lounge with a lovely 1945 mural of the Everglades covering all four walls, and a restaurant that serves three meals daily.

Down the street, try to catch dinner at **Robbie's Restaurant** on Cracker Night, when catfish, turtle, gator tail, frog legs, quail, and turkey are served.

The **Clewiston Museum** tells the story of early Clewiston, including the arrival of the railroad, the Herbert Hoover Dike, and the sugarcane industry. It's open Tuesday through Saturday.

The **Okeechobee Scenic Trail** is approximately 110 miles long. It encircles Lake Okeechobee on top of the Herbert Hoover Dike. Part of the 1,300-mile Florida National Scenic Trail, it is popular for hiking, bird watching, biking, fishing, and photography. There are more than a dozen camping areas on or adjacent to the two-track gravel roadway, including United States Army Corps of Engineers primitive campsites and campgrounds operated by local governments in Pahokee, Belle Glade, Okeechobee, and South Bay.

All of the following use the 561 area code, except where noted.

 ACCOMMODATIONS

Clewiston Inn—108 Royal Palm Blvd., Clewiston, FL 33440; 800-749-4466 or 863-983-8151

Hutchinson Inn—9750 S. Ocean Drive, Jensen Beach, FL 34957; 800-909-4204 or 229-2000

Mellon Patch Inn—3601 FL A1A N., North Hutchinson Island, Fort Pierce, FL 34949; 800-656-7824 or 461-5231

Roland Martin Lakeside Resort—920 E. Del Monte Ave., Clewiston, FL 33440; 863-983-3151

ATTRACTIONS

Clewiston Museum—112 S. Commercio St., Clewiston, FL 33440; 863-983-2870

Dolphin Watch and Wildlife Eco Tours—1 Avenue A, Fort Pierce, FL 34950; 971-2855

Fort Pierce City Marina—1 Avenue A, Fort Pierce, FL 34950; 800-619-1780 or 464-1245

Fort Pierce Inlet Marina—1010 Seaway Dr., Fort Pierce, FL 34949; 464-8451

Harbortown Marina—1945 Harbortown Dr., Fort Pierce, FL 34950; 466-7300 or 466-0947

Kissimmee Prairie State Preserve—33104 N.W. 192nd Ave., Okeechobee, FL 34972; 941-462-5360

Little Jim's Marina and Fishing Bridge—601 N. Beach Causeway, Fort Pierce, FL 34949; 468-2503

Marina at Fort Pierce—219 Fisherman's Wharf, Fort Pierce, FL 34950; 461-1266

Okeechobee Fishing Headquarters—800-284-2446

Savannas Recreation Area—1400 E. Midway Rd. (Mail: 9551 Gumbo Limbo Lane, Jensen Beach FL, 34957), Fort Pierce, FL 34982; 800-789-5776 or 464-7855

Savannas State Preserve—Scenic Park Dr. off Walton Rd., Port St. Lucie, FL 34949; 468-3985

Smithsonian Marine Ecosystems—420 Seaway Dr., Fort Pierce, FL 34949; 462-FISH

St. Lucie County Historical Museum—414 Seaway Dr., Fort Pierce, FL 34949; 462-1795

Taylor Creek Marina—1600 N. Second St., Fort Pierce, FL 34950; 465-2663

UDT/SEAL Museum (Frogman Museum)—3300 N. FL A1A, North Hutchinson Island, Fort Pierce, FL 34949; 595-5845

CAMPING

Easy Livin' RV Park—4611 US 1 S., Fort Pierce, FL 34982; 461-0800

Holiday Out and Venture III—10701 S. Ocean Dr., Jensen Beach, FL 34957; 229-1300

Okeechobee KOA Kampground Resort and Golf Course—4276 US 441 S., Okeechobee, FL 34974; 800-562-7748 or 863-763-0231

Road Runner Travel Resort—5500 St. Lucie Blvd., Fort Pierce, FL 34946; 800-833-7108 or 464-0969

Savannas Recreation Area—1400 E. Midway Rd., Fort Pierce, FL 34982; 800-789-5776 or 464-7855

Sunnier Palms Nudist Campground—8800 Okeechobee Rd., Fort Pierce, FL 34945; 468-8512

Villages at Nettles Island—9801 S. Ocean Dr., Jensen Beach, FL 34957; 229-1300

 DINING

Clewiston Inn—108 Royal Palm Blvd., Clewiston, FL 33440; 863-983-8151

Harbortown Restaurant—1945 Harbortown Dr., Fort Pierce, FL 34950; 466-7300 or 466-0947

Robbie's Restaurant—711 E. Sugarland Hwy., Clewiston, FL 33440; 863-983-7001

 EVENTS

Monthly—Friday Fest, Fort Pierce

Monthly—Friday Fest, Port St. Lucie

Monthly—Wednesday Marina Magic, Fort Pierce

March—Okeechobee Speckled Perch Festival

April—Clewiston Sugar Festival

October through April—Fort Pierce Farmers' Market

October through May—Port St. Lucie Farmers' Market

 FOR MORE INFORMATION

Clewiston Chamber of Commerce—544 W. Sugarland Hwy., Clewiston, FL 33440; 863-983-7979

Okeechobee County Tourist Development Council—55 S. Parrott Ave., Okeechobee, FL 34974; 863-763-3959

St. Lucie County Tourism—2300 Virginia Ave., Fort Pierce, FL 34982; 800-344-TGIF; www.visitstluciefla.com

Visitors Information Center—482 Indian River Dr., Fort Pierce, FL 34982; 888-465-8243

HIGHLIGHTS

HENRY MORRISON FLAGLER MUSEUM

STRANAHAN HOUSE

BONNET HOUSE

RIVERWALK

MUSEUM OF DISCOVERY AND SCIENCE

BILLIE SWAMP SAFARI

ANNE KOLB NATURE CENTER

During a drive by the lovely estates just visible beyond the gated drives in Palm Beach, or during a boat ride along Millionaire's Row in Fort Lauderdale, where heirs of the Anheuser-Busch, Otis Elevator, and Blockbuster Video companies hang their hats and park their yachts, it's easy to see why this area is called "the Gold Coast." Supposedly, the name originated more than 100 years ago, when treasure was salvaged from shipwrecks off the coast.

Let's start our tour about 12 miles north of Palm Beach on US 1. Located near the Loxahatchee River, the **Jupiter Inlet Lighthouse** is open for tours on Sunday afternoons. The 105-foot brick tower stands 146 feet above sea level. Tours may be arranged at the **Loxahatchee Historical Museum**, housed in a re-created Florida Cracker-style building on US 1 in Jupiter.

One of Florida's billionaires, John D. MacArthur, donated prime oceanfront property in North Palm Beach for a state park. From exhibits in the nature center off FL A1A to nature trails and boardwalks leading to the unspoiled 1.8-mile beach, **John D. MacArthur Beach State Park** is a wonderful remnant of subtropical coastal habitat. Snorkelers find abundant marine life along the reefs in the 535 underwater acres. A good turtle-nesting site, the park's beach is the site of up to 1,400 nests of loggerhead, green, and leatherback turtles during the summer months. Both snorkel tours and turtle walks are offered during the summer.

Henry Flagler is best known in some circles as a wealthy founding partner of Standard Oil—or Exxon, as it's known today. But in Florida, he's known as the man who used his railroads and hotels to develop most of Florida's Atlantic coast.

The Breakers was one of the hotels built by Henry Flagler as his Florida East Coast Railway changed sleepy fishing villages to luxurious tourist destinations.

When his railroad arrived in West Palm Beach in 1894, the town had 1,000 residents. When Flagler opened his first Palm Beach resort, the Royal Poinciana on Lake Worth, its capacity was 1,200 guests. Many members of the social set began to travel from Newport, Rhode Island, to Palm Beach in the winter.

As word of the new resort spread, Flagler built a second hotel, the Palm Beach Hotel, on 140 acres between the Atlantic Ocean and Lake Worth. Through fires and rebuilding, the Palm Beach Hotel emerged as **The Breakers** overlooking the Atlantic in 1926. The exterior is of Italian Renaissance design. Inside are Venetian chandeliers and vaulted and frescoed ceilings in the lobby. No expense was spared in its creation. The Breakers has grown and undergone major renovations while maintaining its reputation as one of the finest resorts in North America. It has 572 rooms and 47 suites. The amenities include everything from children's programs, a spa, lovely gardens, and swimming pools to golf, tennis, snorkeling,

and scuba. Guests enjoy the finest dining available in a town known for its fine dining. Most visitors find there's little need to leave the grounds, unless it's to visit the high-end shops and restaurants on Worth Avenue or to tour the home of the man who built this fantastic edifice as he developed Florida's Atlantic coast.

The seventy-one-year-old Flagler constructed the opulent 55-room mansion he called Whitehall as a present for his third wife, 34-year-old Mary Lily Kenan. Completed in 1902, it cost $2.5 million to build and an additional $1.5 million to furnish. Thanks to the efforts of Flagler's granddaughter, this National Historic Landmark has been restored to its original appearance. It survives today as the **Henry Morrison Flagler Museum**. Visitors can take an excellent guided tour of the home. Flagler's personal railroad car is on display. It's been restored to the way it looked when Flagler took his historic ride to Key West on his newly completed railroad. Whitehall is closed on Mondays. An admission fee is charged.

Henry Flagler built Whitehall, the largest home in Palm Beach, as a gift for his new bride in 1902.

If you're in need of sustenance while you're in Palm Beach, check out the deli sandwiches at **Toojay's** or grab a sidewalk table, a burger, and slice of Key Lime Pie at **Chuck and Harold's**. If you're looking for elegance, try **Café L'Europe**, where you'll need reservations.

Across Lake Worth, Flagler laid out the streets of West Palm Beach, a town meant to provide homes for the laborers and fishermen who took care of the needs of the beautiful people in Palm Beach. One of a series of streets named alphabetically for plants, **Clematis Street** is the heart of West Palm Beach's entertainment district.

Located about 10 miles south of Palm Beach is Boynton Beach. West of town is the largest remaining undeveloped portion of the northern Everglades, the 147,000-acre **Arthur R. Marshall Loxahatchee National Wildlife Refuge**.

Delray Beach has a large public beach, ample public parking, and a section of FL A1A where structures are limited to the area across the street from the beach. A view of the ocean is thus blessedly restored.

As you continue south along FL A1A from Palm Beach toward Boca Raton and Fort Lauderdale, the Atlantic is often hidden from view by condominiums, resort motels, national franchises, and lots of No Trespassing signs. This discouraging monotony is relieved by the Gumbo Limbo Nature Center and Red Reef Park. The **Gumbo Limbo Nature Center** has aquariums, live exhibits, and displays on local flora and fauna. It's open daily except for Thanksgiving, Christmas, and New Year's. Located a few blocks south, the 67-acre **Red Reef Park** is open daily for swimming and snorkeling in the Atlantic.

At 93 acres, **Spanish River Park** is one of Boca Raton's largest. It offers picnicking, swimming in the Atlantic Ocean, fishing on the Intracoastal Waterway, nature trails, bike trails, and an observation tower with views of Boca Raton and the Atlantic.

The **Cloister Inn**, built in Boca Raton in 1926 by Addison Mizner, reflects the Mediterranean style favored by the Palm Beach developer. It is now the heart of the **Boca Raton Resort and Club**. Also part of the resort are a 27-story tower, golf villas, and the Beach Club. In addition to golf, a fitness and tennis center, and a variety of watersports, guests enjoy a full array of restaurants and a trio of bars.

Boca Raton's **International Museum of Cartoon Art** has more than 150,000 ways to make you smile, thanks to images created by more than 1,000 artists from around the world. It is closed on Mondays. The **Boca Raton Museum of Art** showcases works by Degas, Matisse, Picasso, and Klee in its permanent collection. It is open daily. Both museums charge an admission fee.

Before you cross the drawbridge at Pompano Beach, there's a small parking area on the right at Lighthouse Point. This is a good place to get a view of the **Hillsboro Inlet Lighthouse**, which is now on private property owned by the Hillsboro Beach Club. The lighthouse was built in 1907 to mark the northern edge of the infamous Florida reef and complete the navigational aids on Florida's Atlantic coast.

Cap's Place, located on the island off Lighthouse Point, is an unusual adventure in dining. Just getting to the island requires a boat ride. The rustic seafood restaurant was built on top of a barge brought here during the 1920s. The walls are covered with stories about the legendary restaurant's colorful past. You can catch the boat at the end of 24th Street N.E., but it's best to call for directions.

About 10 miles north of Fort Lauderdale, you'll reach Broward County's **Tradewinds Park**, where thousands of butterflies enchant all ages at **Butterfly World**. A butterfly-breeding laboratory displays the butterfly life cycle. Visitors also enjoy the botanical gardens, the café, the gift shop with all things butterfly-ish, and the garden center filled with plants that attract butterflies.

Lauderdale-by-the-Sea is located across the Intracoastal Waterway from the northern end of Fort Lauderdale. Its beachfront location is especially popular with divers. Three distinctive reefs are located here. The first begins 100 yards offshore and lies at a depth of 10 to 30 feet. The second has much better visibility and depths to 40 feet. The third reef is about a mile offshore and requires more experience, given the strong currents and greater depth. The reefs are home to tropical fish and lobsters.

The motels and inns here are generally small and the atmosphere relaxed. We enjoyed our stay at **A Little Inn by the Sea** overlooking the Atlantic. The three-story inn has 29 rooms and suites and a swimming pool. Continental breakfast is served each morning. We had only to stroll down El Mar Drive to the intersection with Commercial Boulevard to find a trio of restaurants and **Anglin's Fishing Pier**.

Bordered by the Atlantic Ocean on the east, the sprawling metropolis of Miami on the south, the elegance of Palm Beach to the north, and a half-million acres of the Everglades to the west, Fort Lauderdale and Broward County have been transformed from a spring-break party town into the heart of area culture and entertainment. Because of its 300 miles of navigable waterways, its man-made canals lined with beautiful homes, and its 40,000 resident yachts, it's easy to see why Fort

Lauderdale is called "the Venice of America." Fort Lauderdale, population 150,000 and growing, is Broward's largest city and the county seat.

Fans of John D. MacDonald's famous Fort Lauderdale sleuth, Travis McGee, have an image of Fort Lauderdale that extends beyond the 1960s film classic *Where the Boys Are*. Even so, they may be surprised to find that the beach communities east of the Intracoastal Waterway have been named among America's cleanest, and that Broward's Port Everglades is the second-largest cruise port in the world.

The area now known as Fort Lauderdale was inhabited by prehistoric people known today as the Glades Cultures, followed by Native Americans known as the Tequestas and eventually the Seminoles.

Fort Lauderdale took its name from Major William Lauderdale and his company of artillerymen and 200 Tennessee Volunteers, who established a fort on the New River in 1838, during the Second Seminole War. When the war ended in 1842, fewer than 300 Seminoles remained in Florida.

Fort Lauderdale's modern history began when Dade County authorized a rock road to be built from what is now North Miami to a ferry crossing on the New River in 1892. Ohio native Frank Stranahan managed the ferry and established a trading post on the New River. Along with the trading post in Everglades City, this was one of the two South Florida landmarks that established trade with the Seminoles.

The **Stranahan House** was built in 1901 on the banks of the New River to house Frank Stranahan's general store. The two-story wooden building had an upstairs community hall that was the scene of dances and other social events. It had

Fort Lauderdale's Stranahan House was an important part of the town's early settlement.

wide verandas that provided sheltered sleeping areas for the remaining Seminole Indians, who gradually emerged from their isolation in the Everglades and came to trade.

By 1906, his business was so successful that he constructed a second, larger store and converted the original trading post into a gracious frontier home for him and his wife, Ivy. The home was the setting for many of Fort Lauderdale's social events. Eventually, Stranahan was overcome by financial failure. He drowned himself in the New River in 1929. Restored to its 1915 appearance, the home is open for tours Wednesday through Sunday.

Hugh Taylor Birch, a Chicago attorney, made his way to Fort Lauderdale in 1893 after a storm in the Atlantic blew him to a safe harbor near the present location of Port Everglades. Believing it to be a sign that this was where God meant him to be, he bought more than three miles of ocean-front property stretching from the beach to what is now the Intracoastal Waterway. At the time, Henry Flagler's railroad ended in Titusville, and Fort Lauderdale was little more than a village.

Part of Birch's seaside estate is preserved in the 180-acre **Hugh Taylor Birch State Recreation Area**, one of his gifts to the people of Florida. His two-story home is now the park's visitor center. With 1.3 miles of hiking trails, canoe rentals for paddling on a freshwater lagoon, and fishing along the Intracoastal Waterway, this urban oasis is popular with joggers, picnickers, and sunbathers. An underpass beneath FL A1A, the coastal highway, provides safe access to the park's beach.

When Birch's daughter, Helen—a musician, composer, poet, and lover of Florida—married Frederic Clay Bartlett—a widower, an accomplished artist who had studied abroad, and an avid art collector—her father presented them with 35 acres stretching from the ocean to the New River on which to build a home. They called their 30-room home the **Bonnet House**, for the yellow bonnet lily growing in the coastal marshes. It was built during 1920 and 1921 using concrete blocks made on-site, native coral, and local wood brought

The grounds of the historic Bonnet House are home to an extensive collection of tropical flora and fauna. Photo courtesy of Greater Fort Lauderdale Convention and Visitors Bureau

to the site by boat. Helen died of cancer about six years after they married, but her husband continued to winter here and remained close friends with his father-in-law. Bartlett eventually remarried. He and his new wife, Evelyn, were both artists, and their home reflects their creative temperaments. Murals are on the ceilings, and sculptures and paintings are on display, as are treasures they brought back from all over the world.

At the time of their marriage, Fort Lauderdale was still sparsely settled, and the property was home to raccoons and wildcats. A panther was even spotted here. Today, the grounds remain a green oasis amid Fort Lauderdale's high-rise condominiums. The place is still home to raccoons, along with Brazilian squirrel monkeys, swans, wading birds, and Florida parrots. The home was donated to the Florida Trust for Historic Preservation in 1983. It is closed during holidays and from mid-August to mid-September but is open for tours Wednesday through Sunday the rest of the year. An admission fee is charged.

Fort Lauderdale's Riverwalk provides a great location for shopping, dining, strolling along the New River, outdoor concerts, and special events.

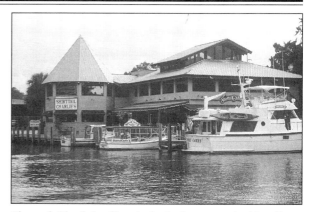

Shirttail Charlie's offers dockside dining on the New River in downtown Fort Lauderdale.

Fort Lauderdale's 22-block arts-and-entertainment district includes Las Olas Boulevard and Las Olas Riverfront. The brick-lined **Riverwalk** meanders along the New River past shops, restaurants including the **River House**, which serves dinner daily and brunch on Sunday, and cultural attractions like the **Fort Lauderdale Historical Museum**, which has displays of local artifacts and photos. The museum, part of an enclave of historical buildings known as **Old Fort Lauderdale**, is maintained by the Fort Lauderdale Historical Society.

Across the river, **Shirttail Charlie's** is a well-liked waterfront restaurant open for lunch and dinner daily. Other popular Fort Lauderdale restaurants include **15th Street Fisheries**, a good place for stone crabs in season, **Charley's Crab**, and **Shooters Waterfront Café**. For upscale dining, try the **Blue Moon Fish Company**, **Mark's Las Olas**, or **Burt and Jack's**, Burt Reynolds's restaurant in Port Everglades.

While exploring Riverwalk on foot is easy, the most entertaining way to get around town is by

The Great Gravity Clock in the atrium of the Museum of Discovery and Science is sure to catch your attention while telling you the time.

water taxi. You may choose a one-way, a round-trip, or an all-day pass for a memorable way to visit restaurants and attractions. Among the 25 scheduled stops are Riverwalk, Port Everglades, and several resorts, including the **Doubletree Oceanfront**, the **Hyatt Regency Pier Sixty-Six Resort**, the **Marriott Fort Lauderdale Marina**, and the **Lago Mar Resort**.

One of the attractions close to Riverwalk is the **Museum of Discovery and Science**. The 52-foot timepiece in the atrium known as the Great Gravity Clock gives a hint of the lighthearted but educational exhibits inside. Florida Ecoscapes introduces Florida's ecosystems. The Discovery Center is especially designed for children up to age seven. You can create your own gallery of sound in the musical kaleidoscope, explore the mysteries of space, or find out what causes a runny nose in the exhibit on Grossology, the impolite science of the human body. The Blockbuster IMAX Theater adjoins the exhibit area. The museum and IMAX are open daily except for Christmas. An admission fee is charged.

A few blocks away on Las Olas Boulevard is the **Museum of Art**, which offers rotating permanent collections that include an exhibit of 20th-century American and European art, a comprehensive exhibit of the works of American impressionist William Glackens, and an exhibit of African, Cuban, Pre-Columbian, and Native American art. The museum is closed on Mondays and major holidays.

Located west of Fort Lauderdale on Griffin Road, **Everglades Holiday Park** offers easy access to the Everglades, airboat rides, fishing, boat rentals, and a campground with RV hookups. A fee is charged for airboat rides and camping.

Two attractions are located still farther west of Fort Lauderdale and north of Alligator Alley, as the portion of I-75 that cuts across South Florida is known. The Big Cypress Seminole Indian Reservation's **Ah-Tah-Thi-Ki Museum** and **Billie Swamp Safari** are venues for a deeper understanding of the heritage of the Seminole tribe of Florida. The museum has the largest collection of rare Seminole artifacts in the world. It is closed Mondays and holidays. An admission fee is

The Ah-Tah-Thi-Ki Museum celebrates the traditions and the culture of the Florida Seminoles.

charged. The safari offers daily swamp-buggy eco-heritage tours, airboat rides into the Everglades, and alligator and snake shows. An overnight stay in a chickee hut may also be arranged.

Attractions south of Fort Lauderdale include the antique shopping district at Dania Beach and the **Anne Kolb Nature Center**, part of West Lake Park in Hollywood. Three walking trails, a canoe trail, a 4,000-gallon saltwater aquarium, and an observation tower guarantee that there's a way for everyone to explore the mangrove forest habitat. A small admission fee is charged on weekends but not on weekdays.

John U. Lloyd State Recreation Area offers a narrow, sandy beach, fishing off the jetty, a self-guided nature trail, canoe rentals, picnic areas, and restrooms. It is open daily. An admission fee is charged.

Another great stop in Dania Beach is the **South Florida Museum of Archaeology**. The museum's 25,000 square feet of exhibit space contain collections from Egypt, Africa, Asia, and Florida that include fossils, minerals, and under-

water artifacts. It's closed on Mondays. An admission fee is charged.

All of the following are in Fort Lauderdale and use the 33316 zip code and 954 area code, except where noted.

ACCOMMODATIONS

A Little Inn by the Sea—4546 El Mar Dr., Lauderdale-by-the-Sea, FL 33308; 800-492-0311 or 772-2450

Boca Raton Resort and Club—501 E. Camino Real, Boca Raton, FL 33431; 800-327-0101 or 395-3000

Breakers—1 S. County Rd., Palm Beach, FL 33480; 800-833-3141 or 561-655-6611

Doubletree Oceanfront—440 Seabreeze Blvd.; 524-8733

Hyatt Regency Pier Sixty-Six Resort—2301 S.E. 17th St. Cswy.; 525-6666

Lago Mar Resort and Club—1700 S. Ocean Ln.; 800-255-5246

Marriott Ft. Lauderdale Marina—1881 S.E. 17th St.; 463-4000

Palm Beach Historic Inn—365 S. County Rd., Palm Beach, FL 33480; 561-832-4009

Riverside Hotel—620 E. Las Olas Blvd.; 800-325-3280 or 467-0671

ATTRACTIONS

Ah-Tah-Thi-Ki Museum—HC-61, Box 21-A, Big Cypress Reservation, Clewiston, FL 33440; 941-902-1113

Anne Kolb Nature Center—West Lake Park, 751 Sheridan St., Hollywood, FL; 926-2410

Arthur R. Marshall Loxahatchee National Wildlife Refuge—10216 Lee Rd., Boynton Beach, FL 33437; 561-734-8303

Boca Raton Museum of Art—501 Plaza Real, Boca Raton, FL 33432; 392-2500

Billie Swamp Safari—HC-61, Box 46, Big Cypress Reservation, Clewiston, FL 33440; 800-949-6101

Bonnet House—900 N. Birch Rd., 33304; 563-5393; www.bonnethouse.com

Butterfly World—3600 W. Sample Rd., Coconut Creek, FL 33073; 977-4400

Gumbo Limbo Nature Center/Red Reef Park—1801 N. Ocean Blvd., Boca Raton, FL 33432; 561-338-1473

Henry Morrison Flagler Museum—Cocoanut Row and Whitehall Way, Palm Beach, FL; 561-655-2833

Hugh Taylor Birch State Recreation Area—3109 E. Sunrise Blvd., 33304; 564-4521

International Museum of Cartoon Art—201 Plaza Real, Boca Raton, FL 33432; 391-2200

John U. Lloyd State Recreation Area—6503 N. Ocean Dr., Dania Beach, FL 33004; 923-2833

Loxahatchee Historical Museum—Burt Reynolds Park, 805 US 1 N., Jupiter, FL; 407-747-6639

Museum of Art—1 E. Las Olas Blvd.; 763-6464

Museum of Discovery and Science—401 Second St. S.W.; 467-6637 or 463-IMAX

Old Fort Lauderdale Museum of History—219 Second Ave. S.W.; 463-4431

South Florida Museum of Archaeology and Natural History—481 S. Federal Hwy., Dania Beach, FL 33004; 925-7770

Stranahan House—335 E. Las Olas Blvd.; 524-4736

Tradewinds Park—3600 W. Sample Rd., Coconut Creek, FL 33073; 968-3880

Water Taxis of Greater Fort Lauderdale—651 Seabreeze Blvd., Ft. Lauderdale, FL 33316; 467-6677

CAMPING

Billie Swamp Safari—HC-61, Box 46, Big Cypress Reservation, Clewiston, FL 33440; 800-949-6101 or 863-983-6101

Everglades Holiday Park—21940 Griffin Rd.; 800-226-2244 or 434-8111

John Prince Park—2700 S. Sixth Ave., Lake Worth, FL 33461; 561-582-7992

DINING

Blue Moon Fish Company—4405 Tradewinds Ave., 33308; 267-9888

Burt and Jack's—Berth 23, Port Everglades, FL 33316; 522-2878

Café L'Europe—331 S. County Rd., Palm Beach, FL 33480; 561-655-4020

Cap's Place—941-0418

Charley's Crab—3000 32nd Ave. N.E., 33308; 561-4800

Chuck and Harold's Café—207 Royal Poinciana Way, Palm Beach, FL 33480; 659-1440

15th Street Fisheries—1900 15th St. S.E., 33316; 763-2777

Mark's Las Olas—1032 E. Las Olas Blvd., 33301; 463-1000

River House—301 Third Ave. S.W., 33312; 525-7661

Shirttail Charlie's—400 Third Ave. S.W., 33315; 463-3474

Shooters Waterfront Café—3033 N.E. 32nd Ave., 33308; 566-2855

TooJay's—313 Royal Poinciana Way, Palm Beach, FL 33480; 561-659-7232

EVENTS

First Sunday, January through December—Jazz Brunch

February/March—Baltimore Orioles spring training

April—Fort Lauderdale Seafood Festival

May—Cajun/Zydeco Crawfish Festival

September—Las Olas Art Fair

October—International Film Festival

December—Winterfest Boat Parade

FOR MORE INFORMATION

Greater Fort Lauderdale Convention and Visitors Bureau—1850 Eller Dr., Suite 303; 800-227-8669 or 765-4466; www.sunny.org

Palm Beach County Convention and Visitors Bureau—1555 Palm Beach Lakes Blvd., Suite 800, West Palm Beach, FL 33401; 800-833-5733 or 561-233-3000; www.palmbeachfl.com

HIGHLIGHTS

BARNACLE STATE HISTORIC SITE

VIZCAYA MUSEUM AND GARDENS

CAPE FLORIDA LIGHTHOUSE

MIAMI SEAQUARIUM

SOUTH BEACH ART DECO DISTRICT

A generation of television viewers watched as cameras panned across Biscayne Bay toward the glittering hotels each week as Jackie Gleason proclaimed Miami Beach the "sun and fun capital of the world." Miami has long been synonymous with wealth, corruption, and/or a decadent lifestyle. The truth may be that it's all the above and more.

The Tequesta Indians lived on the Miami River for 15 centuries before Europeans arrived. In 1763, the remaining Tequestas traveled with the Spaniards to Havana, disappearing from Florida forever as Britain assumed control.

In 1890, the area that is now Miami was little more than a pioneer outpost with a few hundred hearty souls. The two principal landowners in the area were Julia D. Tuttle and William B. Brickell. Afraid that Henry Flagler might stop his Florida East Coast Railroad at West Palm Beach, they offered him lucrative land incentives to come to Miami. The story goes that Flagler was finally convinced when Mrs. Tuttle brought him a healthy Dade County orange blossom following

Miami and Miami Beach have numerous beaches and marinas for enjoyment of water sports.

the great freeze of 1894-95, which destroyed most of Florida's citrus crop.

The first trains arrived during the spring of 1896. Flagler opened the Royal Palm Hotel, although he reportedly had doubts that the town would amount to much. Nevertheless, he paved roads, built a sewage system, and did so much that the city might have been named Flagler. When he turned down that honor, it was incorporated as Miami.

Promoters, touting South Florida for its healthful climate, soon began to use photos of tanned bathing beauties on sandy beaches to lure tourists. Long before it became known as "the American Riviera," developer Carl Fisher offered free beach property to anyone who would build in Miami Beach. Ten years later, in 1925, the place had more than 50 hotels, three golf courses, and nearly 200 apartment buildings.

The entire state enjoyed inflation in land prices during the early 1920s, Miami and Dade County leading the way. The peak came in 1925, when land in Miami fetched a whopping $25,000 per acre. It seemed that everyone who could afford to—and some who couldn't—bought land in sunny Miami. In some cases, land was sold before it was dredged above the water line.

In 1926, the real-estate boom hit the skids when a major hurricane hit the area, completely covering Miami Beach and flooding downtown Miami. The ensuing publicity quelled the public's desire for speculative Florida acquisitions. The entire state plunged headlong into economic depression well in advance of the national stock-market crash on October 29, 1929.

During the 1930s, large numbers of Jewish residents from New York City settled in Miami and Miami Beach, as did thousands of others wishing to escape the bitter Northern winters. They were followed during the late 1950s and early 1960s by middle- and upper-class Cubans fleeing Fidel Castro's revolution. Miami, like the entire state, became the home of a large population of relative newcomers.

To find your way around town, it helps to understand that Miami's streets are laid out in a grid pattern. Streets and terraces run east and west, with Flagler Street dividing the city into north and south. Avenues, courts, and places run north and south, with Miami Avenue dividing the city into east and west. The smaller the number of the street address, the closer it is to downtown Miami.

Beginning with the downtown area, the neighborhoods and towns of most interest to visitors include Little Havana, Coconut Grove, Coral Gables, and Key Biscayne to the south and South Beach and Miami Beach to the east.

In addition to the monoliths of steel and glass, downtown Miami is home to the **Metro-Dade Cultural Center** and its **Historical Museum of Southern Florida** and **Miami Art Museum**. The historical museum displays 10,000 years of South Florida history, while the art museum is a mix of modern and contemporary art.

Calle Ocho, or Southwest Eighth Street, is the last leg of the famed Tamiami Trail, which linked Tampa and Miami in 1928. It is also the main street of **Little Havana**, a Cuban residential community where English is definitely the second language. The heart of Little Havana lies between 12th and 27th Avenues, with most of the commerce on or near Calle Ocho. Cigar shops offer glimpses of traditional cigar rollers at work and samples of their efforts for sale; area restaurants serve a full range of Latin American foods; and Latin music reigns supreme on the streets and in the record shops.

Cape Florida Lighthouse keepers and their families homesteaded Coconut Grove, South Florida's oldest settlement, during the 1830s. It was home to Bahamians, Conchs, artists, writers, and bohemians on its way to becoming the lively, colorful community it is today.

Ralph Middleton Monroe, a native New Yorker, was 30 years old when he brought his wife and sister-in-law to the shores of Biscayne Bay in 1882. His wife had tuberculosis and died after the long trip, and his sister-in-law died on the way back north. Nonetheless, Monroe continued his winter visits to the wilds of South Florida. In 1891, he built a home that adhered to his twin tenets of simplicity and love of nature. The two-story home and five surrounding acres at **Barnacle State Historic Site** are what is left of Monroe's vision of Florida's Walden Pond. The home is open for scheduled tours Thursday through Monday. An admission fee is charged.

You can visit **Vizcaya Museum and Gardens** on South Miami Avenue in Coconut Grove to step out of the bustle of modern South Florida into 1916, when the wealthy co-founder of International Harvester, James Deering, chose native limestone to build his opulent Italian Renaissance mansion. The doors, ceilings, fireplaces, art, and furnishings were brought from Europe. The ten acres of gardens include both formal gardens and native plantings overlooking Biscayne Bay. The house is open daily. An admission fee is charged.

Across the street, the **Miami Museum of Science and Planetarium** explores the mysteries of the universe with hands-on exhibits and astronomy shows. The museum's wildlife center houses reptiles and birds of prey. The museum is open daily. An admission fee is charged.

Visitors to Coconut Grove have a wide choice of national franchise hotels and motels. At the **Cherokee Rose Lodge**, guests can choose a suite or a cottage by the pool at a private estate.

CocoWalk, located at 3015 Grand Avenue in the heart of Coconut Grove, has retail shops, bars, and restaurants, including the delightful **Café Tu Tu Tango**, a prime spot for people who like to enjoy the work of local artists adorning the walls while they dine.

Coral Gables was the dream of the son of a Massachusetts minister. The Reverend Solomon Merrick bought 160 acres southwest of Miami. Around 1906, he built a house his wife, Althea, designed, which had gables they mistakenly believed were made of coral, rather than limestone. Merrick's son, George, knew the two-story house as Coral Gables. It was this name George gave to the dream city he envisioned. The **Coral Gables House** has been restored and is open for tours on Wednesday and Sunday afternoons. A self-guided tour of the garden points out some of the original plantings. An admission fee is charged.

George Merrick built the luxurious 26-story **Biltmore Hotel** in 1926, only months before a devastating hurricane struck. It had hundreds of rooms—all with private baths—grand ballrooms, and the largest swimming pool in the world. The historic hotel stood unbowed before the hurricane, but the Florida land bust that followed threw George Merrick into bankruptcy. The Biltmore has been restored to its original grandeur. It offers 280 rooms and suites, an award-winning restaurant, an 18-hole golf course, lighted tennis courts, and a spa. The famous swimming pool is considered the largest in the continental United States.

Today, Coral Gables has lush golf courses, specialty shops, restaurants, and a large historic district with beautiful Mediterranean Revival and

Spanish Colonial homes that stand as a monument to Merrick's vision.

Located farther southwest, **Miami Metrozoo** is a totally cageless 290-acre complex. An air-conditioned monorail gives you the big view of the park, while moats keep lions and tigers, among others, at bay when you explore on foot. The zoo is open daily. An admission fee is charged.

The southern end of the island now known as Key Biscayne was discovered by explorer John Cabot in 1497 and named "the Cape of the End of April." When Spanish explorer Ponce de Leon came across it in 1513, he called it the Cape of Florida. Known for its ferocious storms, treacherous reefs, and many shipwrecks, Cape Florida was one of the first areas in the Florida territory to receive a lighthouse. A 65-foot tower was built in 1825 to mark the reef four miles offshore. During the Second Seminole War, Indians attacked the lighthouse and set fire to it. The lighthouse keeper was injured and his assistant killed before a navy rescue ship arrived. The present **Cape Florida Lighthouse** was built in 1846 and raised to its current 95 feet in 1855.

In addition to the scenic lighthouse, **Bill Baggs Cape Florida State Recreation Area** has a beach that was voted one of the top 10 in the United States. It also offers picnic areas, a café, and a concession that rents bikes, kayaks, and windsurfing equipment. It's located at the end of Rickenbacker Causeway on Key Biscayne between the Atlantic Ocean and Biscayne Bay.

Miami Seaquarium is open daily for those who'd like to take a look at one of four shows featuring dolphins, sea lions, and Lolita, the resident orca. More classic than cutting edge today, the Seaquarium's golden dome was designed by Buckminster Fuller. It is home to the sea lion show.

Among the other attractions are a 750,000-gallon saltwater aquarium and shark, manatee, alligator, and crocodile exhibits. You may also register for an interactive program with dolphins.

Lunch and dinner at the **Rusty Pelican** come with a gorgeous view of downtown Miami. Much more rustic, the **Bayside Seafood Restaurant** is popular with locals. It also serves lunch and dinner daily.

Biscayne National Park is one of America's few aquatic national parks. Most of its 180,000 acres are underwater, surrounding 44 keys, or islands, constructed mainly of fossilized coral rock. The keys stretch 18 nautical miles south toward Key West. As you might expect, snorkeling, scuba diving, canoeing, and kayaking are popular activities here. Narrated glass-bottom boat tours are also offered. The complex coral communities are home to hundreds of species of brilliantly colored tropical fish. The 14 miles of mangrove shoreline is the longest stretch remaining on the East Coast. The Convoy Point visitor center is open daily. You may rent from the park concession or bring your own canoe to paddle among the mangroves and neighboring islands. A sea kayak is best for the seven-mile paddle to Elliott Key. Accessible only by boat, Elliott Key has a ranger station with restrooms and a 1.5-mile loop trail. Tent camping is allowed on Elliott Key and Boca Chita Key.

Glittering Miami Beach is located on a barrier island east of Miami across Biscayne Bay. South Beach, or SoBe, occupies its southern tip. SoBe attracts sun and water worshipers, as well as the young, the hip, the rich, and the famous, who come for the legendary nightlife.

A post-Depression Art Deco building boom left behind a National Historic District in South Beach that is the crown jewel of this architectural

The first fifteen blocks of Ocean Drive in South Beach's Art Deco District form the heart of the most talked-about beach scene in Miami.

style. More than 800 structures remain in the district, which is bounded by the Atlantic Ocean and Lenox Avenue between Sixth and 23rd Streets. The Art Deco style, which emerged after the 1925 Paris Exposition, usually features a stucco wall surface and stylized natural and geometric motifs used as decorative elements on the walls, towers, and other projections above the roofline. Add to the mix Egyptian motifs, Mediterranean Revival

influences, nautical motifs, and pastels as pretty as a plate of after-dinner mints and you have a recipe for a great walking tour. If you want to participate in an organized tour, head for the **Art Deco Welcome Center** on Ocean Drive.

In addition to beautiful people, New York transplants, yuppies, gays, lesbians, Hasidic Jews, and Cuban immigrants, you'll find a sizable European tourist contingent here. You're almost as likely to hear German or French spoken on the streets of SoBe as English or Spanish. In fact, more than 5 million international visitors arrive in the greater Miami area each year.

Many small hotels have been refurbished and glamorized; others cling to their faded glory like dowagers on limited incomes. We visited the classic **Governor Hotel**, located one block from Ocean Drive and the beach on the quieter, less trendy, and less expensive northern end of South Beach. Although the accommodations might be considered spartan by Miami Beach standards, the pool was glorious, surrounded as it was by exotic, lush foliage. Parking, which is at a premium in the hustle-bustle farther south, was never a problem here.

At the lively south end of Ocean Drive, people-watching is a popular spectator sport from a sidewalk table at the **News Café**, open 24 hours a day.

In addition to the Art Deco hotels across the street from the beach along the first 10 blocks of Ocean Drive, there are beachfront hotels a few blocks farther north. Several of the finer hotels are a block or two off the beach. Among them is the **Albion Hotel**, built in 1939. Its creator described it as "a luxury liner on dry land," a reference to its classic curving facade complete with "smokestack." The hotel's 100 guest rooms and

Sidewalk tables are premium spots to enjoy the view at the News Café.

suites include penthouse suites with private open-air solaria perfect for eliminating tan lines.

Lincoln Road once aspired to become the Fifth Avenue of the South. It thrives today as a pedestrians-only center of art and commerce crowded with restaurants, nightclubs, boutiques, and art galleries. From October through May, Lincoln Road hosts an **Antiques and Collectibles Market** two Sundays each month.

South Beach is home to a trio of interesting museums. The **Sanford L. Ziff Jewish Museum of Florida** houses more than 200 years of Jewish experience in a former synagogue on Washington Ave. It is closed on Monday. The **Wolfsonian** at Florida International University showcases the thousands of artifacts collected by Mitchell Wolfson, Jr., as he traveled the world. It is closed on Wednesdays. The **Bass Museum of Art** has a permanent collection of European paintings from the 15th through the 20th centuries, an outdoor

sculpture terrace, and a café. All three museums charge an admission fee.

As you might expect, the dining choices in South Beach are as varied as its visitors. **Monty's** serves fresh Appalachicola oysters, stone-crab claws, and delicious lobster in an upscale setting overlooking the marina or in a casual outdoor raw bar; it is open for dinner. A tradition since 1913, **Joe's Stone Crab Restaurant** draws long lines on weekends for those wanting to splurge on jumbo crab claws during stone-crab season from mid-October to mid-May; it serves lunch and dinner. Other well-known, colorful, or highly recommended restaurants include **B.E.D.** on Washington, the award-winning **A Fish Called Avalon** in the refurbished Avalon Hotel on Ocean Drive, the **Cheeky Monkey** in the Blue Moon Hotel, and **Grillfish**, which serves fresh seafood prepared simply. Colorful ethnic creations are the order of the day at Gloria and Emilio Estefan's **Larios on the**

Beach, which features Cuban/Latin dishes for lunch and dinner, and **Opium**, which serves Asian cuisine with an attitude. **Wolfie's**, the best deli imaginable, serves a delicious Ruben that seems six inches tall and Cheesecake of the same proportions. The **Front Porch Café** is in the Penguin Hotel on Ocean Drive; like Wolfie's, it serves breakfast, lunch, and dinner.

If you drive north toward Fort Lauderdale along FL A1A, you'll wind through a veritable canyon of concrete-and-glass condominiums that threatens to block the sky as well as the sea. There's a change of scene at the 1,052-acre **Oleta River State Recreation Area** overlooking Biscayne Bayne in North Miami. A sandy beach, a fishing pier, and a concession renting canoes, kayaks, and paddleboats present plenty of opportunities to enjoy the water. Quite a few visitors come to try out the 10 miles of off-road bike trails. For those wanting to spend more than a day here, there are 14 rustic cabins and a group campground that can handle 90 tent campers.

All of the following are in Miami and use the 33131 zip code and 305 area code, except where noted.

ACCOMMODATIONS

Albion Hotel—1650 James Ave., South Beach, FL 33139; 531-6588

Avalon Hotel—700 Ocean Dr., South Beach, FL 33139; 800-933-3306 or 538-0133

Biltmore Hotel—1200 Anastasia Ave., Coral Gables, FL 33134; 800-727-1926 or 445-1926

Blue Moon Hotel—944 Collins Ave., South Beach, FL 33139; 800-673-2262

Cherokee Rose Lodge—3734 Main Hwy., Coconut Grove, FL 33133; 858-4884

Fontainbleu Hilton—4441 Collins Ave., Miami Beach, FL 33140; 538-2000

Governor Hotel—435 21st St., South Beach, FL 33139; 800-542-0444 or 532-2100

Hotel Place St. Michel—162 Alcazar Ave., Coral Gables, FL 33134; 444-1666

ATTRACTIONS

Barnacle State Historic Site—3485 Main Hwy., Coconut Grove, FL 33133; 448-9445

Bass Museum of Art—2121 Park Ave., South Beach, FL 33139; 673-7530

Bill Baggs Cape Florida State Recreation Area—1200 S. Crandon Blvd., Key Biscayne, FL 33149; 361-5811

Biscayne National Park—P.O. Box 1369, Homestead, FL 33090; 230-7275 or 230-1100

Coral Gables House—907 Coral Way, Coral Gables, FL 33134; 442-6593

Miami Metrozoo—12400 152nd St. S.W.; 251-0400

Metro-Dade Cultural Center—101 W. Flagler St.; 375-2665

Miami Museum of Science and Planetarium—3280 S. Miami Ave., Coconut Grove, FL 33133; 646-4200

Miami Seaquarium—4400 Rickenbacker Causeway, Key Biscayne, FL 33149; 361-5705

Oleta River State Recreation Area—3400 N.E. 163rd St; North Miami, FL 33160; 919-1846

Sanford L. Ziff Jewish Museum of Florida—301 Washington Ave., Miami Beach, FL 33139; 672-5044

Vizcaya Museum and Gardens—3252 S. Miami Ave., 33129; 579-2813

Wolfsonian—1001 Washington Ave., Miami Beach, FL 33139; 531-1001

 DINING

B.E.D.—929 Washington Ave., South Beach, FL 33139; 532-9070

Café Tu Tu Tango—3015 Grand Ave., Coconut Grove, FL 33133; 529-2222

Cheeky Monkey—944 Collins Ave., Miami Beach, FL 33139; 534-2650

Fish Called Avalon—700 Ocean Dr., South Beach, FL 33139; 532-1727

Front Porch Café—1418 Ocean Dr., South Beach, FL 33139; 531-8300

Grillfish—1444 Collins Ave., South Beach, FL 33139; 538-9908

Joe's Stone Crab Restaurant—11 Washington Ave., South Beach, FL 33139; 673-0365

Larios on the Beach—820 Ocean Dr., South Beach, FL 33139; 532-9577

Monty's—300 Alton Rd., South Beach, FL 33139; 673-3444

News Café—800 Ocean Dr., South Beach, FL 33139; 538-6397

Opium—136 Collins Ave., South Beach, FL 33139; 674-8630

Rusty Pelican—3201 Rickenbacker Causeway, Key Biscayne, FL 33149; 361-3818

Sunday's on the Bay—5420 Crandon Blvd., Key Biscayne, FL 33149; 361-6777

Wolfie's—2038 Collins Ave., South Beach, FL 33139; 538-6626

 EVENTS

January—Orange Bowl

January—South Beach Art Deco Weekend

January—Little Havana Three Kings Parade

February—Coconut Grove Art Festival

February—Miami Art Festival

March—Carnival Miami Festival

March—Calle Ocho Festival

June—Coconut Grove Goombay Festival

August—Miami Reggae Festival

September—Festival Miami

October—Caribbean Carnival

November—The Ramble

November—Miami Book Fair International

December—Orange Bowl Parade

 FOR MORE INFORMATION

Greater Miami Convention and Visitors Bureau—701 Brickell Ave., Suite 700; 888-766-4264; www.miamiandbeaches.com

Miami Beach Chamber of Commerce—1920 Meridan Ave., Miami Beach, FL 33139; 672-1270

Homestead-Everglades National Park-Flamingo

Homestead and Florida City are the gateway communities to the eastern portion of Everglades National Park, including the Royal Palm Visitor Center and Flamingo Lodge on Florida Bay. We suggest you allow time for a stop in Homestead, especially if you're interested in antique shopping.

Located about 30 miles southwest of Miami, Homestead was incorporated in 1913. It came to the national consciousness following the devastation left by Hurricane Andrew on August 24, 1992. As Andrew crossed South Florida, it left a path of destruction 25 miles wide and 60 miles long. About one-fourth of the royal palms and one-third of the pine trees in nearby Everglades National Park were broken or damaged, although the vast saw-grass prairies in the interior wetlands suffered little lasting effect. Amazingly, Andrew also had little effect on the wildlife in the Everglades. Sooner than anyone who saw the news footage could have imagined, Homestead, like the Everglades, started to repair and rebuild.

Today, restored buildings, inviting restaurants, and more than a dozen interesting antique shops join the stately palm trees along Krome Avenue in downtown Homestead. If you happen to come through in February or October, keep an eye out for **Sally Through the Alley**, Homestead's semi-annual antique street festival.

The **Redland Hotel**, constructed in 1904, has been recently renovated. It offers all the latest amenities, including nonsmoking guest rooms with private baths, cable TV, DSL internet connections, a restaurant that serves three meals daily, and a pub in the former library.

In an area with many natural treasures, Homestead is the home of one of the most unusual man-made attractions imaginable, the **Coral Castle**. This National Historic Site is an amazing feat of engineering accomplished by a lovelorn man, Ed Leedskalnin.

Born in Latvia in 1887, Ed left his homeland when he was rejected by the love of his life, a sixteen-year-old named Agnes. He wandered for several years through Canada, California, and Texas before finding his way to Florida City around 1920. There, on the acre of ground he had

Coral Castle is one of South Florida's most unusual tourist attractions.

purchased, he began to carve a coral castle dedicated to his "sweet sixteen." Working alone and using only hand tools, he cut and moved blocks of coral weighing many tons, fashioning them into chairs, tables, and even a rocking chair.

An intensely private man who never revealed the secrets of his methods, Leedskalnin decided to move a few miles up the road when development threatened his privacy at the Florida City location. He purchased 10 acres in Homestead. A friend with a tractor helped him move his huge coral carvings, but no one ever saw how he loaded or unloaded them. Once here, he began to cut

coral to construct walls that were three feet thick and eight feet tall to enclose his creation. He built a two-room, two-story coral castle complete with a twin-sized bed for the wife he still dreamt of, a coral cradle for the child that was never born, and tables and chairs for meals that were never served. Among the many coral carvings on display are a remarkable 30-ton telescope focused on the North Star, a sundial that accurately determines Standard time within one or two minutes a year, a 5,000-pound heart-shaped table, and a gate weighing 18,000 pounds that is so flawlessly balanced that one finger is all that is needed to open it.

Of course, the Everglades is the main attraction in this part of Florida. Marjory Stoneman Douglas said of the Everglades, "They are unique . . . in the simplicity, the diversity, the related harmony of the forms of life they enclose." She began writing *Everglades: River of Grass,* considered a Florida classic, at the age of 52. The book was published in 1947, the same year President Harry S Truman dedicated Everglades National Park. Until she died at the age of 108, the writer and conservationist remained a champion of her beloved Everglades.

Once covering 8 million acres, the Everglades has been reduced to half its original size. Of the remaining 4 million acres, a total of 1.5 million acres form **Everglades National Park**.

An International Biosphere Reserve, Everglades National Park is unsurpassed as a biological preserve. So complex are the associations among climate, water, fire, and inhabitants that even ecologists are not certain of all the intricate relationships here. The beauty of the Everglades tends to seep into your consciousness gradually. The sun chases clouds across sweeping vistas of saw grass that look as solid as a Western plain, but looks are deceiving. A closer inspection reveals that the saw grass sits in a vast river six inches deep and fifty miles wide that is steadily progressing toward the sea in a riverbed that slopes two or three inches per mile. Here and there appear tufts of treetops that manage to gain a solid footing in hammocks ranging in size from a few square feet to several acres.

Everglades National Park is a sanctuary and a breeding and feeding ground for more than 300 species of resident and migratory birds. Bird watching is a popular activity here. In addition, 99 species of butterflies, including many found nowhere else in America, have been documented. Besides the ubiquitous raccoon population, some 40 species of mammals, including bobcats and white-tailed deer, are here. Then, of course, there are the more than 50 species of reptiles, including alligators, which are now so plentiful they're no longer a threatened species in Florida. Alligators create holes and clear them of plants and muck, so the depressions in the limestone gradually fill with water. These gator holes then become essential for the survival of other freshwater-dependent species during the dry season. The rare American crocodile, distinguished by its narrow snout and olive-brown coloration, is occasionally seen in the mangrove swamps and creeks of Florida Bay.

If Marjory Stoneman Douglas was the mother of the Everglades, then Ernest F. Coe was surely the father. The Connecticut landscaper and his wife moved to nearby Coconut Grove during the 1920s. His shock at the destruction of rare birds and orchids led to the creation of the Tropical Everglades National Park Association and a proposal for a national park that took 20 years to come to fruition.

A paved road leads 38 miles from the Everglades National Park Ernest F. Coe Visitor Center to Flamingo.

The **Ernest F. Coe Visitor Center**, one of four entrances to Everglades National Park, is a good place to learn about the Everglades and the guided activities offered by park rangers. This is the only automobile entrance that gives access to Flamingo. An admission fee valid for seven days is charged to enter the park at this point. The bookstore at the visitor center offers a good selection of titles about the Everglades and information about the other entrances to the park—at Everglades City on the western park boundary, at Shark Valley at the northern boundary (see the chapter on Naples and Everglades City), and at Chekika, a campground accessed at the end of Southwest 168th Street in Homestead.

Although most activities in the park are available year-round, the vast majority of visitors wisely choose the cool, dry winter months, when the insect population is at its lowest. If you are advised that mosquito levels are heavy when you arrive, you've probably turned up during the summer or early fall, when mosquitoes and a host of biting flies are at their highest levels. Effective countermeasures other than bathing yourself in insect repellent include covering every part of your body with light-colored, lightweight clothing, finding any breeze you can, and avoiding grassy and shady areas. During peak mosquito season, a mosquito-net jacket and pants are the height of functional fall fashion in the Everglades. Luckily, they're usually for sale in the gift shop. Unlike most of Florida, regular mosquito spraying is not conducted inside the park. The little buggers can be maddening in their ability to chase you, biting every step of the way, inside your car, the restaurant, your room, and even the shower. That said, would we miss an opportunity to visit the Everglades in October? Absolutely not, but unless we come during the winter, we'll be wearing our very own mosquito-net suits next time.

From the Ernest F. Coe Visitor Center, a 38-mile paved road leads toward the Flamingo Visitor Center. Along the way, some short trails and overlooks give visitors glimpses into the mysterious Everglades.

About four miles down the road from the Ernest F. Coe Visitor Center, there's a smaller cen-

The Anhinga Trail follows a man-made canal to one of many freshwater sloughs found in the Everglades National Park.

ter at Royal Palm, where the park's first visitor facility was located. The park's nucleus consisted of 4,000 acres donated to the National Park Service by the Florida Federation of Women's Clubs. This center is also open daily.

The half-mile **Anhinga Trail** is one of the park's most popular trails. It offers a good chance to spot wildlife, including the anhinga, or "snakebird," as it's also known. The anhinga swims with only its long, snaky neck sticking out of the water as it searches for fish. After dining, the anhinga sits in a tree with its wings extended, drying its feathers. Occasionally, river otters are spotted in the spring. Alligators, herons, and egrets are commonly seen here.

The other trail at Royal Palm, the **Gumbo Limbo Trail**, winds through a tropical hardwood hammock island high enough above the water level to support royal palms, gumbo-limbos, nicknamed "tourist trees" for their red, peeling bark, and poisonwood trees, which are capable of causing a persistent rash that can be even worse than

The road through the Everglades National Park ends in Flamingo overlooking Florida Bay.

that caused by their relative, poison ivy. This is also a good area to see wild orchids.

Next comes Long Pine Key, which is literally an island in the wide, shallow river that forms the Everglades. Long Pine Key contains one of the park's two campgrounds. It has 108 sites, restrooms, drinking fountains, picnic tables, grills, and parking pads but no water, electrical, or sewage hookups. Sites are assigned on a first-come, first-served basis or may be reserved from November through April. More than 28 miles of trails cut through the pinelands, where white-tailed deer are commonly seen, as well as an occasional bobcat.

Another nine miles bring you to the **Pa-hay-okee Overlook**. *Pa-hay-okee* means "grassy river," which describes what you'll see from the elevated wooden platform at the end of a short boardwalk. Red-shouldered hawks and vultures are commonly seen overhead.

Fifteen more miles bring you to Paurotis Pond. This is a primary nesting area for the endangered wood stork. There's a small launch for nonmotorized boats.

The next stop gives access to the first of several canoe trails of varying lengths. The trails visit such sites as Nine Mile Pond, Noble Hammock, Hells Bay, and West Lake, where a half-mile boardwalk leads into a mangrove forest. Swallow-tailed kites may be seen overhead in March as they return from South America.

The granddaddy of them all, the **Wilderness Waterway**, starts at Flamingo and is open to powerboats under 18 feet in length, canoes, and kayaks. It's estimated to take six to eight hours by motorboat and eight to ten days by canoe. This is one of the best ways to see the incredible sights in the Everglades.

The road comes to an end at Flamingo, the site of a marina overlooking Florida Bay and the only lodging inside the park. Flamingo was a fishing village in the 1800s. It became part of Everglades National Park in 1947, but the marina is still popular with anglers fishing Florida Bay. In addition to basic marina services, the offerings include canoe and small-boat rentals, bike rentals, houseboat rentals, charter fishing boats, regularly scheduled sightseeing trips aboard the *Bald Eagle* into Florida Bay, and back-country cruises aboard the *Pelican*. The marina even rents binoculars.

The Flamingo campground has tent and trailer pads, drinking water, restrooms, picnic tables, grills, and cold showers. The ranger station and visitor center offer information about back-country camping permits and local canoe trails; the visitor center may be staffed intermittently during the summer. The back-country campsites are of several types—coastal shell beaches, slightly elevated ground sites along interior bays and rivers, and chickees, which are elevated 10-by-12-foot wooden platforms with roofs and self-contained toilets.

Regularly scheduled sightseeing trips offer visitors to Flamingo a chance to explore Florida Bay aboard the Bald Eagle.

If you're not quite ready to head into the wilderness, there are overnight accommodations year-round in 24 cottages and 103 rooms at the **Flamingo Lodge**. The cottages have fully equipped kitchens, air conditioning, a living room, a bedroom, and a bath. Guests have swimming-pool privileges, no small thing since the pool is the only place you'll want to swim while you're here, given the alligators in the fresh water and the sharks in Florida Bay. Although dogs are not allowed in most of the park, pets under 40 pounds are welcome at Flamingo Lodge. They must be declared upon check-in and kept on a leash when outside.

At Flamingo, **Flamingo Lodge Restaurant** overlooking Florida Bay serves breakfast, lunch, and dinner during the peak season, which runs from November to April. Or you can try the **Buttonwood Café**, which offers mixed drinks, pizza, salads, and sandwiches from December to April

and limited food service during the summer. During the summer off-season, sandwiches and salads are available at the marina store.

More than a half-dozen hiking trails originate at Flamingo, including the 7.5-mile **Coastal Prairie Trail**, which runs along an old roadbed once used by cotton pickers and fishermen. The half-mile **Eco Pond Trail** leads to a freshwater pond and a wildlife viewing platform with ramp access. Roseate spoonbills, the only large pink birds you'll see at Flamingo, visit Eco Pond with their young as their nesting season ends in March, about the time alligators start building their nests.

When you're ready to leave this exotic, watery world, return to civilization by the same road you traveled to Flamingo.

All of the following use the 305 area code, except where noted.

ACCOMMODATIONS

Flamingo Lodge, Marina, and Outpost—Everglades National Park, 1 Flamingo Lodge Hwy., Flamingo, FL 33034; 800-600-3813 or 941-695-3101; www.flamingolodge.com

Redland Hotel—5 S. Flagler Ave., Homestead, FL 33030; 264-1904; www.redlandhotel.com

 ATTRACTIONS

Coral Castle—28655 S. Dixie Hwy. (US 1), Homestead, FL 33030; 248-6345

Everglades National Park—40001 CR 9336, Homestead, FL 33034; 242-7700; www.nps.gov/ever

 CAMPING

Everglades National Park—40001 CR 9336, Homestead, FL 33034; 800-365-2267 or 242-7700

 DINING

Main Street News Café—128 N. Krome Ave., Homestead, FL 33030; 245-7575

Redland Hotel—5 S. Flagler Ave., Homestead, FL 33030; 264-1904

White Lion Café and Antiques—146 Seventh St. N.W., Homestead, FL 33030; 248-1076

 EVENTS

February and October—Sally Through the Alley

 FOR MORE INFORMATION

Homestead-Florida City Chamber of Commerce—43 N. Krome Ave., Homestead, FL 33030; 248-6344

Tropical Everglades Visitor Center—160 US 1, Florida City, FL 33034; 245-9180

HIGHLIGHTS

JOHN PENNEKAMP CORAL REEF STATE PARK

BAHIA HONDA STATE PARK

KEY WEST LIGHTHOUSE MUSEUM

ERNEST HEMINGWAY HOME

AUDUBON HOUSE AND TROPICAL GARDENS

KEY WEST SUNSET CELEBRATION

Although not technically a tropical region, since the Tropic of Cancer lies south of Key West, the Keys are often referred to as "Florida's Caribbean Islands." Visitors who ooh and aah their way down US 1 to Key West are treated to an incredibly beautiful, ever-changing palette of shimmering waters that constantly shift from turquoise to deep blue to green and back again.

The Florida Keys include dozens of islands that form an arc stretching south of Miami at Biscayne Bay for approximately 150 miles to Key West. To the east lies the Atlantic Ocean, to the west is Florida Bay, and to the south is Cuba. Divided into the Upper, Middle, and Lower Keys, they're all gorgeous, though they differ a bit geologically. The Upper and Middle Keys, which stretch from Key Largo to Marathon, are composed of ancient fossilized coral reefs that were exposed as the ocean receded during the Wisconsin Ice Age about 100,000 years ago. The Lower Keys are largely composed of Miami oolite, a type of limestone with egg-shaped particles.

The Calusa Indians inhabited the area long before Juan Ponce de Leon spotted the islands on May 15, 1513, and gave them a strangely portentous name. The islands' shapes looked like suffering men to the Spaniards, who christened them Los Martires, or "The Martyrs," an ominously appropriate choice, given the disasters that would befall ships and sailors in the treacherous waters of the nearby Florida Reef. So many ships foundered on the perilous coast that an industry was spawned and fortunes made in recovering sailors, passengers, and cargo by bold Key Westers known as "wreckers."

According to Charlton W. Tebeau in *A History of Florida*, there were no permanent residents in Key West in 1821, although it had been used earlier as a base for fishermen, spongers, and pirates. Key West was given to Juan Pablo Salas, a Spanish officer, in a land grant in 1815. Six years later, Salas sold it to John W. Simonton of Mobile for $2,000, and it became the first permanent settlement in the Florida Keys.

Two roads lead from the mainland to the Keys. The less-traveled is Card Sound Road. The more popular one, US 1, known locally as the Overseas Highway, runs from mile marker 126 at Florida City to mile marker 0 at Key West. Along the highway, a steady parade of green mileposts with white numbers tick off the distance to Key West. Directions in the Keys usually reference mile markers, written as "MM," and specify "bay side," or west, and "ocean side," or east. Card Sound Road, the back road to the Upper Keys, joins US 1, but before it does, you'll have the chance to stop by **Alabama Jack's** for some of the best conch fritters in the Keys.

The first community you'll encounter is Key Largo, or Cayo Largo, meaning "long island." Key Largo was known as Rock Harbor until portions of the 1948 movie *Key Largo*, starring Humphrey Bogart and Lauren Bacall, were filmed here at the **Caribbean Club**, located at MM 104 bay side. If you stop by the Caribbean Club, grab a cold beer and head to the back deck overlooking Florida Bay to see the beautiful sunset.

Just down the road at MM 100 ocean side, the original *African Queen*, made famous in another Bogart movie, is usually berthed at the Holiday Inn, if it is not on a promotional tour.

John Pennekamp Coral Reef State Park, named for a *Miami Herald* newspaperman and dedicated conservationist, is located at MM 102.5 ocean side in Key Largo. This was the first undersea park in the United States. North America's only coral barrier reef lies about six miles offshore and parallels the Keys. The park harbors living coral gardens, sea-grass beds, sponges, crabs, lobsters, shrimp, turtles, and nearly 600 species of fish. The slow-growing coral reefs in this area, the most biologically diverse marine ecosystems in the

world, thrive in warm, nutrient-free ocean waters.

The visitor center at John Pennekamp has a large, circular aquarium; interesting exhibits about this marine ecosystem; two short nature trails; picnic tables; a campground with 47 sites, a bathhouse, restrooms, and electrical hookups; and a concession that sells books, souvenirs, and tickets for a glass-bottomed boat tour designed for those who want to see the reef with dry feet. Visitors may also rent canoes, kayaks, and snorkeling equipment. The dive shop offers a full range of courses, scuba tours, and equipment rentals.

The water on both sides of the Keys forms the **Florida Keys National Marine Sanctuary**, which supports aquatic life of many kinds. Encompassing 2,800 square nautical miles, this is the second-largest marine sanctuary in the United States. Most areas of it are open for recreational use by snorkelers, divers, and boaters.

One of the more unusual lodges you're ever likely to run across is at MM 103.5 ocean side. **Jules' Key Largo Undersea Lodge** is permanently anchored in 30 feet of water, so you'll have to take a swim to get to your room. Once you arrive, you'll find your two-bedroom suite much like a regular resort. The rooms have comfortable beds and furnishings, telephones, VCRs, and air conditioning. The fish swimming outside your window give new meaning to the phrase "ocean view." Best of all, the lodge offers unlimited diving for certified divers.

One of our favorite spots in the Keys, the **Kona Kai Resort**, is in Key Largo at MM 98 bay side. This beautifully landscaped resort has an art gallery open to the public, featuring works of noted Florida artists and selected European artists for sale.

This adults-only, nonsmoking resort is like a

Kona Kai Resort in Key Largo offers a vacation getaway in a tranquil setting overlooking Florida Bay.

little bit of heaven overlooking Florida Bay. The owners continue to refine and improve services for their guests. They recently discovered that having a no-guests-under-16 policy allowed them to create a unique home-away-from-home environment. The 11 guest rooms and suites have CD and VCR players, living plants, sculpture, and original art. You'll even find real silverware and china in the suites with kitchens.

The lovely garden at Kona Kai is not only pretty to look at but tasty as well. It produces 20 different fruits, including *monstera deliciosa*, a cross between a pineapple and a banana that looks a lot like corn on the cob. There are more than 100 palms of 43 different kinds on the grounds. The sunset views are wonderful. Guests enjoy the pool open from sunrise to sunset, the small dock out back, and the tennis court complete with practice wall. When you've had enough rest and relaxation, the owners will happily arrange activities such as an Everglades fishing trip or a back-country tour with a marine biologist. They'll also help you make plans for a day trip to Key West.

The **Florida Keys Wild Bird Center**, located at MM 93.6 bay side, provides homes for injured, ill, and orphaned birds until they can be rehabilitated and released. Some, unable to survive in the wild, have found their way here to live out their golden years in large cages sponsored by concerned individuals, where they're cared for by a host of volunteers. The center is open to the public. Donations are accepted.

Located at MM 92.5, Tavernier was the first stop along Henry Flagler's Overseas Railroad. Other than Key West, most of the Keys have few historic buildings. Tavernier is an exception. Its substantial historic district includes cement Red Cross houses built as relief housing following a devastating 1935 hurricane.

Visitors find the **Old Tavernier Restaurant** a great spot to enjoy fresh seafood, steaks, veal, chicken, and lamb.

The community known as Islamorada is the heart of an area made up of several offshore keys and parts of Plantation Key, Windley Key, Upper Matecumbe, and Lower Matecumbe. Islamorada was settled in the 1850s by homesteaders who planted limes and pineapples. By the time

Flagler's work crews arrived, the area was still so inaccessible that workers on the Overseas Railroad were housed in boats—at least until a hurricane in 1906 made barracks on dry land seem like a much better idea. The railroad arrived in 1907.

Unfortunately, cheaper pineapples and limes arriving by ferry from Cuba forced Islamorada to search for other sources of revenue. The tourists who came to fish and relax were the ticket to the emergence of a new economy. This stunning spot, known as the "Sportfishing Capital of the World," offers both offshore and back-country guides and tournaments almost every month. Baseball legend Ted Williams came here to fish during the off-season in the 1950s. Several presidents—including Hoover, Roosevelt, Truman, and both Bushes—have fished here as well.

In the middle of the Great Depression, a tragedy of unimaginable proportions struck both the railroad and Islamorada. It was September 2, 1935, and hundreds of World War I veterans were working on a highway being built alongside the Overseas Railroad. Their foreman correctly read storm-warning signs and called the Florida East Coast Railway in Miami asking that a train be sent down to evacuate the men. Settlers, too, hoped for rescue. When the train crew was called back from its Labor Day holiday, the winds were starting to gust. By the time the train arrived, the barometer had crashed to the lowest reading ever recorded in the Northern Hemisphere. Settlers and their children fought alongside the veterans to make their way to the train through the rising surf and wind. Suddenly, a 17-foot storm surge washed hundreds of helpless people out to sea. At Islamorada, 577 bodies were recovered. One family lost 63 of its 74 members. While they grieved, they built funeral pyres. After holding up

The classic Cheeca Lodge and Spa offers today's vacationers an outstanding ocean-front retreat. Photo courtesy of Cheeca Lodge and Spa.

against the fury of three prior hurricanes, Flagler's Overseas Railroad was no match for the Labor Day Hurricane, the worst of many that have swept through the Keys.

The Hurricane Monument at MM 81.6 ocean side guards the ashes of many who died in 1935. The other monument to that terrible storm is one that managed to prevail. While nearly everything else was swept out to sea, the statue of an angel at the Pioneer Cemetery at what is now Cheeca Lodge was left standing.

Today, **Cheeca Lodge and Spa**, built in 1946 as the Islamorada Olney Inn, is an extraordinary oceanfront haven. The 27-acre property was bought by heirs of the A&P grocery stores, Carl and Che-che Twitchell. They totally rebuilt the resort, combined their names into Cheeca, and maintained the property for many years as an exclusive retreat for wealthy sportsmen.

The ocean-view guest rooms and suites have balconies overlooking a 525-foot fishing pier and one of the longest stretches of private beach in the Keys. Inside, you'll find all the creature comforts you could possibly want. Cheeca's award-winning **Atlantic's Edge Dining Room** features freshly caught Islamorada seafood in an elegant setting with sweeping views of the Atlantic. The **Ocean Terrace Grill** offers casual dining in an open-air room with an outdoor terrace. It overlooks one of Cheeca's three swimming pools. A friendly egret named Sam strolled in through an open door when we visited, no doubt looking for a bit of breakfast like the rest of us. For those needing an extra dose of pampering, the **Avanyu Spa** offers everything from massages to mud wraps and manicures. It has steam rooms in both the men and women's dressing rooms, Cheeca's second freshwater swimming pool, and an exercise room. A full-service dive center with its own dive/snorkel boat, guided fishing trips, six tennis courts, and a nine-hole golf course guarantee that there's something for everyone to do. Family-friendly **Camp Cheeca** provides marine activities ranging from snorkeling to catch-and-release fishing. Its programs, developed by camp counselors for children ages six to 12, are offered during peak family visitation periods.

If your idea of enjoying marine life consists of sitting down to good, fresh seafood and a cold drink, you're in luck. There are lots of good restaurants in Islamorada. One of the local favorites is the **Lorelei Restaurant and Cabana Bar**, where the food is as good as the view and as interesting as the people who wander in for the sunset celebrations at the bar. The Lorelei is open daily. Breakfast and lunch are served in the bar and dinner in the restaurant. **Papa Joe's**, located at MM 79.5 bay side, is a local landmark that has served the area since the 1930s. **Dino's** serves lunch and dinner daily from a menu that includes seafood, pasta, and gourmet pizzas. It offers an extensive wine list.

If you'd like to get a special gift for the angler in the family, look no farther than the **World Wide Sportsman** for a great selection of gear and outdoor clothing or the **Redbone Gallery**, located at MM 81.5, for artwork with a marine theme. We left with treasures from both.

Nearby, the remnants of an ill-fated Spanish treasure-ship convoy rest in 18 feet of water a little more than a mile south of Indian Key. Now known as the **San Pedro Underwater Archaeological Preserve**, it is one of nine shipwrecks on the **Florida Keys National Marine Sanctuary Shipwreck Trail**.

There are three parks in the area, two reachable only by water and one reachable by land. **Lignumvitae Key State Botanical Site**, located on the bay side, offers protection for native forests of tropical trees, two Indian shell middens, and a house built in 1919 that is now a museum. **Indian Key State Historical Site** is an 11-acre island off Lower Matecumbe. Jacob Housman bought the island in 1825 and set up his wreck salvage business here. Things went well until 1840. By that time, Indian Key had nearly 40 buildings, but an attack by the Seminole Indians dealt the community a fatal blow. Now, only ruins and streets remain. To see Lignumvitae or Indian Key, arrange for a boat ride Thursday through Monday from **Robbie's Marina** at MM 77.5. While you're at Robbie's, check out the hand-fed tarpon that prowl beneath the docks. Children especially get a kick out of watching the tarpon in a feeding frenzy brought on by the buckets of fresh baitfish that Robbie's offers for sale. **Windley Key Fossil Reef Geological Site** offers you the chance to stand in the fossilized remains of a coral reef.

Another local attraction is the **Theater of the Sea**. Created from a quarry used by Flagler's men in 1946, it offers boat rides, continuous shows featuring marine life, and special programs like swimming with dolphins or sea lions.

About halfway down the Florida Keys, you'll find **Long Key State Park**, located at MM 67.5 ocean side. The park offers camping overlooking the Atlantic. It has 60 sites with electrical hookups, showers, restrooms, and a dump station. Henry Flagler's exclusive Long Key Fishing Club, built here in 1908, hosted celebrities like famed Western author Zane Grey until it was destroyed in the 1935 Labor Day hurricane. The 965-acre park located here now offers a couple of short nature trails, canoe rentals, and a canoe trail through a shallow lagoon.

Hawk's Cay Resort and Marina on Duck Key offers interactive dolphin programs, special activities for children, and weekend classes in fly-fishing, sailing, and scuba diving. The lovely accommodations here include rooms and suites in the inn, along with two-bedroom villas. Several restaurants and a marina offering water-craft rentals are also on the premises.

Grassy Key is home to the **Dolphin Research Center**, a not-for-profit educational and research facility at MM 59 bay side. It's easy to spot because of the giant dolphin statue out front, but few who pass by know that one of television's original Flippers is buried beneath here. The center is now home to a family of Atlantic bottlenose dolphins and California sea lions. Dolphins are no longer collected from the wild; over half of the dolphins in residence were born at the center. Activities available to the public include a structured swim program and a Splash Program, in which people can wade in the water and meet

the dolphins. Reservations for either program must be made about a month in advance. Dolphin Lab is a week-long program for adults and teens that can be taken for college credit.

Swimming, snorkeling, sunbathing, fishing, and picnicking are popular activities at **Curry Hammock State Park**, located on Little Crawl Key at MM 56 ocean side. This is one of the best sites in the world for seeing peregrine falcons, which migrate from as far north as Alaska to as far south as South America each fall. Other raptors observed in the park include sharp-shinned hawks, broad-winged hawks, and the American kestrel, nearly 1,000 of which have been seen here on a single day.

At the center of the Keys is Key Vaca, home to a community supposedly given its name by Flagler's railroad workers in Camp Number 10, who complained that building the railroad was a regular marathon.

Marathon, one of the largest communities in the Keys, is home to the Museum of Natural History of the Florida Keys, the Children's Museum, and the Adderly Village Black Historic Site, known collectively as the **Museums of Crane Point Hammock**. This site is open every day. An admission fee is charged.

The grounds include nearly two miles of nature trails winding through Crane Point Hammock, a 63-acre tropical hardwood hammock that contains 160 species of native plants and what is probably the last virgin Florida thatch palm hammock in North America. Included in the native tree population is the poisonwood, vitally important to the endangered white crowned pigeon found here but toxic to humans. Poisonwood is capable of causing a persistent rash much worse than its relatives, poison ivy and poison oak.

Among the oddest plants is the strangler fig, which begins life as an epiphyte, or air plant, when a seed is deposited in the top of a host tree. After the seed sprouts, it sends down aerial roots that entwine and often strangle the host. When the roots reach the ground, it changes from an epiphyte to a terrestrial plant.

The centerpiece of the **Adderly Village Black Historic Site** is the tabby house built by George Adderly, a native Bahamian, between 1904 and 1906. Tabby is a building material composed of sand, lime obtained from burning seashells like the queen conch, and crushed shells or rocks.

The **Museum of Natural History of the Florida Keys** presents a series of dioramas of all Keys creatures, whether they live on land, in the sea, or in the air. Other exhibits are designed to introduce visitors to Native Americans, pirates, wreckers, and railroaders in the Keys.

The **Children's Museum** offers lots of hands-on activities, including dressing up in clothes pulled from the treasure chest of a make-believe pirate ship.

The Museum Store at Crane Point Hammock has housewares, candles, books, toys, jewelry, and, of course, pirate hats.

Marathon served as the southern terminus of Flagler's Overseas Railroad from 1908 to 1912, while engineers and workmen constructed what was the longest over-water bridge in the world at the time. It spanned the seven-mile gap between Knights Key and Little Duck Key.

A short wooden bridge was built from Marathon to **Pigeon Key**, a five-acre island that became a railroad work camp that housed about 400 workers, wives, and children at its peak. The camp was a vast improvement over the barges that had been used. Initially, huge houseboats called "quar-

The National Historic Site at Pigeon Key figured prominently in the construction of Henry Flagler's Overseas Railroad to Key West.

ter boats" were used for workers' housing. This proved disastrous during the October 18, 1906, hurricane, when the quarter boats were blown apart at sea. Survivors drifted for hours and in some cases days, clinging to wreckage and praying for rescue. At least 130 men died. After that, wooden barracks were built on shore. In some cases, families lived on-site, but they had to leave when hurricane season started in August. It's a good thing they did, because another hurricane hit in September 1909, damaging the bridge being constructed and killing another 40 men.

Sharks, alligators, and hurricanes were menacing, but the hordes of mosquitoes were inescapable. Conditions were so bad that a majority of the 20,000 workers had to be recruited from Northern skid-row districts for the price of a $2 train ticket and $1.25 a day. Of the half that didn't jump the train, hundreds died before the railroad was finished.

Today, this National Historic Site is open to visitors who ride the shuttle bus over or walk the

The Bahia Honda State Park is the only Florida state park offering cabin rentals in the Keys.

bridge. An admission fee is charged. A small museum inside the Assistant Bridge Tender's House features a model of the Seven-Mile Bridge under construction and lots of photos of Pigeon Key.

Bahia Honda is Spanish for "deep bay." The channel at Bahia Honda Key, one of the deepest in the Keys, required yet another bridge. **Bahia Honda State Park**, located at MM 36.9, has one of the prettiest beaches in the Keys. It has a nice overlook and a road that runs along Loggerhead Beach, where the snorkeling is said to be very good. Unfortunately, a storm had just passed when we visited, and both Loggerhead Beach and Sandspur Beach were heavily strewn

with sea grass. For an excellent view, walk onto the Old Bahia Honda Bridge beyond the concession and dive shop and the education center.

The park encompasses 653 acres, including a large stand of threatened silver palms. You can see them along the **Silver Palm Trail**, which begins at the end of the road on the Atlantic side past Sandspur Beach. Diving and snorkeling are best from April to November, and birding is best during March and April and from September to November. The park's three camping areas have a total of 80 sites. Two campgrounds overlook the Atlantic. The other is bay side, as are the six rental cabins. It will take luck and timing to catch a cabin vacant, since Bahia Honda is the only state park in the Keys with rental cabins. The park's marina has tour boats and fishing guides, in addition to boat and equipment rental.

The Lower Keys are the site of the **National Key Deer Wildlife Refuge** on Big Pine and Little Torch Keys. The pint-sized Key deer are about two feet tall and weigh less than 75 pounds. They're related to Virginia white-tailed deer. If you want to try to see one, turn on Key Deer Boulevard at MM 31.5 and follow the sign to the visitor center for more information.

The lodging choices on Big Pine Key include the **Barnacle Bed and Breakfast and Dive Resort**, located four miles from Looe Key. In addition to guest rooms with private baths, the inn offers an introductory scuba course that you start at home with a CD-ROM before you arrive at the Barnacle for your in-water training. **Casa Grande Bed and Breakfast** has three tropically decorated rooms with private baths, a garden patio where breakfast is served and a hot tub awaits, and, best of all, a private beach. The classic **Old Wooden Bridge Fish Camp** has one- and two-bedroom cottages with the basics—i.e., twin beds, air conditioning, free launching and dockage for cottage customers, and very reasonable rates.

At the end of the road is Key West. Only two miles by four miles in size, it's packed with attractions, lodging, dining, and tourists who come to enjoy it all. If New Orleans is the Big Easy, then Key West has got to be the Little Easy because of its laid-back, anything-goes style. The whole town seems to move with a languid saunter that gathers momentum as it flows along the shops and restaurants lining Duval Street north toward Mallory Square as the sun begins to get low in the sky.

Besides being a party town, Key West has a lot to offer those with an interest in history. During the 16th century, Spanish explorers discovered human remains on an island and named it Cayo Heuso, or Bone Island. The British later distorted the name to Key West. By the 1800s, pirates were well established in Key West. Commodore David Perry of the United States Navy was sent to dispatch them in 1822 so serious settlement could begin. Next, wreckers arrived to brave the rough seas and save sailors, passengers, and valuable cargo from sinking ships. The construction of lighthouses and the departure of the Spanish Treasure Fleet spelled a downturn in the wrecking industry. During the 1830s, cigar makers arrived from Cuba and established Key West as a trade center for fine Cuban cigars until labor issues forced manufacturers to move to Tampa and Ybor City.

Key West is constantly subject to the forces of nature. The hurricane of 1846 dealt it a serious blow. The great fire of 1886 swept through two-thirds of the town. Another hurricane hit in 1909.

In 1889, Key West had more income per

The Key West Lighthouse was built in 1848 on the highest ground in Key West.

capita than any city in America. But in the 1930s, it declared bankruptcy. Fortunately, the town has more lives than the multitude of cats that freely roam its streets. Tourism proved to be the answer. Key West began to attract the rich and famous with its diverse culture and picturesque isolation.

Be sure to stop by the visitor information center, located on US 1 as you enter town, for maps.

You might want to start your museum tours with the **Key West Lighthouse Museum** on

Ernest Hemingway lived a colorful life in Key West, but wrote some of his best-known works in the eight years he was here.

Whitehead Street. Here, you'll get a bird's-eye view of Key West. The lighthouse was built in 1848 to replace one destroyed by a hurricane in 1846. It was originally 70 feet tall, but 20 feet were added in 1894 because the trees and buildings of Key West had grown so tall that the light couldn't be clearly seen. The lighthouse keeper's cottage is now a museum. Both the lighthouse and the museum are open daily. An admission fee is charged.

Across the street is the **Ernest Hemingway Home**. Hemingway visited the Keys for the first time in 1928, when he was invited by Western writer Zane Grey to come down and fish.

Hemingway was born in Oak Park, Illinois, and spent his summers at a cottage on Walloon Lake in Michigan, where his dad often took him fishing. By age six, he'd acquired a love of fishing and hunting. He learned the fishing skills necessary to land the big ones from Sloppy Joe Russell of Key West, proprietor of the famous **Sloppy Joe's Bar**, a popular spot for Hemingway fans to raise a cool one and toast "Papa."

The tour of the house and gardens is fascinating. Our guide not only gave us detailed information about the house, its furnishings, and Hemingway's life, but also introduced us to a number of cats that are direct descendants of Hemingway's cats. Lounging about were Ava Gardner and her daughter, Susan Hayward, who were joined on the porch as the sun climbed high in the sky by Ethel Merman, Pablo Picasso, and Charlie Chaplin. Hemingway, we were told, was obsessed with cats, including a six-toed feline supposedly given to him by a sea captain.

There's a great gift shop for bibliophiles, and the gardens are shady and cool. The Ernest Hemingway Home is open daily. An admission fee is charged.

A tour of Key West aboard the **Conch Train** has been obligatory since 1958. You may board the train at Mallory Square or Flagler Station, an interesting spot to visit if you're a railroad-history buff. Even more of Flagler's incredible story is told here.

The Conch Train is a popular way to see the sites of Key West.

President Harry S Truman found the much-needed rest and relaxation his doctor ordered at his Little White House in Key West.

Consider visiting the **Harry S Truman Little White House** on Front Street. After 11 months in office, the 33rd president of the United States became so exhausted that his physician ordered him to rest. Admiral Chester Nimitz suggested he try the submarine base at Key West. Truman made his first visit in March 1946. In all, he visited 11 times during his presidency. He said he had a notion "to move the capital to Key West and just stay." He spent time at the nearby beach that bears his name, played poker on the south porch, and joked with the press, who called him "Truman the human." He said that besides Independence, Missouri, Key West was his favorite place in the world.

You can have lunch at **Kelly's Caribbean Bar, Grill, and Brewery** across the street or continue to the **Audubon House and Tropical Gardens**. John James Audubon visited the house during the spring of 1832. The owner, John Geiger, lived here with his wife and nine children. He was a ship's pilot and later a very successful wrecker.

While he was in the area, Audubon discovered 18 birds he had not previously observed. The second floor of the house displays all 18 of the original paintings he did of them. The third floor houses the **Audubon House Gallery of Fine Arts**. Here, original hand-painted lithographs completed between 1840 and 1859 are for sale. The lithographs are part of Audubon's Royal Octavo series. The house is open daily. An admission fee is charged.

If treasure hunting floats your boat, visit the **Mel Fisher Maritime Heritage Society Museum** to see a portion of the $400 million trove discovered by Key West's most famous treasure hunter after a 16-year search. If you get bitten by the gold bug, you can buy an artifact recovered from the *Atocha* by Fisher and his crew. The museum is open daily. An admission fee is charged.

The **Oldest House/Wreckers Museum** on Duval Street provides insight into Key West's historic wrecking, or salvaging, industry. It is open daily. An admission fee is charged.

Across the street is the **Key West Museum of Art and History** at the Custom House. The first floor has art galleries. Upstairs are the Hemingway Room and an exhibit about the USS *Maine* that is housed in the courtroom where the famous case was tried. "Remember the *Maine*" became the rallying cry that launched the Spanish-American War.

Next door, you'll find yourself in the heart of downtown activity. The old sponge market, shops, restaurants, the **Key West Aquarium** (the first tourist attraction in town), and the **Key West Shipwreck Historeum** will all compete for your attention. The aquarium and the historeum are open daily and charge admission.

Immediately behind this area at **Mallory**

Square is the nightly gathering of street performers, vendors, tourists, and residents known as the **Key West Sunset Celebration**. There's no admission charge, but performers pass the hat.

All the way at the other end of the island is the often-photographed, larger-than-life buoy at Southernmost Point, which is only 90 miles from Cuba and 150 miles from Miami. The **Southernmost House**, the **Key West Butterfly Conservatory**, a host of shops, small bed-and-breakfasts, and **Wyndham Casa Marina Resort**, the magnificent hotel built by Henry Flagler, are found in this area.

Two area attractions are of special interest to Civil War buffs.

Fort Zachary Taylor State Historic Site, located on the southwestern edge of Key West, is a National Landmark. During the Civil War, it was an important Union outpost for detaining Confederate blockade-running ships. Guided tours are offered daily. An admission fee is charged.

You'll need a plane or ferry ride to reach **Dry Tortugas National Park**, located about 70 miles west of Key West. The park is a cluster of seven coral reefs amid 64,657 acres sometimes referred to as the "Atlantic Galapagos." The park is now famous for its birding and snorkeling. Boat and air taxi services in Key West offer trips to the Dry Tortugas. You can make the journey aboard the *Yankee Freedom II*, a high-speed catamaran that serves breakfast and lunch and provides snorkeling equipment and professional guides at sea and at the park.

Two lighthouses remain within the park. One is a 151-foot brick tower on Loggerhead Key. It was built in 1858. The other was constructed on the walls of Fort Jefferson on Garden Key in 1876. The fort was a prison for Union deserters during the Civil War. The most famous of its prisoners was Dr. Samuel Mudd, who was convicted for setting the broken leg of John Wilkes Booth, not knowing Booth was the assassin of President Lincoln. Dr. Mudd was pardoned in 1869 after caring for men at the fort during a terrible yellow-fever epidemic. Thirteen campsites are available year-round on Garden Key.

Key West is blessed with lovely bed-and-breakfasts, including the **Key Lime Inn** on Truman Avenue, two blocks off Duval Street. This 37-room historic inn offers accommodations in several buildings dating from 1854 to 1949. Thanks to its queen- and king-sized beds, its private baths, its continental breakfast served each morning near the swimming pool, its off-street parking, and its location within easy walking distance of Key West attractions, gift shops, and restaurants, this makes a great headquarters. **Merlinn Inn** on Simonton Street has a swimming pool and offers a variety of accommodations from rooms and suites to one- and two-bedroom cottages. The **Blue Parrot Inn**, the **Mermaid and the Alligator**, the **Conch House**

Key West is blessed with an abundance of historic bed-and-breakfast inns, including the Key Lime Inn.

Heritage Inn, the **Curry Mansion Inn**—the list of fine bed-and-breakfasts goes on and on.

You've seen the T-shirts. Now it's time to check out the places they advertise. The **Hog's Breath Saloon** and **Sloppy Joe's Bar** are popular tourist destinations. Other local favorite restaurants include the **A & B Lobster House** on Front Street and **Louie's Backyard Restaurant** on Waddell Street, a hands-down favorite for fine dining at lunch or dinner. Regardless of where you eat, remember that conch is pretty tough, so it's either pounded and tenderized, cut into small pieces and served in chowder, salad, and fritters, or breaded and fried as a steak. If they're in season, you owe it to yourself to try Florida lobster and stone-crab claws. And remember that good Key lime pie should be creamy, tart, and always yellowish in color, never green.

Each April, the brief 1982 "secession" of Key West from the United States is commemorated in a series of hilarious events known as the **Conch Republic Independence Celebration**. The secession, which lasted all of one minute, was launched in response to the establishment of a United States border patrol blockade on US 1 that prevented residents of the Keys from driving freely onto the mainland. As a result, Key West Mayor Dennis Wardlow felt compelled to lead the civil rebellion that officially established the Conch Republic. Activities range from tattoo contests to drag races featuring—you guessed it—the Conch Republic's best-known drag queens. There's a bed race down Duval Street that's purported to be the most fun you can have in a bed with your clothes on. The parade gathers folks from cars and bars as it goes.

On a final note, even the **Key West Cemetery** is filled with humor. Its most famous epitaph is this: "I told you I was sick." The cemetery is open daily from sunrise to dusk.

Most directions given in the Florida Keys begin with the closest mile marker on US 1. For that reason, they are included in the addresses below wherever appropriate. All of the following use the 305 area code, except where noted.

 ACCOMMODATIONS

Barnacle Bed and Breakfast and Dive Resort—1557 Long Beach Dr., Big Pine Key, FL 33043; 800-465-9100 or 872-3298

Blue Parrot Inn—916 Elizabeth St., Key West, FL 33040; 800-231-2473 or 296-0033

Casa Grande Bed and Breakfast—1619 Long Beach Dr., Big Pine Key, FL 33043; 872-2878; www.floridakeys.net/casagrande

Cheeca Lodge and Spa—MM 82, P.O. Box 527, Islamorada, FL 33036; 800-327-2888 or 664-4651

Conch House Heritage Inn—625 Truman Ave., Key West, FL 33040; 800-207-5806 or 293-0020

Curry Mansion Inn—511 Caroline St., Key West, FL 33040; 800-253-3466 or 294-5349

Hawk's Cay Resort and Marina—61 Hawk's Cay Blvd., Duck Key, FL 33050; 800-432-2242 or 743-7000

Jules' Key Largo Undersea Lodge—MM 103.5, 51 Shoreland Dr., Key Largo, FL 33037; 451-2353

Key Lime Inn—725 Truman Ave., Key West, FL 33040; 800-549-4430 or 294-5229

Kona Kai Resort—MM 98, Key Largo, FL 33037; 800-365-7829 or 852-7200; www.konakairesort.com

Merlinn Inn—811 Simonton St., Key West, FL 33040; 800-642-4753 or 296-3336

Mermaid and the Alligator Bed and Breakfast and Tropical Gardens—729 Truman Ave., Key West, FL 33040; 800-773-1894 or 294-1894

Old Wooden Bridge Fish Camp—Rt. 1, Box 455, Big Pine Key, FL 33043; 872-2241

Pilot House—414 Simonton St., Key West, FL 33040; 800-648-3780 or 293-6600

Wyndham Casa Marina Resort—1500 Reynolds St., Key West, FL 33040; 800-626-0777 or 296-3535

 ATTRACTIONS

Audubon House and Tropical Gardens—205 Whitehead St., Key West, FL 33040; 877-281-2473 or 294-2116

Bahia Honda State Park—MM 36.5, 36850 Overseas Hwy., Big Pine Key, FL 33043; 872-2353

Caribbean Club—MM 104 bay side, Key Largo, FL 33037; 451-9970

Conch Train—P.O. Box 1173, Key West, FL 33040; 294-5161

Curry Hammock State Park—c/o Long Key State Park, P.O. Box 776, Long Key, FL 33001; 664-4815

Dolphin Research Center—58901 Overseas Hwy., Grassy Key, FL 33050; 289-0002 or 289-1121

Dry Tortugas Ferry—240 Margaret St., Key West, FL 33040; 800-634-0939 or 294-7009; www.yankeefleet.com

Dry Tortugas National Park—P.O. Box 6208, Key West, FL 33041; 242-7700

Ernest Hemingway Home—907 Whitehead St., Key West, FL 33040; 294-1136

Florida Keys National Marine Sanctuary—email: floridakeys@noaa.gov

Florida Keys Wild Bird Center—MM 93.6, 93600 Overseas Hwy., Tavernier, FL 33070; 852-4486

Fort Zachary Taylor State Historic Site—P.O. Box 6560, Key West, FL 33041; 292-6713

Gallery at Kona Kai—MM 98, Key Largo, FL 33037; 852-7200

Harry S Truman Little White House—111 Front St., Key West, FL 33040; 800-868-7482 or 294-9911

Indian Key State Historical Site—P.O. Box 1052, Islamorada, FL 33036; 664-2540

John Pennekamp Coral Reef State Park—MM 102.5, 10261 US 1, P.O. Box 487, Key Largo, FL 33037; 451-1202

Key West Aquarium—1 Whitehead St., Key West, FL 33040; 296-2051

Key West Lighthouse Museum—938 Whitehead St., Key West, FL 33040; 294-0012

Key West Museum of Art and History—281 Front St., Key West, FL 33040; 295-6616

Key West Shipwreck Historeum—1 Whitehead St., Key West, FL 33040; 800-868-7482 or 292-8990

Lignumvitae Key State Botanical Site—MM 77.5, P.O. Box 1052, Islamorada, FL 33036; 664-4815 or 664-2540

Long Key State Park—MM 67.5, P.O. Box 776, Long Key, FL 33001; 664-4815

Mel Fisher Maritime Heritage Society Museum—200 Green St.; Key West, FL 33040; 294-2633

Museums of Crane Point Hammock—MM 50 bay side, 5550 Overseas Hwy., Marathon, FL 33050; 743-9100

National Key Deer Wildlife Refuge—MM 31.5, Big Pine Key, FL 33043; 872-2239

Oldest House/Wreckers Museum—322 Duval St., Key West, FL 33040; 294-9502

Redbone Gallery—P.O. Box 273, Islamorada, FL 33036; 877-534-7423 or 664-2002

Robbie's Marina—MM 77.5; 664-9814

San Pedro Underwater Archaeological Preserve—P.O. Box 1052, Islamorada, FL 33036; 664-2540

Seaplanes of Key West—3471 S. Roosevelt Blvd., Key West, FL 33040; 800-950-2359 or 294-0709

Theater of the Sea—MM 84.5 bay side, 84721 Overseas Hwy., Islamorada, FL 33036; 664-2431

Windley Key Fossil Reef Geological Site—MM 84.5 bay side, P.O. Box 1052, Islamorada, FL 33036; 644-2540

World Wide Sportsman—81576 Overseas Hwy., Islamorada, FL 33036; 664-4615

 CAMPING

Bahia Honda State Park—MM 36.5, 36850 Overseas Hwy., Big Pine Key, FL 33043; 872-2353

John Pennekamp Coral Reef State Park—MM 102.5, 10261 US 1, P.O. Box 487, Key Largo, FL 33037; 451-1202

Long Key State Park—MM 67.5, P.O. Box 776, Long Key, FL 33001; 664-4815

DINING

A & B Lobster House—700 Front St., Key West, FL 33040; 294-5880

Alabama Jack's—58000 Card Sound Rd., Key Largo, FL 33037; 248-8741

Ballyhoo's—MM 98.7, Key Largo, FL 33037; 852-0822

Dino's—MM 81 ocean side, Islamorada, FL 33036; 664-0727

Fish House Restaurant—MM 102.4, Key Largo, FL 33037; 451-4665

Hog's Breath Saloon—Duval and Front Streets, Key West, FL 33040; 800-826-6969 or 296-4222

Islamorada Fish Company—MM 81.5, Islamorada, FL 33036; 664-9271

Kelly's Caribbean Bar, Grill, and Brewery—301 Whitehead St., Key West, FL 33040; 293-8484

Lorelei Restaurant and Cabana Bar—MM 82 bay side, Islamorada, FL 33036; 664-4656

Louie's Backyard Restaurant—700 Waddell St., Key West, FL 33040; 294-1061

Mangoes—700 Duval St., Key West, FL 33040; 292-4606

Old Tavernier Restaurant—MM 90.1 ocean side, Plantation Key, FL 33070; 852-6012

Papa Joe's—MM 79.5 bay side, Islamorada, FL 33036; 664-8756

Sloppy Joe's Bar—201 Duval St., Key West, FL 33040; 800-437-0333 or 294-5717

Snapper's Waterfront Saloon—MM 94.5 ocean side, Key Largo, FL 33037; 852-5956

EVENTS

January, February, and March—Key West House and Garden Tour

March—Marathon Seafood Festival

April—Conch Republic Independence Celebration

July—Hemingway Days

September—WomanFest

October—Florida Keys Birding and Wildlife Festival

October—Fantasy Fest

November—Cuban American Heritage Festival

December—Key West Lighted Boat Parade

FOR MORE INFORMATION

Florida Keys and Key West Visitors Bureau—P.O. Box 1147, Key West, FL 33041; 800-FLA-KEYS; www.fla-keys.com

Greater Marathon Chamber of Commerce—MM 53.2, Marathon, FL 33050; 800-262-7284

Islamorada Chamber of Commerce—MM 82.5, Islamorada, FL 33036; 800-322-5397

Key Largo Chamber of Commerce—MM 106, Key Largo, FL 33037; 800-822-1088

Key West Chamber of Commerce—402 Wall St., Key West, FL 33041; 800-LASTKEY

Lower Keys Chamber of Commerce—MM 31, Big Pine Key, FL 33043; 800-872-3722

Index